DEPENDENCY ROAD:
Communications, Capitalism, Consciousness, and Canada

COMMUNICATION AND INFORMATION SCIENCE

A Series of Monographs, Treatises, and Texts

Edited by
MELVIN J. VOIGT

University of California, San Diego

William C. Adams • Television Coverage of International Affairs

William C. Adams • Television Coverage of the Middle East

Hewitt D. Crane • The New Social Marketplace: Notes on Effecting Social Change in America's Third Century

Rhonda J. Crane • The Politics of International Standards: France and the Color TV War

Herbert S. Dordick, Helen G. Bradley, and Burt Nanus • The Emerging Network Marketplace

Glen Fisher • American Communication in a Global Society

Edmund Glenn • Man and Mankind: Conflict and Communication Between Cultures

Bradley S. Greenberg • Life on Television: Content Analyses of U.S. TV Drama

Robert M. Landau, James H. Bair, and Jean Siegman • Emerging Office Systems

John S. Lawrence and Bernard M. Timberg • Fair Use and Free Inquiry: Copyright Law and the New Media

Robert G. Meadow • Politics as Communication

William H. Melody, Liora R. Salter, and Paul Heyer • Culture, Communication, and Dependency: The Tradition of H.A. Innis

Vincent Mosco • Broadcasting in the United States: Innovative Challenge and Organizational Control

Kaarle Nordenstreng and Herbert I. Schiller • National Sovereignty and International Communication: A Reader

Dan Schiller • Telematics and Government

Herbert I. Schiller • Who Knows: Information in the Age of the Fortune 500

Dallas W. Smythe • Dependency Road: Communications, Capitalism, Consciousness and Canada

In Preparation:

William C. Adams • Television Coverage of the 1980 Presidential Campaign

Mary B. Cassata and Thomas Skill • Life on Daytime Television

Ithiel de Sola Pool • Forecasting The Telephone: A Retrospective Technology Assessment

Oscar H. Gandy, Jr. • Beyond Agenda Setting: Information Subsidies and Public Policy

Bradley S. Greenberg • Mexican Americans and the Mass Media

Cees J. Hamelink • Finance and Information: A Study of Converging Interests

Vincent Mosco • Pushbutton Fantasies

Kaarle Nordenstreng • The Mass Media Declaration of UNESCO

Jorge A. Schnitman • Dependency and Development in the Latin American Film Industries

Indu B. Singh • Telecommunications in the Year 2000: National and International Perspectives

Jennifer D. Slack • Communication Technologies and Society: Conceptions of Causality and the Politics of Technological Intervention

Janet Wasko • Movies and Money: Financing the American Film Industry

Osmo Wiio • Information and Communication Systems

DEPENDENCY ROAD:

Communications, Capitalism, Consciousness, and Canada

by Dallas W. Smythe
Simon Fraser University
with a foreword by Herbert I. Schiller

Ablex Publishing Corporation
Norwood, New Jersey 07648

Acknowledgments

Appreciation is expressed to the following who generously allowed extended quotations from the works mentioned:

Marx, Karl, *Grundrisse: Foundations of the Critique of Political Economy*, translated by Martin Nicolaus. Copyright 1973. Reprinted by permission of Random House, Inc.

From William J. Baumol and William G. Bowen, *Performing Arts: The Economic Dilemma*. Copyright © 1966 by the Twentieth Century Fund, Inc. Reprinted by permission.

Absentee Ownership and Business Enterprise in Recent Times, by Thorstein Veblen. Copyright 1923 by B. W. Huebsch, Inc., renewed 1951 by Ann B. Sims. Reprinted by permission of Viking Penguin Inc.

American by Design: Science, Technology and the Rise of Corporate Capitalism, by David F. Noble. New York: Alfred A. Knopf, Inc., 1977. Reprinted by permission of Random House, copyright holder.

Power and Imagination: City States in Renaissance Italy, by Lauro Martines. New York: Alfred A. Knopf, Inc., 1979. Reprinted by permission of Random House, copyright holder.

The Economic Implications of Advertising, by O. J. Firestone. Toronto: Methuen Publications, 1967. Reprinted by permission of O. J. Firestone, copyright holder.

Public Relations, by E. I. Bernays. Copyright 1952 by the University of Oklahoma Press, publishing division of the University. Composed and printed at Norman, Oklahoma, USA, by the University of Oklahoma Press.

The Struggle for National Broadcasting in Canada, by E. A. Weir. Reprinted by permission of the Canadian Publishers, McClelland and Stewart Limited, Toronto.

The Effects of Mass Communication, by Joseph T. Klapper. Pages 7–8, 49–51, 120–121. Copyright © 1960 by The Free Press, a corporation. Reprinted by permission of Macmillan Publishing Co.

The Sponsor, by Erik Barnouw. Copyright 1978. Reprinted by permission of Oxford University Press.

Intermedia, Vol. 6, No. 6, by E. Ploman. Reprinted by permission of *Intermedia*, journal of the International Institute of Communications, London.

"The Political Character of Science," by D. W. Smythe in Mattelart, A. and Siegelaub, S. (Eds.), *Communication and Class Struggle: 1. Capitalism, Imperialism*. New York: International General, 1979. Reprinted by permission of the publisher.

ABLEX Publishing Corporation
355 Chestnut Street
Norwood, New Jersey 07648

Dedication

To people everywhere who struggle for a fully human life.
You are wonderful.

Table of Contents

PREFACE

It is arbitrary to acknowledge help received from friends in a long life preceding this first book. Many not mentioned here possibly should be.

Peter R. Saunders, then Manager of College Sales for McClelland and Stewart, Toronto, encouraged me to write this book and provided useful information concerning publishing. By a bitter irony (given the book's title), when the manuscript was finished eighteen months later that Canadian publishing house had been forced by the pressure of American competition to reverse his decision to publish it, forcing me to seek an American publisher. Thanks, Peter. I thank my friend, colleague, and chairman, William H. Melody, for his encouragement and for the privilege of teaching our large introductory class in Mass Communications at Simon Fraser University, where students gave my draft manuscript the invaluable and constructive test of use as a textbook. Thanks, Bill. Joseph K. Roberts, University of Regina, helped me by negotiating arrangements which extricated me from academic administration there after I had chaired the Division of Social Sciences in its formative first five years. He also encouraged me to pursue the theory and practice of research on communications at the world level. Thanks, Joe. And Herbert I. Schiller, colleague since the 1950s, provided intellectual and moral support in many ways in the work which produced this book. Thanks, Herb.

Concerning the substance of the book, I am grateful to Bill Livant, University of Regina, for unremitting hard criticism and support regarding the theoretical aspects of the audience commodity and of capital. The institutional analysis of the relation of capitalism to communications and Canadian dependency reflects what I learned from two groups of people. Three of my teachers in economics at the University of California, Berkeley, were especially significant. The most pervasive in his helpful insights was Professor Melvin M. Knight whose teaching assistant in economic history I was from 1928 to 1933. Cogent and lively advice came from him in his nineties when I was writing this book. Robert A. Brady, and Leo Rogin set me standards of rigorous work which I cherish. The other group were friends and working associates while I was Chief Economist for the Federal Communications Commission (Washington, D.C.). I must mention Clifford J. Durr, Charles Clift, Daniel Driesen, Joseph Kehoe, Geraldine Shandros, Jennie Newsome, Bill Bender, and Joseph Selly in that connection. We all engaged in struggles against monopoly capitalism which were rich in developing theoretical understanding and with some practical results.

On a more personal level, I am boundlessly grateful to Beatrice Bell Smythe and Jennie Newsome Smythe, who successively and lovingly tolerated the inroads my professional work made on my behavior as husband and father. Thank you, Jennie. Thank you, Bee. I owe to my parents, John W. and Emily C. Smythe such capacity as I have to love people and the world and to identify with the underdog. Finally, I acknowledge my love for my children, Sandra, Susan, Roger, Pat, and Carol and their children whose welfare it has been my compelling purpose to improve in some way through my work.

Dallas W. Smythe

September, 1980
Burnaby, B.C.
Canada

INTRODUCTION

This is a study of the process by which people organized in the capitalist system produced a country called Canada as a dependency of the United States, the center of the core of the capitalist system. Rooted in the realistic history of how monopoly capitalism was created in the United States and Canada simultaneously, it focuses on the role of communications institutions (press, magazines, books, films, radio and television broadcasting, telecommunications, the arts, sciences, and engineering) in producing the necessary consciousness and ideology to seem to legitimate that dependency.

If Canada's dependency is my concern, why do I devote so much space to developments in the United States? Because the Canadian people and their development over the past one-hundred-and-fifty years have been substantially assimilated to the latter country. Beginning about the mid-nineteenth century, the processes by which capitalism transformed itself into monopoly capitalism operated across the 49th parallel almost as if no border were there. Indeed, Canada's military-industrial complex is a subset of the American military-industrial complex, integrated into it by corporate connections and special tariff arrangements. If Canada's vast and sparsely settled territory be thought to set it apart from the United States, this has come to be an illusion. Canada's natural resources are as much integrated with those of the United States as are those of, for example, Alaska and Hawaii. So Canada is effectively part of the United States core of monopoly capitalism.

Canadians typically either enjoy the American presence or regard it as a passing source of irritation, to be overcome by pulling themselves up by their idealistic bootstraps. With respect to the automobiles they drive, the movies they see, the popular music they listen to, the popular television programs they watch, the prescription and nonprescription drugs they take, and the junk food they eat at fast-food chains, Canadians are comparable to Californians. They are citizens of a distinct region with its own short historical tradition and its own flag; but they are part of the "continental" scheme of things. Wryly, Canadians often say, "when the United States catches a cold, we get pneumonia." Pierre Trudeau said in 1968 that Canada is no more independent of the United States than is Poland of the Soviet Union; we have 10 percent independence and can maneuver with that degree of freedom.

That Canada has its own state apparatus tends in Canada to be mistaken for national autonomy. The rhetoric of Canadian federal politics has typically emphasized the need for, and even asserted the existence of, the unity or identity of people living in the country. The mere assertion of such a need passes as surrogate for action to establish effectively such unity and identity—as a dozen or more reports by royal commissions created to investigate the need for various kinds of national policy attest. The ruling establishment in Canada has chronically avoided taking the hard measures which would have provided the basis for a modest, limited, but real autonomy of the order of that enjoyed by Belgium, the Netherlands, or the Scandinavian states.

This tendency to mistake state apparatus for autonomy has been reinforced by the tradition of Canadian scholarship in history and the social sciences. Canadian scholars adopted with facility the juridical formalism which has characterized their ruling class's attitude toward Canadian culture. Because Canada has borders and the inherited British constitutional form, it *must* be an independent country and studied as such. Even Harold Innis's work on the staples was a study of the period of mercantile capitalism which governed Canada's early development as a British colony. It might equally well have been applied to the lower thirteen colonies. He conspicuously missed the main point of Canada's industrial development at the hands of American monopoly capitalism. From the 1870s on, Canada experienced the application of science to optimize the efficiency of giant corporations, integrated from raw materials to consumer and fronted for by the mass media. But Innis showed no awareness of the dynamics of science harnessed to greed in the growth of a business bureaucracy sheltered by direct investment in his country. When he dealt with "technology," it was in idealist terms unfocused on the going concern that melded Canada into the American system.

Canada's nominal autonomy has been vastly overrated internationally where it is often regarded as neutral. Canada served as a testing ground for, or instrument of, American foreign policy in major respects since 1945, for example, in the exploitation of the Gouzenko "spy case" in 1945–1946 in starting the Cold War; in Canada's unneutral membership in the International Control Commission to monitor the application of the Geneva accord regarding Vietnam after 1954; in recognizing the Peoples Republic of China in 1971 as preparation for United States rapprochement with that country, etc.

Canadians, however, *undervalue* their state apparatus because they so rarely try to use it to assert Canadian needs when these needs conflict with American wishes; the history of the Canadian film, book, magazine, and radio-television broadcasting industries offers examples. Membership in the United Nations and its specialized organs, direct diplomatic relations with foreign countries: these are advantages which Canada might have used to repair its own damaged sovereignty. Yet Canada prefers "quiet diplomacy" (i.e., private, submissive negotiations) in its relations with the United States.

This book may be read from the standpoint of Canadians concerned with their identity problem, but it is also an analysis of how the United States developed its largest and most loyal colony. It analyzes an aspect of American history—even American economic history—which is little understood in the United States.

I regret that limits of time and space prevented me from exploring fully the policies and structures of Consciousness Industry and the mass media as they deal directly with Third World and socialist countries although the analysis of cultural screens and "technology" in Chapter 10 and Appendix A deal with that topic. People in those countries will find that those policies and structures produce dependency on the capitalist core and may benefit from understanding how Canada's dependency came about over the past century and a half. True, probably no other country in the world has had experience analogous to that of Canada. Populated by European invasion at about the same time as the United States, with a common language for its dominant group, Canada in fact passed from being a British to being an American colonial appendage. But the process by which the United States came to control Canada was the same as that by which the United States developed its worldwide economic-cultural empire after 1945.

Even though capitalism has prospered by its capacity to organize the production of goods and services in the short run, its survival as a system depends upon its ability to produce people ideologically willing to support it in the long run. Its success to date in both respects arose from the transformation of competitive capitalism into monopoly capitalism. That transformation was not restricted to the United States and Canada, but it took shape earlier and more completely in this core area than in Europe or Japan. In those countries, the surge of change which created monopoly capitalism was dampened and delayed by a combination of factors: chief among these were the persistence of traditional class structures, bureaucratic hangovers from feudalism, nineteenth-century-style class struggle, and the devastation wrought by two world wars, from which America profited mightily in economic and military power.

The heart of the analysis presented here of the transformative process which developed monopoly capitalism concerns the growth of giant corporations and the means by which they achieved control over not only the resources and labor for physical production of commodities but also over the creation of demand for commodities. It was equally necessary to establish scientifically based methods of producing physical goods, as to create the marketing institutions by which consumer demand for goods could be managed. At the same time, it was necessary for the security of the giant corporations that they establish hegemony over the state apparatus.

The mass media of communications were a *systemic* invention of monopoly capitalism. Their purpose is to set a daily agenda of issues, problems, values, and policies for the guidance of other institutions and the whole population. They mass produce audiences and sell them to advertisers. These audiences work on, and are consumed in, the marketing of mass-produced consumer goods and services to themselves. This is what Baran and Sweezy called the "Civilian Sales Effort." The audiences also work on, and are consumed in, the marketing of political candidates and public policies. This work includes what Baran and Sweezy called the "Military Sales Effort." Absent the production, consumption, and work of audiences, the mass production of consumer goods and services and the creation and growth of the military establishment would have been impossible. The structural result has been the creation of the corporate capitalist system in which a small number of giant corporations is fronted by the complex of industries, led by the mass media industries, which I call *Consciousness Industry*.

The main effect of this transformation of capitalism in the past hundred years in the core area is the tendency to blur or erase the difference between the world of message-images (embodied in both the abstract symbols of communication and the design and packaging of physical commodities) and the nature of the "real" world as it is understood by the whole population. The main contradiction between people and capital (on both a national and world scale) is between, on the one hand, the ability of capital to maintain and extend its power positions through the influence of the message-images and, on the other hand, the resistance and initiatives of people struggling to control the terms of their own lives (and of nonhuman resources). Far from either the message or the medium being the principal aspect of communications, it is people with whom communications begin and end.

The site where the struggle goes on between people and the mass production of message-images day by day, and hour by hour, is where people are made into audiences, and where they take actions then or later which may be said to be the "work" they do as a result of their participation in audiences. The *mass-produced* audience is a new major institution which now holds a central place in the interwoven complex of institutions—the family, workplace, school, church, and state. I contend that in creating the mass-produced audience, monopoly capitalism produced not only its own chief protagonist (and agenda setter), but its major antagonist in the core area, displacing organized labor from that role.

The monopoly capitalist system has enjoyed impressive success in creating and using the mass media for its purposes in many respects since the 1890s. This occurred first in its core area, and then by extending the scope of Consciousness Industry in the interest of cultural domination in peripheral regions and into the socialist countries. The continued growth and prosperity of the several hundred biggest transnational corporations, operating flexibly around the world yet mostly rooted in the United States, sustains the monopoly capitalist system despite the decline of American power relative to other monopoly capitalist formations (Western Europe and Japan especially) since the 1960s. The rivalry for control of energy, mineral, and other resources—especially in peripheral countries— since the early 1970s has created waves of disruptive inflationary pressures throughout every aspect of the capitalist system. In this situation, people in the audiences of the core nations resist the dissolution of social reality into a world of subjective images.

How does communications relate to the struggles raging on the world scene? In a real sense every politico-economic system rests on the power to control the use of information. Mature industrial countries had the advantage of being first to develop electronic communication using the radio spectrum. This use became the indispensable foundation of the capitalist politico-economic system. With respect to the use of electronic communications, as with other resources, the relations between the capitalist core area and both Third World nations and socialist countries are asymmetric. The core area has, however, put its eggs into a fragile basket. Both military and nonmilitary activities of the advanced industrial countries (capitalist and socialist) depend upon teleprocessing of data via the radio spectrum. Yet for one nation or class of user to use the radio spectrum, all nations and classes of users which have the minimally necessary technical equipment and skill to do so must also be able to use it. Cooperation of all nations, working through the International Telecommunications Union, is an inescapable prerequisite for any nation to use the radio spectrum. It is now known that the organization and technique for using the radio spectrum for teleprocessing is very vulnerable to accidental and unintended disruption. The possibility obviously exists that, if backed by ITU regulations, the opponents of aggressor countries were to deny intentionally the use of the radio spectrum to their adversaries, physical and cultural domination of one country by another might be stopped. Although such sanctions are probably not now technically, politically, nor legally available, they may be possible at some future time when ongoing struggles make such actions feasible. The nonviolent nature of such sanctions may make them particularly appealing to opponents of violent aggression. In short, as the monopoly capitalist system's manifold contradictions intensify, it becomes increasingly evident that its weakest feature is that upon which it most depends for its power: communications.

The methodology here is critical, historical materialism. I advance views which currently are or may become controversial on a range of Marxist theories and concepts, the most obvious of which are these:

1.   Materiality of production means something more than processing raw materials from nature. The implicit Physiocratic premise in Marx and Engels seems outdated. "Consumers'" awareness of the ecological consequences of aerosol sprays plays no less potent a part in determining the policy of corporations in the initial material production than the advice of industrial chemists. I assert that production and productive work in the capitalist system take place in the work of exchange, marketing, and consumption of consumer goods as well as in factories where they are initially fabricated. *Materiality* today in Marxism should mean the actual processes which link people together in social production and social consumption.

2.   It is mandatory that Marxists pay attention to the peculiar nature of social production and social consumption under the constraints in the monopoly capitalist system, as distinct from the competitive capitalism which Marx and Engels knew. The most striking feature of monopoly capitalism is the role of giant integrated corporations (usually transnational corporations—TNC hereafter) in using scientific management to manage demand (the audience front) as well as to manage the job front.

3.   In order to manage demand, monopoly capitalism "invented" the mass media of communication, the principal product of which is audiences to be sold to advertisers. The audience power bought by advertisers finishes the production of commodities by marketing them and finishes the production of political candidates and national and international policies by taking actions in the political process, including the ballot box.

4.   The base/superstructure dichotomy as currently accepted is ahistorical and unrealistic. Evidence of its unrealism is the fact that the mass media of communication which Marxists tend to place in the "superstructure," when they notice them at all, are a principal part of the "base." This is so because their *principal* product is audiences which perform a materially productive service in

accomplishing the mass marketing of mass-produced consumer goods and services.

5. The issue of the process by which labor power is produced needs to be reconsidered in light of the salience of the audience commodity. Here we face no economistic reductionism: in producing their own labor power, audience members experience the dialectical tension between their two "faces," i.e., that which deals with their work as audience members in choosing brands and candidates, and that which deals with their non- or anticapitalist values in living and raising children.

6. "Technology" is not determinative of anything except a pernicious mystification of bourgeois domination. Neither the "medium" nor the ostensible "message" in the ostensibly nonadvertising component of the mass media is the realistic basis of mass communication. The prospective audience beckons the mass media into the form it takes as well as the content it conveys. Put negatively, the sequence is no audience, no message; no medium, no advertiser. Mass communications theory begins and ends with audiences, prospective and produced (and consumed).

7. Ideology, consciousness, and hegemony are areas of Marxist thought today which tend to be saturated with subjectivism or positivism. They should be treated dialectically as interconnected with people's activities which always link some level of thought, language, and physical actions in a context of politico-economic-social institutions. The post-World War I defeat of revolutionary movements by reactionary and fascist regimes turned European Marxists to subjective, manipulative explanations of ideology and consciousness (Gramsci and the Frankfurt School especially). It was no novelty to discover that dominant class formations used the state, the church, the educational system, and the mass media to supplement the use of force in domination. Whatever the concept of "hegemony" contributed to crystallizing our understanding of the process seems to me to have been more than offset by its rigid, stereotypical usage. Rather than perennially rediscovering the wheel (class domination as "hegemony") and employing content analysis of media free lunch to coin in-group "buzz words," it seems more useful to get on with the job of developing tools which work at describing and analyzing the processes of dialectical tension between the private-sector "face" of workers and their public sector "face." For, in inventing the mass media and the mass audience as its principal protagonist, monopoly capitalism has created its chief potential antagonist in the capitalist core area.

8. Just as material production for Marxists should be liberated from the bourgeois disguise of "technology", so should the arts

and science be liberated from their bourgeois class trappings and re-conceptualized in dialectical terms.

To develop the eight foregoing propositions adequately with necessary source citations would require a book itself and its audience would be mostly Marxist theorists. The present work was planned not as one about the debates on theory which may take place, but rather to demonstrate the need for such debates. Or to put it differently, instead of writing a book about theory I have tried to write one which demonstrated theory in practice. The theoretical and factual content in it seems to "work," at least for students. Used over the past three years in draft form as a textbook, the student response has been encouraging.

Dallas W. Smythe

Burnaby, British Columbia
September, 1980

FOREWORD

Dallas Smythe's professional life spans a period in which the United States' business system has become totally dependent on communications for its domestic and international operations. It would be merely coincidental if the increasingly vital role of communications occurred parallel to Smythe's professional career. It is our good fortune that much more than parallelism is involved.

Canadian born, Smythe moved into communications work in the middle of the Second World War, taking up the position of chief economist for the Federal Communications Commission in 1943. Here, he was well-located to observe the tremendous burst of American power into the global arena at that time, and to note the increasingly prominent place of communications in the fusion of corporate and governmental power.

Expansionist policies which sent American troops to bases around the world and private U.S. capital into the former colonial holdings of Europeans, were packaged neatly for public consumption. Fighting or containing communism were the spritely wrappers. Though this was not a totally convincing marketing operation, it did not prevent most government professionals from following and contributing unhesitatingly to the imperial drive abroad and the intellectual repression at home.

Smythe left the government in 1948 and continued his work at the University of Illinois in Champaign-Urbana. Here he organized what may have been the first university course on the political economy of mass communications. He also directed graduate studies in communications. In the early 1960s, he returned to Canada and continued his work first at the University of Saskatchewan in Regina and then at Simon Fraser University in British Columbia. In 1980 he moved to Temple University in Philadelphia.

These biographical details are mentioned to provide a personal, historical frame for appreciating the scientific enterprise in which Dallas Smythe has been engaged for more than four decades, and which culminates in this book. Communications, as a subject of study, has moved from marginality to centrality in this period and the questions Smythe has dealt with now occupy a prominent place on the international policy agenda.

Indicative was the creation at the end of 1977 of the International Commission for the Study of Communications Problems (The McBride Commission), largely as a consequence of mounting dissatisfaction in the less developed world with the state of international communications. In the Commission's Final Report, issued in the Spring of 1980, the Commission made some general comments about the kind of communications research it felt should be undertaken—research that might contribute to an international information order that supported and practiced non-exploitative relations between nations and peoples. I quote these comments at some length:

> Current and future research should broaden its focus in order to deal with the truly fundamental problems of our time. It should not be content to serve to implement a given communications policy, or just to "support" the media establishment, in order to make an existing system or various parts thereof more effective, regardless of its validity or of the possible need to rethink certain dominant values or to suggest alternative means or ends. Research, instead of dealing with value-free micro-questions, must therefore endeavor to apply independent critical criteria and to explore the potential of new forms and new structures. However, the transformation or adaptation of structures, institutions, and types of communications organization is not an end in itself. They may also prove to be quite inadequate. It is with a completely open and challenging mind that they must be investigated and judged for it cannot be assumed that a given complex of structures is by itself necessarily and inevitably consonant with the best interests of all individuals in a given society.
>
> To this end, research must aim to draw closer to the emerging consideration of communication as a social process which entails studying the media institutions not in isolation but in their relationship to other institutions in broad, social, national, and international contexts, i.e., conceptually in terms of structures, ownership, organization, socialization, participation, etc., potentially leading to a reappraisal of existing systems, institutions, structures, and means. . . .*

These comments, in my estimation, are a fitting description of Dallas Smythe's research and work in communications.

Smythe has not been content to support unquestioningly *any* media establishment. He has concerned himself not with "value free micro-questions," but with the fundamental issues of the social economy. At all times, he has insisted that communication is a social process. He has consistently and unwaveringly concentrated his analyses on media institu-

---

Many Voice, One World: Communication and Society: Today and Tomorrow, Report of the International Commission for the Study of Communication Problems, UNESCO and Kogan Page Ltd., Paris and London, 1980, pages 225–226.

tions and their connection to underlying economic structures and social systems.

Dependency Road: Communications, Capitalism, Consciousness and Canada is the outcome of a lifetime's work and thought. The book stands on its own. Yet in reading it, it may be helpful to understand that it represents more than the customary allocation of time and energy to a serious study, much as this usually is. It is additionally, the accumulation of years of government experience, familiarity with many of the important figures in communications research over the period, and, most significantly, the intellectual search of someone who does not back away when the general political, or for that matter, the research climate, becomes stormy.

Dependency Road takes up several of the most demanding questions that have accompanied the massive social transformations since the beginning of industrialism, two centuries ago. These reappear continuously, often in new guise. The central theme in Smythe's study is "the growth of great corporations and the means by which they achieved control over resources and labor for physical production of commodities *and* over the creation of demand for commodities." (Introduction, page 12)

It is corporate capitalism's creation of consumer demand that most occupies Smythe's analytical interest and which probably will be regarded as the most provocative part of the book. It is his contention that the production of consciousness has become a major site of human labor, one that is totally unacknowledged. He claims that audiences work at their own ideological production and reproduction, under the stimulus of an industry devoted to the manufacture of consciousness. The most apparent, but not exclusive, component of this industry is advertising, which Smythe declares is wrapped around the "free lunch"—the entertainment, news, drama, etc. programming on television, in magazines and newspapers and radio.

This emphasis supplies a much needed supplement to "effects" studies and similar audiences and programming analyses.

On technology, Smythe is unmatched. Repeatedly, and it cannot be too often, in my opinion, he insists that communication cannot be equated entirely with the technology nor the messages it carries. Social relations determine what kind of messages will be transmitted and influence as well the means by which they are conveyed.

The Shah of Iran, despite multi-billion dollar American information technology at his disposal, was toppled in an instant. Cuba, with no hard technology to speak of, overcame mass illiteracy with the intense dedication of thousands of youthful teachers. And Vietnam, on whom was imposed a monstrous, American-designed electronics battlefield, side-stepped and defeated the sophisticated military communications of the superstate with its popular mobilizations.

These successes and failures of communications in recent history, do not mean that communication technology is unimportant. They suggest instead that what actually constitutes the technology, and who will be using it for what ends, are matters of social control and class power.

Smythe's discussion of technology is especially applicable to the choices and decisions that must be made in the years ahead by less developed nations and by the most industrially advanced ones, as well. By what social standards should computerization, satellite communications, cable TV, and all the other instrumentation promoted assiduously by the corporate system, be regarded, evaluated, and, under what circumstances, introduced?

National development, the creation of dependency, and the State as a complex ruling class instrument, are other major areas analyzed in *Dependency Road*, with the Canadian-American connection supplying the specifics. Canada's economic and cultural-informational subordination to its "southern neighbor," is seen as an inevitable outcome of a process in which Canada has been compromised at every turn, to powerful United States interests, by its own dominating ownership class. The Canadian case is exceptionally instructive to other dependent countries because Smythe details some of the options that might have been taken had Canada's leaders desired to have their nation genuinely independent.

Dependency Road will help students, teachers and general readers understand better the multiple crises of advanced capitalism, as they work their way into everyday life. As social upheaval and revolution erupt in one country after another, and as waste and ecological destruction and unemployment and inflation grow more intense in the heartlands of the system, communications and communication technology increasingly will be relied upon to maintain, transform, and reinvigorate the world business order. Their uses will include: global surveillance; military intervention; economic rationalization to cut labor costs in the fierce world market capitalist competition; the containment of global audiences with entertainment and diversion and ideological massage; and, providing the underpinning for a new international division of labor.

Dependency Road can reveal, and assist in combatting, some of these uses. As the crises quicken and deepen, the book will not lose its relevancy. It will have a contribution to make, in at least indicating the choices that have to be made, in many places in the time ahead, in finding a different road to social development and individual emancipation.

Herbert I. Schiller
La Jolla, California
September, 1980

DEPENDENCY ROAD:
Communications, Capitalism, Consciousness, and Canada

1

THE ROLE OF THE MASS MEDIA
AND POPULAR CULTURE
IN DEFINING DEVELOPMENT

The mass media of communications (television, radio, press, magazines, cinema, and books), the related arts (e.g., popular music, comic books), and consumer goods and services (clothing, cosmetics, fast food, etc.) set the daily agenda for the populations of advanced capitalist countries and increasingly for Third World nations. It follows, therefore, that the policy which governs what appears on the daily agenda produced by these institutions has a special role in defining the process of "development" for those populations.

What do I mean by *agenda*? As Ortega y Gasset remarked, "Living is nothing more or less than doing one thing instead of another." Individuals daily live by giving *priorities* to their problems. Whether implicitly or explicitly, they use their time and resources to attend to their problems according to some ordering of these priorities. It is when they act as part of *institutions* that the agenda-setting function becomes a collective rather than an individual process.

Human beings are human because and by means of the relationships or process that links them together. Institutions are social habits—systematic and perpetuated relationships between people. Institutions have specialized agendas for their own actions. Thus, the family is primarily concerned with the nurture of children. Work organizations (factories or farms) are primarily concerned with "production" activities. Military and other security institutions specialize on the use of force to perpetuate a particular class structure's control of people and other resources. The formal educational system is primarily concerned with instructing the next

1

generation in the techniques and values of the dominant social system. Medical institutions are principally concerned with the treatment of illness and accidents. Religious institutions have a special concern with theological and ethical aspects of birth, life, and death.

Each of these institutions also embodies in its actions and propagates the agenda which follows from the ideological theory and practice of the whole social system of which it is a part. Therefore each of these institutions incidentally to its prime purpose states and reinforces priorities in the systemic agendas to which the population gives attention. For example, the military discipline instructs young people in the values of private property and individual subordination to a hierarachy of authority. All these institutions are very old, dating from prehistoric times. As compared with them, the mass media of communications are very young institutions (printing since the late nineteenth century, electronic media since the early twentieth century). What has been distinctive about the capitalist mass media is their *specialized function* of legitimizing and directing the development of the social system. For example, the western mass media propaganda had a major role in the capitalist system's replacement of the "detente" between the capitalist core countries and the USSR during World War II with the violent Cold War policies between 1945 and 1950. This was only an incidental function of the older institutions. Because of their relative youth, this special function of the mass media is not yet generally appreciated.

The real world context for the present dominant institutional structures developed over the past four centuries is that of capitalism. It is a system based on private property in the means of production and consumption and on the appropriation of the surplus product of labor by the owners of capital. It is a worldwide system of interrelated markets for commodities. These markets, through more or less monopolistic prices, determine *what* is to be produced, *how much* is to be produced, *for whom* it is to be produced, and *how* it is to be produced. The answers given through these markets to the *how* question determine the kind, amount, and location of specialization of work and production, as well as the kind, timing, extent, and location of invention and innovation of new products and techniques of productive activity.

The two basic building blocks developed to control and operate in the worldwide interrelated markets for commodities are the nation-states (of varying degrees of strength) with their subordinate state apparatuses (military, educational, religious, "cultural," etc.) and business corporations. The latter have come to giant size in the "developed" countries, clustered in groups of three to ten in most industries, and through their power, dominating those industries. Some 200 or more of these giant corporations (mostly domiciled in the United States) operate in a number of countries and are known as *transnational corporations* (TNCs). National state structures are controlled by the dominant class alone or through symbiotic relations with other class formations, although there is an ongoing struggle between that capitalist class and workers of different degrees of intensity in different countries. This struggle is the basis of change in the system of both the nation-state structures and the whole world order. The principal contradiction is between workers and capital, but a number of massive contradictions exist within it: those between dominant and subordinated races and ethnic groups, between men and women, between broad age groups (youth vs. middle-aged, the old vs. the middle-aged), between religious faiths. There are also significant contradictions within the ruling class.

The United States (with its Canadian colony), the United Kingdom, West Germany, France, and Japan have constituted the *core* of the capitalist system since World War II. The "socialist" countries (USSR, the East European socialist countries and Cuba linked with the USSR, China and North Korea, Vietnam, Laos and Cambodia) are, to varying degrees, connected with the TNCs, even if only because all do some trading in the capitalist world market structure. The remainder are Third World nations. They have more to gain than others by changing old and new colonial dependency relations. As we consider in more detail later, "development" of a country (e.g., Canada) at the hands of the capitalist power structure means typically cultural subordination of the "developing" nation in the service of TNCs and the capitalist core. Indeed, the capitalist core developed itself through profitably exploiting the material and natural resources of the rest of the world. Today the core, with only 30 percent of the world's population, consumes 80 percent of the world's energy production (the United States—with 6 percent consumes 30 percent) (Cook, 1973, p. 135). Before the breakup of empires over which flew a single flag and which were represented by a single color on a world map (that is until about 1918–45), control of empires was formal and politically visible—through open control of state structures by the mother country. Since the advent of mass communications, however, imperial control may be and is exercised more simply and quietly through cultural domination via Consciousness Industry supported by the military power of core nations (most often the United States). The myth that formal independence from imperial core countries for former colonies after 1918 meant they were now autonomous as against their former imperial masters does not correspond to reality.

Canada is a case in point. With the disappearance of the British Empire, Canada appeared to become autonomous. In reality, Canada merely shifted from dependency on Britain to dependency on the United States. In capitalist terms, Canada is a "developed" country; as such it is the world's most dependent developed country. At the same time it is the world's richest underdeveloped country and becoming more underdeveloped every year. We shall return to explore these statements more fully in Chapter 5, but before doing so it is necessary to analyze further how the mass media are connected with the kind of development or underdevelopment which takes place in a country. And especially to understand the role of Consciousness Industry.

Today, the mass media (press, television, radio, magazines, books, cinema) are the central means of forming attitudes, values, and buying behavior—consciousness in action, to put it succinctly. They are the "shock troops" of Consciousness Industry. It is obvious to all—and is the main concern of liberal and radical critics—that the way the mass media select and present news, portray ethnic groups in the "entertainment," and handle public controversial issues powerfully affects people's behavior. Such influence is *not* the main concern of this book although its importance is not minimized. Here we are concerned to show that the mass media have a more basic influence on our lives and our ideology because they, together with advertisers, take a central part in the process by which the monopoly-capitalist system grows or declines in strength. In the core area, the mass media *produce* audiences and *sell* them to advertisers of consumer goods and services, political candidates, and groups interested in controversial public issues. These audiences *work* to market these things to themselves. *At the same time*, these audiences have their basic human concerns, and part of the *work* they must do is to reproduce their labor power. This work embodies their resistance to the power of Consciousness Industry. That power appears to them through the total mass media *message* (consisting of advertising, entertainment, information, news), through the physical consumer goods, political candidates, and through tangible evidences of social relations problems.

At the same time as people experience the contradictory pulls of the need to conform to the demands of the capitalist system and the need to live as human beings—and running parallel to that dialectical tension—there is an analogous contradiction built into all commodities. That contradiction is between the physical-and-symbolic potential of each commodity for individual or collective welfare. Just as individuals and groups differ greatly in the way they experience their internal struggles over their internal contradictory tendencies, so also commodities differ greatly in the "mix" of material incentives which they contain toward individual or collective welfare. (See the analysis in Chapters 10, 11, and 12.) In this sense all commodities resemble teaching machines, some more obviously than others. Thus music and wire service news agencies produce commodities which seem entirely to affect consciousness in one way or another (see Chapter 12 for definition of *consciousness*). Thus people in the capitalist core area have come to understand that the automobile biases them toward selfish individualistic actions, although it also has the (relatively damaged) potential for necessary collective action (transportation). The material reality seems to be that (to oversimplify it) we have two parallel sets of dialectical tension: that within individuals (and groups), and that within commodities, *plus* the intersecting dialectical tension between people *and* commodities. Recall the ancient observation that what is one man's meat is another's poison; my friend is allergic to clams, I am not. I argue that the processes of these three sets of dialectical tensions are the detailed location of the production and reproduction of ideology. And therefore Consciousness Industry must include all consumer goods and services.

Why not also include all producers goods and services, or indeed the whole economic order in Consciousness Industry? After all, nuclear power generation and the production and use of pesticides are now well-known to embody conflicts between the selfish private interest and social welfare. Maybe in time our theoretical understanding will develop to the point of coping with that perspective. For the present, I include consumer goods but exclude producer goods from Consciousness Industry because my objective is to explore the relation of people as audience members to the physical and symbolic goods and services which they market to themselves. Concretely then, what does Consciousness Industry consist of?[1]

Although the mass media began the *mass* production of information, they are linked through interlocking business organization and a complex of largely managed, i.e., oligopolistic, markets with a much broader base of information production and exchange. The whole complex is Consciousness Industry. Advertising, market research, photography, the commercial application of art to product and container design, the fine arts, teaching machines and related software and educational testing, as well as the formal educational system, are all part of it. The mass media are also linked through corporate ties and intersecting markets with professional and amateur sports, the performing arts, comic books, toys, games, the production and sale of recorded music, hotels, airlines, and a

---

[1] Hans Magnus Enzensberger was the first publicly to identify Consciousness Industry in *The Consciousness Industry* (1974), and to put the concept on the agenda of Marxist and other media critical analysts. He defined it to include radio, cinema, TV, recording, advertising, public relations, publishing, fashion and industrial design, religions and cults, opinion polls, "simulation," tourism, and education. He did not, however, relate it to the power structure of monopoly capitalism, demand management, and the fact that the mass media were a systemic invention for the production of audience power for sale to advertisers. That is, he took the conventional view that the free lunch was the principal product of the mass media and that it operates manipulatively.

wide variety of consumer goods industries (automobiles, clothing, jewelry, cosmetics, etc.) through "tie-in" contracts and their advertising service to these industries. They are also mutually interdependent with telecommunications operations (point-to-point electronic communications), the computerized storage, transmission, retrieval, and processing of digital information and the industries which produce the equipment for telecommunications and computer operations and which conduct research and development in electronics, physics, and chemistry. The information sector of the United States government and military is at least as large as the civilian telecommunications sector, and both are linked with the mass media by giant corporations. The telecommunications and computer industries dwarf the mass media in terms of revenues and assets and simultaneously generate technical innovations (e.g., television, teleprocessing of data) and enlarge their economic and political power by doing so.

Still another dimension of the complex consists of the banking, finance, and insurance industries which produce and deal in information. To many writers it is sufficient to characterize banking, finance, and insurance as producers of power. But although power is the cause and the result of their actions, the stuff on which they are based is the information generated in these industries. Surrounding all and penetrating this information complex are the gambling industry (illegal and legal) and the grey areas of organized and white-collar crime. In 1967 this "primary information sector" (exclusive of gambling and crime) accounted for 25.1 percent of GNP production in the United States. *This primary information sector plus the consumer goods industries constitutes Consciousness Industry.*

A *secondary information sector* consists of the information-concerned activities of agriculture and producers of goods *other than information* (e.g., missiles and producers' goods, such as iron, steel, and trucks), and the service industries. This secondary information sector accounted for a further 21.1 percent of GNP. The remainder of GNP—less than half—is all that remains of the once predominant agriculture, manufacturing, and service sectors. In terms of workers, the primary and secondary information sectors just described comprise about 47 percent of the total work force and earn 53 percent of total employee compensation in the United States (Porat, 1977, 1978).

This is a totally different situation than that which, as late as 1875, characterized the Canadian and American scene. For the preceding several centuries, the function of "information" transfer was conducted by the post office and by the newspaper, magazine, and book industries with narrow, mostly elite markets and almost no manipulative advertising. In the past century Harold Innis observed, "The Western Community was atomized by the pulverizing effects of the application of machine industry to communication" (Innis, 1951, p. 79).

But the policies of the family, the churches, the educational institutions, the medical institutions, and the military are still saturated with the assumptions and attitudes of a long-gone reality. These hangovers are called *institutional lag*. Much of what follows in later chapters attempts to dispel the myths and confusion in this institutional lag.

Every social institution works through its agenda. Whether the source of the agenda be from the top down, or determined democratically, every institution has an agenda which gives priorities to the problems it faces and the actions it might take. The agendas are both long range (as in a national constitution) and short range (what actions to take today, in what order of importance). They may be formal and written, or informal and aural. As noted, every individual has such agendas, but for the purpose of this book we consider the major institutions because they represent and affect all individuals in one way or another and because they wield decisive influence on the policies determined for the state and for the capitalist system as a whole. What is left off the agenda gets little or no attention and just what gets on the agenda and in what form determines our collective definitions of reality—and of what is possible, what impossible of accomplishment.

The capitalist system, like other social systems, has its unique agenda which claims the attention of its constituent institutions and population. And through words and actions, its population spends its daily lives according to how their real conditions, with all the contradictions and conflicts which such real conditions produce, are affected by the demands of that agenda. For most people, most of the time, the substance of the capitalist daily agenda is painfully manifested by the wage/price squeeze, by unemployment and inflation, by their unmet needs for medical attention, for care in old age. Most people, much of the time, are incidentally instructed in the meaning of the daily agenda through their contacts in, and with, organizations specialized for work, religion, police, schools, and health. But for virtually all the people, all the time, the agenda which directs their attention is that which comes to them from the mass media segment of Consciousness Industry. Priorities in their personal agendas are the outcome of the contradictions between the priorities assigned to topics or themes in the mass media and their own human requirements. This educational process begins in infancy and ends with death.

The secret of the growth of Consciousness Industry in the past century will be found in (1) the relation of advertising to the news, entertainment, and information material in the mass media; (2) the relations of both that material and advertising to real consumer goods and services, political candidates, and public issues; (3) the relations of advertising and consumer goods and services to the people who consume them; (4) the effective control of people's lives which the monopoly capitalist corporations dominating the foregoing three sets of relationships try to establish and maintain. The capitalist system cultivates the illusion that the three streams of information and things are independent: the advertising merely "supports" or "makes possible" the news, information, and entertainment, which in turn are *separate* from the consumer goods and services we buy. This is untrue. The commercial mass media *are* advertising in their entirety. Advertising messages provide news (that a particular product or sponsor has something "new" to deserve the attention of the audience), entertainment (many television commercials are more entertaining than the programs in which they are imbedded), and information about prices and alleged qualities of the advertised product of the "sponsoring" organization. And both advertising and the "program material" reflect, mystify, and are essential to the sale of goods and services. The program material is produced and distributed in order to attract and hold the attention of the audience so that its members may be counted (by audience survey organizations which then certify the size and character of the audience produced) and sold to the advertiser.

This neglected fact was stated in startling terms by the Canadian Special Senate Committee on Mass Media:

> What the media *are* selling, in capitalist society, is an audience, and the means to reach that audience with advertising messages. As Toronto advertising man, Jerry Goodis, who appeared before the Committee, put it: "The business side of the mass media is devoted to building and selling the right audience . . . those who buy and, more importantly, those who can choose what they will buy, those whose choice is not dictated by necessity." In this sense, the content—good or bad, timid or courageous, stultifying or brilliant, dull or amusing—is nothing more than the means of attracting the audience. It seems harsh, but it happens to be utterly accurate, that editorial and programming content in the media fulfills precisely the same economic function as the hootchy-kootch girl at a medicine show—she pulls in the rubes so that the pitchman will have somebody to flog his snake oil to. . . . Yes, advertisers are concerned with content, but only insofar as it serves to attract an audience. . . . In other words, the pitchman would naturally prefer a slender, 17-year old hootchy-kootch girl to a flabby, 45-year old hoofer (Canada, Special Senate Committee on the Mass Media, 1970, pp. 39–40).

As we show in later chapters, readers and audience members of advertising-supported mass media are a commodity produced and sold to advertisers *because they perform a valuable service for the advertisers.* This is why the advertisers buy them. What is the valuable service audiences perform? It is three kinds of work:

1. They market consumer goods and services to themselves.

2. They learn to vote for one candidate (or issue) or another in the political arena.

3. They learn and reaffirm belief in the rightness of their politico-economic system.

A threadbare myth which is still part of the propaganda of capitalism is that of *consumer sovereignty*—that the consumer is in charge and in fact chooses freely between the many thousands of different commodities daily pressed on him/her. The people are told that they can always "switch off" if they do not like a program, newspaper, or magazine. And the use of "ratings" to decide which commercially sponsored programs will be continued and which dropped is sometimes called *cultural democracy*. After all, should not the majority rule? These propaganda themes ring hollow when one realizes that businessmen are not throwing their money away when they pay for advertising. And when one pursues the question, what kind of "work" is it which audiences do for advertisers?

What sort of *work* is it which is not paid money wages, must continue from childhood to death, and must wait for the next hour or day before it is presented to the workers? The only comparable form of labor is slavery. It is tempting to think of referring to audience power as *mind slavery*. Slavery however, means *ownership* of the person. And the term must be rejected as applying to audience members in the core area because they are legally "free" to try to control their own lives.

Audience power work for Consciousness Industry produces a particular kind of human nature or consciousness, focusing its energies on the consumption of commodities, which Erich Fromm called *homo consumens*—people who live and work to perpetuate the capitalist system built on the commoditization of life. This is not to say that individuals, the family, and other institutions, such as labor unions and the church, are powerless. They resist the pressures of the capitalist system. As we develop in Chapter 12, they daily express this resistance in individual and collective actions which embody essential human qualities of love, creativity, and the struggle to assert dignity. But for about a century the kind of human nature produced in the core area has, to a large degree, been the product of Consciousness Industry. People with this nature exist primarily to serve the system; the system is *not* under their control, serving them.

Typically when a "new" model of a consumer good or service is innovated, the process begins where it ends—in market considerations. It begins with market research into the characteristic features of a hypothetical product, candidate, or service which will "sell." This means doing research which simulates the offering of the proposed new product to samples of audience-member-consumers. And it involves the most sophisticated methods of psychological testing. Initially, in its cruder beginnings, market research concentrated merely on numbers of people in the potential market. At a second stage (reached roughly in the 1960s), research techniques were extended to the *demographics*—determining the age, sex, income level, race, education, and urban or rural or farm location of the market to be created. As Erik Barnouw says:

> Network executives now tended to survey their schedules in terms of demographic product demands. Negotiations resembled transactions to deliver blocs of people. An advertising agency would be telling a network, in effect: "For Shampoo Y, our client is ready to invest $1,800,000 in women 18–49; other viewers are of no interest in this case; the client does not care to pay for irrelevant viewers. But for women 18–49 he is willing to pay Z dollars per thousand. What spots can you offer? (Barnouw, 1978, p. 71).

The refinement of survey methodology and development of more refined psychological theory resulted by the mid-1970s in the perfection of "psychographics" by which markets and audiences may be produced according to psychological types of people. It is thus now possible for an automobile manufacturer to design and market a range of models designed for, and marketed by, audiences composed of known psychological types which correspond to the models (e.g., one model designed and advertised to "swingers," another for "geriatrics," etc.). Such products and advertising are not accepted uncritically by audiences as the recent difficulties of Chrysler autos and the notorius failure of the Ford Edsel attest.

When the market research has been digested and the new product or service is decided upon, then the next stage is to design it, drawing on engineering research to incorporate into it controlled obsolescence and optimum appearance features. Considerations of the actual product's potential saleability are matched by equal concern with the design of the container. That design is linked to the anticipated level of the shelves and location in the supermarket where, according to market research, the prospective customer will be most likely to transfer it semiconsciously to the shopping cart as a result of subliminal cues.

Following this, the final marketing plan (test markets, promotional plans, selection of type of media for advertising to reach the target market described in terms of age, sex, ethnic composition, income level, geographic location, and psychographic considerations) is perfected. Finally the physical production process is itself activated and the whole "campaign" put into operation.

If we would understand how and why the agenda of modern capitalism's system, including particularly the mass media which articulate this agenda, is what it is, we must look to the features of modern capitalism which give it its distinctive character. The United States empire differs from earlier empires in that it rests on cultural domination rather than on formal political control, as Herbert Schiller (1976) has shown. The centrality of Consciousness Industry was emphasized by John Foster Dulles, architect of United States empire in the 1950s, when he said, "If I were to be granted one point of foreign policy and no other, I would make it the free flow of information (Schiller, 1976, p. 25). Since World War II, the United States empire has been strategically on the defensive, following the adoption of socialist systems by about one-third of the world's population. But it has been tactically on the offensive with the means of cultural domination. Economically, the successes of United States-dominated monopoly capitalism in developing markets and investments in Western Europe, Africa, Asia, and Latin America have been very great. Militarily, the empire is protected by massive destructive power, supplemented since the late 1950s by substantial ability to deny indigenous liberation movements the power to control their own future development in such areas as the Dominican Republic, Indonesia, Brazil, the Congo, and Chile. Each such intervention, however, by arousing world and domestic public opinion against it, progressively limits American use of such force.

The principal basis of sustained growth in Western monopoly capitalism since 1945 is the spontaneous cooperation of the relatively few giant monopoly corporations (less than 1000 for Western Europe, the United States, Canada, and Japan) of which the few hundred transnational corporations operate in worldwide markets. In each major industry, the controlling giant corporations accumulate and cherish the surplus derived from their managed markets because of the relative autonomy and security that surplus affords. The deliberate collusive avoidance of price competition between giant corporations engaged in consumer goods production provides built-in guarantees against deflation and supports the system in a condition of *stagflation* (simultaneous inflation and cutbacks in production and employment) in periods of business depression. The continued growth of surplus—for the corporation and for the system—depends on the innovation of new models of familiar products and of "new" products and services. Replacement markets are generated by designing obsolescence into consumer goods.

The necessity for consumers to buy new products is guaranteed by (1) style changes; (2) quality control in manufacture, not to maximize product life but to produce product lives which will end shortly after warranty periods expire so that there is predictable "junking" of products because it would cost more to repair than replace them. And the stylistic features of all consumer goods and services are based on calculated manipulation of public taste so that increasingly consumers pay for images rather than use-values. Having analyzed the American development of science, capital equipment, and production, Professor David Noble of MIT begins his *America by Design*:

> Modern Americans confront a world in which everything changes, yet nothing moves. The perpetual rush to novelty that characterizes the modern marketplace, with its escalating promise of technological transcendence, is matched by the persistence of pre-formed patterns of life which promise merely more of the same. Each major scientific advance, while appearing to presage an entirely new society, attests rather to the vigor and resilience of the old order that produced it. Every new, seemingly bold departure ends by following an already familiar path (Noble, 1977, p. xvii).

There are two broad classes of markets in which giant corporations make the "sales effort" which stimulates the realization of surplus that powers the monopoly-capitalist system. First, and most easily recognizable, is the Civilian Sales sector where ordinary civilians buy their consumer goods and services. But if left to depend on this sector alone for its growth, the monopoly-capitalist system would be plunged into ruinous depression. The Military Sales and Welfare sector must be maintained as a giant and increasingly generous "pump primer" in order to compensate for the "leakiness" of the system—the tendency for surplus to be accumulated (or hoarded) by corporations and their direct beneficiaries rather than distributed to workers so that they in turn could buy the consumer goods and services produced. Of course the Military Sales effort also serves to ensure the security of the capitalist system against dissidents and criminals at home and liberation movements in the economic colonies around the world.

This simple summary ignores the massive contradictions between the central core area of capitalism and other major capitalist power centers as well as peripheral Third World nations and their Nonaligned Movement, which are outside the scope of this book. The latter persist in trying to take control over their own societies from the ties which link them to old and new colonial masters. The capitalist system itself generates instability because of the endemic inflation which its oligopolistic practice produces. The cost of maintaining its worldwide gendarme apparatus from 1945 to the 1970s forced the United States to devalue the dollar beginning in 1971 and destroyed international monetary stability. This coincided with strong capitalist hegemonic tendencies in Japan, the European Common Market, and the Soviet Union, leading to a polycentric system less dominated by the United States than in the preceding generation. Increasingly, United States participation in the world system takes place through the TNCs which earn most of their profits outside the United States and are thus essential parts of United States monopoly capitalism while creating destabilizing conditions both within the American market and throughout the world.

In this context, we identify the agenda-setting role of the mass media and Consciousness Industry in the broader sense. The prime item on the agenda of Consciousness Industry is producing *people* motivated to buy the "new models" of consumer goods and services and motivated to pay the taxes which support the swelling budgets for the Military Sales effort. We should recall the fable about the king who wore no clothes and the unwillingness of his subjects to admit the fact publicly. For the suppressed facts are (1) the monopoly-capitalist system gets the people to market both the new models of consumer goods and the ever-growing military establishment *to themselves through advertising*; (2) there is interplay between advertising and real commodities and services and the news, entertainment, and information in the mass media.

In economic terms there are three types of commodities: primary commodities (e.g., wheat), intermediate products (e.g., flour), and end products (e.g., bread). In economic terms, the audiences of the mass media are intermediate products. Like other factors of production, they are consumed in producing, i.e., selling, the end product; their production and use by the advertiser is a marketing cost. The end product of the giant corporations in the consumer goods and services sector is those consumer goods and services. The audiences produced by the mass media are only part of the means to the sale of that end product. But at the larger, systemic level, people, working via audiences to market goods and services to themselves, and their consciousness ultimately are the *systemic* end product: *they* are produced by the system ready to buy consumer goods and to pay taxes and to work in their alienating jobs in order to continue buying tomorrow. The message of the system is a slogan in fine print on a full-page advertisement in the *New York Times*: "Buy something." That way you help keep up the GNP and perhaps keep your job and paycheck so that next time around you will still be able to "buy something."

The media function of producing audiences is not limited to audiences designed to market consumer goods and services. It also includes the production of audiences designed to produce the end product: votes for candidates for political office, and public opinion on "political" matters. For example, the long conflict between Richard Nixon and the press in the United States focused on Watergate was a struggle to produce public opinion on one side or the other. For Nixon, his worst enemies were the producers of the "liberal" press and television audiences; in fact, it was the public opinion mobilized by the mass media which precipitated his resignation. Nixon's election campaigns in 1968 and 1972 were designed and administered by the same methods employed in the production of consumer goods markets. He had said in 1957 that the public buys names and faces, not platforms, and that a candidate for public office must be merchandised in much the same way as any television product. He had been a pioneer in manufacturing public opinion for anti-Communism, beginning with his news management of the trial of Alger Hiss with his memorable use of fraudulent "pumpkin papers." Nixon provides a conspicuous example of what is termed *news management*.

The practice of news management is universal on the part of party candidates, heads of states, government agencies, business corporations, and their organized pressure groups often working through trade associations for the various industries and government intelligence agencies (CIA, etc.). Political parties and candidates advertise heavily in the mass media, and their relation to audiences is the same as that of consumer goods manufacturers. The content of news space in the print media, television, and radio is mostly the result of press releases and publicity-getting events which are staged in order to *make* news. Advertising agency executives have estimated that as much as 85 percent of news is "planted" through the staging of pseudo events (press conferences, publicity stunts, etc.) rather than the result of the initiative of editors and reporters. The objective of political advertising and news management is the same as that of advertisers of consumer goods. It is to produce people who are ready to support a particular policy, rather than some other policy, be it buying brand X rather than brand Y of automobile, or "supporting" one or another political candidate, or supporting employment preference for ethnic minorities or WASPS, or supporting Israel or the Arabs in their long struggle in the Middle East. The mass media thus daily set the agenda of issues and images to which everyone pays some attention.

What are the similarities and differences between the advertisements and the "nonadvertising" content of the mass media? It is important to get a firm foundation for the answer to this question. Humphrey McQueen says:

> To make sense of Australia's media monopolies, it is essential to get the relationship between the media and advertising the right way round: commercial mass media are not news and features backed up by advertising; on the contrary, *the commercial mass media are advertisements which carry news, features and entertainment in order to capture audiences for the advertisers.* . . . It is a complete mistake to analyse the relationship between media and advertising by supposing that the media's prime function is to sell advertised products to audiences. On the contrary, the media's job is to sell audiences to advertisers.[2]

---

[2] McQueen, Humphrey, *Australia's Media Monopolies* (Camberwell, Victoria, Australia: 3124, Widescope, P.O. Box 339, 1977), pp. 10–11. Emphasis in original. This is an important Marxist study of the mass media.

To be effective, advertising, like the avowedly news, entertainment and information interlarded between the advertisements, must have the same qualities as the ostensibly nonadvertising content: it must catch and hold audience attention and present its message in an entertaining way; that is, it must tell an effective story of some kind. Advertising is storytelling. So also is the news. No matter the claims that news is "objective"; obviously it is not. It has a subjective perspective—determined by stylized customs. Even weather reports on television tell a story about what tomorrow's weather will be. And of course, the so-called entertainment programs on television are stories told in stylized, commoditized ways. TV advertisements cost more than the surrounding program material by a factor of from eight to ten to one per minute of air time. They therefore contain the *concentrated* entertaining and informative qualities which are spread out more thinly in the nonadvertising program content.

A second reason for treating advertising and the surrounding program content as inextricably intermixed is, as alluded to, that the advertisers require that the program content be suited to the advertisements. For example, advertisements for foreign travel in newspapers *must* appear adjacent to the "news stories" of the tourist attractions of visiting Hawaii, or Europe, or if you are in the United States, visiting Canada. And there are very many examples of television programs which reached the air only to be canceled (or never passed the "pilot" stage) not because they were not entertaining, but because they did not produce the particular audience demographics which advertisers demanded. A third reason, which applies particularly to news, is that the great bulk of the news is itself produced by business enterprises, government agencies, and occasionally other institutions (churches, labor unions, and special interest groups, e.g., environmental protection associations)—and hence has the same manipulative intentions as does explicit advertising.

A fourth reason for treating the advertising and nonadvertising content of the mass media as essentially connected with each other is that the business organizations which operate them so consider them. In the early years of the mass media, as Chapter 4 explains in greater detail, the press in fact generally allowed advertisers to supply directly the news which the latter wished to see published. Only by a long struggle to eliminate the cruder manifestations of such direct dictation have the mass media achieved limited "believability" for the autonomy of the editorial side of the media. (In newspapers the travel and real estate sections still commonly allow advertisers to determine the editorial content.) Edward L. Bernays declared:

> At its 1888 convention, the American Newspaper Publishers Association openly worried about the effects of press agentry. . . . But there was no real

effort to eliminate free publicity until about twenty years later (Bernays, 1952, p. 61).

How different from the nonadvertising content of the mass media which are openly dominated by advertising is the content of other branches of popular cultural industry, such as motion pictures, popular music, paperback books, and comic books? After all, the customers pay for them at the box office or cash register and not indirectly by working for advertisers. From a broad systemic point of view, however, the content of these popular cultural industrial products is *not* different from that in the advertiser-dominated mass media. It is axiomatic in the trade that if a story has what it takes to sell, it matters not whether it first appears in a book, a popular song or musical genre (like rock music), in a movie, or in television-radio. Cross-marketing of nonadvertising material is essential to capitalist popular culture. The Beatles' records dominated radio station programming for a time. "Hit songs" in the juke boxes are takeouts from Hollywood film sound tracks. *Roots*, beginning as a book, was a successful television series. *Peyton Place* was profitable in television, cinema houses, and as a paperback. And the connections noted here are not confined within the media, no matter how broadly defined, but extend to tangible commodity markets. The "Daniel Boone" and "Davy Crockett" television series had spinoff markets for coonskin caps, T-shirts, etc. The motion picture "Cleopatra" had spinoff markets in jewelry, perfumes, hairstyling, and clothes. Automobiles are given to be used in police dramas on television as "free" advertising. And the jewelry and clothes invented by the counterculture of the 1960s made their way into television situation comedies where they provided unpaid advertisements for the apparel industry. Readers may amuse themselves by extending the list indefinitely. The point is not merely that these specific cultural commodities were cross-marketed, but that the qualities of form and content which made them successful in one or another branch of cultural industry, whether explicitly advertiser-dominated or not, are deliberately cultivated by *all* branches of cultural industry.

The *whole* content (and form) of the mass media is involved in an extremely complex struggle by contending institutions and groups of people. Moreover, in a given country like Canada, the whole content and form of the mass media represents and guides the capitalist system of which Canada is a part. In doing so, the mass media content and form teaches people the ideology of that system. Of a number of conflicting definitions of *ideology* I prefer Lenin's: the system of values with which people support or attack a particular class-dominated social system (see Kellner, 1978, p. 41). The mass media screen in the values of the capitalist system and screen out other values—a function which Nordenstreng terms the

"hegemonic filter." The agenda set by the mass media is explicitly or implicitly (in much so-called entertainment, e.g., professional sports)—
although traditional contradictory elements are included in it—ideologically loaded to support the system. A condensed summary of such values
illustrates.

Human nature is portrayed as fixed ("you cannot change human
nature"). It is typically and incurably selfish. Therefore, "look out for
number one." Let the other fellow take care of himself. In every area,
what is private is better than what is public. Private business is clean and
efficient. But some people are dishonest and mean and they will be
punished by a heroic individual or the efficient military or police forces.
Public government is inherently dirty and inefficient, and of course, politics is a dirty business. It follows that prices charged by private business
are good because private businessmen "have to meet a payroll" and are efficient. But taxes (which in economic terms are indistinguishable from
prices) are bad; and because public officers need not "show a profit," they
are inefficient. Private property is virtually sacred. And public planning
which would tell private owners what to do with their property is inherently bad. But sometimes bad, miserly landlords should be punished by
the community. In fact, that government is best which governs least,
leaving everything possible to be provided by the "market." We should be
"objective" and respect each other's opinions, unless the others are Communists. In that case they are part of a bad international conspiracy.
They are not good Canadians or Americans and ought to be sent back
where they came from.

The difficulties which capitalism experiences in Third World countries, such as Vietnam, Chile, the Congo, Angola, Rhodesia, etc., are stirred
up by Communists. When our TNCs' interests in the Third World are
threatened by discontented peasants or workers who want to elect governments which would serve their interests rather than those of the TNCs, we
should support military takeovers under which our friends can pursue
their policies (as in Chile, Brazil, for example). Force is the only thing
Communists understand. But foreign policy is too complex for citizens to
understand and therefore decisions should be made by the head of state
and his military advisers. Technology and winning are the most important values for us enlightened individuals. As we learn from professional
sports, "nice guys finish last." Our high moral ends justify our means. We
are the defenders of the "free world" and will accept any nuclear risks to
preserve our system. Any such summary of dominant values is deliberately simplified. The texture of the ideology is more complex. In TV, for example, family values are emphasized as against individualism. And
similarly, small groups are given meaning as against raw individualism
(as in "Mary Tyler Moore" and "MASH").

Although its core values are static and rigid, the capitalist system has the necessary flexibility to cope with internal structural conflicts which would otherwise be disruptive. This is a particular virtue of the policy of the mass media which air and coopt such drives. Thus the mass media facilitated the move to the Right which the capitalist system initiated with the Cold War anti-Communist inquisition inaugurated by Richard Nixon and associates in the United States in 1946. And the Black civil rights movement, the anti-Vietnam–war movement of the late 1960s and the exposure of the corruption of President Nixon in the Watergate matter were also facilitated by the mass media. Symptomatic of this cooptative capacity of the system was the full-page advertisement in the *New York Times* for a bank. It featured a blown-up photograph of Che Guevara and the copy ran about as follows: "We would hire this man if we could. For we are making a revolution in banking." Through this cooptative flexibility, individual and ethnic alienation is kept within tolerable limits for the system. Consciousness Industry *leads* in the cooptation. The distinctive clothing, jewelry, hairstyling, and music of the counterculture of the 1960s was quickly adopted and profitably mass produced and mass marketed. This effectively liquidated its cultural characteristics of "protest" and completed the erosion of potential for structural change or revolution which the young radicals of the 1960s hoped to develop.

The enormous mass of advertisements and other mass media content which bombards the individual in the advanced capitalist state from *all* the mass media has the systemic effect of a barrage of noise which effectively exhausts the time and energies of the population. This is a powerful deterrent to consideration of the possibilities of alternative systems of social relationships. As Robert Merton and Paul Lazarsfeld wrote in 1948, in a scene which did not yet include mass television, the net effect is to "dysfunctionally narcotize" the population:

> For these media not only continue to affirm the *status quo*, but, in the same measure they fail to raise essential questions about the structure of society (Lazarsfeld and Merton, 1949, p. 459).

By attending to the agenda set for them by the mass media, the actions of audiences working for advertisers, narcotizes the population. People are diverted from giving high and continuous priority to the political, economic, and social crises which are marginally on or off the agenda and not dealt with, such as the ecological disasters which the rape of natural resources, environmental pollution, and the threat of extinction of life by nuclear weapons make very real possibilities. Biologist Barry Commoner finds that the options are rapidly narrowing and force the choice on humanity of barbarism or a fundamental social reorganization which eliminates the capitalist system (see Commoner, 1971, especially chap. 13).

If the role of the mass media and popular culture today is to define development, what do we mean by *development*? Countless United Nations, UNESCO documents and commissions, as well as individual scholars have defined it in terms such as these: Development is the process of creating the conditions for every individual to live in such relations with other human beings and his/her fellow animals and the remainder of the physical environment as will realize the potential of all. It is also the only tenable definition of *peace*. Because we have not yet in the multimillion year evolution of life on this planet approached an awareness of the qualities inherent in that potential, it is impossible now to describe the objective of development more exactly.

Life proceeds through a process of contradictions and the struggles which embody them. The common denominator which runs through these struggles through recorded history to date appears to be the efforts of some social formations to oppress and exploit other social formations (men vs. women, boss vs. workers, rich vs. poor, white vs. nonwhite, for example). The terms *developed* nations, *developing* nations, *underdeveloped* nations have entered our vocabulary within the past 35 years as a result of the struggles focused in international forums such as the United Nations. The concept of development in these terms has been shaped by experience to date. And that experience has been mostly that of the capitalist world order (for the past 400 years at least). It therefore is not surprising that for the greater part of the world's population today, *development* is defined by the capitalist system through the agenda set by its Consciousness Industry, with the communications media as the leading edge of the process. In the comparatively short history of the efforts to establish socialism since the Russian Revolution in 1917 and the Chinese Revolution in 1949, a *process* of defining and achieving development on lines which might be more in keeping with the objective of development has been institutionalized to some degree (about one-third of the world's population now lives in countries loosely grouped as socialist). It is, however, premature to judge that process except tentatively.

Regardless of the immediate achievements of capitalist or socialist systems, the rivalry between them reveals for all to see the *processual* nature of development. Now everyone has a real basis to ask questions like these: Who will determine the kind of development which is to be pursued? How? When? Why? And most fundamentally, for whose benefit, i.e., for the benefit of which class of people? The answers given to these questions will describe the *development* any people will experience. In the total power struggle between class interests which *is* the process of development, the peculiar technical forms of power embodied in the mass media where they themselves are developed will play the agenda-setting role in all ideological systems. The mass media, as the specialized institutions created for this purpose, will guide (but not decide in any determin-istic fashion) the evolving struggle between contradictory power concentrations within the system. What is *omitted* from the agenda set daily by the mass media for people's attention will hardly shape the strategic level of policy determination for that society. What is generally unconsidered or discontinuously considered cannot enter into mass consciousness. At the tactical level, e.g., the eve of forcible revolution, the revolutionary forces must overcome by other means the technical advantage which control of the mass media confers on the defenders of the *status quo*. Seizure of radio and television stations, the telecommunications net and mass production newspapers is an immediate imperative in every *coup* or revolution. Symbolically and practically, this act sums up the role of information in maintaining or overthrowing a social system. In a fundamental sense, control over the means of informing people is the basis of political power—whether those means be the mass media of communication, informal political education, or the barrel of a gun. As Alfred Sauvy put it, the power to build television stations is like the medieval power to build castles along the Rhine (Sauvy, 1959).

Is "modern technology" necessary for development? Despite the prevalence of the assumption that the answer to this question is affirmative, the proposition requires critical examination. In the past 30 years, the ex-colonial dependencies of nineteenth-century empires have been given aid and advice to adopt advanced technology in order to develop. As Joan Robinson suggests, the purpose and effect of such aid is to perpetuate the systematic underdevelopment of those ex-colonial countries (Robinson, 1966, p. 25). Indeed, as the work of Andrew Gunder Frank and others has demonstrated, such countries have suffered regression as a result. For example, they now import through TNCs denatured junk foods and soft drinks while the mass production by "agribusiness" of such genetic achievements as square tomatoes lacking in flavor but designed to stand the rigors of exportation to Canadian and American markets forces rural populations into slum ghettoes around huge cities (see, for example, Frank (1969); Schumacher, 1973). What does "technology" mean? As I demonstrate in Chapter 10, *modern technology* is a mystifying term which describes the ongoing capitalist system, nothing more. In fact, the idea *appears* to be nonpolitical although, in reality, it is one of capitalism's most potent propaganda weapons in the struggle between the rich and the poor nations and the rich and the poor within nations.

This chapter has served a double purpose. It introduces generally the remaining chapters. It also has shown how all social systems depend upon specialized institutions which, in addition to providing their specialized services or products, incidentally instruct people according to that particular social system's agenda. At the leading edge, as a specialized institutional complex whose principal purpose is the statement and reiteration of that agenda, the mass production by communications institutions integrate and promote the interests of Consciousness Industry. It has argued that "development" as practiced by capitalist Consciousness Industry substitutes an illusory and mystified version of reality for *bona fide* development. And that a fundamental contradiction exists between the cultural domination by Consciousness Industry and the great bulk of the population in Canada and throughout the world.

2

ON THE AUDIENCE COMMODITY
AND ITS WORK

Obviously communications and their equipment, and labor and its equipment are inseparable except in the mind. Both complexes are useful and
marketable, therefore commodities, whatever the theoretical assumptions
may be (M. M. Knight, letter to author, 23 January 1978).

To suggest that the mass media audience is a commodity and that audiences "work" is to raise many questions which unsettle established ways
of thinking. As most audience "work" centers in the home, all the other
functions of the family become involved in considering the implications of
the proposition. Marital relations, child care and development, leisure
time activities, consumer expenditure decision making—all these functions are somehow involved with audience work. Beyond these, for possible consideration, are the relations of family life and of audience work to
alcoholism, drug and tranquilizer addiction, crime and violence—all of
which in one way or another focus on the family. In raising these issues in
the context of the North American capitalist core, I cannot answer many
of the significant questions which are generated. Indeed, so complex and
unanalyzed are the issues I shall be discussing that it may be as much as
can be done on this occasion to try to pose the "right" questions. Traditional behavioral research (and its popular handmaiden, market research)
is simply tangential, self-interested, and irrelevant to the complex dialectical processes of contradictions which are working before our eyes. In
order to analyze our largely commoditized society, we must beware
thinking of people and commodities as disconnected things and see them
as relationships in a social process.

What is the principal product of the mass media? To answer this central question one needs tools—theories. There may be two modes of theory: subjective, idealist concepts, or objective and realistic concepts. Until now, all theory relevant to our principal question has been subjective and idealist. My argument is that this is so and that an objective and realistic theory is needed. Before entering into explanation of such a realistic theory, it is necessary to state why theory concerning the mass media and their principal product has been subjective and idealist. It is easy to see why conventional, bourgeois theory about communication is idealist. The entire literature—bourgeois and Marxist alike—about mass communications has defined the principal product of the mass media as "messages," "information," "images," "meaning," "entertainment," "education," "orientation," "manipulation," etc. *All* these concepts are subjective mental entities; all deal with superficial appearances, divorced from real life processes. The concepts of entertainment, education, orientation, and manipulation do not even refer to any aspects of mass media content but to its *effects, or purpose.*

Of course, this is not to say that abstract, subjective processes are not real. Much of the work that audience power does for advertisers takes place in the heads of audience members. My argument, however, is that there is a material base of work which people must do under monopoly capitalism. Food, clothing, etc., must be bought, and it is this aspect of audience work which "pays off" for the advertiser. At the same time, with inadequate income to meet the demands on the family budget, sacrifices must be made in order that the values of family life may be achieved. Parents postpone some expenditures on their own needs in order that the children or grandma may receive dental care. There is a dialectical tension between the work for advertisers and the effort necessary to put into practice the values which people believe are necessary to make a home, a community, and a nation of which they can be proud. Practical consciousness (awareness of what it means to live—to put it briefly) is objectively and realistically powerfully affected by the outcome of this dialectical contradictory process. (See Chapter 11.)

Naturally, the general literature about economics has, for the past century, had opportunity to recognize and analyze the significance of the mass media, advertising, audiences, and Consciousness Industry. None of it deals with the role of the markets for audiences, produced by the mass media, bought and used by advertisers. It is not surprising that this is true of neoclassical marginal utility economists whose interest concerns imaginary competitive models which correspond to nothing significant in the real world of oligopolistic reality. Those in the Keynesian tradition do notice advertising but only in subjective psychological terms as aimed at "control of the buyer's consciousness" (Chamberlin, 1931, pp. 113–34).

But having noticed it they then disregard it. Some bourgeois economists, increasingly since the 1960s, have shown interest in developing theories of taste and buying behavior, joining in management's interest in market research or in efforts to enforce antimonopoly laws. Without exception, they ignore the role of demand management by monopoly capitalism and the role of the mass media in producing the marketing agent (the audience) for it. Instead they treat advertising expenditures in relation to firm profitability in purely statistical terms as if nothing real was being purchased or used.[1] Among institutional economists, J. K. Galbraith alone has pursued the matter of demand management by giant corporations by means of advertising but stops short at the brink of discovering the audience market:

> The present disposition of conventional economic theory to write off annual outlays of tens of billions of dollars of advertising and similar sales costs by the industrial system as without purpose or consequence is, to say the least, drastic. No other legal economic activity is subject to similar rejection. The discovery that sales and advertising expenditures have an organic role in the system will not, accordingly, seem wholly implausible (Galbraith, 1967, p. 205).

Unfortunately he does not explore that "organic role," nor describe and analyze the relation of mass media, audiences, and advertisers to each other (Smythe, 1980).

How does it happen that Marxists have not pursued a materialist, realistic theory of communications? Marxists from Marx down to about 1920, and including Lenin, could hardly be expected to recognize and deal with the demand-management function of advertising and mass communication on behalf of monopoly capitalism because it was hardly evident until after World War I. In the period of newspaper and magazine development before the 1880s, the press was mostly supported by money and influence from political parties—not advertisers. The press which politicians subsidized thus seemed to influence audiences toward the point of view of the subsidizer through the editorial content (everything but the relatively insignificant advertisements). Because the only market substantially involved in the sale of newspapers and magazines was that in which people bought them, it was easy for them to fall into a psychological, subjective answer to the question, what does the press produce. It produced newspapers and magazines and sold them; no organized market for the production and sale of audiences then existed. So for Marx-

---

[1] This literature is reviewed in Simon (1970); Schmalensee (1972); also, Pollak (1978); Pessemier (1978); and Marschak (1978).

ists the press was lumped together with educational and other high culture institutions of the state as part of its "superstructure," while productive *work* took place at the base—the "infrastructure"—where people were paid for working. After 1920, Marxists continued to assume that the principal product of the mass media is influence.

Gramsci, the Frankfurt School (Adorno, Horkheimer, Lowenthal, Marcuse, Habermas), Raymond Williams, Poulantzas, Althusser, and Marxists concerned particularly with the problems of countries peripheral to the capitalist core (e.g., Samir Amin, Clive Y. Thomas)—none addresses the Consciousness Industry from the standpoint of its historical-materialist role in making monopoly capitalism function through demand management (advertising, marketing, and mass media)[2]. Baran and Sweezy in *Monopoly Capital* (1966) do indeed emphasize the importance of demand management by monopoly capitalism but they unfortunately stop short of analyzing realistically *how* it takes place, contenting themselves with a manipulative assumption about the mass media and advertising. The same blind spot afflicts communications scholars who take a more or less Marxist view of communications (Nordenstreng, Enzensberger, Hamelink, Schiller, Murdock, Golding, and me until recently). Because they do not take account of how the mass media under monopoly capitalism produce audiences to market commodities, candidates, and issues to themselves, theory and practice regarding the production of ideology continues on a subjective, unrealistic, and essentially

---

[2] Raymond Williams comes closer than many Marxists to a realistic treatment of communications and may be singled out for comment. In his *Marxism and Literature* (1978) he sees the full range of "cultural industry," including entertainment, as "necessary material production." He does not include advertising in cultural industry and is vague as to what, if any, activities besides official "culture" are included in it. He criticizes the base-superstructure dichotomy in twentieth-century Marxism and shows that it derived from Plekhanov, not Marx. Williams' *Television: Technology and Cultural Form* (1975) is disappointing. Broadcasting was called into existence by "a new way of life." The innovation of broadcasting is similarly mystified. It is traced to "no more than a set of particular social decisions, in particular circumstances, which were then so widely if imperfectly ratified than it is now difficult to see them as decisions rather than as (retrospectively) inevitable results" (p. 23). By whom, why, in what circumstances, the decisions were made he doesn't say. "Ideological control" was vaguely a purpose, again with no indication of how or who was involved. He never defines "technology" and uses the term as politically neutral. He sees broadcasting in technical terms, worldwide in scope, and advertising as ". . . a feature not of broadcasting itself but of its uses in a specific society [unnamed]" (p. 68). He does a fair critical analysis of McLuhan, not noticing that he himself had given us a line from McLuhan (". . . the means of communication preceded their content," p. 25). In reality, of course, it was the prospective audience which beckoned both the means and the content into existence. In neither book does he recognize the media as producing audiences for sale to advertisers or that advertisers use the audience power to complete the marketing of their consumer goods production. In neither does he recognize demand management by TNCs in monopoly capitalism—terms strangely lacking from his books.

ahistorical basis. *Why* they continue to suffer this blind spot it is not my present task to determine.[3]

The answer given in Chapter 1 to the question, what is the principal function which the commercial mass media perform for the capitalist system was essentially to set an agenda for the production of consciousness with two mutually reinforcing objectives: (1) to mass market the mass-produced consumer goods and services generated by monopoly capitalism by using audience power to accomplish this end; (2) to mass market legitimacy of the state and its strategic and tactical policies and actions, such as election of government officers, military thrusts against states which show signs of moving toward socialism (Vietnam, Korea, Cuba, Chile, Dominican Republic, etc.), and policies against youthful dissent ("Middle America"). The answer to the question, what is the principal product of the commercial mass media in monopoly capitalism was simple: audience power. *This* is the concrete product which is used to accomplish the economic and political tasks which are the reason for the existence of the commercial mass media. Let us consider this strange commodity, audience power.

Because audience power is produced, sold, purchased and consumed, it commands a price and is a commodity. Like other "labor power" it involves "work." So at the outset let us consider what we mean by *work*. By common usage under capitalism, *work* may be defined as whatever one does for which one receives pay (wages, salaries, etc.). (Let us defer for the moment the fact that audience members do not get paid for the use of their audience power.) As such it has come to be regarded generally as doing something which you would prefer not to do, something unpleasant, alienating, and frustrating. It also is thought of as something linked with a job, a factory, an office, or a store. It was not always this way. At its base, work is doing something creative, something distinctively human— for the capacity to work is one of the things which distinguishes human beings from other animals. "By changing the world they live in through labor, human beings *at the same time* alter their own nature, for the lives of people *are influenced both by what they* produce and how they produce" (Rinehart 1975; emphasis added).

It seems that with other animals (e.g., beavers, ants, bees) work skills are programmed through the genes, whereas with human beings, they are learned after birth—i.e., are social products. This fact conceals a secret which explains both the unlimited creativity of which human beings are

---

[3] I first addressed this criticism to Marxist theories in "Communications: Blindspot of Western Marxism" (1977). Also see Murdock, Graham, "Blindspots about Western Marxism: A Reply to Dallas Smythe" (1978) and my "Rejoinder to Graham Murdock" (Smythe, 1978), and Livant (1979a).

capable in their work and their alienation in the processes of work under capitalism. The secret is that for human beings, work involves both thinking and the application or testing of ideas in practice. The link between thinking and practice (or theory and practice)—that *thinking may be joined to, or separated from, practice*—is basic to the power struggle between capital and labor. (Parenthetically, it is the grasp of this fact which gives the thought of Mao Zedong and the Chinese people the basis of their amazing accomplishments.) (Mao Zedong, 1968) The revolutionary success of capitalism as a system rests on the division of labor and its command of capital to multiply the "productivity" of work using ever more sophisticated machines, at the human cost of effectively denying the creative process by fragmenting workers' practice and divorcing it from the interaction of thought and practice. This is the practical effect of "scientific management" (see Chapters 3 and 4).

Let us pose and answer some questions which should serve to identify and describe the audience commodity more precisely:

What do advertisers buy with their advertising expenditures? As hardnosed businessmen they are not paying for advertising for nothing, nor from altruism. What they buy are the services of audiences with predictable specifications which will pay attention in predictable numbers and at particular times to particular means of communication (television, radio, newspapers, magazines, billboards, and third-class mail) in particular market areas.[4] As collectivities these audiences are commodities. As commodities they are dealt with in markets by producers and buyers (the latter being advertisers). Such markets establish prices in the familiar mode of monopoly capitalism. Both these markets and the audience commodities traded in are specialized. The audience commodities bear specifications known in the business as "the demographics". The specifications for the audience commodities include age, sex, income level, family composition, urban or rural location, ethnic character, ownership of home, automobile, credit card status, social class, and, in the case of hobby and fan magazines, a dedication to photography, model electric trains, sports cars, philately, do-it-yourself crafts, foreign travel, kinky sex, etc.

Are audiences homogenous? By no means, although all of them have the common features of being produced by mass media and priced

---

[4] One of my critics argues that a better term for what advertisers buy would be *attention*. At our present naive stage concerning the matter, it does *seem* as if attention is indeed what is bought. But where people are paid for working on the job, should one say that what the employer buys is "labor power" or "the manual dexterity and attention necessary for tending machines?" Where I refer to audiences as being produced, purchased, and used, let it be understood that I mean "audience power," however it may turn out upon further realistic analysis to be exercised.

and sold in oligopolistic markets to advertisers for whom they perform services which earn their keep, i.e., keep advertisers advertising because the expenditure is productive from the advertisers' standpoint. Audiences produced for sale to advertisers fall into two groups: those produced in connection with marketing consumers' goods and those for producers' goods. The latter are typically produced by trade or business media (magazines, newspapers, or direct mail). The buyers of producers' goods are typically institutions (government, in the case of the "military sales effort," or private corporations) which presumably buy on specifications of objective qualities. Moreover, such advertising is a relatively small part of the total; hence, the following analysis disregards this category of audience. The second and strategically most important class of audiences is produced for advertisers marketing consumers' goods. Again, these audiences fall into two classes: The first of these are for producers of what Julian L. Simon (1970, p. 71) calls *homogenous package goods* (HPG) which have certain common features:

> (1) Slight or no objective physical difference between the brands, (2) Low unit cost, (3) Short time period between repeated purchases, (4) Large total dollar volume for each product industry, (5) Except for liquor, heavy use of television as an advertising medium, and (6) Large proportions of sales spent for advertising.

In the HPG category are soft drinks, gum, candy, soaps, cleaners, waxes, etc., tobacco products, beer, wine, liquor, gasoline, patent drugs, perfumes, cosmetics, deodorants, razor blades, etc., as well as fast foods and restaurants. The second subclass of audiences for consumers' goods is that for durable consumer goods. Here are automobiles, snowmobiles, clothes, boats, shoes, hobby equipment (e.g., cameras, sports equipment, household tools), household appliances, etc. Although objective qualitative characteristics are ascertainable, annual style changes dominate them. It is the consumer goods advertisers whose audiences are produced by the mass media to generate the "demand" which can increase GNP.

How are advertisers assured that they are getting what they pay for when they buy audience power? After all, the skeptic asks, how does the advertiser know that I am in his audience? And even if I am in the room when the television set is on, why does he think that I am paying attention to the commercials (I may time my visits to the refrigerator or toilet to coincide with the appearance of the commercials)? The answer is simple. The advertiser is assured that he/she gets the audience power that is paid for in just the same way that an insurance company profits by insuring your life. You may drop dead the day after taking out the policy, or you may pay premiums for 50 years. The insurance company "gambles" on the probability of your living a certain number of years. Probability, working with large numbers, removes the risk from the gamble. Similarly with advertising, the assurance lies in the law of large numbers and the experience with audience probabilities which yields the basis for prediction on which the price of audience power is based. So it matters not if some audience members withdraw their attention; that is expected and discounted in advance by the advertiser.

As to the statistical basis of the experience and prediction of audience size: that is the specialized business of a subindustry sector of the Consciousness Industry which checks to determine audience size. The behavior of the members of the audience under the impact of advertising and the other content of the mass media is the object of market research by a large number of independent market research agencies as well as by similar staffs in advertising agencies, in the corporations which advertise, and in media enterprises. The raw data for their demographic and psychographic research are gathered by intensive interview studies and extrapolated to estimates of total audiences, using reports from A. C. Nielsen and a host of competitors who specialize in rapid assessment of the delivered audience commodity. Scientific sampling yields results as reliable for audiences as it does for grain, sugar, and other basic commodities which also can be "graded" only on the basis of probability and experience.

What institutions produce the commodity which advertisers buy with their advertising expenditures? There seem to be two levels to the answer to this question. The first, immediate level is the media enterprises and the family which is the nexus of audiences. Media enterprises include those which operate commercial television and radio stations (and networks of such stations), newspapers, magazines and which produce billboard and third-class mail advertising. The second, deeper level is that of the factor supply services for the media. Feeding these media enterprises with what might be thought of as the producers' goods which support the commercial media "side" of the production process are all the advertising agencies, talent agencies, package program producers, specialist firms in producing commercial announcements, film producers, the wire services (AP, UPI, Reuters, Canadian Press, etc.), "syndicators" of news columns, writers' agents, book publishers, motion picture producers and distributors.

But powerful institutions feed the audience production process from the family or audience side as well. Here the role of the educational institutions, especially at the primary and secondary levels, is important. Preparation of children for their role in audiences in those institutions is both explicit in classroom experience which "educates" children as to how media and business function (e.g., classes in business English or other vocational skills related to salesmanship, advertising, etc.) and implicit in the submissiveness to authority which the schools impart. Obviously, underlying both the media side and the audience side of the process of producing audiences is the electronics-photography industry complex which conceives, produces, and markets both the "software" (package programs, wire service copy, for example) and the hardware (high-speed presses, porto-pak television cameras, home receivers for television, radio, etc.).

How are prices for audience power determined? Monopoly and oligopoly characterize the supply of audiences produced by the newspaper industry. Single newspaper ownership is practically universal in American and Canadian urban areas, and the only effective ceiling on audience prices demanded by newspaper publishers is the opportunity cost to the advertiser of using alternative media (direct mail, billboards, radio and television). Cross-ownership of radio and television stations by newspaper publishers is so common as to inhibit intermedia competition in the sale of audience power (see Chapters 6 and 8). Moreover oligopolistic price setting is supported by long-established trade associations for each of the media. Prices are differentiated according to types of demand for audience power. Basic to newspaper pricing is the separation of "national" from "retail" advertisers, with the former being charged substantially higher rates than the latter. A separate price schedule governs sales to "classified" advertisers. Within the retail category, different prices are commonly charged for different classes of advertisers, e.g., on "business pages"—main financial pages, notices of dividends, corporate meetings, etc.—or listings of restaurants, amusements, books, resorts, etc. Quantity reductions are commonly granted for larger spaces; frequency discounts, for multiple exposures over time. The levels of rates are set on the basis of ability to pay (Simon, 1971, pp. 146–147). Magazine prices for audiences are classified as "national" for magazines producing nationwide audiences, and "local," for magazines with more limited geographic scope.

The markets for radio and television audiences, except for the relatively small proportion served only by single stations, display more competition for the advertisers' expenditures than do those of newspapers. For television audiences, the competition between networks is intense. Audiences for television (and radio before radio networks atrophied after television was innovated) command different prices according to whether they are priced as a network package or the product of a single station. They were originally priced differently if they were sold as produced by a "sponsored program," or as spot announcements *between* programs. By the 1970s, few "sponsored" programs were broadcast (mostly soap operas and one-time "specials" in prime time); the great bulk of audience time on both television and radio is now sold via spot announcements—mostly those sold by networks, but some directly by stations through "station representatives" to advertisers.

Erik Barnouw (1978, pp. 69–70) describes the television market for audience power in terms analogous to markets for spot and future transactions in commodities like wheat or copper:

> A central point was that a sale designated a particular *program*—not merely a time period. The advertiser had taken the position that he must have program settings suitable to his messages and purposes, and the networks had accepted this as reasonable. From this flowed many consequences.
>
> One was the disappearance of fixed prices. The rate card became virtually obsolete. A slot in a program that had, at the moment, a top Nielsen or Arbitron rating could be sold for a higher price than a slot in a program with a lower rating. Thus the business gravitated toward endless bargaining. Prices fluctuated as on a stock market.
>
> A sharp rise in ratings brought a rise in asking price. When NBC decided in 1970 to schedule a series around the comedian Flip Wilson—then a relatively unknown quantity—network time salesmen began by selling 30-second slots for about $35,000 each. As the program won unexpected success and climbing ratings, the asking price went to $40,000, $45,000, $50,000 and beyond. On a single broadcast, one slot might have been sold at the lowest, earliest price; others at later prices. On some series, ratings and prices went down instead of up.
>
> The buying and selling was generally done in clusters or packages. In view of the staggering number of spots involved, this seemed inevitable. For the sponsor it was also a way to hedge his bets. Unexpected failures could be balanced by unexpected successes. There was a safety in this "scatter" buying. In the bargaining process, a sponsor might indicate through his advertising agency that he was ready to invest $1,400,000 in time purchases for Mouthwash X; the network was asked to provide a suggested list of available slots. Some would be rejected as unsuitable, others accepted. Eventually there would be agreement on a spectrum of spots, and on a package price. A specific dollar value would be assigned to each spot; this was essential because a program cancellation would require the network to make a refund, or provide a comparable spot. The spots in a package might have wildly diverse price tags, reflecting their ratings and other bargaining factors. They might include 30-second slots in a football bowl game at $90,000 each; in a popular mystery series at $55,000 each; in an evening news series at $18,000 each; in a documentary prime time special at $14,000 each; and in an early morning show at $4,000 each.
>
> A documentary special, even in prime time, was likely to go at a "bargain price" unless some sensational element was involved. A special could not have a track record, so its ratings could only be guessed at. And most sponsors were in any case reluctant to consider a slot in what might prove controversial; some flatly refused to take the risk.

To see that audience power is literally a commodity, consider the following packages of audience power available in the Vancouver, British Columbia, area for local television advertisers in May 1978:

For One 30-Second Spot on Bulk Basis
(Dollar cost per 1,000 persons)

	M*A*S*H (prime time)	Hockey Night in Canada (prime time)	Batman (Saturday AM)
Total viewers	2.32	1.99	0.96
Adults, total	3.00	2.29	—
Men	5.84	3.45	—
Women	5.13	5.98	7.35
Teenagers	25.39	42.44	3.85
Children	50.78	50.78	1.89

If the demographic and psychographic characteristics of women in these audiences in this market fitted the demand-management needs of an advertiser, M*A*S*H would be a better buy than either of the other programs. Similarly, if the advertiser's marketing strategy was aimed at children, the best buy of the three would be the Batman program on Saturday morning.

These audience power markets establish prices in the familiar oligopolistic mode of monopoly capitalism. And an advertiser's power in the audience market has been a significant factor in building monopoly corporate empires. A sympathetic expert on advertising, Julian Simon (1970, pp. 222–223) says:

> At the corporate level, advertising sometimes has led to increased concentration by diversification because of multiproduct volume discounts on advertising time and space. For example, the FTC record revealed that Procter & Gamble could buy television time for 5 percent less than could the Clorox Company and this was an admitted motivation in Procter & Gamble's purchase. . . . Blake and Blum (1965) have compiled their relevant data on these volume discounts and provide compelling analysis to show that they must have been an important reason for firms that advertise heavily to seek mergers and reduce the cost of advertising.

> This effect is illustrated by a recent trade-paper story: "The proposed Cadbury-Schweppes merger, which sees economies in advertising and overseas expansion as its chief benefits, will create (if the Board of Trade permits) the United Kingdom's fourth largest food group, with estimated sales of $600,000,000. Savings would come from the group buying of television time, which accounts for at least 75% of the companies' joint budget in that medium. In 1968, the two companies put out $13,650,000 for advertising, the second largest in the country. . . ." (*Advertising Age*, March 3, 1969, p. 26).

Simon also points out that the better the advertiser's ability to measure the productivity of his purchased audience power, the more sensitive the advertiser will be to rate changes. And he uses as example, the case of mail order advertisers who buy magazine audience power:

> Mail order advertisers have an almost perfect measure of the effect of their advertising, and they receive sharp discounts below the rates paid by general advertisers. (Simon, 1970, p. 146).

Who pays how much for the production of audience power?   On the surface it seems as if the exchange of audience power for commercial media content is equal or perhaps is even tilted in favour of the audience. You audience members contribute your unpaid work time and in exchange you receive the program material and the explicit advertisements. What better way to spend those "leisure hours" anyway? Especially, if as audience research suggests, television audience behavior since the mid-1960s increasingly tends to treat television as aural-visual wallpaper: the set is left on and audience members either attend to it or drift between the television room and adjacent (or remote) rooms, "glimpsing" the television set in passing and monitoring it auditorily all the while. (Lyle, 1972, p. 23). Is there inconsistency between the concept of audience power as a commodity and such disrespectful behavior? Of course not. Is the tendency of workers on the production line to skimp or sabotage their work processes inconsistent with the fact that they have sold their labor power to the boss?

If we would understand the full audience contribution to producing their own audience power in a capitalist system, we must start by asking what value the system places on that audience power. And we shall find (in the next two chapters) that it is of vital importance to the system which could not survive without it. But, and the contradiction is significant, the system gets it "dirt-cheap."

Regarding television and radio broadcasting, advertisers spent in Canada in 1976 about $417 million on television and $279 million on radio.[5] For the 6,684,000 Canadian households with television sets in

---

[5] These estimates are made by applying to Canadian time sales by television and radio the same ratio which such time sales bear to total advertising expenditures on television and radio in the United States. In the United States in 1976, 77 percent of advertising expenditures on television went for network and station time ($5.198 billion), and 22 percent for production of program and advertising content; in radio 87 percent ($2.019 billion) went to network and station time and 13 percent to program and advertising content. In Canada the official statistics are nonsensical. Statistics Canada reported total advertising expenditures on television of $341.8 million; time sales of networks and stations to advertisers were given as $322.6 million. For radio, $111.1 million advertising expenditures were reported; time sales of networks and stations to advertisers (which represent only part of advertising expenditures) were given as $241.8 million. I have assumed that Canadian practice followed the United States model.

1976 (and they were 97 percent of all households), advertisers spent $62 per household. Assuming a 23-hour week for television viewing per household (a very conservative figure), advertisers paid 5.2 cents an hour for the audience power of the average television household in 1976. Similarly, the 6,918,000 Canadian households with radio (100 percent saturation) cost the advertisers an average of $40 per household per annum. Assuming 18 hours per week of radio listening per household, this equaled 4.2 cents per household per hour of radio listening. Even without sophisticated productivity analysis of these costs, it is evident that the productivity of audience power need not be very high for all the individuals in the audience in order for it to be profitable for advertisers to recoup the costs—to them—of putting audience power to work.

From the standpoint of the audience, however, it bears much heavier costs than the advertisers. For what? For the privilege of working without pay as audience members, marketing consumer goods and services to themselves. And these heavier costs ignore the hidden costs they incur through commodity purchases. Table 2–1 compares the direct cost to audiences in Canada and the United States of commercial television and radio programming. It shows that, in 1976, Canadian audience members paid $2.188 billion as the direct cost of owning and operating their television receivers, whereas advertisers spent a mere $417 million. In other words, for every dollar spent by advertisers to buy media-produced television audiences, Canadian householders spent five. And whereas the depreciated investment in property, plant, and equipment of the combined over-the-air and cable television industry and the over-the-air radio broadcast industry in Canada was $645 million in 1976, the audience's depreciated investment in television and radio receivers was $3.905 billion. (Because CBC does not report investment in television and radio property separately, it is necessary to combine them.) In other words, for every dollar invested by the television-cable and radio broadcast industry in plant and equipment, Canadian householders had invested more than six dollars in their television and radio receivers.

In the United States, audience members paid $21.949 billion to own and operate their television receivers in 1976; advertisers spent $6.721 billion to buy the television audiences—a ratio of three dollars spent by the audience to one by the advertisers. A similar ratio of three to one existed between costs for radio receivers ($2.330 billion) and advertiser expenditures to buy radio audiences ($8.040 billion). Curiously, although these ratios for operating costs were lower in the United States than in Canada, the ratios for depreciated investment by audiences were higher. Thus for television, audience investment was $32.670 billion, but over-the-air television depreciated investment was $850 million—a ratio of 33 to 1.

Table 2-1
Comparative Cost of Television and Radio
in Canada and the United States, 1976

	Canada		USA	
	TV	Radio	TV	Radio
Audience Costs, Direct:				
Basic Data:				
Number of receivers (000)*	9,895	23,400	121,000	402,000
Average purchase price (est. $)	600	80	540	72
Average useful life (est. years)	7	7	7	7
Average remaining useful life (est. years)	3.5	3.5	3.5	3.5
Interest rate on investment (est. %)	10	10	8	8
Average cost of power (est. $)	15	4	15	4
Average cost of repairs (est. $)	70	3	60	3
Annual Costs per Set ($):				
Depreciation (1/7 of price)	86	11	77	10
Interest (on 1/2 of price)	30	4	22	3
Power	15	4	15	4
Repairs	70	3	60	3
Total	201	22	174	20
Total Audience Cost (total cost per set times number of receivers/million $ per year)	1,989	515	21,054	8,040
Add cable costs for cabled households (million $ per year)†	199	—	895	—
Total Audience Cost (million $)	2,188	515	21,949	8,040
Advertiser Costs (million $ per year)‡	417	279	6,721	2,330
Audience and Industry Investment:				
Depreciated audience investment (1/2 original cost, million $)	2,969	936	32,670	14,472
Depreciated investment in broadcast property, plant and equipment (million $):				
Over-air industry (except CBC)§	101	56	850	504
Over-air industry (including CBC)§		409	—	—
Cable industry†	236	—	?	—
Total Cable and Over-Air (Canada)		645		

Table 2-1 (Continued)
Comparative Cost of Television and Radio
in Canada and the United States, 1976

	Canada		USA	
	TV	Radio	TV	Radio
Profitability of Industry:				
Net profit before taxes (million $):				
Over-air industry§	60	36	1,546	158
Cable (Canada)†	36	—	—	—
Rate of return (%)				
Over-air industry	59	65	182	31
Cable (Canada)	15	—	—	—

* UNESCO *Statistical Yearbook*, 1977, pp. 996, 1016.
† Statistics Canada, *Cable Television*, Cat. 56, 205, 1976; United States Bureau of the Census, *Statistical Abstract*, 1978. Aspen Institute, *The Mass Media*, 1978, p. 215.
‡ For Canada, see footnote 5 (in text); for United States, Aspen Institute, *The Mass Media*, 1978, p. 203.
§ For Canada, Statistics Canada, *Television and Radio Broadcasting*, Cat. 56, 204, 1976; for United States, Federal Communications Commission, *Annual Report*, 1976, pp. 130, 141; Aspen Institute.

And for radio broadcasting, audience investment was $14.472 billion as against $504 million by the radio broadcast networks and stations—a ratio of 33 to 1.

If one examines the basic data on audience receiver costs in Table 2-1 closely, it is evident that I have had to make rough estimates for all of them. The estimates appear to be conservative. At any event, the gross imbalance between audience costs and investment on the one hand, and expenditures by advertisers and investment by television and radio broadcast industries is obvious. Even if the real costs of depreciation, interest, power, repairs were a third less than my estimates suggest, television audiences in Canada and the United States would still be paying twice as much as advertisers.

What seems surprising from this analysis is that this preponderant investment and expense by audience members is virtually unnoticed by them and by scholars working in the mass media field. By what magicians term *misdirection*, attention is so focused on the exotic performances and lives of media stars and the showbiz glamor of program production and network and station operations that the real situation is mystified out of existence, as far as popular consciousness is concerned.

Who pays how much for the production of audience power other than via television-radio? For newspapers and magazines, advertisers pay the great bulk of the cost—typically from 70 to 90 percent. Audience subscription and newsstand purchase payments cover approximately only the delivery cost of the newspapers and magazines. "Community" and "shopping" newspapers which have no subscription price are paid for entirely by advertisers. Direct mail advertising materials are at the expense of advertisers, subsidized by heavy drains on revenues from first class mail and general tax revenues through below-cost postal rates. A similar postal subsidy for magazines and newspapers has shifted substantial portions of the costs of magazines and newspapers to the postal service in Canada and the United States since the last quarter of the nineteenth century.

What is the nature of the content of the commercial mass media under monopoly capitalism? In Chapter 1, we considered the many ways in which there is unity between the apparently advertising and the apparently nonadvertising content of the commercial mass media. Both types have the same features. But it would be a serious error to ignore the importance of the formal difference between the "advertising" and the "program" or "editorial" content. The fiction that the advertising supports or makes possible the news, entertainment, or "educational" content has been a public relations mainstay of the commercial mass media. The professional *esprit de corps* of journalists hinges on it. And the textbooks, courses of instruction, teachers, and researchers in the mass media accept this fiction as defining the boundaries of their concerns. Either they deal with editorial content (in the case of newspapers and magazines) or program content, or they are hived off into textbooks, research, etc., about advertising. The only connection commonly made between advertising and the nonadvertising content of the media is to raise and dispel the suspicion that advertisers commonly tell the editorial departments of newspapers and magazines or the program producers of television and radio what *not* to say in the nonadvertising portions. (Of course, they seldom do this; it is not necessary because the editorial policy of the media selects people for employment and predetermines the limits of what is "acceptable" noneditorial content.)

As a necessary consequence of the prevalence of this fiction, audience members and social scientists have come to regard the nonadvertising content as the sufficient attraction which warrants audiences spending time attending to the whole media product. So A. J. Liebling's (1961) point that the nonadvertising content is the "free lunch" does have a solid basis in public consciousness, a basis cynically reinforced by the newspapers' practice of referring to the space between the advertisements as the *holes* which must be filled with appropriately sized chunks of "news." The appropriateness of the analogy is manifest. As with the *hors d'oeuvres* or potato chips and peanuts given to the customers of the pub, bar, or cocktail lounge, the function of the free lunch is to whet the appetite. In this case, to whet the prospective audience members' appetites and thus (1) attract and keep them attending to the program, newspaper, or magazine; (2) cultivate a mood conducive to favorable reaction to the advertisers' explicit and implicit messages.

In the policy of the mass media, the characteristics of the free lunch must always be subordinated to those of the formal advertisements, because the purpose of the mass media is to produce audiences to sell to the advertisers. Therefore a program which is more arousing than the adjacent advertisements will not survive; it could survive the preliminary screening only because of faulty judgment on part of the media management and advertisers. The cost per unit of time or space of producing an explicit advertisement is many times the cost per unit of time or space of producing the free lunch (in a ratio of 8 or 10 to 1 in television) which is a rough index of the relative attention paid to the arousal qualities of the two.

There is, of course, a market for the free lunch, and this market spans not only the totally advertiser-dependent media (television and radio) but also the cinema, magazines, newspapers, and book industries. A particular commodity in the free lunch market (*Roots*, for example) will appear in more than one of these media, sometimes simultaneously (as with the book and film, *China Syndrome*), often successively, in each case appropriately edited to fit the media's needs.

Qualification is necessary regarding the free lunch. On the one hand, in the case of newspapers and magazines, many readers buy the publication *because* they want the advertisements. This is especially true with classified advertisements and display advertising of products and prices by local merchants in newspapers. It is also true of most "hobby" magazines where the product information in advertisements may be as much an inducement as the free lunch to prospective readers. On the other hand, cable television, coupled with commercial television broadcasting, results in audience members paying directly for *both* the free lunch *and* the advertisements, as inescapably they will for pay-television —if and when that becomes widespread and able to prempt mass appeal free lunch programs, such as championship sports events.

By emphasizing the economic role of the free lunch in media content, I by no means wish to minimize its importance in its own right. As a social institution with the agenda-setting role which it has, the mass media free lunch puts into words and images the view of events in the local community, the region, the country, and the world which journalists produce and media entrepreneurs publish. That the mass media in Canada and the United States on occasion expose and attack corruption and otherwise critically examine the working of the present social system is undeniable. We need not expand on that here because the literature on the mass media amply celebrates these efforts. But as is demonstrated in Chapter 11, the overwhelming tendency of the free lunch is to reaffirm the status quo and retard change.

Nor should one minimize the propaganda value of the free lunch. Its production by Consciousness Industry is a process of interpreting and homogenizing the entire cultural heritage in current commoditized terms. (A sign over a Hollywood publicity agent's desk reads, "You never lose money by underestimating the level of popular taste.") As and when bourgeois literature, drama, art, and music, and traditional folk cultural materials (e.g., Calypso music) provide profitable opportunities, it all becomes raw material for commercial media free lunch and advertising content. The ideological basis of it all is possessive individualism with the corollaries described in Chapter 1. Beginnings are being made in the exploration of the concrete reality of how the process works (Dorfman and Mattelart, 1975; Schiller, 1969, 1973, 1976; Kellner, 1979; Gitlin, 1979). The range and subtlety of the propaganda is evidenced by the following testimony before a United States congressional subcommittee, "On Winning the Cold War," by Dr. Joseph Klapper. Although it is an evaluation of a form of propaganda addressed to foreigners, it is equally applicable to domestic media content:

> Now, of course the broadcasting of popular music is not likely to have an immediate effect on the audience's political attitude, but this kind of communication nevertheless provides a sort of entryway of Western ideas and Western concepts, even though these concepts may not be explicitly and completely stated at any one particular moment in the communication. In addition, and simply because the communication does fill a need which the audience enjoys having filled, it probably serves to build up a certain credibility and respect for the source of that communication. . . . And this building of source credibility is one of the numerous possible preparatory steps toward the eventual clinching moment of persuasion (U.S. Congress, House, 1967, pp. 64–65).

The free lunch thus provides material which, taken jointly with the explicit advertising, gives the audience material to work on.

What is the nature of the service performed for the advertiser by the members of the purchased audience? In economic terms, the audience commodity is a nondurable producers good which is bought and used in the marketing of the advertiser's product. The work which audience members perform for the advertiser to whom they have been sold is learning to buy goods and to spend their income accordingly. Sometimes, it is to buy any of the class of goods (e.g., an aircraft manufacturer is selling air transport in general, or the dairy industry, all brands of milk) but most often it is a particular "brand" of consumer goods. In short, they work to create the demand for advertised goods which is the purpose of the monopoly-capitalist advertisers. Audience members may resist, but the advertiser's expectations are realized sufficiently that the results perpetuate the system of demand management.

People in audiences, we should remember, have had a rich history of education for their work as audience members. As children, teenagers, and adults they have observed old and new models of particular brands of products on the street, in homes of friends, at school, at the job front, etc. Much time will have been spent in discussing the "good" and "bad" features of brands of commodities in hundreds of contexts. A constant process of direct experience with commodities goes on and blends into all aspects of people's lives all the time. Advertisers get this huge volume of audience work (creation of consumer consciousness) as a bonus even before a specific media free-lunch–advertising program appears on the tube face and initiates a new episode in audience work. (See Chapter 11, pp. 263–69)

While people do their work as audience members they are simultaneously reproducing their own labor power. In this respect, we may avoid the trap of a manipulation-explanation by noting that if such labor power is, in fact, loyally attached to the monopoly-capitalist system, this would be welcome to the advertisers whose existence depends on the maintenance of that system. But in reproducing their labor power, workers respond to other realistic conditions which may on occasion surprise and disappoint the advertisers.

The nature of audience work may best be approached through successive approximations. At a superficial level it looks like this: "Customers do not buy things. They buy tools to solve problems," according to Professor T. N. Levitt (1976, p. 73) of Harvard Business School. The nature of the work done by audience power thus seems to be to use the advertising free lunch combination of sensory stimuli to determine whether s/he (1) has the "problem" the advertiser is posing (e.g., loneliness, sleeplessness, prospective economic insecurity for loved ones after the breadwinner's death, etc.), (2) is aware that there is a class of commodities which, if purchased and used will "solve" that problem (e.g., shampoo, nonprescription sleeping drugs, life insurance) and that people like him/her use this class of commodity for this purpose, (3) ought to add brand X of that class of commodities to the mental or physical shopping list for the next trip to the store. This is the advertisers' rational basis. For audience members, however, their work is not so rational.

There is an *ever-increasing* number of decisions forced on audience members by new commodities and their related advertising. In addition to the many thousand of different items stocked by a typical supermarket at any one time, more than a thousand new consumer commodities appear each year. Literally millions of possible comparative choices face the audience member who goes shopping. As a long line of books stretching back to the 1920s has argued (for example, Chase and Schlink, 1927), the consumer is totally unable to *know* either the craftsman's sense of quality or the "scientific" basis of quality as built into consumers goods by modern mass production techniques. Imagine yourself entering a toilet-goods section of a modern department store in which every product was in a similar glass container and the containers bore only the chemical description of the contents and the price. Unless you were a very experienced chemist specializing in cosmetics and other toiletries (and even then you would have to do a lot of thinking), how could you know which was a "best buy," or even what the product was intended to do: be a shampoo, deodorant, skin-care cream, or what? Lacking the product brand name, the shape and symbolic decoration of the package, you would be helpless.[6]

It must be assumed that when most people go shopping, even for H.P.G., there is real necessity moving them. The refrigerator needs restocking. Soap is needed for washing, and so on. And that they are increasingly aware of the squeeze of increasing cost of living versus inadequate income. The recent appearance of "no-name brand" commodities is a response of monopoly capitalism to consumer resistance to the usual brand pricing practice. In the 1950s there was a flurry of "discount stores" where "standard" brand merchandise (acquired from bankrupt stores, from usual sources, or from thieves) was sold at substantial discounts. This was a tactical response of the system to consumer resistance. And with the artificial prosperity of the Vietnam war period these stores disappeared. It is probable that "no-name brand" merchandise is a similar, temporary tactical concession. In any event, "no-name brands" amount in fact to new "house brands" with, for the present, reduced prices.

Your work, as audience member, has to do with how your life's problems interact with the advertising-free-lunch experience. But how? How, in light of that experience do you decide whether you really have the "problem" to which the advertiser has sought to sensitize you? And if the answer to this question be affirmative, how do you decide that the class of commodities which have been produced to cope with that problem will really serve their advertised purpose? And if the answer to that question be affirmative, how do you decide whether to buy brand A, B, or n? *The process contains a monstrous contradiction. It is totally rational from the advertisers' perspective and totally irrational from the audience members'.*

---

[6] I am indebted to William Leiss for this hypothetical and chastening idea. See his *The Limits to Satisfaction* (1976, p. 81).

Faced with the necessity to make some decisions as to what classes and what brands of commodities to put on the shopping list (if only to preserve a shred of self-respect as one capable of making one's own decisions), it seems that Staffen B. Linder (1970, p. 59) may be correct in saying that the most important way by which consumers can cope with commodities and advertising is to limit the time spent per purchase in thinking about what to buy:

> Reduced time for reflection previous to a decision would apparently entail a growing irrationality. However, since it is extremely rational to consider less and less per decision there exists a rationale of irrationality.

"Impulse purchasing" has increasingly become the practice of Consciousness Industry, as market researchers have studied the effect of store layout, shelf-level display, and commodity package design and artwork on customers pushing their basket-carts through supermarket aisles. Studies of eye-blink rates indicate that a semihypnotic condition of the customer results in impulse purchases for which no rationale can be remembered when the customer returns home. "Consumers" produced and delivered by Consciousness Industry are in the position of trying to cope with a giant con game. They know that they do not really have all the problems which advertisers press them to solve by buying their products. Placed in a time- and income-spending bind, the impossibility of making rational shopping decisions forces consumers to "take a chance." The lottery is perhaps the best model for explaining what happens at the moment of truth when the customer reaches for the package from the shelf. And it is perhaps significant that lotteries, so long excluded from socially sanctioned practice, have recently become legal and generally used in North America. For consumers accustomed to taking a chance on a $9.99 item on the supermarket shelf, the option of a statistically sheer random "chance" to win a million dollars can be very attractive and compelling. Yet the rationale of irrationality (Linder's) is unsatisfactory as an explanation of audience work. It may serve as a first approximation to an explanation. But we must dig deeper into the process of which audience work is a part.

How can audience power be "work" when it takes place in "free" or "leisure" time? What becomes of the labor theory of value if audiences are working? Is it not true that what people do when not working at the job front (where they are paid money for their work) is their free or leisure time *by definition?* Is it not true that "you can do as you please" in this "free" time? Have not "modern" household appliances relieved women of household work?

At the outset it is important to note that the idea of such free or leisure time is a hand-me-down from the upper classes in bourgeois society. It derives from the upper-class notion of leisure for the enjoyment of "official culture" (see Chapter 9). At the height of imperialist power toward the end of the nineteenth century, it took the form of emulating the *conspicuous* consumption of the rich and powerful, as Veblen so bitingly revealed in *The Theory of the Leisure Class* (1899). As transformed by monopoly capitalism, it meant the imitation of *expensive* consumption, for, as Veblen also pointed out, the policy of monopoly capitalism was to be "a competition in publicity and scarcity" (see Chapter 3). David Riesman (1950) and Stuart Ewen (1976) focused on the illusory semblance of reality in such "leisure" and "free time."

It is necessary to state clearly that just as people are rarely totally controlled by Consciousness Industry, so marketed commodities rarely have absolutely no use value. Repeatedly, in different ways I emphasize that most people embody a dialectical tension: they feel it necessary to cooperate with the monopoly-capitalist system in a variety of ways and for a variety of reasons; yet at the same time, as human beings they resist such cooperation in a variety of ways, for a variety of reasons. An analogous internal dialectical tension seems to exist *within* most commodities under capitalism. The gas-guzzling, overpowered, dangerous private automobile *also* transports you from home to work and back again; when suitably "hotted up," it may even lure into a lasting relationship a commoditized person of the opposite sex, just as the advertisements promise. The relative strength of the repressive and emancipatory ingredients in a commodity obviously differs greatly as between different commodities, e.g., an adulterated drug as against ordinary packaged milk. As we shall see in Chapter 10, this dialectical conflict within commodities exists within producer goods as well as consumer goods, which is the reason that the term *technology*, with its assumed neutral quality, is dangerously misleading. For most people in the core area today, leisure or free time, like technology, are propaganda devices which obscure and confuse the real contradictions between the respects in which people cooperate with and resist the monopoly-capitalist system and its commodities.

Except for those people who have been so rich that they did not have to work, all people have always had to work—one way or another—when not at the job in order to prepare themselves to work *tomorrow*. *Before* the mass production of consumer goods—roughly before 1875—in capitalist core countries, people's work to prepare themselves to work tomorrow (e.g., to reproduce their labor power) was done under conditions of cottage industry. For example they baked their own bread using flour which they might have ground themselves and yeast which they cultured for themselves. But with the mass production of consumer goods, their work to reproduce their labor power depends on buying and using consumer goods *in end-product form*. They have become dependent on factory-baked bread. And if sophisticated durable goods, e.g., vacuum cleaners, have relieved them of the necessity to sweep with brooms, it has required them to spend time buying filters and other equipment and arranging for maintenance of such equipment by "service men." And the endless proliferation of new commodities which clamor for their place in household consumption (e.g., electric can openers, electric carving knives, power lawn mowers, etc.) demands so much of so-called free time to buy, use, and maintain them that the idea of "free time" has become ridiculous. Consider what has happened to the time available to workers and the way it is used in the past century.

In 1850, under conditions of cottage industry, i.e., unbranded consumer goods, the average work week of employed men was about 70 hours per week in the United States.[7] The average worker could devote about 42 hours per week to such cottage industry types of reproduction of his labor power. By 1960, the time spent on the job was about 39.5 hours per week—an apparent reduction in time spent on the job of about 30 hours per week (to which should be added 2.5 hours as a generous estimate of the weekly equivalent of paid vacations).

Advertisers and home economists regularly argued that the apparent reduction in "work" hours created new leisure time for workers and housewives between 1910 and 1940, as Stuart Ewen's *Captains of Consciousness* (1976) demonstrated. Consumer durable goods like washing machines, vacuum cleaners, etc., were said to *free* housekeepers from work. Some time was indeed freed from drudgery in this way, but the illusion that most people had large blocks of free time was a myth created by Consciousness Industry. Upon close inspection, as we shall argue, leisure time for most people is work time. As Marylee Stephenson (1977, p. 32) puts it "over 90% of 51% of the adult population is engaged in . . . wageless labor (known as housework) for their entire adult life. . . ."

In fact, the meaning of the almost 30 hours per week by which the *job* work week shrank between 1850 and 1960 was transformed doubly by monopoly capitalism. One transformation removed huge chunks of people's time from their discretion by metropolitan sprawl and by the nature of unpaid work which workers were obligated to perform. For example, recently travel time to and from the job has been estimated at 8.5 hours per week; "moonlighting" employment at a minimum of one hour per week; repair work around the home at another five hours per week; and men's work on household chores and shopping at another 2.3 hours per week. As I write this the postman drops through the slot a piece of direct

---

[7] The following analysis of time use is based on de Grazia (1964).

mail advertising for a *Do-It-Yourself* manual. It tells me that owning this manual:

> . . . is like having the experts at your side . . . but without having to pay for them! You can save the expense of countless calls for cabinetmaker, carpenter, decorator, electrician, heating expert, locksmith, mason, painter, paperhanger, plasterer, plumber, roofer, rug cleaner, tile layer.

And it lists more than 50 "projects you can build for your home or garden" with the manual.

A total of 16.8 hours per week of the roughly 32 hours of time supposedly "freed" as a result of "modernization" is thus anything but free. A further 7 hours of the 32 hours of "freed" time disappears when a correction for part-time female employment is made in the reported hours per week in 1960.[8]

A second transformation involved the pressure placed by the system on the remaining hours of the week. If sleeping is estimated at 8 hours a day, the remainder of the 168 hours in the week after subtracting sleeping time and the unfree work time identified earlier was 42 hours in 1850 and 49 hours in 1960. The apparent increase in "free" time has thus shrunk to 7 hours per week (instead of about 30 hours). We lack systematic information about the use of this increased free time for both dates. We do know that certain types of activities were common to both dates: personal care, making love, visiting with relatives and friends, preparing and eating meals, attending union, church, and other associative institutions, including saloons. We also know that in 1960 (but not in 1850) there was a vast array of *branded* consumer goods and services pressed on workers through advertising, retail establishment displays, and peer group influence. Attendance at spectator sports and participation in such activities as little leagues, bowling, camping, and "pleasure driving" of the automobile or snowmobile—all promoted for the sake of equipment and energy sales by the Consciousness Industry—now takes time that was devoted to noncommercial activities in 1850. In-house time must now be devoted to deciding whether to buy and to use (by whom, where, under what conditions, and why) an endless proliferation of goods for personal care, household furnishings, clothing, music reproduction equipment, etc. And thus far we have not mentioned mass media *use*, although it

---

[8] Part-time workers (probably more female than male) amounted in 1960 to 19 percent of the employed labor force in the United States and they worked an average of 19 hours weekly. If we exclude such workers in order to get a figure comparable to the 70 hours in 1850, we consider the weekly hours worked by the average American male who worked at least 35 hours per week. We then find that they averaged 46.4 hours (as against 39.5 hours for all workers). For the sake of brevity, I omit the counterpart calculation of "free time" for women jobholders. No sexist implications are intended.

should be noted that workers are guided in all income and time expenditures by the mass media—through the blend of explicit advertising and advertising implicit in the program content.

Let us now introduce mass media use as it relates to the seven hours of "free" time thus far identified (ignoring the pressures on the audience to use its time and income referred to in the preceding paragraph). How much time do most people spend as part of the audience product of the mass media—their time which is sold by the media to advertisers? David Blank, economist for the Columbia Broadcasting System, found in 1970 that the average person watched television for 3.3 hours per day (23 hours per week) on an annual basis, listened to radio for 2.5 hours per day (18 hours per week), and read newspapers and magazines for 1 hour per day (7 hours per week) (Blank, 1970). Recent years show similar magnitudes. If we look at the audience product in terms of families rather than individuals, we find that in 1973 advertisers in the United States purchased television audiences for an average of a little more than 43 hours per home per week.[9] By industry usage, this lumps together specialized audience commodities sold independently as "housewives," "children," and "families." In the prime time evening hours (7:00 PM to 11:00 PM), the television audience commodity consisted of a daily average of 83.8 million people, with an average of two persons viewing per home. Women were a significantly higher proportion of this prime time audience than men (42 percent as against 32 percent; children were 16 percent; teenagers 10 percent).

Let us sum up these figures. Television, radio, and newspapers plus magazines take up 48 hours per week, for the average American! And they have only seven hours more free time than in 1850! Obviously some doubling up takes place. So let us estimate that half of the radio listening takes place while traveling to or from work; perhaps another quarter while doing the personal care chores at the beginning and end of the day. As for television, perhaps a fourth of it (on average) is glimpsed while preparing meals, eating, washing dishes, or doing other household tasks or repair/construction work. Estimate half of newspaper and magazine reading as taking place while traveling between home and job, while eating, etc. Our reduced exclusive audience time with the four commercial media is now down to 22 hours per week. Obviously more doubling takes place between audience time and other activities, and the reader is invited to make more precise estimates based on (perhaps) some empirical research. On television broadcasts of commercial sports events in the United States one sees some spectators *in the stadia* who are simultane-

---

[9] *Broadcasting Yearbook*, 1974, p. 69.

ously watching the live event and portable television sets (for the "instant replay" in stadia not blessed with huge overhead television screens for that purpose), or listening to the radio (for the sportscaster's instant comments on the play just completed).

Perhaps the only conclusion to be drawn at this time on this point is that there is no free time devoid of audience activity which is not preempted by other activities which are market-related (including sleep which is necessary if you are to be fit to meet your market tests on the morrow). In *any* society, sleep and other nonwork activities are necessary to restore and maintain life and labor power. Work itself is not intrinsically oppressive. It is the inclusion in so-called leisure time of commodity-producing work under monopoly capitalism which creates the contradiction between oppressive liberating activity in time for which people are not paid.

The bitter reality for most Canadians and Americans is that the commodity rat race—as they call it—makes a mockery of free time and leisure, both during their years at the job and after retirement.

What time is *not* work time in the mature capitalist core area? For the great majority of the population—all except those who are so rich that they can afford to have their shopping done by servants—24 hours a day is work time. Modern machinery requires maintenance when idle between shifts. The human body requires rest, time for reflection, time for the cultivation of the arts (see Chapter 9), time for the subtleties of raising children, time for community activities, etc. But the pressures for audience-oriented work exerted by Consciousness Industry are relentless. George Allen, famous American football coach, tells his players, "Nobody should work all the time. Leisure time is the five or six hours you sleep at night. You can combine two good things at once, sleep and leisure (quoted in Terkel, 1974, p. 389)

How does the view that all time of most of the people in the capitalist core countries is work time relate to Karl Marx's theory of labor power? As Bill Livant puts it, the power of the concept of surplus value ". . . rests wholly on the way Marx solved the great value problems of classical political economy, by *splitting the notion of labour in two*, into labour in productive use and labour power (the capacity to labor)."[10]

Labor in productive use in the production of commodities-in-general was Marx's concern in the three volumes of *Capital* (except for Vol. 1, chap. 6) and scattered passages in the *Grundrisse*. It is clear from those exceptions that Marx assumed that labor power is produced by the laborer and by his or her immediate family, i.e., under the conditions of hand-

---

[10] Livant (1975c); Bill Livant, University of Regina, has helped to develop the analysis of the audience commodity and I acknowledge this emphatically.

icraft production prevailing when he wrote. In a word, labor power was "home made" (in the absence of dominant brand name commodities, mass advertising, and the mass media which monopoly capitalism had not yet invented). In Marx's period and in his analysis, the principal aspect of capitalist production was the alienation of workers from the means of producing commodities-in-general. Today and for some time past, the principal aspect of capitalist production has been the alienation of workers from the means of producing and reproducing themselves.

The prevailing Western Marxist view today still holds the incorrect assumption that the laborer is an *independent* commodity producer of labor power *which is his to sell.* But

> What often escapes attention is that just because the labourer sells it (his or her labour power) does not mean that he or she produces it. We are misled by fixating on the true fact that a human must eat and sleep into thinking that therefore the seller of labour power must also be the producer. Again the error of two combines into one (Livant, 1975b).

> Livant goes on to say that a Marxist view: . . . sees leisure time correctly as time of production, reproduction and repair of labour power. This production, reproduction and repair are activities. They are things people must do. As such they require labour power. To be sure, this latter labour power you do not have to sell directly to capital. But you do have to use it to produce labour power in the form you do have to sell.

(Chapters 3 and 4 discuss just how the contradictions within capitalism produced monopoly capitalism, Consciousness Industry, and the mass media.)

Under capitalism your labor power becomes a personal possession. It seems that you can do what you want with it. If you work at a job where you are paid, you sell it. Away from the job, it seems that your work is something you do not sell. But there is common misunderstanding at this point. At the job you are not paid for all the labor time you do sell (otherwise interest, profits, and management salaries could not be paid). And away from the job, your labor time *is* sold (through the audience commodity), although you do not sell it. What is produced at the job where you get paid are commodities used for consumption or for further production. And what is produced by you away from the job is your labor power for tomorrow and for the next generation: ability to work and to live (Livant, 1975a).

The point to be pursued here is that the ruling groups cultivated "high" or bourgeois culture (in the fine arts) both for their own enjoyment and as an invaluable ideological feature of monopoly capitalism (itself dealt with in Chapter 9). Liberal notions about "leisure" to which a substantial amount of effort by bourgeois sociologists has been devoted (see, for example, Kaplin, 1960, 1975) perpetuate the mystification of leisure, treating it "apolitically." In fact, the system used labor unions, religious organizations, and community arts organizations (musical, painting, sculpture, literary, poetic, etc.), to turn the "high culture" from Greece on down into a means of attaching workers loyally to the system. A considerable literature about "popular culture" and "mass culture" deals with this relationship, which is also dealt with in Chapter 9 (see, for example, Garnham, 1977). The unrelenting pressures of Consciousness Industry, however, reveal the yawning gap between high culture notions of leisure, which are the stuff of establishment propaganda regarding "national identity," and the vulgar, atomized, and capitalized exploitation of leisure as a cover for an ever-expanding range of commodity markets.

Audiences for the commercial mass media are a strange type of institution. They are more a statistical abstraction than are, for example, the audience of the live or motion picture theater because they have no possibility of simultaneously and totally interacting internally to create an audience mood or affect. Yet we know that they are far from merely being statistical abstractions. Orson Welles' "Invasion from Mars" radio broadcast precipitated mass hysteria (Cantril et al., 1940). And the record industry depends on radio stations to produce "hit parades" which mobilize fans of popular music stars to buy records on a mass scale. We are far from having a full understanding of the audience commodity, but there is no doubt that it is a qualitatively new major social institution, a collectivity, and a commodity. As Bill Livant (1979a, p. 103) says:

> Virtually everyone is organized into the complex tapestry of these audiences, whose underlying properties we are just beginning to understand. For one thing, the production, destruction, division and recombination of audiences is a vast and turbulent motion. For another, the Audience Commodity is a multipurpose capacity. It is the other side of the labour power that Marx discovered in the production of commodities-in-general, and it is as Protean in its capacities.

> The *first* great form of the organization of this commodity [is] the Audience Commodity as a Market. This form emerged first historically and with the greatest clarity in the United States. . . . This form is the first, *but not the last.*

We can already observe that the audience commodity has changed the social form for political party electoral behavior in the capitalist world. Murdock (1978, p. 117) refers to the changing form of social conflict in Europe:

> The expansion of consumerism was accompanied by a dampening down of industrial conflict and class struggle. The contradiction between capital and labour receded from the centre of attention and its place was taken by con-

flicts grounded in age, in gender, in nationality, in race, and above all in the yawning gap between the developed and underdeveloped worlds, between the colonizers and the colonized.

The rationalization by Consciousness Industry of the process of conducting elections through mass media "pseudo events" and advertising is, through the telltale demographics, evidence of the audience commodity, having been produced for the election market and paid for by the parties, at work in ways quite familiar in the North American scene. Richeri (1978) has linked the rapid transformation of the Italian political constituency system to the rapid introduction of the production of audiences by commercial television and radio stations in recent years. An analogous transformation of the electoral process took place in the United States and Canada between the mid-1930s and 1960s as political campaigning/advertising via radio broadcasting, public opinion polling, and interlocking ownership interests in radio (and later television) stations between politicians and newspaper publishers were substituted for nineteenth-century modes of mobilizing people for elections. Richard Nixon's flat statement in 1957 that political candidates must now be merchandised like any other consumer product recognized the reality. Europe, lagged by a decade or so, has now experienced the same transformation more quickly.

The work of the audience commodity poses severe problems for Marxist theory derived from Europe and based upon the analysis of competitive capitalism, nineteenth-century style. The *base* or *infrastructure* in that theory was defined as the job front where pay was received for productive work. There were two main reasons for this: (1) The factory system of nineteenth-century capitalism embodied mass production of (almost all unbranded) commodities with all the improved efficiency traceable to the Industrial Revolution. (2) The tradition in economic theory begun by the Physiocrats and running through Marx that production was closely allied to natural resources and especially agriculture. The superstructure in that theory was where the ruling class in the state inculcated ideology by its press, its educational and religious institutions, and its monopoly of force (police and military).

The clear dichotomy between base and superstructure was no longer possible under monopoly capitalism, with Consciousness Industry buying audiences comprising virtually the whole population to aid it in managing demand for its commodity output. For the audiences are engaged in production which is an essential to the capitalist system as was the production at the job front in the early nineteenth century. Perhaps the audience market even takes priority away from the job front because the former "beckons" the latter into action very directly through the mode of operation of giant integrated corporations. The superstructure (in nineteenth-century terms) is thus decisively engaged in production. And increasingly, as welfare programs of employers have engaged people at the job front in all manner of popular cultural activities and vocational training, it seems as if the old "infrastructure" has taken on in part the ideological training functions previously associated with the old "superstructure." (See Chapters 3 and 4.) It is not clear now how Marxists will resolve the anomalies in their theory as it applies to core area monopoly capitalism, especially because current Marxist theorists do not recognize that the audience commodity even exists.

It appears, as will be argued further in Chapters 11 and 12, that in seeming to perfect its system for managing demand through producing and consuming audiences in order to market its products, monopoly capital has produced its principal antagonist in the core area: people commodified in audience markets who are consciously seeking noncommodified group relations. A symptom may be apparent in a downward trend in television viewing in 1977 and 1979 in the United States after 30 years of rising viewing.[11]

It has long been noticed that all traditional social institutions (family, church, labor union, political party, etc.) have been stripped of much of their traditional purpose by the impact of mass-produced communications. The mysticism attached to technique (and "technology") has incorrectly assumed that the medium basically defines the audience. But as a historical analysis of the rise of the mass media will show, the opposite has been true: the availability and actions of the audience is the basic feature in the definition of the media, singly and collectively. By placing the contradiction between advertisers/media on the one hand and audiences on the other on the level of social relations we are on solid ground and can repudiate the mysticism of the technological trap by which audiences are tied to hardware, software, and technique (as in Innis, McLuhan, and others).

In order to dig deeper into the process of which audience work is a part, it is necessary to consider how we got this way. In other words, we must review some history of monopoly capitalism. This will be the burden of Chapters 3 and 4.

---

[11] *Time*, 12 March 1979, p. 57.

3

ON HOW CONSCIOUSNESS INDUSTRY DEVELOPED I: THE JOB FRONT AND THE HEGEMONY OF BIG BUSINESS

Preacher (on a southern state side road): My good man! Don't you know you shouldn't beat that mule with a two-by-four? You should be kind to him.

Redneck Farmer: I aim to do just that, Reverend. But first I've got to get his attention. (Traditional story).

The argument thus far has been that in the capitalist core countries most of the people spend most of their time working and that the work people do as audiences of advertising is *bona fide* work, albeit unpaid. Further, that the role of mass media of communication is preeminently to establish daily the agenda which defines "reality" for the people. They do this by a mix of advertising–free-lunch production of what we call *news, entertainment,* and *information,* all of which has the form of commodities. We analyzed the nature of the service performed by audience power and found it to be essential to mass production of goods and services. The capitalist system requires people to work on the media content in order that monopoly-capitalist corporations may manage demand for such civic purposes as "democratic" elections, and in order that people may be indoctrinated in the virtues of the capitalist system. We observed that in TV and radio the remarkable feat has been accomplished of getting people to ple to invest many times as much capital in electronic equipment as do the media enterprises, and to bear many times the annual expense of those enterprises, simply in order to qualify themselves to deliver audience power to the advertisers. Lastly, we penetrated the nature of the "work" done by audiences only deeply enough to note that it seems to involve "parsing" the media content in an irrational way, because only through doing so could they rationalize the expenditure decisions forced on them by the marketers of consumer goods and services. But we recognized that this was only a first-approximation explanation of the nature of audience work. Next, we need to ask, was it always this way (as the media system seems to say)? If not, how did we get this way? We now turn to analysis of the economic history of production and consumption in the capitalist core countries for the answer to this question.

Work in the emerging modern capitalist system of Western Europe in the fifteenth and sixteenth centuries, like work in the medieval period, tended to be located at or close to home, whether in agriculture or in cities, or towns. The immediate predecessor of the Factory System was the Domestic or Putting-out System for manufacturing textile, leather, or metal products. With the breakup of the medieval guilds, the Domestic System was a mode of organizing work in which capital in the form of raw or partly processed materials was provided by a merchant capitalist commonly to skilled workers who did the work on the products in their homes. In this pre-factory system, workers' families worked as teams in the production both of goods to be sold in the market by the capitalist, and also of a substantial part of the goods consumed in the workers' homes (e.g., cereals, meat, clothing). Even if the raw materials for such household-produced consumption goods had to be purchased, they were mostly processed and prepared in the home. In rural districts, domestic production of consumption goods was practiced even more fully than in the towns and cities where more pronounced division of labor took place through market relations. This was no idyllic situation because the struggle for subsistence was severe among workers and the position of women was subordinated to traditional male domination. The alienation of women and men from the product of their labor, however, was less evident than later on. The household production of most consumption goods meant that the role of women (and men, too) around the home could afford them the satisfaction of creative work, integrated somehow with their child-rearing roles. There was neither the degree of alienation of men nor women which later attended their work in factories under the discipline of industrial capitalists.[1]

With the Industrial Revolution and the rise of the factory system in Western Europe in the eighteenth and nineteenth centuries, the struggles between capitalists and labor became centered on work at the factory where division of labor and development of tools and machines became the basis for ever larger-scale production and standardization both of

---

[1] See Knight et al. (1928, p. 286), the chapters on "The Beginnings of European Expansion" and the "Commercial Revolution," and the works by W. Cunningham and Henri See cited there.

work and of products. This "production" front dominated the lives and thinking not only of capitalists and workers, but also of the classical economists and Marx and Engels as well. All concerned *assumed* down to the last quarter of the century that workers and their families would largely produce their own consumption goods in final form from the flour, "yard" goods, and other materials needed for basic family living. *Luxuries* were defined in upper-class terms. Workers' consumption of alcohol was an anodyne to the miseries of slum existence. A close reading of Marx and Engels suggests that they assumed that the "reproduction of labor power" took place in the family under handicraft-production conditions. Advertising and branded merchandise were conspicuously absent from the writings of the classical economists *and* Marx. For this there was good reason. The dynamism which was transforming the industrial landscape did not depend on advertising or brand names. Such was the scarcity of the "commodities in general" produced by the factory system—producers' goods, such as railway equipment and steamships, and the unbranded staples of food, clothing, and shoes—that it seemed as if the transition from *household* production of consumables to *industrial* production of them warranted the anticipation of market expansion which would satisfy real needs (i.e., without the artificial stimulation of advertising and branded goods). In Marx's days of active work—from roughly the 1830s to the 1860s—the course of development of capitalism seemed predictable: from his standpoint, capitalists would be expropriated by a proletariat which was conscious of its own class identity and oppression. The capitalist establishment, despite the roseate veneer of optimism provided by the liberal apologists for an enlightenment based on bourgeois power acted as if they thought Marx's expectations were correct. For them the reality was frustrating and insecure (cf. Hobsbawm, 1967, 1975).

In the heyday of Victorian liberalism, the role of competition between enterprises was dialectical. It facilitated the rapid development of markets and extended them to the whole world (as Marx predicted). And it destroyed itself. To operate most profitably, mass production had to be increased, capital equipment to become more elaborate, and investment larger. A reciprocal relation of larger production, lower prices, more extensive markets, greater profits, capital accumulation, more efficient producers' goods, larger production, etc., ensued. In the middle decades of the nineteenth century, the swings of the business cycle, generated by the whole market-directed structure of competitive capitalism became more severe. In the liquidation phases of the business depressions which began in 1837, 1857, 1871, and 1893, the self-destructive aspect of competitive capitalism was painfully apparent to workers and capitalists alike. The pressure of overhead costs arising from more and more capital investment in plant produced epidemics of cutthroat competition which shook the foundations of the system as bankruptcies, bank failures, unemployment, and falling prices took place.

> The threat of excess capacity appears to have been a primary stimulus to initial combinations in most American industries. But why did factories have difficulty in using fully their available resources in a period of swiftly growing markets? The answer seems to be that the rapid increase in the output of many small enterprises exceeded immediate demand. Each firm expanded because its executives hoped, particularly during the boom periods after the Civil War and again after the depression of the 1870s to profit thereby from the new markets. Then, as the market became glutted and prices dropped, the many manufacturers became more and more willing to combine in order to control or limit competition by setting price and production schedules (Chandler, 1962, p. 30).

As far as consumers' goods producers were concerned, competition destroyed competitive enterprises because commodities produced by different producers were readily substitutable for each other. Flour was flour, yard goods were yard goods, and as far as businessmen could see, the "circulation" of commodities made the swings of the business cycle inevitable. If, however, a partial monopoly could be created for the product of a particular manufacturer, a partly captive market could protect that manufacturer's product from price competition and might avoid the losses and possible bankruptcy which followed in periods of the cyclical depression. Advertising of brand names was the means to that partial monopoly and security in the selling market for a commodity—to which we will return shortly.

When the businessman looked backward towards the markets for the factors of production he also faced an unstable and insecure prospect. The production process, from start (in basic materials) to finish (at end-product markets), was market-directed to be sure, but the size and degree of capital application in industries was irrational as compared with the certainties now enjoyed by vertically integrated producing enterprises. Moreover, the same disruptive and destructive effects of overhead costs produced cutthroat competition in producers' goods industries as in consumers' goods industries.

So it was that in the second half of the nineteenth century, capitalism faced a crisis, not only structurally but—and this was of decisive importance—politically. The labor supply was on the verge of making the very revolution which Marx and Engels predicted. The horrible abuses of children, women, and men in the factory system produced militant radicals. Thus, a member of the House of Commons reported from his investigations:

> The cotton trade has existed for ninety years. . . . It has existed for three generations of the English race, and I believe I may safely say that during that period it has destroyed nine generations of factory operatives.[2]

After a few decades, the protests of workers and their politically oriented unions forced the English government to regulate the hours and safety conditions of work, first for children and later for adults. But the remedies came too slowly and too feebly.

The tide of revolution which erupted on the Continent in 1848 was symptomatic of the potential for revolutionary action. Not only were workers restive. They also possessed too much technical knowledge and political organization for their employers' security. In the early phase of the Factory System, labor had been marshaled in buildings and subjected to some division of labor, attending the current generation of machines powered by steam and water. But the master-craftsman-journeyman-apprentice formation inherited from the medieval guilds survived the Domestic System and was incorporated in the factories which made complex products.

The issue was knowledge and information for whose benefit—the workers' or the capitalists'? The ability to control the flow and use of information, i.e., communication (this time within the industrial organization) was the basis of economic and ultimately political power. Literally, the master craftsman steel-maker or machinist in the factory had more knowledge about the production process than did his employer. When, as happened in the middle decades of the nineteenth century, men with this crucial technical knowledge became active in labor unions with revolutionary political objectives, the power of capitalists was gravely threatened (Stone, 1974, pp. 113–173). This lack of control over essential information about the productive process, of course, was subversive of discipline within the factory. Also, and more importantly in the long view, it prevented the capitalists from being able to make use of the improvements which they suspected the rapid progress in the physical and chemical sciences would make possible as the century wore on. Lacking a full understanding of the productive process within his factory, the employer could hardly plan and execute innovations which would reduce costs and further increase productive capacity. And for decisively significant firms and industries, and also incidentally for the capitalist system as a whole, this was intolerable. The issue of controlling information and its movement was thus specific to the individual firm. But its roots lay in the institutional structure of industry. And in the relation of that structure to the state. The *potential* existed for an expansion of mass production at

---

[2] Quoted in Marx, Karl, *Capital*. (1959; Modern Library edition; Vol. I, p. 293).

ever lower unit costs which could be sold to the great bulk of the population which had never previously been able to afford more than the bare minimum required for subsistence. The profit potential seemed unlimited. If demand had always previously exceeded supply, if commerce had always previously dominated industry, it was possible in the late nineteenth century to envisage the reverse.[3] And as David F. Noble (1977) has shown, scientists and engineers at that time were articulate and even utopian in foreseeing an economy of abundance for all.

The principal contradiction faced by capitalism in the last quarter of the nineteenth century was that between the enormous potential for expanding production of consumer goods (spurred by the fantastic profits thus to be realized) and the overt political hostility of the workers and a fair proportion of the middle class. The solution which the system provided to this problem was a classic example of Mao's principle: "One divides into two." In the resolution of the principal contradiction, two problems were identified and solved: (1) The need for an unquestionable conquest by the business system of control of the state and its ideological apparatus—the military, educational system, communications system, etc.—in short the formal political system of the bourgeois state. (2) The task of winning the automatic acquiescence of the population to a "rationalized" system of monopoly capitalism. The achievement of these twin objectives would give the business system hegemony—i.e., effective domination of the nation-states.

But a prerequisite to solution of these problems was a suitable means to be used. The previously typical individual proprietorship or the partnership form of business organization was too limited to small-scale operations to meet the new situation. The giant corporation or trust was the organizational instrument which served to solve both these problems, and *was* the building block of monopoly capitalism. As Veblen (1923, pp. 98–99) said,

> That period which has here been called the "era of free competition" was marked by a reasonably free competitive production of goods for the market, the profits of the business to be derived from competitive underselling. . . .
> In practical effect it tapered off to an uncertain close in England about the middle of the century, in America something like a quarter-century later. . . . It meant a competition between producing-sellers, and so far as the plan was operative it inured to the benefit of the consumers.

What we now know as a *corporation* had been illegal under English common law from the Middle Ages until around 1850, except for the infre-

---

[3] Knight et al. (1928); Veblen (1903, 1904) saw this as a conflict in which a class- and craft-conscious caste of engineers threatened to overthrow capitalism, nineteenth-century model.

quent chartering of companies of merchants (e.g., Hudson's Bay Company) by the Crown (from the sixteenth century on). With the protection of "limited liability" for stockholders, by mid-nineteenth century the corporation became the common vehicle for "captains of industry" (Vanderbilt, Astor, J. P. Morgan, et al.) to accumulate capital and monopolize markets. As it gained control of key industries—railroads, steel, coal, oil, chemicals, and telegraph (and later telephone) in the last quarter of the nineteenth century—a fundamental change in function took place:

> Doubtless, such freely competitive production and selling prevailed only within reasonable bounds even in the time when it may be said to have been the rule in industrial business, and with the passage of time and the approaching saturation of the market the reasonable bounds gradually grew narrower and stricter. The manner of conducting the business passed by insensible degrees into a new order, and it became an increasingly patent matter-of-course for business enterprise in this field consistently to pursue the net gain by *maintaining prices and curtailing the output.*

> It is not that competition ceased when this "competitive system" fell into decay, but only that the incidence of it has shifted. The competition which then used to run mutually between the producing-sellers *has* since then increasingly *come to run between the business community on the one side and the consumers on the other.* Salesmanship, with sabotage [i.e. "quality control in the interest of planned obsolescence"], has grown gradually greater and keener, at an increasing cost. *And the end of this salesmanship is to get a margin of something for nothing at the cost of the consumer in a closed market.* Whereas on the earlier plan the net gain was sought by underselling an increased output of serviceable goods in an open market. The old-fashioned plan, so far as it was effective, might be called a competition in workmanship; *the later plan, so far as it has gone into effect, is a competition in publicity and scarcity* (Veblen, 1923, p. 99; emphasis added).

Veblen, in 1923, clearly saw the difference between the polity of competitive capitalism and that of monopoly capitalism. He also noted that Marx, as much as the classical economists, failed to conceive ". . . the industrial system at large as a going concern. He had not dealt adequately with the institutional forms of capitalist accumulation" (Veblen, 1923, pp. 270–271, f.n. 5). In practical terms the difference was that sheer competitive market power was the basis of the enterprise's strength in the mid-nineteenth century. By 1920 *intentional* and effective control of markets for labor and consumption was becoming the power base of the giant corporation.

The growth of giant corporations began shortly after 1850 in the United States as predatory tactics and mutual interest eliminated competitive business. One of the earliest was Western Union Telegraph Company which, until the 1890s commanded the only electronic nationwide communication system. Closely tied to the scores of railroad companies on whose rights of way its lines ran, Western Union served a coordinating role for monopoly capitalism. On its board of directors sat captains not only of the railroads but also the leading investment bankers like J. P. Morgan who planned and executed many major mergers, including the formation of the United States Steel Corporation. This informal "general staff" of the ruling class in 1890 included Jay Gould, Russel Sage, William W. Astor, J. P. Morgan, P. R. Pyne, C. P. Huntington, Chauncy M. Depew, Henry F. Flagler, Cyrus W. Field, A. B. Cornell, John Hay, and many others (Parsons, 1899, p. 60). One of Western Union's many advantages to the aspiring monopolists was its relation to the Associated Press. As the only nationwide telegraph system, Western Union had a mutual aid understanding with the Associated Press by which Western Union protected the Associated Press and its affiliated local newspapers from competition by refusing wire service to others who sought to establish news wire service for the use of new newspapers in their local markets. In return, the Associated Press (and necessarily its affiliated newspapers) took its policy on news, and hence political matters, such as the issue of public ownership of telegraphy and railroads from Western Union (Parsons, 1899). It was a rough but efficient means of managing the news to control the agenda set by the mass media of the late nineteenth century—which calls for historical analysis unlikely to be forthcoming from United States schools of journalism.

Some means of coordination of the policies of big and little business enterprises was needed to cure the problems they faced. And for this purpose the trade association form was adopted generally in advanced capitalist countries at about the same time: the mid-1890s (Brady, 1943, pp. 1–17, chap. VI). In the United States in 1870 there were not more than 40 chambers of commerce; by 1930 there were about 3000. Trade associations identified with particular industries grew simultaneously, ostensibly to protect medium and small businesses from the giants. The second edition of the Encyclopedia of American Associations in the early 1960s listed 2314 trade associations. There are even one or more *associations of trade associations*, intended to coordinate activities at the highest level. The main vehicle for big business coordination, however, has been the National Association of Manufacturers (from 1895 on). It is roughly analogous to the form and policy of the Federation of British Industries, and the "peak associations" in pre-Hitler Germany (the *Spitzenverbände*). Through this dense structure of business associations, "private" corporate enterprise formulates and executes policies on a wide range of issues: how to beat and control unions, lobbying for or against tariff legislation, desirable government regulation of business, government aid in expanding foreign markets, etc. In short, the structure is used to mobilize the power of capitalists for all politico-economic issues affecting the "bottom line" of business in the era of monopoly capitalism. With this structure a-building, the system's efforts to cure its systemic ailment, the contradiction between profitable potential development and the hostility of a large proportion of the population (workers, farmers, at least) could be resolutely attacked on two levels.

1. The contradiction between the sphere of private (economic) power and the resistance encountered in the formal democratic political and governmental process was attacked frontally by the new general staff of monopoly capitalism, and the state became unequivocally an instrument of big business. In Britain, France, and Germany, the class struggle of workers won social insurance measures: collective bargaining; labor legislation protecting women and minors in industry, etc. In the United States, the conquest of the state by the business system was more difficult because the Constitution of 1789 had built-in features protecting the rights of individuals which had been institutionalized through the Jeffersonian and Jacksonian traditions. The constitutional authority of the states supported the anti-Wall Street populism which pervaded the South, and Middle West and Western states. And the tide of popular sentiment ran strongly toward nationalization of basic industries in the 1890s.[4] Class struggle between insurgent farmer-labor-civic-improvement groups and the conservative upper class was sharp. The struggle against exploitation by "Wall Street" through high interest rates, high and discriminatory railroad rates, the exactions of the "trusts," and stock swindles raged within the formal political process. Monetary policy (bimetallism vs. the gold standard) focused the struggle between populist forces working through the Democratic Party and their enemies (using the Republican Party) in the 1890s. Control by big business of the Associated Press and the editorial policy of the most aggressive newspapers—Hearst and the rest of the "yellow press"—was used to launch the United States toward offshore imperialism of the nineteenth-century variety when in 1898 the war to capture the Philippines and Cuba was begun under the self-serving slogan that America's "Manifest Destiny" required it. A defensive effort for pacifism and social democratic socialism continued down to the outbreak

---

[4] In the 1890s the Public Ownership League counted two political parties and more than two million men who by vote and petition had supported a government telegraph. The Farmers' Alliance and Industrial Union, the National Grange, the Knights of Labor, the American Railway Union, the American Federation of Labor, the International Typographical Union, the Peoples Party had supported it. Chambers of Commerce and Boards of Trade in New York, Philadelphia, Denver, Pittsburgh, Richmond, Kansas City, Jersey City, and other cities supported it. At least four state legislatures had petitioned Congress for it. Judges, governors, senators, and prominent economists supported it (Parsons, 1899).

of World War I—an effort represented by many millions who linked pacifism with the egalitarian morality of populism and naive socialism.

The tactics employed by the ruling group were two-edged. Reformism was coopted, i.e., given token reality in legislation which *appeared* to regulate the railroads (the Interstate Commerce Act, 1887, and a number of state railroad commissions, especially in areas like Wisconsin and Michigan where radicalism was strong among transplanted German and other Continental enclaves familiar with Marxism). In reality, the "regulatory" commissions generally shielded the railroads and later other public utilities (telephone, telegraph, electricity, etc.) *from* criticism. The enactment of the Sherman Anti-Trust law (1890) defused poplar hostility to the growing trust movement while not seriously impeding its growth. The radical potential among the Blacks was emasculated by brutal white domination and racism. This racism was "legalized" by court interpretations which effectively nullified the constitutional amendments adopted for their protection at the close of the Civil War and by the submissive reformist program ostentatiously begun with Rockefeller money by Booker T. Washington.

Meanwhile, harsh repression was used to defeat politically conscious unions. Military/police attacks on workers were launched in Chicago (Haymarket, 1886), in steel (Homestead, 1892), in railroads (Pullman, 1893), in coal (Colorado Fuel and Iron Co., Ludlow, 1913). Coming as they did on the heels of repression of strikers in the 1870s, these battles openly identified the McCormicks, the Carnegies, the railroad barons, and the Rockefellers with the use of the state to serve big business. At the same time, the "pork chop" unionism of Samuel Gompers and the American Federation of Labor was tacitly encouraged by employers because of its disavowal of political objectives and devotion to immediate economic payoffs. To redirect workers' energies in ideologically safe channels was the role of the YMCA and the YWCA with their emphasis on muscular Christianity. Joining with a ruling class initiative originating in Europe, the Olympic games were invented to develop cadres of physically fit and patriotic men for national defense. In all, during the period from the 1880s to 1914, what Kolko calls "the triumph of conservatism" was orchestrated and accomplished by seizing and occupying the central organs of the state and its ideological apparatus. It was, as Kolko (1963, pp. 279–305) says, a synthesis of economics and politics. The formal political conditions for ensuring the security of capital in its quest for markets in which to profitably exploit the productive potential of its science were successfully established.

This sketch of the politico-economic context for the rise of Consciousness Industry in the heartland of monopoly capitalism—the United

States—illuminates the Canadian context as well. Thanks to the Canadian Tariff of 1878, (a feature of the National Policy commonly credited with "nation-building" in Canada), branch plants of major United States giant corporations securely occupied Canadian basic markets long before World War I. Telephones were innovated in Canada in the 1880s by a branch plant of the United States Bell Telephone system. International Harvester, Edison Electric, Singer Sewing Machine, Westinghouse, Gillette, and some 444 other American branch plants were operating in Canada before 1913. And the class struggle between capital and labor ignored the border as well. Under the common influence of worker problems in both countries, Canadian unions had benefited from organizational help from south of the border from the 1860s to around 1900 and had affiliated with "international unions." After about 1900, the class-collaborationist character of the AFL (and later the CIO) made international unions allies of the branch plant managements with whom they negotiated. At the same time, militant IWW unionism entered Canada, to be crushed by the power of Canadian employers (Howard and Scott, 1972; Scott, 1975). Observing the triumph of conservatism in the United States from the 1870s to 1913, the ruling group in Canada overcame whatever doubts it might have had earlier about the populist radicalism of the United States to welcome United States transnational corporate investment in Canada. What later was known as *continentalism* was already firmly established by 1913 although masked by the older political symbols of identification with the British Empire. That Prime Minister King had "earned his spurs" in labor relations work for the Rockefellers growing out of the Ludlow Massacre in Colorado before 1920 is a suitable feudal metaphor for the ideological relations between the countries.

2. The second level was the long-range problem confronting the emerging monopoly-capitalist system in the last quarter of the nineteenth century, i.e., that of establishing institutional relations which would win the acquiescence of the population. And because its successes were earliest in the United States-Canadian theater, our attention properly focuses there. As Veblen correctly noted, this problem was one of establishing the hegemony of the business system over people as "consumers." It was a problem of linked competition in *publicity* and *scarcity*, to use Veblen's terms. It was a problem of establishing domination of consciousness through culture and communication.

The context thus far sketched for the emergence of Consciousness Industry has been in broad terms: the growth of the merger and trust movement, the taking of control of the formal political government and the ideological apparatus of the state (especially the military and educational apparatus). These aspects represented the immediate and superficial (though essential) preconditions for the growth of Consciousness Industry. Veblen, indeed, interpreted the merger movement as a market-directed mobilization of enterprises motivated and rewarded by the immediate and enormous profits reaped by Morgan and other "Robber Barons" out of the corporate manipulations which produced the giant integrated corporations (see Veblen, 1903, 1904). In order to make the expropriation of technical knowledge from skilled craftsmen by corporate managers profitable, and indeed to cure the basic contradictions which produced the insecurities of competitive enterprises described earlier (i.e., insecurities stemming from market uncertainties both "forward" toward consumers and "backward" toward factor supplies, including labor) both qualitative and structural changes were necessary. It was urgent to *rationalize* the *whole* of that major share of the economy which the new giant corporations could control *absolutely*. The basis of rationalization was at hand in the name of *science*. In the name of science, knowledge and the production and regulation of information were to be appropriated by the new giant corporations. Science would be applied in the beginning both to *manufacturing* and to *marketing*. Workers, having had their craft skills expropriated by corporate management, were faced by "scientific management" at the job front. The same workers and their families on the home front were faced with scientific marketing, spearheaded by the invention of monopoly capitalism: the mass media of communication and the unpaid work which audiences perform for advertisers.

Harry Tipper, advertising manager of Texaco and a teacher of advertising, noted that with the introduction of mass production techniques, "Consumers had to be taught to use more than they formerly used, and to discriminate between different sellers or sections in order to aid in control of the market."[5]

Scientific management, originally pioneered by Frederick Taylor, was the unifying policy for dealing with workers both at the job and at home. Thanks to the enormous technical progress and multiplication of consumer commodities which resulted, it was blessed with the term *modernization*, and—more subtly still—technology with a capital "T." David F. Noble (1977, p. xxi) correctly refers to ". . . the concurrent emergence of modern technology and the rise of corporate capitalism as two sides of the same process of social production in America." Was scientific management the best way to do work in general? No, it was not, because that was not its purpose. Its purpose was to provide the best way for capitalists to control and profit from alienated labor and from alienated "consumers." Ideologically, it served to conceal that work is a collective affair whether the work be at the production line in a factory or the production line

---

[5] Pope (1973, p. 41); the quotation is from Tipper, Harry, *The New Business*, N.Y., 1914, p. 13.

forming at the supermarket cash register where "audience power" earns its keep from advertisers. The selection and carrying of commodities to the cash register now done by consumers in droves was formerly a function of salaried store employees. So the collective nature of work was turned inside out ideologically by the way scientific management embodied in work and life the values of possessive, competitive individualism and the myth that the "insatiable wants" of consumers must spur them to endless consumption of commodities as the sufficient objective of life. That the Soviet Union from the 1920s on tended to organize work on Taylorist lines was yet another triumph for the propaganda of the capitalist system at the nitty-gritty level of commodity production and consumption.

The systemic objective of scientific management has now become clear. It is much more than merely the production of physical machines and commodities. In the long run its objective clearly was to rationalize the production and control of *people*. On both the job and home fronts, the objective is the same: to control minds and bodies of people. The difference between the emphasis on *bodies* and minds of workers at the job front, and *minds* and bodies at the home front where audience power is used, is merely one of degree and institutional design. This is not the place to analyze in detail the application of scientific management to the job front, but enough must be said to demonstrate the systemic integrity of the ideological instruction given there.

Having broken the militant unions and fired most all-around craftsmen, the next step was "job-breakdown" (in the jargon of personnel managers). The operative principle derived from Charles Babbage in 1832: never pay for skilled labor if it is scientifically possible to avoid doing so.[6] Complex work processes were analyzed (with the aid of stop watches and time and motion studies) to determine the maximum contribution which new machinery could efficiently make, and which detailed and unskilled "tasks" must still be performed by human beings. Having designed, invented, and innovated the machines, productivity of unskilled workers was stimulated by replacing hourly rates with piece rates, which seemed to mean that the harder one worked the more one earned. Workers were quickly antagonized because the new assembly lines could be speeded up (Recall Charles Chaplin in *Modern Times*.)

Strikes and more labor union militancy led to the involvement of psychologists and sociologists as part of scientific management. The new formulation of the problem was how to convince workers that, as individuals, their interests coincided with those of the employer and were opposed to those of their fellow-workers. More sophisticated pay arrangements provided both standard pay by the hour/day plus bonus rates for produc-

---

[6] For an exact formulation, see Braverman (1974, pp. 79–80).

tion in excess of "norms." The dead-end tasks of tending the machines were arrayed on "job ladders," with distinctive titles for different rungs but trivial differences in pay. "Promotion from within" was introduced; that reinforced the "ladders" and saved management the expense of recruitment and training to replace labor turnover. The objective was to encourage worker competition within the plant, dependency on the company, and acceptance of the system. This was also the purpose of a wide span of welfare plans: pensions, stock subscription plans, safety programs, health programs, company housing, sports programs, schools, music programs, etc. A necessary consequence was a reduction of horizontal labor mobility (between employers) and erection of strong barriers to industrial unionism and the class consciousness of workers.[7] Scientific management of the sort just described permeated basic United States Industries (steel, electrical, chemicals, and automobiles) by the end of World War I. It also included industrial and scientific standardization (from nuts and bolts to time zones), reform of the patent system in the interest of the corporations, the establishment of integrated industrial and university research, and the takeover of public school and university educational planning (Sinclair, 1923, 1924; Veblen, 1918). And power and profits accrued from the production of a host of new consumer goods and services.

The next chapter continues the analysis of the development of Consciousness Industry. In it we consider the development of scientific mass marketing and the invention of the mass media.

---

[7] Braverman (1974) is excellent on scientific management but naive in regard to technology and advertising. See also Stone (1974, pp. 113–173) and Palmer (1975, pp. 31–49).

4

ON HOW CONSCIOUSNESS INDUSTRY DEVELOPED II: SCIENTIFIC MASS MARKETING AND THE INVENTION OF THE MASS MEDIA

When a famous English painter, W. P. Frith (R.A.) protested because his painting of a little girl holding a garment had been purchased and used by a soap company to advertise its soap, the editor of *Magazine Art* replied (1889): "Art, like Truth, can only dignify and beautify that with which it comes in contact. . . . Commerce has everything to gain and nothing to lose. . . . To sum up, artistic advertising is . . . a forceful weapon for disseminating good art in the most public manner possible" (Presbrey, 1929, pp. 99–100).

The rationalization of the marketing process was no less revolutionary than that of the physical production process under the policies of monopoly capitalism. Typically characterized by unbranded consumer goods (flour, apples, yard goods, freshly killed and dressed meats, poultry, fish, etc.) the marketing process of mid-nineteenth-century America and Canada was not greatly different from that of the Middle Ages. Most consumer goods were or could be homemade, at least in the stage of final processing:

> . . . while only about ten percent of the total bread consumed in 1850 had been baked commercially, the ratio increased to 25 percent by 1900 and about 60 percent by 1930 (Pope, 1973, p. 25).

If not locally produced and supplied, they came via the "circulation of commodities" with which Marx was so familiar. Hardware items and other metal consumer goods (e.g., brass bedsteads) and staples like salt, spices, distilled liquors, etc., "circulated" rather freely from the manufacturer to the retail outlet via a chain of wholesalers, brokers, sales agents, etc. Before the era of widespread "brand" marketing of consumer goods, the means of salesmanship were traveling salesmen (drummers) who "called on" the retailers. Retail general stores in turn were supplemented by door-to-door peddlers, ranging from the pushcart peddlers of the city slums to horse-drawn vehicles making house-to-house calls.

Transport facilities and the rates charged for hauling commodities limited the geographic scope of consumer goods markets. Commodities which were small in bulk and weight in relation to their market prices were therefore the first to enjoy regional and national markets. Patent medicines were a prime example. Such advertising as there was in mid-nineteenth-century Canada and America was of two kinds: The older was predecessor of our "national brand" advertising. Patent medicine elixirs of life seem to have been the earliest users of the brand name technique associated with "secret" formulas and a heavy infusion of imaginary qualities "hawked" by the spellbinder, who incidentally, often "worked" fairs, city street corners, etc.[1] Other advertising was usually of the simple "announcement" variety, e.g., "the arrival of a shipment of high quality shoes" (or stoves) announced in newspapers. These ads, resembling modern classified advertisements, commonly appeared in newspapers from the eighteenth century on. The retailer was more often identified in the ads than the manufacturer. Magazine (periodical) advertising was ill-suited to informative advertising of the type carried by newspapers because of its relative infrequency of publication and tendency to have broader geographic sales than the markets that advertisers were able to command with their products. It is not surprising, therefore, that on a sporadic basis precursors of national advertising of branded commodities appeared in English magazines as early as the Napoleonic War period: Presbrey (1929, p. 85) could find one example—"Warren's Shoe Blacking" thus advertised as early as 1820. But the marketing of consumer goods was typically competitive and lacking in "vertical" industrial organization. What "display" advertising there was tended to be confined to billboards and magazines. This is another way of saying that the last stage in the production of consumer goods typically was a domestic affair as late as the middle of the last century.

As noted earlier, so acute an observer as Karl Marx took it for granted that this was so. From what he did say that was relevant to the conditions under which labor power was produced, as well as from what he did not, it is clear that Marx assumed that labor power was then produced under "handicraft" conditions (not those imposed by Consciousness Industry)

---

[1] Presbrey (1929, p. 65) speaks of an ad for "Stoughton's Great Elixir" in a London broadsheet or popular newspaper, *London Postman*, in 1706. But brand name advertising was then uncommon; see also Lynd and Lynd (1929).

and that workers would use their common sense in buying consumer goods despite the blandishments of capitalists.[2]

Although Marx apparently paid no direct attention to advertising, his conception of production and consumption would have supported a realistic view of advertising by monopoly capitalism:

> *Consumption produces production in a double way . . . because consumption creates the need for new production, that is it creates the ideal, internally impelling cause for production, which is its presupposition.* Consumption creates the motive for production; it also creates the object which is active in production as its determinant aim. . . . No production without a need. But consumption reproduces the need, but it also supplies a need for the material. As soon as consumption emerges from its initial state of natural crudity and immediacy—and, if it remained at that stage, this would be because production itself had been arrested there—it becomes itself mediated as a drive by the object. The need which consumption feels for the object is created by the perception of it. The object of art—like every other product—creates a public which is sensitive to art and enjoys beauty. Production thus not only creates an object for the subject, but also a subject for the object. *Thus production produces consumption (1) by creating the material for it; (2) by determining the manner of consumption; and (3) by creating the products initially posited by it as objects, in the form of a need felt by the consumer. It thus produces the object of consumption. Consumption likewise produces the producer's inclination by beckoning to him as an aim-determining need* (Marx, 1973, pp. 91–92; emphasis added).

It is clear, first, that the exchange of activities and abilities which takes place within production itself belongs directly to production and essentially constitutes it. The same holds, secondly, for the exchange of products, insofar as that exchange is the means of finishing the product and making it fit for direct consumption. Thirdly, the so-called exchange between dealers and dealers is by its very organization entirely determined by production, as being itself a producing activity. Exchange appears as independent and indifferent to production only in the final phase where the product is exchanged directly for consumption (Marx, 1973, p. 99).

---

[2] A close reading of the three volumes of *Capital* and the *Grundrisse* discloses no awareness of the role which advertising (which is hardly mentioned at all) might play in the further development of capitalism. Thus, ". . . the worker's participation in the higher, even cultural satisfactions, the agitation of his own interests, newspaper subscriptions, attending lectures, educating his children, developing his tastes, etc., his only share of civilization which distinguishes him from the slave is economically only possible by widening the sphere of his pleasures at the time when business is good, where saving is to a certain degree possible. . . ." (Marx, 1973, p. 287). He saw that the accumulative process would multiply commodities: "Capital's ceaseless striving towards the general form of wealth drives labour beyond the limits of its natural paltriness (*Natürbedurftigkeit*), and thus creates the material elements for the development of the rich individuality which is as all-sided in its production as in its consumption" (Marx, 1973, p. 325). That he apparently slighted advertising and branded commodities remains surprising; perhaps as yet unpublished writing which will fill the gap will appear in time.

These then were the conditions in which the "mass media" emerged. In the last quarter of the nineteenth century, the corporations *needed* some means of expanding the outlets for the mass-produced consumer goods they were able to manufacture with their new-found rationalization of the "productive" process. But how to mass market vastly increased quantities and varieties of mostly unbranded goods? The expansion of activity by door-to-door peddlers was logistically ridiculous. Mail-order marketing had been started but clearly was inadequate. And left to itself, the melange of wholesalers, brokers, commission merchants, etc., and retailers was so diffuse as to frustrate the corporations' need to *manage* "consumer" demand (the term *consumer* came into common use only through Consciousness Industry practice). Handbills had been used for advertising since the seventeenth century, but sporadically, and in any event, their random distribution and evanescent physical nature limited them as a marketing medium. Billboards also had been used for rough poster art and advertising, but their power was also limited. There remained newspapers and magazines as possible mass marketing agents if they could be modernized. "Advertising men as early as the 1870s were portraying advertising as a modern, lower cost alternative to personal selling" (Pope, 1973, p. 15).

The technique of producing newspapers and magazines had hardly changed from Gutenberg's time to the beginning of the nineteenth century. The high cost of rag paper and the small press runs possible meant high prices and a small circulation among the upper class, clergy, intelligentsia, and businessmen. Such was the political power potential of the press that it seems safe to say it has *never* been supported and controlled by its readers' market. At first it was monarchical and clerical power which licensed printers/publishers as monopolies, taxed and supervised them in the seventeenth and eighteenth centuries. As political parties (contemporary style) took shape in Britain and America in the period from roughly 1690 to the 1840s, their political and financial backers controlled the press. Also by means of regular state subsidies through free or virtually free postal rates, the parties from the eighteenth century on, shifted an appreciable portion of the cost of the press to the taxpayers. And when the press became "free" of monarchical, clerical, and rigid party controls (but not free of the postal subsidies which continue today) during the middle decades of the nineteenth century, the market control which took its place was quickly dominated by advertising. The pretense that the nonadvertising content of the press was produced in the interest of the people who bought the newspapers and magazines free of controls was *always* a hoax if one looks at the whole system.

Beginning about the end of the Napoleonic Wars, a series of technical innovations made possible a cyclical, reciprocal process which dramatically developed the number of newspapers and magazines in North

America and Britain, increased their total circulation, and lowered the prices charged to readers while profiting the publishers. The logic of the process was: technical improvement leading to increased pressruns leading to lower unit costs, leading to greater profits for the publisher, leading to capital accumulation, and the entry of competitive publishers into the market, leading to further technical improvement, leading to still larger pressruns and methods of reproducing pictures, leading to lower unit costs and further increases in profits, and so on. For our purposes the identity of the publishers who pioneered these innovations and built large fortunes and reputations (especially in the innumerable journalism textbooks which celebrate them in romantic, turgid pap) need not be repeated here.

What is important is that while the "leading" respectable newspapers and magazines in the mid-nineteenth century continued to appeal to an upper-income or bourgeois readership at 6 cents a copy (a high price in terms of current price levels), very successful ventures developed a low-priced newspaper with editorial content which was "sensational" rather than substantive. This happened earlier in the United States—with the New York *Sun* in 1833 and the New York *Herald* in 1835—than in Britain. In the second half of the nineteenth century, the reciprocal spiraling process accelerated greatly; by the 1880s, the form of the present stereotypical North American-British newspaper enterprise was mature. Patterned on the sensational "editorial" content associated with the names of Pulitzer and Hearst in the United States, and Northcliffe and Pearson in Britain, and conceived of as a marketing mechanism to produce readerships for sale to advertisers, the mass media had been systemically innovated.[3] Now, as Veblen said, publicity and scarcity could power a false simulation of abundance for all.

With advertisers paying most of the cost of producing and distributing newspapers and magazines, were the advertisers to be responsible for providing and paying for the "free lunch" as well as the advertisements? We noted in Chapter 1 that down to about 1908 the answer seemed to be affirmative; publicity handouts from advertisers constituted a large pro-

---

[3] If one avoids the trap of considering press history in terms of romantic "star" reporters, editors, or publishers, another trap too often diverts attention: the economics of the technique of the press and paper, fascinating as it is. In his valuable essay, "Technology and Public Opinion in the United States of America," Harold Innis did a good job of analyzing the technical factors in the complex process which I have deliberately passed over lightly. He quite failed to perceive the economic role of advertising and the mass media for monopoly capitalism. He came only this close to it: "In actively supporting a policy of holding down the price of newsprint and of increasing production, newspapers favoured a marked extension of advertising. The economy became biased toward the mass production of goods which had a rapid turnover and an efficient distributing system. The advertiser was concerned with constant emphasis on prosperity" (Innis, 1951, p. 187).

portion of the "news" in the press. E. L. Bernays (1952, pp. 60–61) reports that a tremendous increase in advertising—patent medicines, soaps, breakfast foods, gas companies, classified ads, etc.—took place. As a consequence "a flood of press agentry . . . got the press to publish advertisements in the guise of news." Such disguised ads cost the advertiser more than unconcealed advertisments. The Standard Oil Company and the leading manufacturers of patent medicines were conspicuous in this regard.

News management is deliberate actions by organizations and individuals outside the mass media which shape the agenda and content of the free lunch. It is designed to place on (or exclude from) the agenda determined by the media information, issues, or points of view which are helpful (or harmful) to the interests of those who take such actions. There were (and are) several reasons that media enterprises have accepted and published as part of the free lunch, reports and information provided to them by outside sources. In the first place, the expenses of operating the media are thereby reduced because space (or time) is filled with material which would cost money to replace. In the second place, a community of interest between media management and the external news managers leads the former to regard the news provided at the latter's expense as equally deserving of free lunch status as if it had been produced by the former's staff. In the third place, material rewards (trips, gifts, and money) induce them to do it.

In the United States there have been waves of exposure and public criticism of the regular practice of such news management by corporations which grossly promote their own interests in this way, e.g., by Lincoln Steffens (1920), Ida Tarbell (1904), and Upton Sinclair (1920). The "muckraking" movement from the 1890s on exposed how railroads, meat packers, the Rockefeller oil empire, etc., spent many millions to control the "free lunch" in the press. In response the publishing industry partially eliminated the cruder forms of direct planting of free lunch material by nonmedia organizations.

A new "profession" which came to call itself *public relations counsel* developed from the early efforts of T. N. Vail and the American Telephone and Telegraph Company to influence public opinion in the first decade of the twentieth century (U.S. Federal Communications Commission, 1937, 1939; Daniellian, 1939; Bernays, 1952). On a very sophisticated level the news management efforts of corporations and trade associations, including the National Association of Manufacturers and the United States Chamber of Commerce, have since then been conducted in a context of using *all* means to influence public opinion. Publicity events, press releases, free trips and favors for reporters and editors, motion pictures produced for public relations purposes (played at no cost by theaters and television stations), books written to order, but purporting to be by independent authors, and *institutional* advertisements (as where an aircraft manufacturer advertises that its aircraft bring the peoples of the world closer together) are among the kit of tools in the "PR" agency's repertoire. The essence of the PR effort, to paraphrase an AT&T explanation, is so to conduct the corporation's relations with the mass media when the corporation does *not* need help from them that, when it *does* need help from the media, the most natural thing in the world is for the media people to *ask* the corporation for advice as to how to handle the problem. It would be wrong, however, to think of PR as limited to the design and conduct of tactical efforts to influence the public. Giant corporations rely on their vice-presidents in charge of public relations and their outside PR consultant firms on even the most basic structural issues involving their long-term profitability. For example, advice from the PR consulting firm of Earl Newsom prompted the Ford Motor Company in the 1940s to reorganize itself to offer the public the opportunity to buy common stock in the company, while at the same time spinning off enormous surplus capital into the tax-exempt Ford Foundation, which was then created.

The tradition of muckraking continued in the work of George Seldes, I. F. Stone, Ralph Nader, etc. And with monotonous regularity, investigations of private sector and intelligence agencies activities in news management reveal briefly the perennial effort of privileged groups to protect and advance their privileged position by (among other means) influencing the free lunch. The massive manipulative campaign by the electric light and power industry in the United States to oppose public ownership or effective public regulation of the industry in the 1920s was exposed by a Federal Trade Commission investigation. The Federal Communications Commission investigation of the Bell System has already been mentioned. Congressional investigations of the role of the CIA in overthrowing the Allende regime in Chile disclosed the use made of the wire services and *Time* magazine in news management. The Pentagon Papers case in the federal courts revealed United States government news management regarding the Vietnamese war. And so on.

The portion of the free lunch which is devoted to debate on controversial public issues in the broadcast media originated in the *Mayflower* decision of the Federal Communications Commission in the late 1930s where the commission held that merely because it was the holder of a radio broadcast license, a corporation was not free to employ its programs to advocate its owner's private interest. It held that if the owner wished to use the station for such a purpose it was obliged to present "other sides" of the issue in question. Out of that case grew the "fairness doctrine" which still exists and which was imitated by a small number of newspapers in their "Op-Ed" page. As the experience of Edward R. Murrow revealed, however, the freedom of creative media investigative reporters to present analyses of controversial public issues was very limited by private, corporate power (Friendly, 1967; Halberstam, 1976). Murrow was forced off the air by its pressure. The range of examples is too large to be analyzed here. But one will suffice. It is now obvious to all that the so-called peaceful uses of atomic energy pose grave dangers to the future of human beings. Yet, thanks to the government-industry complex which controlled the development of nuclear power in the United States from 1945 to the end of the 1960s:

> . . . nothing seen or heard on television could lead viewers to think that atomic energy involved risks of any serious kind. Documentaries and public service messages had come overwhelmingly—perhaps exclusively—from those who had a stake in promoting the industry (Barnouw, 1978, pp. 164-165).

As Barnouw (1978, pp. 140-146) also discloses, the numerous, allegedly "public service announcements," sponsored by the Advertising Council are in fact controlled by a peak organization of major advertisers. Far from being the product of disinterested public concern they are the result of an essentially political screening process designed to perpetuate the *status quo* while seeming to be disinterested.

The production of newspaper and magazine audiences for sale to advertisers made possible rationalized marketing of mass-produced consumer goods and services. The great expansion of the newspaper and magazine industry which followed the adoption of those institutions as marketing agents is well known. In numbers of newspaper and magazine publishers the expansion was very great in the capitalist heartland. Circulation figures reached astronomical proportions and the poundage of individual papers (especially in the United States and Canada with their lavish use of newsprint) soared.

The role of advertising (and advertisers and advertising agencies) in developing what Veblen called the "going concern" character of monopoly capitalism, so sadly neglected by economists (neoclassical and Marxist alike), must be emphasized. Table 4-1 shows, for selected years beginning with 1867, the growth of advertising in relation to population for the United States. (Canada does not publish statistics which would make possible a parallel analysis.) Because of the great inflation in the price level (i.e., fourfold since 1867), it is the deflated figures in column (4) which are meaningful for our purpose. Expressed in dollars of *constant* purchasing power (i.e., 1977 prices), total United States advertising expenditures in 1977 were 176 times what they were in 1867, while the population grew just under six times. Or putting it in per capita terms (column 5), the United States economy spent $5.80 *per capita* in 1867 and

$175.74 in 1977 on advertising—*30 times* as much. The growth of Consciousness Industry since World War II is reflected in the fact that since 1948, advertising expenditures per capita more than doubled.

Table 4-1
United States Advertising Expenditures and Population
(selected years, 1867–1977)

Year	Population (millions)	Cost of Living Index (1977:100)	Total Advertising Expenditures (dollars)		
			Actual (millions)	In Constant Dollars (millions)	Per Capita (constant dollars)
	(1)	(2)	(3)	(4)	(5)
1867	37.4	23	50	217	5.80
1880	50.2	16	200	1,250	24.90
1890	63.0	15	360	2,400	38.09
1900	76.0	14	542	3,871	50.93
1914	99.1	17	1,302	7,659	77.20
1919	104.5	28	2,282	8,150	77.99
1929	121.8	28	3,426	12,236	100.46
1933	125.6	21	1,302	6,200	49.36
1948	146.6	40	4,864	12,160	82.95
1970	204.9	64	19,600	30,625	149.46
1977	216.8	100	38,100	38,100	175.74

Sources:
Column (1) Bureau of Census, *Historical Statistics of the United States, Colonial Times to 1970.* Washington, D.C.: United States Government Printing Office, 1975, pp. 10–12; *Statistical Abstract,* 1978.
(2) *Historical Statistics,* 1975, p. 210; *Statistical Abstract,* 1978, p. 478. (Converted to base 1977.)
(3) *Historical Statistics,* 1975, p. 856; *Statistical Abstract,* 1978.
(4) By dividing column (3) by column (2) and multiplying by 100.
(5) By dividing column (4) by column (1).

The mainstay producer of audience power for advertisers (as measured by the expenditures of advertisers) was from the beginning the newspaper industry. In 1935 (the earliest year for which data exist), newspapers accounted for 45 percent of all United States advertising expenditures; magazines, 8 percent; direct mail, 17 percent; radio, 7 percent; outdoor and farm publications, less than 2 percent each; and miscellaneous, 18 percent. Between 1935 and 1975, the major shift in audience producers was the rise of television to 19 percent of all advertising expenditures. Much of this appears to have been at the expense of newspapers, reduced to 30 percent (still significantly more than television), and magazines (down to 5 percent). Radio (7 percent), direct mail (15 percent), business papers (3 percent), outdoor (2 percent), and miscellaneous (18 percent) remained stable in their shares of total advertising.[4]

From the standpoint of Consciousness Industry, the role of the advertising agencies has been of pivotal importance in demand-management. Although advertising agencies existed from early in the nineteenth century in both England and the United States, their function changed dramatically in the 1880s and 1890s. Originating as buyers at *wholesale* of newspaper (and magazine) advertising space (and therefore audience power) their main function originally was to serve as brokers in reselling that space to particular advertisers. They did not prepare advertising copy or perform the "creative" role in commodity- and package-creation that now distinguishes their contribution to the mass marketing of consumer goods. And their compensation was in the form of a commission *from* the media whose audiences were being sold to the advertiser. After the last two decades of the nineteenth century, their role was transformed; increasingly they assumed the market research, copy-writing, sales-planning function which they have performed conspicuously since the 1920s. Only their mode of compensation (typically 15 percent of the advertising budget) remains as a token of their origin although it too is slowly yielding to negotiated fees for services rendered.[5] By an unremarked sleight of hand, the "client" became the advertiser as the systemic dependency of the media on advertisers made itself felt since the 1890s.

A process of merger and integration took place among advertising agencies which parallels the similar process among giant corporations. The resulting concentration of control of the agency business has facilitated the integration of Consciousness Industry's mass marketing and production and use of audience power. As Herbert Schiller (1973, pp. 128–133) pointed out, in 1971 10 percent of the agency firms received four-fifths of the United States billings; international billings are even more tightly concentrated. Jerry Goodis, a Canadian advertising agency entrepreneur, reports angrily just how the tight connections between the

---

[4] *Historical Statistics*, 1975, pp. 855–856; and *Statistical Abstract*, 1977, p. 845.

[5] See Presbrey (1929) for a sympathetic account of these systemic changes. Goodis (1972) criticizes the 15 percent agency commission tradition vigorously.

New York head office of the big United States agencies with their clients, the giant TNCs, lead to the establishment of branch plant offices of the American agencies which automatically preempt the advertising business of the branch plants of the TNCs in Canada. He referred to the "merger" between branch plants of American advertising agencies and Canadian agencies: "It would be as appropriate to speak of a merger between a cannibal and a missionary" (Goodis, 1972, p. 111). And Jeremy Tunstall (1977) reports that 4 of the largest 5 and 13 of the largest 20 Italian advertising agencies are American branch plants. Advertising agencies are an essential component in the "central nervous system" by which monopoly capitalism practices cultural domination through culture—and communications.

The model of the mass media as mass producers of audience power for the use of mass producers of consumers' goods and services was set with the conversion of newspapers and magazines to serve that role.[6] It would be natural in the context of the lusty expansion of Consciousness Industry in the first half of the twentieth century to find it picking up attractive technical possibilities for expanding its mode of audience production. And radio communication was an irresistible temptation to the monopoly-capitalist system. The original applications of the technique of radio communication were to transmit encoded messages between shore stations and ships at sea and between ships at sea for military operational purposes from the turn of the twentieth century to World War I. In that period a capability to produce radio equipment developed in the technically advanced nations of the capitalist world. The inescapable necessity of international cooperation in regard to frequency allocation, equipment standards, and operational procedure and the character of the radio spectrum placed radio under international law and regulation from 1906 onward.[7] During World War I, military necessity produced rapid increase in research and development, including especially the capacity to transmit voice by radiotelephone. The giant electronics firms (AT&T, General Electric, Westinghouse, et al.) were the contractors which developed expertise in radio at taxpayers' expense.

---

[6] As early as 1909, advertising amounted to 64 percent of total newspaper revenues in the United States. The proportion rose until by 1973 it was 76 percent. For magazines the proportion has been consistently in the range of 59–67 percent (Newspaper Advertising Bureau, using Census of Manufactures data).

[7] The near monopoly control by the British Marconi Company and its competitive practices (e.g., refusing to communicate with non-Marconi-equipped ships) led directly to the first international conference on radio in Berlin in 1903. This conference was attended by Austria, France, Germany, Great Britain, Hungary, Italy, Russia, Spain, and the United States. Tighter rules were adopted by the first International Radio-telegraph Convention, Berlin, 1906. The first United States law on radio was adopted in 1910. A similar sequence occurred in Britain. (Smythe, 1957, reprinted in Kittross, 1977, Vol. 2).

In all the major warring powers, the coming of peace in 1918 found private industry with the technical knowledge with which to "spin off" nonmilitary uses of radio technique, as well as further to develop its military applications. The institutional form for pursuing civilian uses of radio was then fluid. In the United States which was quick to assert international leadership in radio development, the struggle to determine the institutional form was between the waning populist-democratic forces which had continued to fight for public ownership and operation of communications and private commercial interests. President Wilson had appointed a commission which had recommended government ownership of all radio communications in 1914 (U.S. Congress. Senate, 1914). During the war, all commercial radio stations were taken over and operated by the United States Navy which, in addition to military operation, provided commercial transmission of news and a daily shipping bulletin of maritime news. And when, in July 1918, Congress considered a joint resolution under which the President assumed control of the telegraph, telephone, and cable systems, both the Secretary of the Navy and the Postmaster General testified that the control should be permanent. In the event, the probusiness forces won this struggle handily, thanks to the masterly political abilities of T. N. Vail, president of AT&T, and his man in Washington, Walter Gifford, "loaned" as secretary to the wartime industrial mobilization agency of the federal government (see Daniellian, 1939). The communications industry used the brief wartime government "takeover" of telephone and telegraph operations to obtain desired concessions on rate increases and accounting policy from the state regulatory commissions and to block public ownership. The way was then clear to solve the impasse created by mutually interfering patent positions, market occupation, and development plans. Under the leadership of General Electric, a cartel divided the domestic American electronic communications market between a new entity created by General Electric (the Radio Corporation of America), AT&T, General Electric, Westinghouse Electric, and United Fruit Company. The same cartel agreements divided international markets between the American companies and British Marconi (Smythe, 1957, pp. 46–53).

The impetus for the innovation of radio broadcasting was the prospective profits to be made by radio equipment manufacturers from producing and selling radio receivers and transmitting equipment—a market which we noted in Chapter 2—is heavily weighted on the side of receivers. Inevitably, the receiver manufacturers employed radio programs to produce audiences to market their own products, and incidentally those of consumer goods and service manufacturers. Thus in the early 1920s, the institutional base of radio broadcasting was joined with that of newspapers, magazines, and other advertising media for both Canada and the United States. In Britain, the upper class cultural legacy was sufficiently resistant to the grossness of Consciousness Industry to resist it with the British Broadcasting Corporation service supported by a license fee paid by listeners. The same model was adopted in France, Germany, Italy, and Spain and spread to the colonies of the European powers. In Canada, as we demonstrate in Chapter 8, the enduring pattern for radio broadcasting (and later television) was established in the 1920s on the United States model. The Canadian Broadcasting Corporation was a belated and unsuccessful attempt to graft a BBC model onto the established American-based Canadian system.

Because the radio spectrum is a unique natural resource, whose successful use rests on its *not* being reduced to private property status, there is a tension about radio (and later television) quite alien to the other mass media (see Appendix). Publishers of the printed press, shielded by the constitutional barriers erected in the eighteenth century to protect the interest of the rising business class against capricious monarchical "censorship," had virtually carte blanche to run the press free of government interference when advertisers' control became dominant. But it was legally impossible for a radio (or television) station to own its radio frequency license. Somehow, a reconciliation was necessary between the demands of private business corporations to operate radio stations as they pleased in their own interest (as in the case of the press) and the demands of "politicians" and "voters" in the formal political apparatus of the state that the private licensees operate in the "public interest." The result was a perennial guerrilla war between naked "bottom line" interests on the one hand, and outraged public protests on the other. In this struggle which regularly erupts over issues of obscenity, violence, the right-of-reply concerning controversial public issues, etc., the "regulated" radio (and later also television) broadcast industry enjoys a privileged position of power vis-á-vis the regulators (frequently recruited from the ranks of broadcasters, and never intentionally recruited from the ranks of known critics of Consciousness Industry).

World War II was a turning point in the development of monopoly capitalism. Before World War I, the United States was not a first-ranked power (in military terms), as compared with Britain, Germany, and France. As a result of the war the economic strength of American capitalism was vastly increased because that of Britain and France was greatly weakened while Germany was deprived of its colonies and suffered under a heavy burden of reparations. When World War II began, the United States monopoly-capitalist order was prepared for the giant military-economic mobilization which decisively helped turn the tide against the Axis powers whose strength had been sapped by Soviet resistance. And in 1945 when World War II ended, the United States had the means to try to make itself the ruling world power. By then Britain and France were reduced to second-class power; Germany was devastated and divided; and the Soviet Union impoverished by its losses of people and productive equipment of all kinds. Apart from its preeminence in nuclear weapons and conventional military arms, the largest single asset the United States had in 1945 in asserting its claim to world leadership was its demonstrated ability to produce and market goods, especially consumer goods, and to produce, market, and operate the means of publicity (press, cinema, radio and television) to all countries to which it could get access. The stage was set for Consciousness Industry's most free-wheeling period of powering monopoly capitalism's hegemonic thrust worldwide. The "free flow of information" (in one direction) was unimpeded.

The basis of the power of the United States and the rest of the core area of monopoly capitalism since 1945 has been the Civilian Sales Effort and the Military Sales Effort. For the United States some indicators of the effects of these efforts are offered in Table 4-2 for selected years beginning with 1934, a depression year. The data are presented in terms of dollars per capita. First the effect of changing price levels was eliminated by using the Consumer Price Index; then the resulting constant dollar figures were divided by total population. Per capita expenditures on consumer goods and services—the result of the Civilian Sales Effort—rose over the whole period, 1934–1977: slowly until the end of World War II, then more rapidly, until by 1977 they were three times what they had been in 1934. This increase was made possible by two processes: pump-priming by government expenditures, and consumer borrowing of which installment credit has been the most active element. National defense expenditures—reflecting the Military Sales Effort—rose faster than other federal government expenditures between 1934 and 1938 as the American military prepared for World War II. But it was the vast increase in national defense spending during the war years which prepared the ground for the postwar expansion in consumer expenditures. In the last full year of the war (1944) national defense expenditures were 107 times as large as in 1934. Because of the acute shortage of consumer durable goods between 1941 and 1946 (civilian automobile production having been stopped, for example), the increased consumer income resulting from full employment went partly for consumer services (motion picture attendance then reached an all-time peak) and consumer nondurables. The latter were in short supply because of wartime cutbacks and rationing and the remaining unexpended income went into savings (war bonds especially), and to pay off consumer installment credit. Consumer installment credit in 1944 was much lower than in 1934 and less than half what it had been in 1938.

Table 4-2
United States Consumer Expenditures, Consumer Installment Credit, Federal Government Expenditures, and National Defense Expenditures, Selected Years, 1934–1977
(per capita in constant dollars, 1977 level)

	1934	1938	1944	1946	1955	1977
(1) Consumer expenditures	$1857	$2132	$2735	$3231	$3464	$5586
Relative to 1934	100	115	147	174	187	301
(2) Consumer installment credit outstanding	$ 67	$ 122	$ 54	$ 92	$ 396	$ 999
Relative to 1934	100	182	81	137	592	1492
(3) Total Federal government expenditures*	$ 213	$ 279	$2504	$1461	$1005	$1854
Relative to 1934	100	131	1178	687	473	872
(4) National defense expenditures	$ 20	$ 34	$2130	$1107	$ 520	$ 450
Relative to 1934	100	173	10769	5593	2628	2272
(5) Other Federal government expenditures	$ 193	$ 245	$ 374	$ 354	$ 485	$1404
Relative to 1934	100	127	193	183	251	727

*Note that this and national defense relate to the federal government only.

Source: For all series, actual (current) dollar figures converted to value of dollar in 1977 by dividing by Consumer Price Index, multiplying by 100, and using the Consumer Price Index converted to 1977 equals 100. Per capita figures derived by dividing these values by total population, including members of armed forces.

All basic data from United States Department of Commerce, Bureau of the Census, *Historical Statistics of the United States* (Washington, D.C.: 1975), p. 225, for all years except 1977; 1977 data from Bureau of the Census, *Statistical Abstract*, 1978, p. 261.

After "reconversion" to civilian production the American people used their savings, current income and installment credit to finance continually rising consumption. Enormous postwar expansion resulted. Increasingly consumption relied on installment credit: by 1977, that was 15 times what it had been in 1934, 9 times what it had been in 1929 ($102 in 1977 prices), and 37 times what it had been in 1919 ($27 in 1977 prices). When one considers the ratio of consumer installment credit outstanding to consumer expenditures, it is obvious that increasingly present expenditures are possible only by pledging future income. This ratio rose from 3 percent in 1934 to 18 percent in 1977. The impact on this vast pyramid of consumer borrowing of the sharp rise in interest rates after 1975 would be drastic. Consumer borrowing will fall, and with it consumer expenditures. The Civilian Sales Effort will falter for this reason. Substantial increased support from the Military Sales Effort was provided beginning after 1948 (when national defense expenditures dropped to $278 per capita in 1977 prices). Defense spending during the Cold War, Korean War, and the aerospace race rose by 1955 to 26 times the 1934 level. Heavy dependence on military spending continued: in 1977 it was 23 times the 1934 level. The pump-priming effect of military spending, however, has lost much of its direct impact on workers' incomes and hence their consumer expenditures. Increasingly since World War II, military spending is devoted to "high technology" electronic and weapons development and production. Such spending benefits professional and managerial employment and corporate profits without giving rise to as large a proportion of employment as when military procurement involved mainly small weapons, ammunition, tanks, clothing, and food.

The foregoing analysis has been limited to the United States because of the unavailability of most of the comparable information for Canada. Table 4–3 presents information (per capita, after eliminating the influence of changing price levels) on Canadian personal consumption expenditures and short-term consumer credit outstanding. It is possible to compare the change between 1955 and 1977 in Canada with that in the United States between the same years (but not, of course, to compare absolute data, expressed in Canadian and United States dollars, respectively). Personal consumption expenditures in Canada increased to twice the 1955 level by 1977; by that year, short-term consumer credit increased to three and a half times the 1955 level. The comparable changes in the United States (from Table 4–2) were a little more than half for consumer expenditures, and two and a half times for consumer installment credit outstanding. Canadian consumption expenditures and use of short-term consumer credit thus increased at a substantially higher rate than American between 1955 and 1977. Moreover, the ratio of consumer installment credit to consumer expenditures in Canada was at a higher level in both years (15 percent in 1955, 25 percent in 1977) than in the United States (11 percent in 1955, 15 percent in 1977). Canadian consumption was thus even more dependent on installment credit than that of the United States in this period.

Table 4–3
Canadian Personal Consumption Expenditures
and Short-term Consumer Credit,
1955 and 1977
(per capita in constant prices, 1977 level)

	1955	1977
(1) Personal consumption expenditures	$2643	$5304
Relative to 1955	100	201
(2) Short-term consumer credit outstanding	$ 388	$1345
Relative to 1955	100	347

Source: *Canada Yearbooks.*

The vast expansion of research and development of radio communications (and thefore all electronics) during World War II provided the giant corporations which possessed this know-how with potentially immense markets for civilian products and services (television, land, marine, and aeronautical radiotelephone, citizens' band mobile radiotelephone, and computers). In this context monochrome television and later color television broadcasting were innovated by the giant corporations with the aid of their peak trade associations and with a modicum of rivalry between the giants (e.g., the bitter struggle between RCA and Columbia Broadcasting System over the engineering standards and frequency allocations for monochrome and color television, 1943–1950). This innovation process revealed some interesting aspects of Consciousness Industry. First, the innovations were primarily struggles for control of markets in which audience power would market to itself new broadcast equipment. The technical basis of monochrome television had been laid in the 1920s and 1930s and owed little to World War II research and development. Second, the role of the regulatory agency of the national government was limited to rationalizing the technical and organizational planning for the television systems. Third, the venture capital required for financing the new television broadcasting industry was largely provided from accumulated profits from radio broadcasting networks and stations, newspapers and magazines, and to a lesser degree, from motion picture producers anxious to join their own industry's destructive rival. To a substantial degree, general taxpayers subsidized the new investments in television through the written-off plants which the electronics industry, "converted" to war production (of shells, small arms and ammunition, etc.), had operated on a cost-plus basis during the war. These plants were donated or sold at token prices by the government to the industry at war's end for instant conversion to assembly lines to produce television and radio receivers.

The systemic process of innovating television by Consciousness Industry was (as just indicated) marked by intercorporate rivalry which sometimes erupted in open conflict. It also revealed consistency (or systemic integrity?) in innovation, of which the case of broadcast facsimile is a shining example. From the early days of radio broadcasting, the technique had developed by which record communications could be broadcast either multiplexed (carried piggyback) on sound carrier waves or separately on very narrow channels. During World War II the navies of the Western powers had employed the technique to distribute weather maps, operational plans, etc., to diverse points. By 1943 when the major postwar planning for development of electronics industry began, it was evident that broadcast facsimile was ripe to deliver electronically a newspaper to the home either with or without aural radio accompaniment.

A clear alternative mode of newspaper production and delivery was in hand and it was one with many advantages. The plant required to produce and broadcast a facsimile newspaper was cheap (a maximum of $10,000 for a facsimile transmitter, plus electromatic typewriters to set up copy, located in about 3000 square feet of space which could be in the upper floors of cheap buildings). By contrast a metropolitan newspaper needs expensive and extensive downtown real estate and several million dollars worth of typesetting and printing equipment plus a delivery system of trucks, substations, and much direct labor input. The receiving component for a broadcast facsimile newspaper was cheap and rugged (John V. L. Hogan, pioneer radio inventor told me in 1948 it could be mass produced to sell at no more than the cost of a portable typewriter, to which it was technically comparable). The chemically sensitized paper for use in the receiver could be mass produced and distributed cheaply.

The prospect meant that a city which by then had only from 1 to 3 newspapers could readily support as many as 15 or 20 broadcast facsimile newspapers. Rural delivery, where inclement weather, rugged terrain, or sparsely distributed population impeded or prevented conventional newspaper distribution, could be accomplished with the speed and geographic range of radio waves. All in all, a competitive, rugged, and inexpensive mode of providing a "free marketplace" of news was available. Between the 1920s and 1950s almost every major United States newspaper conducted experiments using broadcast facsimile and some (e.g., the Knight chain newspaper in Miami) made a bold public attempt to get one started. The Federal Communications Commission had authorized its commercial licensing.

The failure of Consciousness Industry to innovate broadcast facsimile illustrates how politico-economic considerations produce *the kind of* "technology" which will be innovated—and preclude others. Patents clearly were one element in accounting for the failure of broadcast facsimile to achieve innovation. All the needed technique was available free of patent control, the patents long since having expired. No giant corporation could hope to gain a competitive advantage over its rivals by innovating facsimile (as RCA did with monochrome television). But a more compelling reason for absence of interest in innovating broadcast facsimile is to be found in the interlocking interests of the newspaper industry and the giant corporations which mass market consumer goods. For the latter, broadcast facsimile would shatter the pattern of vertical control of audiences produced by the newspaper, radio, and television media. The space and time buyers in the giant consumer goods producing corporations would have faced a *locally* competitive structure of newspaper, radio, and television audience producers in which the share of audiences produced would be volatile, rendering "scientific" mas marketing so complex and unstable as to be practically impossible. It threatened a return to the very unstable conditions of marketing which the system had begun to cure in the last two decades of the nineteenth century.

Also to be noted in analyzing why broadcast facsimile "failed" of innovation is the fact of bureaucratization—both in the giant advertising corporations and in the print media in general—extending from senior staff levels "down" to the unions of craftsmen who for centuries, have clung to physical modes of print production (U.S. Federal Communications Commission, 1948; Hills, 1949; Jones, 1949; Hogan, 1941). So, despite its obvious advantages, broadcast facsimile was systemically shelved. In considering the ideological aspects of "technology" (Chapter 10), we refer to broadcast facsimile again: was its noninnovation and the runaway innovation of television the result of some primordial "scientific" teleology, the result of some mystical invocation by a "global village," or the result of monopoly capitalism as a going concern?

To round out this analysis of the systemic inventions and innovations of mass media, it must be noted that the innovation of communications satellites and data processing was made at public expense as part of the Cold War, and as a "civilian" spin-off from the military aerospace "race" between the United States and the Soviets. Their role in United States imperial strategic policies of cultural domination has been demonstrated by Herbert Schiller (1969, chap. 9; 1976).

A companion innovation—at the polar opposite position—cable television—grew at the level of the local community in the more traditional pattern of first, small business risk-taking and demonstration of profits followed by the "hedging" investments of over-the-air television and radio broadcasters, newspaper, magazine, and motion picture enterprises. Here the spun-off transistors, printed circuits, and fiber optics, etc., from the aerospace race research and development have presented Consciousness Industry with problems yet to be solved:

1.   The innovation of multiple, interactive services to cabled homes—including banking, marketing, etc., as well as broadcast services—requires massive institutional reorientation from traditional modes of operation (as with banking, for example) and very heavy equipment expenditures by consumers. In a period when runaway inflation, soaring interest rates, and unemployment afflict the core area, innovation of such services is problematic at best.

2.   The innovation of pay-television depends upon the *ultimate* willingness of people to pay heavily to receive the *same* type of program they now *mostly* use from advertising-laden television. If and when the buying power of pay-television entrepreneurs is large enough for them to outbid "commercial television" for popular sports events, this type of programming will be monopolized by pay-television. Then the cost of bringing to pay-television audiences these very expensive kinds of free lunch will initiate the process which has prevailed in commercial broadcasting (and now even in United States Public Broadcasting) of introducing advertising—first modest institutional sponsorship announcements; then as audiences become desensitized to that level of advertising, harder and harder advertisements. To my knowledge no prospective pay-television entrepreneur has guaranteed or will guarantee *not* to superimpose advertising on top of the fees to be paid by the audience member.

After this extended analysis of the application of science in marketing—the systemic invention of the mass media to serve advertisers—it is necessary to return to its twin: the application of capitalist science to product fabrication. The process of merging and amalgamating competitive factory enterprises, competitive wholesalers, etc., into horizontal and vertical giant corporations was discussed in Chapter 3. In the 1870s and 1880s, early efforts at achieving the anticompetitive purposes of the merger movement had often fallen apart from lack of internal cohesion and centralization of decision making (Chandler, 1962). And as Chandler says:

> The years from the end of the depression of the 1870s until the turn of the century witnessed an enormous surge in American industrial output. By 1900 industrial capacity surpassed that of any other nation. During this same period of growth, the most dynamic and most significant of American industries had become dominated by a few great vertically integrated enterprises operating in national and often world markets. . . .

In the last two decades of the nineteenth century, American industrialists concentrated their imagination and energy on the creation of these industrial empires. They became engrossed in planning the strategies of expansion and in securing the resources—the men, money, and equipment—necessary to meet the needs and challenges of a swiftly industrializing and urbanizing economy. *The powerful captains*—the Rockefellers, Swifts, Dukes, Garys and Westinghouses—and their able lieutenants *had* little time and often little interest in fashioning a *rational and systemic design for administering effectively the vast resources they had united under their control. Yet their strategies of expansion, consolidation, and integration demanded structural changes and innovations at all levels of administration* (Chandler, 1962, p. 36; emphasis added).

By about 1914 in the United States scientific management had taken over operations on the "factory floor" of heavy industry and was being imitated in light industry. As a necessary result an immense amount of information about the production process had been generated—which had to be processed by white-collar clerks in administrative offices. Similarly, investigation of sources of raw materials, and marketing and public relations activities piled up paper work in administrative offices. Efficient rationalized management was necessary. As Chandler (1962, p. 37) says, what was needed were ". . . carefully defined lines of authority and communication and . . . detailed, accurate, and voluminous data to flow through these lines." Again, control of the flow of communications was seen to be the basis of power.

The work of the multiplied number of clerks was the next target of scientific management on the job front. Initially the flow of paper was rationalized via pneumatic tubes and systems of wires or belts to move the paper from station to station within and between offices. A second more fundamental method of economizing in clerical work involved application of the Hollerith machines (a mechanical computing machine using 80-column punch cards invented in the United States Census Bureau before 1900) to scientifically handle information (rather than paper bearing information). Linear programming was developed as a means of preplanning whole series of decision-making stations so that intervening clerks were no longer necessary. The introduction of the electronic computer after 1945 and reduction in its cost put this "pipeline" system within the reach of every firm. Most of the clerks who survived this wave of scientific management were "detail workers" (as on the shop floor), mostly women, whose salaries were lower than those of factory operatives. After 1945 scientific management was applied with these patterns to the whole range of service and retail establishments, with similar deskilling and reduction of labor costs and employment. So also for wide sectors of government employment, the administrative aspects of educational insti-

tutions, and the operation of computers themselves. *All* these developments of scientific management are based on communications systems
and techniques in the interest not of the best way to organize work but the
best way to produce profits for monopoly capital (see discussion of scientific management in Chapter 3).

Currently the prototypical application is at the supermarket where
the coming implementation of a "wave" of scientific management will
replace the checker with a computer which will "read" the cryptic symbols printed on the commodity package so that a "bagger" and cashier
function is all that will remain to be performed. Soon, even those details
may be replaced by a credit card and automatic bagging routine. If and
when automatic replenishment of commodities on shelves is mechanized,
the only human beings the working audience member will see in the
modern supermarket will be a manager and occasional maintenance
workers. Division of labor is being carried to its logical conclusion by
scientific management. Each generation of machines requires only
"damaged" labor to tend it. And the information about the work process
disclosed by that generation of machines provides the basis for further deskilling and reduction in wages and employment, leading to the next generation of new machines, and so on. By and large labor unions have been
completely "tamed" by the application of scientific management—even
to the extent of making the rationalization of task ladders and the protection of "seniority" and "promotion from within," which had been forced
on unwilling workers in the 1890s, their own demands to their employers
since the 1930s.

The vertical organization of commodity production and marketing
has proceeded apace, although the backward state of scholarly work on
the history of marketing obscures the reality situation. According to Philip
Kotler (1972, p. 446):

> A change began in the 1890s with the growth of national firms and national
> advertising media. The growth of brand names has been so dramatic that to-
> day in the United States hardly anything is sold unbranded. Salt is packaged
> in distinctive manufacturers' containers, oranges are stamped, common nuts
> and bolts are packaged in cellophane with a distributor's label, and various
> parts of an automobile—spark plugs, tires, filters—bear visible brand names
> different from that of the automobile.

And Joseph C. Palamountain (1969, p. 138) says, "Great increases in the
size of manufacturers or retailers have changed much of the distribution
from a flow through a series of largely autonomous markets to a single
movement dominated by either manufacturer or retailer". Demand management by Consciousness Industry has replaced the "circulation" of commodities with the "induced suction" of commodities.

Ewen (1976, p. 195) correctly declares, "The implementation of 'scientifically' calibrated monotony on the job required the development of a new science to deal with its effect on consciousness." This was the science that Veblen termed "publicity" but which we know better as communications. (Its analysis is in Chapter 11). It was rooted in the behavioral sciences of psychology and sociology in the twenty years after World War I.[8] Implemented through the theory and practice of Consciousness Industry, its practitioners of communications were more concerned with practical results than published theoretical rationalizations. The servile role thus established has continued to dominate work on communications in North America, as scrutiny of the titles and courses taught in hundreds of institutions would demonstrate.

The political rhetoric produced by the executives of Consciousness Industry (with an overt assist here and there from academicians) is the final feature to be analyzed. Evidence to support the preceding analysis of the rise of Consciousness Industry has been hard, realistic material relating to institutions and their operations. I have been chary of using rhetorical claims about the systemic purpose of those acts because, as every historian knows, such claims may reflect either empty puffery or perhaps suspected conspiratorial plans. And although there may indeed have been significant conspiracies in the business and political history of this period, one need not prove their existence in order to establish the main point: that the system, comprised of a few hundred giant corporations each one of which mostly acted in its own interest, became in fact a "going concern" as a coherent and to a large extent cohesive system. To say this is not to imply that the system was free of grave problems. Internally, the fact of the depression (1930 to the beginning of World War II) revealed the hangover of failures in corporate pricing and demand-management policies the need for which had prompted the rise of corporate capitalism half a century earlier. The public activity of the "America First" movement revealed the interest of some major United States corporations (e.g., Ford Motors) to sympathize with Nazi and Italian fascism. And the hard fact that poverty was substantial (Paul Douglas calculated in 1924 that most wage-earning families were at or below the minimum subsistence level) (quoted in Ewen, 1976, pp. 57–58), meant that Consciousness Industry was riding a tiger. To function profitably, monopoly capitalism requires sufficient *ready buyers with income to spend*. Ready buyers without money to spend could spell political trouble. If not revolu-

---

[8] Conspicuously, John B. Watson, founder of American behavioral psychology who left his teaching post at Johns Hopkins to become a senior executive in a New York advertising agency. Rollo May, Floyd Allport, and many others served the same public relations, propaganda, and market research functions. Edward Bernays was a public relations practitioner who did court publicity and published much.

tion, they tend to turn to alcohol, drugs, and crime. The latter could be glossed over. (Remember J. Edgar Hoover and the "ten most wanted list"?) And the necessary income to spend could be stretched increasingly into the future through installment credit which flourished from the 1920s on. But the haunting fear after 1917 was of the contagion of socialism spreading from the Soviet Union and later China.

It was in this context that spokesmen for Consciousness Industry openly espoused the ideology of corporate capitalism in public rhetoric. Of many who might be cited, I quote from one qualified by position to speak for the capitalist system, the President of the United States, Calvin Coolidge, in 1926:

> When we stop to consider the part which advertising plays in the modern life of production and trade we see that basically it is that of education. It informs its readers of the existence and nature of commodities by explaining the advantages to be derived from their use and creates for them a wider demand. It makes new thoughts, new desires, and new actions. *By changing the attitude of mind it changes the material condition of the people.*

> Somewhere I have seen ascribed to Abraham Lincoln the statement "In this and like communities public sentiment is everything. With public sentiment nothing can fail; without it nothing can succeed; consequently he who molds public sentiment goes deeper than he who enacts statutes or pronounces decisions. He makes statutes and decisions possible or impossible to be executed."

> Advertising creates and changes this foundation of all popular action, public sentiment or public opinion. It is the most potent influence in adopting and changing the habits and modes of life, affecting what we eat, what we wear and the work and play of the whole nation. *Formerly it was an axiom that competition was the life of trade. Under the methods of the present day it would seem to be more appropriate to say that advertising is the life of trade. . . .*

> Under its stimulation the country has gone from the old hand methods of production, which were so slow and laborious, with high unit costs and low wages, to our present great factory system and its mass production with the astonishing result of low unit costs and high wages. The preeminence of America in industry, which has constantly brought about a reduction of costs, has come very largely through mass production. *Mass production is only possible where there is mass demand. Mass demand has been created almost entirely through the development of advertising.*

> In the former days goods were expected to sell themselves. Oftentimes they were carried about from door to door. Otherwise they were displayed on the shelves and counters of the merchant. The public were supposed to know of these sources of supply and depend on themselves for their knowledge of what was to be sold. *Modern business could neither have been created nor can it be maintained on any such system. It constantly requires publicity. It is not enough that goods are made; a demand for them must also be made. It*

is on this foundation of enlarging production through the demands created by advertising that very much of the success of the system rests. . . . Those engaged in that effort are changing the trend of human thought. They are molding the human mind. Those who write upon that tablet write for all eternity. . . . It is a great power that has been entrusted to your keeping which charges you with the high responsibility of inspiring and ennobling the commercial world. It is all part of the greater work of the regeneration and redemption of mankind.[9]

The hegemonic, imperial, authoritarian, systemic intention is obvious. The institutional means were ready. In the guise of cultural "democracy," the democracy of commoditized people chasing dollars to mass-market commodities to themselves was to be administered by an authoritarian system of corporate capitalism. The system was perfected with the tight fusion of giant corporations with formal government organs during World War II (Catton, 1948). The systemic invention of the Military-Industrial Complex established in those years provided a means of pump-priming which insured against catastrophic losses of profits, reduction of prices, and the political danger of massive unemployment during business depressions. After a fashion, welfare-state measures patched up the damage done to people. And, thanks to the pervasive redirecting of the full range of social institutions (from church and school to sports), the constant teaching of corporate capitalist ideology was guaranteed. At the core, the ideological instruction in possessive individualism at the job front and at the home front was the focus of the process of producing consciousness and the labor power for the next day and next generation. Corporate capitalism had systemically harnessed scarcity and publicity in the creation of profitable empire through Consciousness Industry's capacity for cultural domination. The hegemony of the monopoly-capitalist system seemed impregnable. Growing resistance to it both in its heartland and in peripheral countries, and grave internal problems, including chronic stagflation and instability of money and credit, suggest, however, that as with other empires, "nothing fails like success." In the dialectical processes of nature, it seems probable that another systemic transformation impends. It is necessary now to consider Canada's specific relations to capitalism, the burden of Chapter 5.

[9] Coolidge, Calvin, address to the Annual Conventon of the American Association of Advertising Agencies, Washington, D.C., 27 October, 1926. (Printed in full in Presbrey (1929, pp. 619–625; emphasis added).

5

THE CONTEXT OF CANADIAN
COMMUNICATIONS MEDIA

Merchants have no country. The mere spot they stand on does not constitute so strong an attachment as that from which they draw their gains. (Thomas Jefferson, letter to Horatio Spafford, March 17, 1814. Quoted in *Monthly Review* (November 1976, p. 61).

The quotation which heads this chapter explains much about why Canada has been a colonial satellite, first of Britain and then of the United States, without ever being an autonomous country. And because Canada's communications media have been shaped mostly during the period of Canada's dependency on the United States, much of the context for the development of Canadian communications media has already been provided in Chapters 3 and 4 which dealt with the growth of Consciousness Industry. In the capitalist core area that industry has been little impeded by the boundary which nominally separates Canada from the United States. Canada, therefore, may be regarded simultaneously as part of the American economy and as a country displaying the elements of underdevelopment typical of peripheral countries.

Canada is the world's most dependent "developed" country and the world's richest "underdeveloped" country. As early as 1964, Canada held 31 percent of all foreign United States direct investment. This was more than all Europe, and more than all Latin America (Levitt, 1970, p. 61). Canada is still far and away the country with the most direct United States investment, although its share had fallen to 22 percent in 1978. Latin America and Europe have been receiving growing shares, but the United Kingdom (the next largest recipient), with 12 percent in 1978, is still far behind Canada. At the same time, Canada is the *source* of heavy direct investment *in* the United States. In 1978 Canadian institutions and individuals owned some $6.2 billion in direct investments in the United States, second only to the United Kingdom with $7.3 billion. Direct investment between the United States and Canada is thus a two-way affair and the Canadian direct investment in the United States is massive. But the balance is, of course, still heavily on the side of United States direct investment in Canada; in 1978 the latter amounted to $38.8 billion.[1]

Canada's share of international trade of all industrialized countries has been declining. The composition of Canadian trade resembles that of underdeveloped countries: it exports mostly raw and partially processed materials (75 percent of the total) and imports mostly manufactured goods (80 percent of imports). For Canada less than 20 percent of exports are end products, whereas for typical Western European countries about two-thirds of exports are end products. The percentage of all manufactured goods in Canadian imports has been rising since the mid-1920s. The percentage of consumer goods in Canadian imports rose steadily since the mid-1950s (Gonick, 1970, p. 59). And as in typical underdeveloped countries the Canadian economy suffers from the diseconomies and inefficiencies of the "miniature replica effect." That is, too many models of products, designed for the much larger United States market, are manufactured and sold in Canada by branch plants of American transnational corporations (TNCs), with too small-scale production of each. Given the predominant control of most consumer goods industries by United States TNCs, this is inevitable because the Canadian market is too small (as compared with the United States) to achieve the economies of scale in production. Consequently, Canadian consumer goods bear excessive costs and allocation of Canadian productive resources is distorted. As is true also of the United States, deskilling of workers in Canada progresses with the steady growth of "scientific management" in the branch plant economy.

In order to achieve an adequate geographic context for the whole development of Canada and its communications media (not only in the period of United States domination), the essential elements in the capitalist system around the world should be identified. They are:

1. Interrelated markets which afford calculations of maximum profitability, which determine the kind, purpose, and amount of productive activity; the kind, amount, and location of specialization; the modes of payment for labor, goods, and other services; the nature, extent, and location of invention and innovation.

---

[1] U.S. Department of Commerce, *Survey of Current Business*, August 1979, Part I.

2.   National state structures of varying degrees of strength and their ideological apparatuses (military, educational, religious, "cultural," etc.) under the control of a dominant class and with struggle between that class and workers.

3.   The 200 or more TNCs and the other business enterprises which operate in the interrelated markets in such a manner that the result is a one-way flow of resources from the periphery to the core of the system.

4.   Equipment, machines, know-how, and policy for producing commodities, including mass media audiences, and communicating information characterized by a one-way flow from core to periphery of the system. This one-way flow is disguised by a number of axiomatic propositions which are essential to the capitalist system. These are:

a.   The law of comparative advantage is good for every country because it is good for the TNCs and the capitalistic system. This is the economic proposition that regional and local *specialization* in economic activity according to the resources available in various countries is the most efficient division of labor possible. It was enunciated by Adam Smith in *The Wealth of Nations* (1776), became a cornerstone of classical economic theory and was generally accepted even by Marxist economists. It is in contradiction to efforts by peripheral and socialist countries to develop significant degrees of economic self-sufficiency and to develop national cultural autonomy, as is argued in Chapters 9 and 10.

b.   The notion that "modernity" requires uncritical acceptance of "technology," which is held to have no political consequences. Chapter 10 argues the contrary.

c.   The notion that "modernity" requires information to be regarded "objectively" as if it also had no political consequences. This book is an argument to the contrary.

d.   The notion that modernity requires a "free marketplace of ideas" and pluralism in political formations. Originally formulated by John Stuart Mill, it was subtly altered later to mean that all values are purely relative, that equally valid arguments may be made for each.

e.   The legal principle essential to monopoly capitalism that the privately owned business corporation has the same rights as an individual.

    f.   Promotion of the ideology of possessive individualism.

    g. Promotion of the use of a single language—English.

    5. The appropriation of the surplus product of labor through three organizational levels:

        a. Where people work, in homes and at jobs.

        b. At the level of country or state where compradors take their cut while passing on the remainder to

        c. The head offices of the TNCs.

    6. The struggle of countries for independence, of nations for liberation from oppression, and of people for human rights, control of the fruits of their labor, and the revolutionary changes in social institutions which these struggles require.[2]

Canada came into existence as a result of the mercantilist policies followed by Western European nations which were developing capitalism in the seventeenth and eighteenth centuries. Specifically, first France and then Great Britain seized and claimed the territory now called Canada, dispossessed its indigenous peoples, destroyed their cultures, and in large measure killed them (Knight et al., 1928; Naylor, 1972; Innis, 1954, 1970). After the British conquest of New France, the colonial system in Canada followed the pattern of mercantilist empire. In contrast to the rampant individualistic democracy south of the border, as Levitt (1970, pp. 142–143) says:

> . . . Canada was an ordered, stable, conservative and authoritarian society based on transplanted British institutions. . . . The arrangements were quite compatible with the interests of the bureaucratic clerical elite of French Canada.

And the church in both English and French Canada played a major role in maintaining colonial control.

The function of the colonial bourgeoisie as ruler is precarious. It must accommodate the colony to its subordinate position in the imperial system, i.e., to serve its imperial bosses. But it must also maintain some kind of legitimacy domestically. As Peter Newman (1975, p. 184) declares, the Canadian bourgeoisie have used nationalism ". . . as a tight rope which will bridge the distance between local and imperial concerns." It has used its government power to rule rather than to build, in the words of Drache. The basis of bourgeois rule is division. It never tried to resolve the French issue any more than it tried to build inclusive and conserving national institutions.

---

[2] In the formulation of these characteristics I borrowed some features from E. Wallerstein and H. I. Schiller (see Schiller, 1976) and the last from Mao Zedong.

Indeed within their framework, national politics, when stripped of pretentious rhetoric, was a holding action where the centre be it Ottawa or Bay Street—that is the English majority, industry and finance—kept the nation "together" by keeping it apart. . . . Leading the country meant playing off French against English, east against west, labour against business (Drache, 1970, p. 10).

The formula has been divide and rule and enjoy power and profits while you stall for time.

There *never* was a time when the dominant groups in Canada pursued policies which would build an autonomous nation. Those groups (whether the Chateau Clique, the Family Compact, the Tories, or the Liberals) all had their power base in commerce, not industry. As merchants their economic base was trade, finance, transportation, and more recently, communications. And when Canadian colonial status in British mercantilism finally ended in the 1920s, it had been replaced by a mini-mercantilism, subordinate to American imperialism, which had been building Canada from 1867 onwards.

With the relative decline of the original "staples" (fur, fish, and timber) after 1815, business enterprise turned toward the United States. As Naylor (1972, p. 20) says, "The essential policy of the Montreal Merchants from 1763 had been strict mercantilism within the British Empire together with free trade with the United States". Two modes of getting free trade with the United States were considered. One was outright annexation of Canada to the United States; the other was reducing tariffs to a level amounting to free trade. *Both* were promoted by segments of the merchant class in Canada between the 1830s and 1860s. The struggle between them was won by the group favoring "reciprocity" in tariff reduction (1854). In addition to the north-south trade axis thus cultivated, Canadian merchants got their cut out of the trade in American products as they transited the St. Lawrence en route to Britain. This economic detente was ruptured by Canada's favoring the losing side in the American Civil War. In 1866 the United States abrogated the reciprocity treaty. The following year, it purchased Alaska, thanks to the diplomatic efforts of Western Union Telegraph Company which had been negotiating with the Tsar of Russia a projected telegraph system to Europe via Canada and Alaska. Thus, as Naylor (1972, p. 12) says, "Canadian Confederation [in 1867] resulted not from a drive for independence led by a dynamic capitalist class but from the inability of the Canadian bourgeoisie to find a new dependency."

The National Policy following 1867 was a unique Canadian form of mercantilism including a strong national government, heavily subsidized transcontinental railway building, and a protective tariff. The latter was a new wrinkle on an old Canadian policy: enjoying the commercial aspects of American industrial production. There were (and are) three ways in which a country can obtain the capital necessary to build its factories, mines, transportation agencies, etc.

1. It can accumulate such capital from the surpluses produced by its commerce in existing industries and in readily available natural resources, such as timber, fish, furs. This route would have meant a slow growth for Canada, and in any event would have assumed that the ruling commercial class would forgo private hoarding and consumption of their net revenues.

2. It can *borrow* capital from abroad. This, called *portfolio*, capital borrowing would be repaid over time, leaving the productive investment of it in factories, mines, etc., under the ownership of indigenous capitalists. Britain was the main source of borrowed capital between the 1860s and 1920s, and these loans were paid off.

3. It can permit or invite foreigners to make direct investment of their capital in the country. This means that foreigners *own* the investment of such capital in factories, mines, etc., initially and forever. The United States was principally interested in direct investment in Canada and such investment was far greater than American portfolio investment.

A combination of 1 and 2—without 3—would have permitted the development of a Canadian economy owned by Canadians. The National Party after 1867, however, deliberately invited American direct investment in Canadian industry, through the establishment of branch plants and takeovers of Canadian-owned investments.

In addition to the inducement of tariff protection, United States direct investment was wooed by federal, provincial, and local governments with all manner of enticements, including free land, tax exemptions, etc. Canadian banks vied with each other to provide working capital to the American branch plants—in effect retailing the portfolio investments which British capitalists made in Canada. Consequently, the United States common stock ownership of the Canadian plants "often represented nothing but . . . the productive technique and the promotional American interest in the project" (Naylor, 1972, p. 23, quoting Viner, 1924, p. 285).

Coincidentally, the Tariff of 1878 came at the very time when the merger–trust-building movement was taking off in the United States (see Chapter 3). The rapidly growing giant corporations which were developing Consciousness Industry in the United States duly took advantage of the Canadian invitation. And direct investment (giving Americans ownership of Canadian property in perpetuity) rose from $15 million in 1867 to $175 million in 1900 and $520 million in 1913 (Levitt, 1970, p. 66).

As noted later, Bell Telephone joined Western Union Telegraph Company in occupying the Canadian telecommunications market and as Michael Bliss (1970, p. 31) says:

> By the early 1900s it was common knowledge that Canada's protective tariff had encouraged such major American companies as Singer Sewing Machine, Edison Electric, American Tobacco, Westinghouse, Gillette, and International Harvester to establish Canadian subsidiaries. By 1913 it was estimated that 450 off-shoots of American companies were operating in Canada. . . .

The significance of this process for the unification of the ideology, consciousness, and economic systems of Canada and the United States is fundamental. Canada, by the end of the nineteenth century, had already demonstrated that empire via direct investment and the domination of culture was a going concern—and the highest stage of imperialism. As Naylor (1972, p. 25) declares:

> The American corporations, forever the innovators, advanced to their highest state, that euphemistically called "multinationality" through direct investment abroad on an enormous scale. Export of direct investment is accompanied by export of industrial organization, consumer taste patterns, social philosophy, and inevitably metropolitan law through the subsidiary.

Canada thus was economically assimilated to the United States economy through the TNCs half a century *before* American monopoly capitalism launched *the same type of cultural offensive* on a massive, coordinated scale against peripheral countries in Latin America, Africa, Asia, and against European countries about 1950. Special conditions invited and made possible this early integration of Canada's economy into the American monopoly-capitalist system.

Unlike the situation in which monopoly capitalism penetrates a traditional society, as in Africa or Asia, or even a semi-Latinized culture as in Latin America, Canada's dominant English-speaking population shared the same ideological and cultural background as that of the United States. In both countries, European migrants dispossessed, killed, and confined to marginal land the indigenous peoples. The tide of migrants from various ethnic origins in Europe (and Asia) in the nineteenth century flowed freely and abundantly into and between Canada and the United States.

After the English conquest of Canada, a common body of ideology was operative on both sides of the border. This ideology had a more class-bound elitist character in Canada than in the United States because the Anglophone ruling class was established in Canada by United Empire

Loyalists—those refugees from the southern thirteen colonies who could not survive the democratic/republican revolution of 1776 against English political arrangements. Possessive individualism, a passionate concern with private property, and a system of business law derived from English common law underlay the ideology of both Canadians and Americans. A common market for entrepreneurial talent and applied engineering embraced both countries and occupational skills fitted easily into jobs for migrant workers moving in both directions. Americans were prominent in building the Canadian railroads, and at least one American railway tycoon, James J. Hill, was a Canadian. Weights and measures, a decimal currency and substantially identical occupational and corporate structures and practices aligned Canada with the United States, not England. So also did "international unions," international organizations of Sunday schools and fraternal orders, etc. The bulk of the Canadian people living in the string of Canadian cities and towns close to the United States border enjoyed markets for the *same* brands of consumer goods as their southern neighbors.

As will be shown in Chapters 6–8, Canadian popular culture has been produced and marketed by businessmen more concerned with short-term profits than with nation-building. By *nation-building* I refer to the unpursued possibilities of directing Canadian development: (1) in economic activity based on Canadian-owned investment, (2) in publishing, film, and later radio and television, to develop industries supported more by the Canadian market and less by the "international market," through deliberate national protective and stimulative measures commonly taken by smaller European countries, (3) in education, to take measures analogous to (2) rather than making an education system as a "feeder" to metropolitan (English and American) universities and values, (4) deliberately to make an early serious attempt to forge a common cultural bond between Francophones and Anglophones, if only as an indispensable bulwark against American influence.

Instead of taking a nation-building road, Canadian businessmen served as agents of cultural submission to the stronger southern neighbor. The impact of the development of Consciousness Industry was similar in Canada to that in the United States. Because it is basic to our later consideration of class consciousness, it is important here to observe the effect of the rising Consciousness Industry on the class formations and struggles in Canada. As Leo A. Johnson (1972, pp. 145–146) declares:

> During the early part of the nineteenth century, Canada's history was dominated by the struggles of the farmers and small businessmen—the classical petite bourgeoisie—against the domination of aristocratic elements such as the Family Compact and the Chateau Clique. By 1848 with the granting of responsible government and the introduction of elective local govern-

ment, most of the ideals of these groups had been achieved. Of course, the landless agricultural workers were still disenfranchised, as were the poorer proletarian urban elements, but the more prosperous crafts workers and skilled tradesmen—in the words of the period, those who had "a stake in society"—had been accommodated.

In the National Policy period small businessmen and crafts workers were smashed by the giant corporations. Again, Johnson (1972, p. 146):

> By the 1870s, however, . . . the development of a [monopoly] capitalist mode of production and distribution with the resultant destruction of the small local manufacturing and distribution centres, and the growing tendency towards monopoly control of prices, tariffs, freight and interest rates, began to force the independent commodity producers to find means of defending their interests against the growing power of the large capitalists.

> At the same time, the crafts workers also were coming under attack by the new capitalist mode of production. By 1872, consciousness of their own interests produced the first major concerted effort to win better working terms by the creation of organizations such as the Toronto Trades Assembly and the Nine Hours League, as well as Canada's first labour-oriented newspaper. By the 1880s, the [monopoly] capitalist mode of production, which utilized large amounts of unskilled labour, had begun to make significant inroads in the ranks of skilled crafts workers, and ancient and respected crafts such as shoemakers (the sons of St. Crispin as they styled themselves) were in serious decay.

Politically, the basis was laid for the later populist and social democratic reform movements (e.g., CCF, Social Credit) which siphoned off militant radicalism into essentially petite bourgeois objectives of making monopoly capitalism work more "fairly" (consumer protection laws, labor standards laws, for example). Meanwhile, as noted in Chapter 3, the IWW and radical unionism in extractive industries were crushed by crude force on both sides of the border.

As might be expected, given the inclusiveness and power of the dependency relationship between Canada and the United States, the rhetoric of the Canadian ruling class is idealistic and mystifying. Drache's condensed paraphrase of innumerable statements by royal commissions and governments says it well:

> . . . Canada can be a country, a nation unto itself, and can survive on the continent as an un-American yet sovereign state by virtue of the fact that the desire is a reasonable one, nonantagonistic to American interests, and because Canada's existence as a nation is recognized by law. . . . Canadian nationalism is essentially a nationalism of, and at one with empire (Drache, 1970, p. 8).

Until the recent spate of critical writings by Watkins, Naylor, Gonick, Teeple, Lumsden, et al., Canadian scholarly work has remained within that idealist frame. Even Harold Innis, who contributed indirectly to the recent critical analysis, misperceived the extent and process of Canadian dependency when he remarked "Canada moved from colony to nation to colony."

Superficially it appeared that Canada came closest to national autonomy about the close of World War I. As was recognized by both the Massey Commission (Canada. Royal Commission on National Development in the Arts, Letters and Sciences, 1951, p. 13) and the O'Leary Commission (Canada. Royal Commission on Publications, 1961, p. 4), two prerequisites for autonomy are control of the nation's military and its cultural defenses. Having developed a significant military capability, 1914–1918, Canada was approaching the substitution of autonomous partnership in the Commonwealth for its colonial status within the British Empire, and supposedly might have played off British and American pressures in pursuit of a modest but independent foreign policy role. As far as the print media and popular culture were concerned, Canada was already identified with those of the United States. But the new electronic media offered, again supposedly, the possibility of being directed to national development. Of course the power structure which dominated Canada pursued neither of these principled options. The electronic media became as tributary to the United States as their print predecessors. As to military defense, Canada gave over control of its military to the United States informally shortly after World War I and formally and permanently in 1940 when Canada placed the Canadian Armed Forces under the direction of the Permanent Joint Board of Defense, Washington, D.C. This was accomplished by the Ogdensburg Agreement which:

> . . . only converted into an explicit alliance the quiet understanding which had grown up between Canada and the United States over the previous twenty years.[3]

The solid underpinning of this failure to assert prime attributes of sovereignty was that between 1913 and 1939, United States investment in Canada multiplied almost fivefold (from $835 million to $4.151 billion) and came to much exceed the British investment which had shrunk appreciably (from $2.818 to $2.476 billion). The growth of the giant United States TNCs in the 1920s had its erosive effect on the earlier pattern of east-west trade when the new staples, oil, gas, iron ore, and nonferrous metals, began moving south in heavy volume. Each of the provinces welcomed United States entrepreneurs to exploit these national resources of which Ottawa relinquished federal control as a result of federal-

---

[3] Sutherland, R. J., "Canadian Defense Research Board," quoted in Warnock (1970b, p. 104).

provincial disputes (with a progressive weakening of federal authority). By the end of the 1920s, most of the American-owned companies now in Canada were established and ". . . Canadian nationalists had either been eliminated from the ranks of Canadian employers or had become clients of American penetration" (Gonick, 1970, p. 62). During World War II (from 1939 to 1946), United States investment increased by about a quarter (to $5.175 billion) while British investment fell by one-third (to $1.688 billion).

The integration of the industrial systems of Canada and the United States was immensely accelerated during World War II. The Ogdensburg Agreement on military operational integration was followed in April 1941 by the Hyde Park Agreement which integrated military procurement between the two countries. During World War II, the United States spent $1.25 billion on military procurement in Canada. The postwar economic boom, exploiting the backed-up demand for consumer goods denied by wartime necessity, spilled over generously into Canada under the "continental" policy managed by King and C. D. Howe. As John Deutsch wrote:

> The stimulus for the boom of the 1950s came wholly from the United States, with the result that the east-west structure of the Canadian economy was fundamentally modified by an almost massive north-south integration. Toward the end of the period Canadian trade statistics revealed the emergence of almost entirely new exports to the United States of iron ore, uranium, oil, and nonferrous metals which rivals and in some cases superseded in size the traditional staples which were sold in overseas markets.[4]

By 1969 there were more than 500 firms in the Canadian wing of the United States military-industrial complex. And Canada has developed a flourishing subimperial arms market to "friendly countries," subject to approval by the Department of Defense in Washington. In order to increase their share in this gravy train, large Canadian firms like Canadian Marconi (formerly English controlled), DeHavilland of Canada, Computing Devices of Canada, and Hawker Siddeley (Orinda Division) sold controlling interests to United States TNCs (Warnock, 1970b).

An unhappy interlude in the Canadian relationship with the United States was the Diefenbaker government, 1957–1963. That Progressive Conservative government dared to differ with the United States on such matters as placing Canadian armed forces on the highest level of alert during the Cuban missile crisis without Canadian authorization, the Bomarc missile program, etc. There followed an exercise in open inter-

---

[4] Deutsch, John J., "Recent American Influence in Canada," in *The American Impact on Canada.* (Durham, N.C., 1959), p. 45. Quoted in Resnick (1970, p. 102).

vention in Canadian federal political activity by President Kennedy, the state department, and the United States Embassy in Ottawa in order to procure the election of Lester Pearson in the 1963 election (Warnock, 1970b, pp. 156–197).

With the election in 1963 of Pearson and following him of Trudeau, amicable relations were restored. Trudeau put it plainly:

> The fact that Canada has flourished for more than a century as the closest neighbour to the greatest economic and military power in the world is evidence of the basic decency of United States foreign policy. When Canada continues to trade in non-strategic goods with Cuba, or proposes recognition of the People's Republic of China . . . the world is given evidence of your basic qualities of understanding and tolerance (Warnock, 1970b, p. 217).

Had Canada's ruling class been other than it was—and still operate within the bounds of capitalism—Canada might have been substantially more autonomous. A range of possible policies which have served to preserve a large measure of autonomy for the smaller European nations could have been adopted in Canada. But the Canadian ruling class did not want to do so. It held power as a means to profits—until the balance of effective decision making passed from its hands and *that* produced its present and unavoidable crisis of legitimacy. When, thanks to the leverage provided by being able to play off pressures from London and New York, it had the means to power and profits at its command (in the nineteenth century), it was so committed to the cruder ideological tenets of capitalism that short-term self-interest in profits prevailed. In this respect the Canadian ruling class acted as did compradors in the typical nineteenth-century colony. As Resnick (1970, p. 94) says, "for the Canadian elite, a deferential, hierarchical society at home found its logical counterpart in deference to imperial policy abroad." And when the center of the capitalist core shifted from London to New York so did its allegiance. E. P. Taylor recently put it bluntly:

> . . . if it were not for the racial issue in the United States and the political problems they have, I would think the two countries could come together.
> . . . I am against this trend of trying to reduce American ownership in Canadian companies. I think nature has to take its course (Quoted in Newman, 1975, p. 184).

This is the politico-economic context of Canada, omitting the communications components from that context. Chapter 6 offers an analysis of the role of the print and film communications media in subordinating Canada to its external masters.

6

MEDIA OF CANADIAN CULTURAL
SUBMISSION I:
PRINT MEDIA AND MOTION PICTURES

The tremendous expansion of communications in the United States has given that nation the world's most penetrating and effective apparatus for the transmission of ideas. Canada, more than any other country is naked to that force, exposed unceasingly to a vast network of communications which reaches to every corner of our land. American words, images, and print—the good, the bad, the indifferent—batter unrelentingly at our eyes and ears (Canada. Royal Commission on Publications, 1961, pp. 5–6).

Economic and cultural policy, rather than geographic factors per se, explains why Canada has been on the receiving end of a one-way "free flow of information" from both Britain and the United States. If this were not so, French Canada would have been homogenized in the "continentalist" culture as has English-speaking Canada. But it has not. The Québécois have maintained a fair degree of cultural autonomy against the one-way flow manifest in the distinctive structures and policies of publishing, film making, and broadcasting in Québec.[1] The extent to which their mass-produced cultural material resembles or is different from the Anglophone cultural material (except in language) is, however, beyond the scope of this enquiry.

Communications institutions have always been tightly controlled by the state in the interest of maintaining and extending the power of the social formations which control it. In the seventeenth and eighteenth cen-

---

[1] Canada. Special Senate Committee on Mass Media, *The Uncertain Mirror* (1970, pp. 95, 122). Hereafter referred to as Davey Report.

turies, the modern bourgeois nation-state was emerging from its feudal womb in convulsive revolutions (e.g., the English Revolution, 1640 onward, the French, from 1789). Two communications institutions were simultaneously being structured and given policies: the postal system and the use of print. In eighteenth-century England the postal system transmitted, collected, and created intelligence. Its officers scattered both domestically and abroad, acted as intelligence agents, reporting on economic conditions, elections, crimes, disorders, suspicious persons, ship movements, naval dispositions, etc. It also conducted several secret operations (called the Secret Office, the Private Office, and the Deciphering Branch). They opened, copied, decoded messages, and resealed them. They had a very restricted clientele (Ellis, 1958, chapter on intelligence). For the first century after its creation in 1635, the English post office was a principal means of distributing propaganda (proclamations, notices, prayers, pamphlets, and newspapers).

Printing and publishing in England were kept under strict state control from the sixteenth to the mid-nineteenth centuries. The number of presses was limited, their use confined to a small number of reliable printer-publishers whose book production was carefully screened by high judges and churchmen, while their rudimentary newspapers and periodical publications were subject to censorship. The process of controlling public opinion became more subtle as increasingly general literacy and the right to vote accompanied the development of a political system comprising two or more political parties—all committed to the constitutional system of the state (Ellis, 1958, pp. 47–59).

The original institutional complex of printer-publisher did not differentiate organizationally a range of products. These included production of the newspaper, the magazine, the book, leaflets and pamphlets, and job printing of stationery, business forms, etc. In the enterprise's retail establishment were sold the books and magazines it and its oligopolistic rivals published as well as writing materials.[2] Political patronage (through government advertising and subsidies), linked with land speculation, and government and party officeholding provided income for newspaper publishing by these undifferentiated enterprises. And free—or virtually free—carriage of the newspapers and periodicals through the postal system simultaneously enriched the publishers and ensured wide circulation of the propaganda of the ruling groups.

This model of the Western European process of print media develop-

---

[2] The printing "conger" of seven firms which controlled English publishing beginning in 1719 was an arrangement similar to that which the Hollywood integrated film producer-distributor-exhibitor firms used to control prices, production, and profits between 1920 and 1948 (Innis, 1951, p. 150; Huettig, 1944).

ment was reproduced in the United States and in Canada. As the business structures became differentiated beginning in the eighteenth century, newspaper publishing took on a centralized character. The writing, printing, and selling (to both advertisers and readers) functions were integrated in one enterprise under the publisher who employed the factors of production, sustained the capital and operating costs, and pocketed the profits. Magazine and book publishing, however, developed primarily on the model of the "putting out" or "domestic" system which it had acquired beginning in the seventeenth century in England. Writers were wholly self-employed ("free lance") in book publishing and mostly so in magazine publishing. Printing and binding for book and magazine publishing were usually done by independent enterprises. Publishers were enterprisers who brought these functions together under contracts rather than in integrated organizations. Marketing of magazines and books tended also to be functions performed by independent distributors, wholesalers, and retailers.

Before railways, the Maritimes and Ontario and Québec were cut off from each other except by water routes. At the request of English merchants who wanted to trade in Canada the first English postal service to Canada was extended by post roads from New York to Montreal and Québec in 1765. Canadian communications dependency on its southern neighbors was established. After the American Revolutionary War, the mails continued to join New York to Canada but direct service from England via Halifax was established in 1783 (Smith, 1918, pp. 37–40). The United States with its earlier development of a rail network provided closer economic and cultural links with each part of Canada than the parts of Canada had with each other. Maritime bookstores, for example, were supplied from Boston (and London), not from Montreal or Toronto.[3]

NEWSPAPERS

Canadian communications media in the period before Consciousness Industry (down to 1890–1900) tended (like American) to be individual proprietorships or partnerships. Canadian newspaper markets (like American) were local, not national or regional. The weekly newspapers which accompanied the Anglophone settlement of Canada in the eighteenth century began in 1752 in Halifax and were established by migrants from the lower thirteen colonies. The designation of one in each town as

---

[3] Gundy, H.P., "Development of Trade Book Publishing in Canada," Royal Commission on Book Publishing, Background Papers (1972, p. 4). Hereafter this will be referred to as Rohmer Report, Background Papers.

"King's Printer" simultaneously assured income and policy control in the interest of the Crown, although more than one sometimes shared the monopoly:

> By 1800 the three [Halifax] news organs enjoyed a friendly press monopoly. They cheerfully shared the printing patronage furnished by the Halifax-based government (Kesterton, 1967, p. 4).

The political controversies ranging from that over the Constitutional Act of 1791, through the Family Compact, the Rebellion of 1837, Confederation, The Riel Rebellion of 1885, to the execution of the National Policy—took place with the aid of newspapers allied with political factions and parties. Revenues of newspapers, down to the 1890s, came from political sources plus subscription sales, plus small amounts of advertising. The newspapers' collective political role and power were clearly very great. In 1867 when the post office became a Canadian federal institution, the decision to reduce the rate on first-class mail from 5 to 3 cents revealed that previously newspapers had been carried free. In 1882, as Smith (1918, p. 143) says,

> An Act was passed "to provide for the free transmission of Canadian newspapers within the Dominion." No discussion on the measure took place in Parliament, and authoritative statements of the reasons inducing the adoption of so generous a policy are not to be obtained; but in well-informed quarters it is held that, in general, the leniency shown to newspapers is not due solely to the acceptance by Parliament of the arguments usually advanced in their favour, plausible and convincing as they probably are to many minds, but has always been dictated more or less by fear of the political power wielded by them; or what is really the same thing, as a result of direct pressure at Ottawa by the newspaper proprietors, based on their influence with the electors or the chiefs of the parties, and exercised in their own interest.

It is not coincidental that this generous subsidy in Canada followed by only three years the passage in the United States Congress without debate or committee recommendation of the act establishing second-class mail consisting of newspapers and periodicals which thereafter would be carried by the postal service at trivial rates, except for free in-county mailing (Heiss, 1946, p. 4). The Canadian Act of 1882 was reversed when the first-class rate was reduced to two cents and newspapers were required to bear only preferential rates.

> Opposition to the change was made on the same grounds as in 1867: that newspapers were the real educators of the people, that the dissemination of intelligence, particularly of political intelligence, was of the utmost importance, and that no impediment should be put in the way of their freest possible distribution (Smith, 1918, p. 145).

Discriminatory rates in favor of newspapers were again introduced in 1908.

The nineteenth century, down to the 1890s, was the only period of significant competition in Canadian newspapers. The number of daily newspapers grew from 1 in 1833 to 23 in 1864 and 121 in 1900 (Kesterton, 1967, pp. 25, 39). In 1900, Canada's 35 largest communities had 2 or more competitive daily newspapers (18 of them had 3 or more). The conversion of the nineteenth-century style competitive newspapers into mass producers of audiences for sale to advertisers (see Chapter 4), took place in Canada almost simultaneously with the United States. The American Samuel E. Moffett (1906, pp. 99–100) said:

> The Americanization of the Canadian newspaper press has been stimulated of late years by the practice adopted by the great American journalists of "syndicating" their matter, especially their Sunday supplements. These supplements are reproduced in the Canadian papers, usually on Saturdays, as the native Sunday paper has not taken deep root in the Dominion. The youths and maidens of Canada are brought up on the adventures of Buster Brown, Foxy Grandpa and the Katzenjammer Kids. They learn how many American heiresses have bought European titles, and what divorces are likely to occur in the course of the season at Newport. There are also colored supplements of Canadian manufacture which imitate those of the American yellow journals as close as possible.

As an advertising pioneer in Canada, H. E. Stephenson, relates, the transformation meant that

> . . . advertising rather than political patronage [came to be] regarded as the logical source of revenue (Stephenson and McNaught, 1940, p. 14).

The bitterness of political controversy was giving way and

> . . . the need for circulation, which in turn attracts advertisers and thus provides the money to finance the increasingly costly business of newspaper publication, was engendering a more temperate and less partisan tone (Stephenson and McNaught, 1940, p. 14).

The first general advertising agency in Canada, A. McKim & Company, was formed in 1889, and one of its first steps was to begin publication of an annual directory of Canadian newspapers, giving circulation, advertising rates, etc. The revolution wrought by Consciousness Industry in both the newspaper industry and the marketing of consumer goods mutually stimulated each other. As Stephenson said,

> . . . the courses of retailing in Canada followed that in the United States. The old general store of the pioneer days split up into specialty stores, selling drygoods, hardware, furniture, drugs, jewellery, and so on. Then the dry-

goods store began to win back something of the character of the old general store, but with the various lines "departmentalized" (Stephenson and McNaught, 1940, p. 38).

And thus the "department store" was innovated during the 1890s. Much later, the "shopping mall" was to reestablish features of convenience provided by the department stores and specialization by different enterprises. Canadian newspaper advertising for giant United States corporations appeared in the 1880s for washing powders, baking powder, coffee, chewing gum, etc., etc.

The merger movement was rapid and complete in newspapers. By 1970 only five Canadian communities had competitive daily newspapers. Not only was *local* competition eliminated in the newspaper industry, but the merger movement produced monopoly on a national scale. By 1970 two-thirds of Canada's 116 daily newspapers were controlled or partially owned by 12 ownership groups. These newspaper chains then had 77 percent of total daily newspaper circulation. By 1970 the three largest chains (Thompson, Southam, and F.P.) controlled 45 percent of total Canadian daily newspaper circulation, as compared to 25 percent in 1958. The newspaper merger movement also dominated the private TV and radio stations in the major "markets." Of 97 private TV stations, the same 12 groups controlled 49 percent in 1970. Of the radio stations, 48 percent.

Monopolistic newspaper enterprises in Canada, as in the United States, have moved to rationalize all aspects of the business from procurement of newsprint, to the manufacturing process, to marketing audiences to advertisers and procurement of the free lunch. Increased investment in new printing techniques has accompanied reduction in employment opportunities. Audience measurement has kept pace with American practice, and close liaison within the newspaper publishing industry through trade associations and between newspapers and advertisers and their agents have been essential components of the rationalization process. Regarding the production of the free lunch, the newspaper industry has relied on a cost-minimizing device: the cooperative management and cost-sharing of a Canadian wire service. The Canadian Press was established in 1910 as a nonprofit cooperative by the big Canadian newspaper publishers. Its function has been essentially to integrate the production of Canadian domestic and international news and to link the latter into the Associated Press system. It provides both an English and (since 1951) a French-language service. Its domestic coverage is gleaned from the domestic newspapers; foreign coverage mostly comes from AP, Reuters, and Agence France-Press. The editing for the CP services is done in its *New York* office, and for 79 of its 103 members in 1970, the CP stories went directly into the newspaper's composing room by teletypesetter. Whoever edits in the New York office determines the foreign component in the free lunch provided by Canadian newspapers, more than 70 of which relied exclusively on CP for out-of-town coverage (Davey Report, p. 230).

How profitable are newspapers? Do they plough back into improving the quality of the free lunch all but a profit margin typical of Canadian industry? The Davey Commission Report showed that in 1966, Canada's daily newspapers as a whole earned annually a return after all expenses (but before income tax) equal to 27.5 percent of the owners' equity in the enterprises, whereas all manufacturing earned 16.9 percent; retail trade, 15.9 percent; all service industries, 17.5 percent; and public utilities, 13.4 percent. As expressed in relation to net investment in fixed assets, the newspapers in that year earned 40 percent (Davey Report, Vol. II, pp. 224–226, 234).

We shall return to analysis of radio and TV in Chapter 8 but it is necessary here to add that they are at least as profitable as newspapers in Canada. The Davey Commission found that the profitability of newspapers and radio and TV broadcasters was "astonishing" and added

> . . . *on the average* media corporations are onto a very good thing indeed. If the brewing industry made profits half this large, and the people knew it, we suspect there would be sit-ins in the beer stores. Most media corporations, fortunately for them, don't have to disclose these earnings. Because their very large profits allow them to pay for expansion and acquisitions out of retained earnings, most continue as private companies. And so we are confronted with a delicious irony: an industry that is supposed to abhor secrets is sitting on one of the best-kept, least discussed secrets, one of the hottest scoops, in the entire field of Canadian business—their own balance sheets!

> The daily newspaper and broadcasting industries make profits that are, on the average, *very* generous . . . In a few cases, the corporations concerned are making genuine efforts to deliver quality editorial content and quality programming in return for their privileged economic position. But the general pattern, we regret to say, is of newspapers and broadcasting stations that are pulling the maximum out of their communities, and giving back the minimum in return. This is what, in contemporary parlance, is called a rip-off (Davey Report, p. 63).

It will be recalled that the newspaper and broadcast sector in Canada is mostly owned by Canadian ruling class interests, not American. (See Chapter 5 for the implications of this fact.)

Is the "astonishing" profitability of Canadian newspapers (and private broadcast stations) a reward for producing the best possible free lunch with which to attract people into the audience product? By no means. The Special Senate Committee gave the only possible answer:

In traditional usage, you have a monopoly rip-off when the corporations concerned use their privileged position to charge their customers more than the traffic would otherwise bear. In the case of the media, we think, the problem is reversed: it's not that the companies are charging too much—but that they're spending too little. The profit margins in broadcasting, for instance, indicate that the industry as a whole can readily afford to supply its audience with the Canadian content that the country has long needed, and which the C.R.T.C. is now demanding. The industry hasn't supplied it voluntarily, for the excellent reason that it can make more money by relying on canned American re-runs. In the same way, many Canadian daily newspapers could readily afford to develop their own editorial page columnists, their own cartoonists, their own commentators. But it's cheaper, far cheaper, to buy syndicated American columnists and reprint other papers' cartoons, and to skimp on staff news coverage in the hope that one of the wire services will do the same job almost as well (Davey Report, p. 64).

English-language Canadian newspapers follow tired and obsolete news-gathering policies:

If it is to be news, there must be a "story." And if there is to be a "story," there must be conflict, surprise, drama. There must be a "dramatic, disruptive, exceptional event" before traditional journalism can acknowledge that a situation exists. Thus the news consumer finds himself being constantly ambushed by events. Poor people on the march all of a sudden? But nobody told us they were discontented. Demonstrations at the bacteriological warfare research station. But nobody told us such an outfit existed in Canada! People protesting pollution? What pollution? The paper never told us. . . . (Davey Report, p. 9).

In Chapter 4, the inclusion of advertising as part of the free lunch was discussed in the American context. Kesterton's generally apologetic *History of Journalism in Canada* discloses the same phenomenon in Canada. Advertisements disguised as news stories "largely disappeared" from newspapers across the country only by 1950 (Kesterton, 1967, p. 149). Bureaucratic routines (the city hall, police court beats for example), and publisher indifference are held responsible in part for the free lunch mess.And particularly penny-pinching employment practice. By contrast it appears that the quality of the free lunch in French-language newspapers, and the dynamism of their staffs' professional development sharply distinguish the French-language press from the English (Davey Report, pp. 95, 122). The Canadian Press does not believe that it should have more staff abroad. "Most of the publishers we questioned think the news we get from three foreign agencies via CP is jimdandy" (Davey Report, p. 233). Yet the Davey Commission recognized that principal reliance on the Associated Press for world coverage was inconsistent with Canadian interests:

Every reporter has a bias. We think it is immensely important that the reporters who give us our picture of the world should reflect the kind of bias that Canadians tend to share, rather than the bias that Americans or Frenchmen or Englishmen tend to share (Davey Report, pp. 233–234).

This analysis of Canadian newspapers may conclude with some findings of a Conference on News Flow between Canada and the United States at the University of Syracuse in 1976. Of foreign news in Canadian dailies, 49 percent is American. Of foreign news in United States dailies, 2 percent is Canadian. Seventy percent of United States news in Canadian papers is written in the United States by Americans. More than one-third of the news about Canada appearing in United States papers is "human interest" (read explosions, hostage dramas, etc.). More than one-third of the news about the United States in Canadian papers is "hard" news (politics, trade negotiations, etc.). In general, it is a case of news flow north, news trickle south.[4]

MAGAZINES

Canadian magazines typically have a short life; only one, *Saturday Night*, founded before 1900 still survives (Kesterton, 1967, pp. 26, 62). From the beginning of Consciousness Industry, 1880–1890, "consumer magazines" have been a major media means of producing audiences for advertisers. As early as the turn of the century the pattern of cultural domination was set. Samuel Moffett (1906, p. 100) then said:

A single American weekly has a circulation of sixty thousand in Canada, which is more than the combined circulations of all the Canadian magazines of general standing. At the newsstands in Canadian hotels American publications fill the bulk of the space.

And in support he quoted editorials from Canadian newspapers:

To abrogate the postal convention would be to exclude from Canada every magazine, newspaper and periodical published in the United States. What then should we read? Where are our Canadian magazines? Where are our great weekly papers? Where, in Canada, have we anything that can fill the place of the American publications that we now buy? Such publications in Canada simply do not exist (*Winnipeg Tribune*, Nov. 24, 1906).

Of Americanizing literature this country is getting altogether too much. Every day carload lots of it in the form of newspapers and magazines are dumped on our market. This foreign reading matter, as was pointed out yesterday, is transported over our railway lines, assorted in our post-offices,

---

[4] *Content*, November 1976, p. 5.

forwarded in local mail bags and delivered at city homes by letter-carriers, all at the expense of the Canadian post-office department, which receives nothing whatever for the service (*Toronto Mail and Empire*, April 26, 1905; Moffett, 1906, p. 101).

Then as now, United States magazines imported into Canada dominated the market for audiences. In 1961 the O'Leary Royal Commission reported that circulation of foreign magazines in Canada (most of them from the United States) outnumbered circulation of Canadian-produced magazines three to one. And the number of different magazines imported was more than 500 as against barely 40 Canadian titles.[5]

A fundamental difference exists between the structure of the newspaper and magazine industries. The former in North America is structured around the production of audiences in specific communities and embraces the whole of such markets. The magazine industry, *per contra*, is structured around the production of segmented audiences (e.g., sports, news weeklies, science fiction, "women's" interests, etc.) but which typically are distributed over a whole country, or as in the case of American magazines, two or more countries. It is thus helpful to think of newspaper audiences as "vertical" geographic units, and magazine audiences as "horizontal" segmental units. Physical distribution of magazines to audience members scattered widely is critical to their survival. This is true even for regionally distributed magazines.

The virtually complete market control exercised by United States magazines has been facilitated because two United States-based firms are the only distributors of magazines in Canada! Small wonder that American magazines get preferred exposure on newsstands; in 1961, major Canadian magazines derived only 10 to 25 percent of their sales through newsstands while major American magazines sold in Canada got 49 percent of their sales that way (O'Leary Report, p. 34).

In 1971, 13 percent (by value) of sales of Canadian-published magazines came via newsstands in Ontario; 64 percent of sales of magazines imported from the United States came that way.[6] Nor has this been the full measure of the generous accommodation which Canada has offered American magazine producers of Canadian audiences. The Canadian postal service was carrying United States magazines free in 1905. In 1961, the O'Leary Commission concluded that a very large part of the postal deficit of $23 million in 1960 was attributable to the free delivery of imported periodicals.

---

[5] Canada. Royal Commission on Publications, *Report* (1961, p. 85). Hereafter referred to as the O'Leary Report.

[6] Canada. Royal Commission on Book Publishing, *Report* (1972, p. 358). Hereafter referred to as the Rohmer Report.

Under such circumstances, it is surprising that any Canadian magazines could survive. The failure rate in Canadian magazine publishing has been very high. In 1970, the Special Senate Committee found that there were only four large-circulation consumer magazines in sound financial condition; and two of them were "Canadian editions" of American magazines: *Time* and *Reader's Digest* (which received 56 percent of all magazine advertising revenue in Canada). That committee remarked that "'Canadian' editions of U.S. magazines are the ultimate refinement in the re-use of second-hand editorial material to provide a vehicle for a new set of advertising messages" (O'Leary Report, p. 39). It recommended that advertising expenditures on Canadian "editions" of foreign magazines be made nondeductible for income tax purposes. This recommendation had been adopted by the government in 1964 but *Time* and *Reader's Digest* had been exempted. Another decade was to elapse before these exemptions were removed. In 1976 *Time* terminated its Canadian edition; *Reader's Digest* got around the barrier by forming a Canadian branch plant "owned" by Canadians. The heavy hand which the United States exercises to establish and maintain its cultural penetration of smaller countries was evident. The Special Senate Committee referred to the prospect of economic retaliation:

> Former Finance Minister Walter Gordon has asserted publicly that the exemptions were granted in the first place as a result of severe pressure from Washington. The Americans are said to have intimated to Ottawa that if *Time* and *Reader's Digest* were kicked out of Canada, it might indirectly affect the course of negotiations on the U.S.–Canada auto parts agreement. It is not unreasonable to anticipate similar pressures this time around, and they need not all be at the quasi-diplomatic level. As Mr. McEachern told the Committee:

> "Remember that in view of the enormous American penetration of Canada, a great many of the big advertising decisions are not made in Canada, but in head offices in the United States. If the Government of Canada were to go ahead and make a move against the two publications named, this would set off a typhoon of criticism. We would be charged with anti-Americanism and all sorts of things; so certainly for a time we would suffer" (Davey Report, p. 162).

As will be discussed under "Books", Canada's two most populous provinces, Ontario and Québec, almost simultaneously around 1970 took or considered taking structural actions to protect Canadian book publishing. One set of measures proposed in Ontario dealt with the problem of United States monopoly control of the distribution of mass-market periodicals and paperback books. It deserves emphasis because it is an example of what Canada might have done (or still might do) to cultivate its cultural identity. The Rohmer Royal Commission on Book Publishing recognized that monopoly existed in the distribution (owned and controlled in the United States) and wholesaling of periodicals and mass-market paperbacks. It advised the government of Ontario to transfer by statute the ". . . monopoly control of geographical wholesalers of periodical literature in Ontario from the national distributors located abroad to the province itself" (Rohmer Report, p. 309). The province was advised to register geographical wholesalers, to determine the market areas they might serve, and require Canadian ownership of them (permitting for each a total of no more than 25 percent foreign ownership, with no more than 10 percent stock ownership by a single foreign owner). Moreover, it was proposed to require such wholesalers to offer to retail news dealers, and to carry reasonable inventories of, all Canadian-edited and Canadian-published periodicals issued four or more times a year (with due regard to French-language periodicals in the areas populated by French-speaking people in Ontario). All national distributors of periodicals and mass-market paperbacks would be required to supply the Ontario wholesalers ". . . on an equal-terms, equal-service basis at all times" on pain of being denied any sales to any wholesaler in Ontario. Retail news dealers in Ontario would be registered, and the same citizenship ownership requirements applied to them as to wholesalers. Finally, no geographical wholesaler would be permitted to acquire an ownership or management interest in any retail news dealer in Ontario. These measures concerning citizenship of wholesale distributors in Canada were adopted by the Ontario government.[7]

Canada's consumer magazines have been unstable and largely unviable, but its "business periodicals" have done better. These periodicals produce audiences with advertising and free lunch directed to segments of the business community (restaurants, chemical industry, etc.). In 1970 they received more advertising revenue than "consumer" magazines. There were 510 such periodicals in 1970 and the Special Senate Committee found them mostly profitable. A high proportion of them are *controlled circulation* periodicals, which means that no subscription price is charged readers, and that circulation is confined to the business sector chosen. Here the sale of the produced audience to advertisers is the sole source of revenue. They too face serious competition from the United States whence came some 1912 U.S. business publications circulating in Canada (free of postage charges and courtesy of Canadian postal rate payers). The audiences created in Canada by these imported business journals are a bonus for the United States-owned branch plants which sell the same branded com-

---

[7] Rohmer Report, pp. 318–320. The Paperback and Periodical Distributors Act of 1971, as amended is the instrument.

modities in Canada as in the United States where the advertising costs are borne by the parent companies. Prior to 1964 some of them carried advertising explicitly directed to Canadian business consumers, but in that year the government acted on a recommendation of the O'Leary Commission and amended the customs laws to prohibit entry of periodicals carrying such advertising. Most of the indigenous Canadian business publications are published by four large firms, notably MacLean-Hunter and Southam Business publications.

A minor but significant segment of the Canadian magazine industry is the "ethnic press"—some 100 periodicals which in 1970 had a total circulation in at least 14 languages of between 2 and 3 million copies. Inevitably in serving up their free lunch, the ethnic publishers are caught in the contradiction: preserve the cultural and linguistic heritage of the old land; or homogenize it into the Canadian commoditized culture. Caught in this dilemma they don't please advertisers:

> Even a superficial glance at a foreign language Canadian newspaper shows a lack of the more obvious consumer ads. The proportion of such advertising has no true relation to the very real buying power among foreign language Canadians. Many potential advertisers would like to go after this buying power—and incidentally, to help the ethnic newspapers remain in business. Yet they feel they cannot afford the gamble. *Until the ethnic publications are able to provide meaningful facts about their readership, the dilemma is likely to remain* (Davey Report, p. 180; emphasis added).

In other words, the ethnic publishers can't or won't provide the necessary demographics or psychographics concerning their audience products. As a result; an industry spokesman said:

> Many of the agencies find it expedient to use the English press rather than the ethnic press. Their rates are higher. The amount of commission is a little more remunerative. There is less production cost; no translation. They know what they are publishing. We often wonder whether it's right or not, but I think they kind of take the easy road out (Davey Report, p. 180).

BOOK PUBLISHING

It was relatively easy for Consciousness Industry to rationalize some industries, such as newspapers. Even in their competitive era, they were centralized enterprises which owned and operated their own printing equipment, held long-term contracts for paper or owned their own pulp mill suppliers, employed their own reporters, and owned and operated their own retail distributor facilities for home delivery. To organize them in chains through mergers was easy. The book industry was so structured, however, as to be very resistant to effective oligopolistic control. Until 1945, it remained fixated with the structure of the "domestic" or "putting-out" system which had provided the model for its development in the seventeenth and eighteenth centuries.

This model had two critical characteristics which explain its resistance to vertically integrated oligopolistic takeover attempts. (1) It was decentralized. Typically the publisher was the entrepreneur who took the risks of combining the necessary products and services to produce and market a book. The principal product was the printed, bound, jacketed book, offered for sale to the reader. To produce it, the publisher acquired the right to publish a manuscript written by an author (who owned it under copyright laws). The publisher controlled and provided editorial services and advertised the book. The publisher typically contracted the physical manufacturing process to an independent book manufacturer, paying for the paper, ink, and other materials required. The publisher then marketed the published book through (typically) independent wholesalers and retailers, except in regard to textbooks and reference books which moved largely to the customer without going through retail outlets. The contribution of the publisher to the whole process was thus intangible: he provided the mental judgment to negotiate in the many different markets involved, plus sufficient loan and equity capital to finance his production and marketing contracts and to maintain inventories of "backlist" books previously published. (2) Barriers to entry were minimal. After the industry had passed beyond the period when prior approval by government was required before a book might be published (typically by the early nineteenth century), the only barriers to beginning operation as a publisher were economic. And they were low. In order to enter the business of publishing a metropolitan daily newspaper in Canada or the United States one needed at least $15 million for fixed capital investment in plant and equipment and as much more for working capital (largely to sustain initial operating losses). But in order to enter book publishing as little as $6000 was deemed sufficient by the Rohmer Royal Commission in 1972. Very little capital, plus a salable title, plus the ability to negotiate the contracts necessary for the physical production, storage, and marketing of the book is all that is required *to start*. Capital cost is thus no barrier to entry in book publishing; but it is to survival if the publisher is to risk unsuccessful titles and to bear the cost of capital and storage of inventories of unsold copies. The result of this second characteristic of book publishing was to produce a highly skewed distribution of publishers, with large numbers of small publishers and small numbers of large publishers.

That each title published is (legally) unique, taken together with the decentralized structure of the industry and lack of financial barriers to entry, *seemed* to make the book publishing industry a durable paradigm of capitalist ideology. Opportunity to write and publish seemed to be available for anyone concerned to produce books of high culture, science, etc. And the lure of author income from royalties from book publication completed the ideological paradigm for capitalism. It seemed, in fact, that book publishing resembled the idealistic objective urged by John Stuart Mill in *On Liberty* (1963) of a free market place for ideas, and that the individual book was responsible for its political and social consequences. Even on the assumption of a fully competitive book industry, however, the opposite seems true. As C. N. Parkinson (1958, p. 9) says:

> The politician who reads it all will have read not only the text which the historian thinks significant but forty-nine other forgotten works of which the historian has never even heard. And if one book appears to have been his favourite it will be because the author recommends what he, the ruler, has already decided to do; or what indeed he has already done. Historically, the book comes afterwards to defend the deed. This is not to say that the book is always *written* after the revolution it seems to justify. It may be written beforehand, gaining its wide circulation only after the event. The books, by contrast, which supported the losing cause have been forgotten, overlooked, destroyed—or else never published. There is thus a natural selection among books, giving to some the popularity and survival which rewards what is relevant to the mood of an age, and ensuring for others the oblivion reserved for all that seems eccentric and out of tune. . . . In England or America the books thus out of step will remain unpublished for lack of expected sales. It is not books which influence political events. It is the events which decide which book is to be pulped and which made compulsory reading in the schools.

Parkinson overstates his case. Obviously the books (published or unpublished, written or unwritten because unpublishable) are part of the larger dialectical contradictions in the social process. They both *are* consequences and *have* consequences in the real world. They favor one side or the other of ongoing struggles (and even a pretended "neutrality" or "objectivity" is not neutral).

In the real world (as distinct from the ideal), the forces of monopoly capital invaded the book publishing industry after 1945 to substantially reduce its competitive character. And as happened in each preceding industry to become dominated by oligopoly, the process was one of promoting mergers. In order to understand how scientific management is serving to rationalize the structure of the book industry, one must see how giant corporations work to manage demand in this as in other branches of Consciousness Industry. The clearest example is popular "trade books" (fiction and nonfiction). Demand is effectively managed by concentrating on the mass marketing of paperbacks (e.g., at supermarkets and shopping malls) *in tandem* with production of motion pictures and TV programs, with due attention to the spin-off of popular music records and tapes—all based on the book. The detailed sequence may run in different directions: from book to motion picture to TV, or as in the case of *Roots*, from TV to book. This obviously entails integration between the publishing of hardcover books, paperbacks and the production of films, TV programs, and recorded music.

This kind of vertical combination took place in the following examples (Chotas and Phelps, 1978, pp. 9–12). Columbia Broadcasting System took over (merged) with Holt, Rinehart and Winston (hardcover books) in 1967, with Fawcett (paperbacks) in 1977. RCA, owner of the National Broadcasting Company, took over Alfred A. Knopf (hardcover) in 1960, Random House (hardcover) in 1966, Ballantine Books (paperbacks) in 1973, and Pantheon (hardcover) in 1961. Gulf & Western, which controlled Paramount Pictures, acquired Pocket Books (paperbacks) in 1966, and Simon & Schuster (hardcover) in 1975 plus three other book publishers. And Music Corporation of America which controlled Universal Pictures took over Berkley Publishing (paperbacks) in 1965, G. P. Putnam and Coward, McCann & Geoghegan (both hardcover) in 1975. Warner Communications (films) bought Paperback Library in 1970. How does it work?

> Mr. Snyder of Simon and Schuster admits that it shares an advantage with other Gulf and Western subsidiaries—Pocket Books and Paramount—in "flow of information." There may be more of advantage than that, for of the 18 Pocket Books that were made into films last year, seven were Paramount's, the highest number made by a single company. Moreover, "Looking for Mr. Goodbar," "Washington Behind Closed Doors" (from John Ehrlichman's novel, "The Company"), and the forthcoming "The Investigation" by Dorothy Uhnak are all examples of a pure conglomerate product, proceeding from Simon & Schuster hardback, to Pocket Book paperback to Paramount movie or Paramount television production (Loercher, 1978b).

But of course, the demand which is sought to be managed is not limited to the foregoing model.

> Historically, mergers within the publishing industry date back to the '40s, but no one paid much attention to them until the '60s when *huge nonpublishing conglomerates* began their colonization. *Seeking to diversify their investments into promising areas such as communications and education,* which were then a growth market, conglomerates such as Litton Industries, the Xerox Corporation, ITT, Raytheon, the National General Corporation, and RCA started taking over publishing houses, particularly those with strong textbook departments (Loercher, 1978a, emphasis added).

Xerox acquired Ginn & Co. (hardcover) in 1968 and 10 other firms in books and learning materials between 1963 and 1974. ITT acquired Bobbs-Merrill (hardcover) in 1961 and 12 other firms in publishing and learning materials. Litton Industries, an aerospace conglomerate, acquired D. Van Nostrand (hardcover) in 1968, American Book Co. (1967), and five other firms in publishing. IBM acquired Science Research Associates (educational tests and teaching materials) in 1964.

Other media conglomerates invaded book publishing in the same period, among them, Corinthian Broadcasting, Cowles Communications, Cox Broadcasting, *Billboard, Filmways, New York Times*, Raytheon, *Time*, Inc., *Times-Mirror*.

A wave of defensive mergers among publishing houses was sparked by these invasions of their industry. Thus Harcourt Brace Jovanovich took over 18 firms in publishing and closely related fields beginning in 1965. Harper & Row acquired eight firms. Houghton Mifflin bought Market Data Retrieval and three other firms. McGraw-Hill merged 11 other publishing and teaching materials firms with itself. Macmillan took over 16 firms in publishing and market research (Standard Rate and Data Service). Lyle Stuart merged with four other publishing houses. Scott, Foresman, with six, and John Wiley & Sons with six. Altogether, according to the editor of *U.S. News and World Report*, there were "more than 300 corporate mergers and acquisitions in the book publishing industry," in recent years (quoted in Loercher, 1978a).

Clearly the structure of the book industry has been transformed, thanks to the aggressive acquisition of it by TNCs—many of which like ITT, Xerox, IBM, RCA, and CBS were already in the forefront of Consciousness Industry's worldwide practice of the means of cultural domination. What are the predictable results of the vertical integration of markets for paperback-hardcover-film-TV, and of textbook-teaching-machines-educational-testing segments of the book industry? The most obvious is that demand management will aim at maximizing profits through vertically integrated successions of markets. And the tested policy for such profit maximization is to aim for and produce "the big book"—the "star" performer which will monopolize the markets for long enough to make a killing. As was true in meatpacking, sugar, oil, and every other industry converted to monopoly capitalism's giant corporate oligopolies, the pressures generated by "rationalization" produce competition which destroys the possibility of competition and results in monopolies. As Oscar Dystel, president of Bantam Books (itself taken over by a West German publishing empire, Bertelsmann) said in 1978:

> I think the economic implications have not been fully felt yet. The competitive forces are almost at a destructive point, of course, the situation is

more acute in the last three or four years because of financial backing—the attitude, "let's go out and get it [the book] regardless of the cost (quoted in Loercher, 1978a).

And the Authors' Guild in 1978 declared that

. . . horizontal acquisitions of separate publishing houses in the same market, such as trade or text, squeeze out independent firms because of their superior financial and operational resources. Vertical acquisitions of a paperback house by a hard cover house has the same effect because the acquired mass-market house has greater resources for promotion and distribution, for outbidding competitors for reprint rights (quoted in Loercher, 1978a).

The purpose is to use market power to establish control of the market. And once that control has been established, sophisticated computer applications permit what the conglomerates call *synergism*. The Rohmer Report explained how the American distributor of mass-marketed paperbacks determines the mix of titles to be displayed by the retailer in Canada, a fair example of synergism.

What determines the time that a mass-market paperback title stays on a display rack is its rate of turnover, just as the quantities and points of distribution for periodicals will be determined exclusively by their profitability. The whole system of distribution is geared to monitor profitability through many different outlets with maximum speed and minimum expense, and it is not surprising that we were told that computerized procedures are being substituted for human decision-making wherever possible (Rohmer Report, p. 306).

More dollar sales for fewer hardcover books; bigger sales of best sellers and fewer nonimitative titles; larger profits from an incestuous interplay between formula-written books, formula-written TV, and formula-written films for the TNCs which manage demand for books and media free lunch. Those are the immediate prospects.[8]

How did and does Canada's book publishing industry relate to the book industry in the capitalist core? British and later mercantilist regulations severely restricted the Canadian book publishing industry. Until 1911, Canada was forbidden by Britain to pass copyright laws in its own interest, which meant that Canadian authors effectively had to be published abroad (Gundy, 1972, p. 15). The British Imperial Copyright

---

[8] The predictable industry defense will be that there have always been formulas in popular fiction (and other branches of book publishing such as travel books). They can point to Ian Watt's *The Rise of the Novel* (1963), with the stereotypical case of Richardson's *Pamela*, which provided the model for popular novels, the soap opera, and Harlequin Romances. The rebuttal is that such kitsch was not a deliberate product of the most powerful economic structures controlling the mainstream of book publishing. The new cross-media TNC monopolies are precisely that.

Act of 1842 prevented Canadian publishers from issuing cheap reprints of English books. Meanwhile American publishers in the nineteenth century generally published pirated editions of English books without regard to copyright and flooded the Canadian market with cheap reprints. The American "one-way" free flow of information policy began in 1890. In that year the "manufacturing clause" in the United States copyright law effectively closed the American market to Canadian-published books manufactured in Canada: books entering the United States in English are denied copyright protection there; manufacture there is required. It may be significant that the first Canadian trade book published was *The Clockmaker*, in 1836, in which the central character was Sam Slick, a Yankee clock peddler.

In Canada book publishing remains a relatively small scale busines because of its organizational and market structure. Publishing markets deal in very large numbers of titles and relatively small production of most of them. The number of titles published annually in Canada about 1970 was 2500; in the United Kingdom, 33,500, in the United States, 37,000. Yet because of its peculiar dependency relations with both countries and because of a common language for most Canadians and those countries, the book industry in Canada sells more United States titles than are available in Britain and more British titles than are available in the United States (with resulting heavy cost of inventories and slow deliveries) (Gundy, 1972, p. 32).

The complexity of Canada's dependency on foreign book markets is suggested by the fact that the label "Canadian," as applied to books, ranges from meaning merely the appearance of the name of a Canadian city following the publisher's name on the title imprint page (e.g., Toronto and New York) of a book manufactured and published in the United States, written by an American and for sale through a Canadian office, to a book written by a Canadian, published in Canada by a Canadian-owned publisher, and manufactured in Canada from mostly Canadian materials. Of total book sales in Canada in 1969 of $222 million, two-thirds ($144 million) consisted of foreign-made books (a) imported directly by Canadian end-users, such as libraries ($33 million); (b) imported by Canadian distributors who are not publishers ($30 million), (c) imported and marketed by Canadian publishers as agents for foreign publishers ($84 million). The remaining one-third is a mix of books "manufactured domestically," which includes an undetermined quantity of books where the original typesetting is done outside Canada and the plates are sent to a Canadian printer for printing and binding, as well as books wholly manufactured in Canada. This mix of books ($77 million) is marketed by "Canadian publishers" (Rohmer Report, pp. 1–2; Ernst and Ernst, 1970, pp. 21, 26).

How Canadian are "Canadian publishers?" Of some 283 publishers in Canada in 1969, 162 published mostly in English and 121 in French. A substantial majority of English-language publishers are branch plants of foreign publishers. Indeed, all except the university presses (which publish 10 to 12 percent of Canadian titles) and rare exceptions, such as Ryerson's, began as branch plants (a cluster of a dozen or more of which became substantial Canadian publishers between 1896 and 1913). Religious orders in French Canada began publishing school textbooks in the 1840s and until a wave of penetration by American and French publishers in the late 1960s, Quebec's publishing was virtually entirely domestically owned. It still is dominated by domestic publishers.

Of the English-language publishers, about one-third (57) are agents for the amazing total of 543 foreign publishers. Some publisher-agents are completely independent of the foreign publishers they represent, frequently being Canadian-owned corporations. Others are incorporated subsidiaries of their foreign parent firms.[9] About half the English-language publishers in Canada in 1970 were "principally Canadian-owned," but a few Canadian-owned "publishers" publish no Canadian-written, or Canadian-manufactured books at all, and do a large import business (Rohmer Report, pp. 59, 84).

How "Canadian" is the authorship of books sold in Canada? No one knows. Because of the "manufacturing clause," a book by the Canadian Bobby Hull, about a Canadian sport, hockey, had to be manufactured in the United States,[10] and a high proportion of Canadian-written textbooks at the university level are published in the United States. The Rohmer Commission found that in 1970, 53 publishers in Canada (excluding government departments) claimed to have 50 or more Canadian books in print and for sale. These 53 publishers accounted for 68 percent of a total of 15,299 Canadian books in print; the open-endedness of the industry is indicated by the fact that several hundred publishers published the remainder (Rohmer Report, p. 1). The commission found that in 1970, 57 Canadian publishers published a total of 631 titles (all of which were written by Canadians or manufactured entirely in Canada). Of these slightly more than half (345) were published by Canadian-owned publishers (again, not all necessarily written by Canadians or entirely manufactured in Canada), and of these 140 were published by two firms. But as the commission observed the number of books by Canadian authors was hopelessly "buried" in the available statistics (Rohmer Report, pp. 1,

---

[9] The vagueness of these two last sentences reflects the Rohmer Report, pp. 2, 14–15. Québec information: Laberge, Georges, and Vachon, Andre, "Book Publishing in Quebec," Rohmer Report, Background Papers, pp. 374–379.

[10] Curry, W. E., "The Impact of the U.S. Manufacturing Provisions," Rohmer Report, Background Papers, pp. 147–148.

59). For French-language publishing, Québec enjoys a much higher proportion of Canadian-written, Canadian-published books.

The core of the economic problem for the Canadian book publishing industry is that the small size of the domestic market (relative to that of the United States) places Canadian publishers in a marginal position in a market where the border is virtually totally open to imported books. The price of materials and labor in manufacturing and distributing books in Canada is no lower than in the United States. American publishers, enjoying the economies of scale in a much larger market, can enter the Canadian market freely, but the "manufacturing clause" prevents Canadian publishers from competing in the United States (Rohmer Report, p. 102).

Confined to a relatively small domestic market, Canadian publishers are constrained to price their books at levels established in continent-wide or international markets. Print runs for the Canadian market are so small as to yield high unit costs—given that the same unions and wage scales exist on both sides of the border. As recently as the 1940s, press runs as large as 2000 copies for trade books by Canadian authors were unusual.[11] The competitive advantages of foreign publishers in Canada are:

1.   Greater scale of production. Hence unit costs are usually lower, even without selling at prices which reflect out-of-pocket costs alone (overhead costs having already been written off), which is a common practice. As two American economists stated ". . . Canada is unusual in that it accounts for over one-third of the dollar volume of U.S. book exports; in fact this country can be viewed almost as a (U.S.) domestic market."[12]

2.   Bigger backlist from the parent abroad. Thus, the backlist of McClelland and Stewart in 1970 was 702 titles, McGraw-Hill in Canada could draw on 10,500, the Oxford University Press, 18,000.

3.   Cheaper operating capital. Branch plants of United States publishers borrow from Canadian banks on loans guaranteed by their parent companies; Canadian competitors have until recently been unable to borrow against inventory from Canadian-chartered banks. The Ontario government, adopting a proposal of the Rohmer Commission in 1971 began supporting loans secured by such collateral in Ontario.

4.   United States publishers have large and more sophisticated sales organizations.

---

[11] Eustace, C.J., "Developments in Canadian Book Production and Design," Rohmer Report, Background Papers, p. 46.
[12] Kapoor, A., and Breisacher, E. H., *Business Quarterly*, University of Western Ontario, Summer 1971; quoted in Rohmer Report, p. 222.

5. Consumer demand tends to be cultivated for United States-published titles by critical reviewers and by TV interviews produced in the United States and seen in Canada. United States book clubs which operate freely in Canada, of course directly preempt the market for Canadian-published books.

6. The larger market and connections with mass-market paperback publishers, the motion picture and TV industry allow United States publishers, therefore, to offer more generous royalty arrangements than can Canadian.

7. The much larger and more sophisticated United States graphic arts industry and book manufacturing industry enjoy the advantages of newer techniques and lower costs than are available to Canadian book publishers and book manufacturers.[13]

As a result of such competitive pressures, books only marginally publishable in Canada would be very publishable in the United States or United Kingdom, whereas books marginally publishable in the latter countries are too speculative for Canadian publishers.[14] For this reason, a rule of thumb in Canadian publishing is that when business is bad (as in the depression, 1930–1939,) original Canadian publishing slumps and publishers rely on promoting sales of popular American and British books.

Three segments of the book industry require further analysis. Retail booksellers in Canada (except in Québec) as in the United States are few and poorly equipped with inventory, workers, and bibliographical aids. In 1970, they numbered 112 trade book stores and 98 university bookstores and accounted for much less than one-third of total industry sales. Much of their sales volume, moreover, is in mass-market paperbacks where they must compete with supermarkets and newsstands.

Mass-market paperbacks (for the total volume of which no statistics are available) are the one segment of the book industry which has been fully exploited by Consciousness Industry. In Canada these paperbacks are distributed by distributors located in the United States through Canadian geographically franchised wholesalers to retail outlets at a 40 percent discount (as compared with 20 percent for hardcover books). The same distributors also distribute magazines to retailers. These paperbacks are usually published in editions of hundreds of thousands of copies as reprints of fast-selling hardcover books under rights leased from the original publisher. The lower cost of paperbacks is mostly due to the low unit costs of mass production; substituting cloth bindings would add no more than 75 cents per copy to the price. The distributor determines the

---

[13] Curry, W. E., *supra.*, p. 143; Rohmer Report, p. 55–56.
[14] See Rohmer Report, p. 126–28 for analysis and examples.

mix of titles to be displayed by the retailer and provides point-of-sale merchandising aids. The "quality" paperbacks usually issued by original publishers (in both Canada and the United States) have been excluded from the mass-paperback distribution channels because of their slower turnover.

The scandalously poor retail bookseller structure in addition to the erosive effect of mass-paperback marketing suffers under another structural handicap: the discount structure adopted by Canada from the United States example. Under this discount structure publishers allow the same discount—commonly 20 percent—to schools, teachers, and libraries as they do to retail booksellers. No wonder schools and libraries "buy around" their local booksellers. Since schools and libraries spent 58 percent of the Canadian book industry's total revenue in 1970, one can appreciate the magnitude of the diversion of revenues from retail booksellers.

The educational and the library markets for books present even more problems to the book industry than that of the discount structure. In the United States book industry, it is axiomatic that comprehensive publishers enjoy secure and substantial markets from the sale of schoolbooks and reference books to educational and library institutions. Indeed they commonly use the profits from those markets to cross-subsidize trade books which they feel should be published but which have uncertain market prospects. Canada's schoolbook publishers have never enjoyed secure nationwide educational and library markets to provide a similar base for trade book publishing. In the nineteenth century, they suffered because school textbooks were almost all imported from the United States, Ireland, or Scotland with ". . . a cosmetic Canadian colouring."[15]

> Even as late as 1950, most Canadian children were learning to read from slightly Canadianized American readers. . . . In elementary or high school, most Canadian children were learning to use American "English"[16]

In Ontario where "Circular 14" (a list of approved textbooks eligible for "stimulation grants" from the province to the local school board) was begun in 1951, Canadian production of Canadian-written textbooks at the elementary and high school level has been successful in providing a more stable base for Canadian book publishing. In 1972, 92 percent of the titles on the list were wholly manufactured and written in Canada. The Ontario "Canadian preference" system for textbook adoption-publication was not imitated in other provinces, with the exception of the Northwest Territories. Some provinces have no policy for Canadian preference. In

---

[15] Eustace, C. J., *supra.*, p. 42.
[16] *Ibid.*, p. 45.

Western Canada, where United States textbooks are virtually universal, there has been the greatest contrast with the Ontario policy. Nevertheless in 1969 sales of textbooks yielded Canada's book industry 50 percent of total revenues, of which a significant fraction was Canadian-written, Canadian-published books.

The "educational revolution" which reached Canada a year or so after it started in the United States in the late 1960s undermined the Ontario Canadian preference system. It meant the cessation of stimulation grants, a drastic devolution of the power to decide on textbooks to the level of the individual teacher, the rapid dissolution of standardized curricula on a provincewide basis and the substitution of local option for textbook selection, fragmentation of curricula, and the hasty choice of a variety of non-textbook teaching resources (film strips, motion pictures, etc.). These AV aids virtually all were imported and sold by the United States producers of audiovisual hardware and software, themselves parts of TNC conglomerates identified earlier. The Rohmer Report emphasizes the changing role of the schools as agenda-setters in this connection:

> The classroom is no longer the prime purveyor of information to children. Whether we welcome it or not, in this selection function television has long since outstripped the school. Today the teacher must help the pupil sort and classify the vast amount of information that is available, information which may be said at one time to have been thrust upon him, and it [sic] must show him how to set about establishing his priorities (Rohmer Report, pp. 188–189).

The struggle to resist United States domination has been largely unsuccessful at the elementary and high school levels. The Symons Commission of the Association of Universities and Colleges of Canada reported:

> While lacking opportunities to learn about their own political system, Canadian students are subjected by the media to a mass of information about the American system. By the time they enter university many think almost completely in terms of American political ideals, terminology, institutions and practices.[17]

The university level text market in Canada in general has always been dominated by foreign-produced books—which provided 87 percent of text sales in 1970 (Rohmer Report, p. 130). Indeed, most Canadian-written university textbooks are published in the United States.

A combination of events in the late 1960s focused a challenge to the policy of passive dependence which had characterized the Canadian book industry. A number of new Canadian publishing firms which came into

---

[17] *The Symons Report*, an Abridged Version of Volumes 1 and 2 of *To Know Ourselves*, the Report of the Commission on Canadian Studies. Toronto: McClelland and Stewart, Limited, 1978, p. 51.

existence and were interested in publishing Canadian authors' books about Canadian topics for the Canadian market organized a Canadian-owned publishers' association to lobby for the Canadian book industry. The "ed-tech" audiovisual invasion of the Canadian textbook market by TNCs shook up some older Canadian publishers whose programs were partly based on that market. And three Canadian publishing firms were purchased by TNCs (Le Centre De Psychologie et de Pedagogie by Encyclopedia Britannica, W. J. Gage—a substantial textbook publisher—by Scott-Foresman of Chicago, and Ryerson Press by McGraw-Hill International). The result, when these events were mixed with the latent Canadian nationalism, were demands that government act to protect the Canadian book publishing system.

The federal government, ignorant of the elementary facts about that system, commissioned a report by a private firm of accountants (Ernst and Ernst) which when tabled in 1970 proved very inadequate. The Ontario government created the Rohmer Commission to study Canadian book publishing (most of which was in that province). Shortly thereafter, the Canadian firm, McClelland and Stewart, announced that it was for sale because of inability to raise necessary working capital. (Canadian banks are forbidden by law to make short-term loans secured by inventories—in this case of backlist books—whereas branch plant publishers when faced with the need for working capital can provide guarantees of their loans from their home offices in the United States and obtain the loans from Canadian banks without difficulty.) The Rohmer Commission recommended, and the Ontario government acted, to make available a working capital loan to McClelland and Stewart at lower than market interest rates. The sale of the firm was averted. The same policy was extended to all Ontario-based, established Canadian publishers.

In February 1971, federal Secretary of State Pelletier reported to the Cabinet on the state of Canadian publishing and made some recommendations for action. His report showed the dominance of foreign ownership and foreign content and noted how distribution of books and magazines was biased toward foreign product. It compared the importance of books and periodicals for the cultural development of Canadian life with that of the other mass media like broadcasting and films in which government invests large funds and in the case of broadcasting regulates the system in an effort to give substance to Canadian identity. It considered such action essential for books. Its proposals included:

     1.   Creation of a Canadian Publishing Development Corporation to provide development funds for publishers;
     2.   Funding of $300,000 for the Canada Council to double its assistance to writing, publishing, and periodicals;

      3.   Support for Canadian involvement in the International Book Year to the tune of $250,000;

      4.   Development of comprehensive proposals for publishing by the secretary of state.

In Québec also in 1971, regulations were adopted for greater Canadian content in bookstores and for the purchasing by public institutions of books through bookstores to strengthen the bookstore distribution system. Encyclopedia Britannica was forced to sell to a Quebec publisher the Québec firm which it had purchased. In 1972, the secretary of state announced the details of the assistance program proposed a year earlier. It included a $1 million program of publisher grants and grants for translations, a $500,000 federal book purchase program, and a $1 million program to aid export of Canadian books. He also promised further remedies.

    The final report of the Rohmer Commission made recommendations which, if implemented, would have protected the *status quo* in book publishing. It proposed an Ontario program of grants to Canadian publishers for trade books similar to that of the federal government through the Canada Council. New foreign branch plants and takeovers by foreign firms of Canadian firms would be prohibited in Ontario, but no steps to repatriate branch plants were envisaged. There would be grants to Canadian-owned publishers in Ontario to stimulate development of new Canadian textbooks. A series of measures was proposed to rehabilitate the eroded Circular 14 policy of Canadian preference in provision of textbooks and library books. And it proposed establishment of an Ontario Book Publishing Board to implement some of the recommendations and to monitor developments on the book-publishing scene. In the event, none of the major proposals was implemented, after an internal evaluation of the recommendations by the Ontario government bureaucracy. This result manifested the lobbying power of the branch-plant publishing houses, which was also reflected in the Ontario government's subsequent decision to subsidize production of new textbooks and to have the government buy copies of newly approved textbooks for the schools. These subsidies were extended to branch plants as well as Canadian-owned publishers. Two takeovers of existing Canadian-owned firms were permitted in 1974.

    At the federal level, the 1972 program which was implemented was not followed by the further remedies promised. A long series of statements of the need for stronger measures has come from the federal government, but no action to put them into effect, apart from a modest increase in the annual grant program to $5.4 million for three years beginning in 1980. In summary: a government policy of nationalist rhetoric, continentalist action has reinforced dependency. In the words of one Canadian publisher, James Lorimer (pp. 20–21):

In the area of books, which many people would consider an absolutely key medium for the development of an independent Canadian consciousness and an independent Canadian culture, both the federal government and provincial governments like Ontario now have continentalist policies in place. The result is domination of the book medium by foreign-owned firms . . . This is a situation which has been deteriorating steadily in the last ten years, during which time Canadian authors' works have gone from 38% of total sales in 1966 to 24% in 1969 and 17% in 1973.

In the case of the federal government, their current continentalist policy involves an absence of ownership legislation regarding book publishers and distribution mechanisms, a copyright act which does nothing to advance national interests in terms of the development of Canadian writing, and an implicit division of publishing into the profit-making educational sector dominated by U.S. multinational corporations and a state-subsidized trade sector of Canadian-owned firms.

In the case of provincial governments like Ontario, their current continentalist policy regarding books concerns mainly the educational field. The provinces have permitted books published by foreign-owned firms (Canadian books published by Canadian-owned publishers accounted for only 3% of the total textbook sales in 1973) though it is obvious that the ultimate ownership of a publishing company affects the contents of the books it publishes. The provinces have permitted schools to make more and more use of texts and library books written by U.S. authors, reflecting American attitudes, values and information, intended for American children. Such policies regarding educational materials must lead to the Americanization of people's minds. . . .

Public policy in this field will remain continentalist in its orientation until the constant fraud involved in the nationalist rhetoric of responsible federal and provincial officials is exposed, and until the groups who share an interest in the nationalist approach to the book medium organize the political muscle to require such measures from government. The groups with a potential stake in this issue are large and powerful: they include writers, publishers, librarians, booksellers, teachers and professors. Many of these groups remain uninformed about the political economy and the politics of Canadian publishing, and they have been misled by the show of attention to publishing by politicians.

MOTION PICTURES

The first nonprint *popular* art form to be developed in Canada as a dependent market for United States cultural imperialism (without even the necessity of establishing United States branch production plants) was the motion picture industry. And the enduring pattern for this no-branch-plant–branch-plant industry was established between 1912 and 1922. By that cumbersome term I mean that Canada has had none of the advantages of having a branch-plant feature film industry (such as employment) while having all of the disadvantages.

The motion picture industry grew out of the ancient traditional mode of the theater. Initially, in the 1890s in many Western capitalist countries it began at the variety-vaudeville-carnival level of theater, appealing to the lower income-level working-class population. As the technique improved (silent cameras, monochrome raw stock, projectors, screens), and as the art of producing, directing, and acting for the medium was learned through practice and deriving some theory from practice, the scale of the industry expanded. What had begun as elaborations of film-loop peepshows had moved through the stage of store-front theaters with moveable chairs, to traditional theater structures. The principal product of the motion picture industry is the sale of a theater seat at a particular place and time in relation to the screening of a particular film. The motion picture industry consisted of the institutions which produce, distribute and exhibit films. It is to be noted that these activities follow in sequence and that they are interdependent. The logic is no film produced, no distribution, no exhibition where the end-product, the seat, is sold to the customer.

Canada and the United States went through the period when experimentation with short films and one-reelers demonstrated the potential market power of the new industry from about 1900 to 1915. Unsuccessful attempts were made to monopolize the three stages of the industry by means of patents on equipment, but relatively competitive market conditions existed by 1915. Short films for exhibition had been produced and marketed in Canada, in various parts of the United States, and of course, in many other countries. With growth in patronage, revenues, and the art of motion picture production, two tendencies emerged.

1. The scale and complexity of operations expanded.   Scriptwriting became necessary as films became longer and plots more complex. "Stars" were created by publicity and audience acceptance, and themselves became the basis for successful attempts to manage demand from the production end of the industry process. They were the means by which producers could ensure the profitability of the *next*, and the next film produced. Stars were and are in fact analogous to advertising brands as means to create partial monopolies in the market. Along with stars, longer and more elaborate productions of film took place. The "feature film" genre was created. D. W. Griffith's *Birth of a Nation*, and *Intolerance* during World War I, with running time of 90 to 150 minutes, required vastly larger investments in production expenses of all kinds than had been the case five years earlier. And to administer production, marketing, and publicity for long features with stars, production enterprises required corresponding central production staffs (administrators, accountants, lawyers, clerks, etc.). Producing organizations needed assured theaters for marketing their films. At the other end of the process, larger theaters with furnishings attractive to the middle class, increased the capital required at the exhibition end. Such theaters, strategically placed in downtown locations represented the probability of regular, heavy attendance, if sufficiently attractive films were made available. They also represented potential partial monopolies of exhibition of films, if they could be assured a regular supply of "first-run" feature films. Exhibiting organizations needed assured supplies of desirable films.

2. *Entrepreneurs at the production end of the process, therefore, attempted to control the distribution of films, and through publicity of stars and movie titles to control the exhibitors.* They therefore sought to establish "franchises" for exhibition of their films which favored theaters might depend upon in the future. They also tended to merge with other producers in order to pool their resources (stars, influence over exhibitors, etc.). At the same time, entrepreneurs at the theater end of the process attempted to form buying alliances with other theater owners in noncompetitive situations (e.g., in other neighborhoods or other cities) to exact more favorable terms from producers for the exhibition of their films. They went beyond this and jointly formed companies to produce films primarily for their benefit. Consequently the period from about 1918 to 1935 in Hollywood (to which production activities had gravitated in North America) and at the exhibition end of the motion picture industry was one in which competitors eliminated competition and substituted an oligopolistic structures.

At the production end, five giant corporations (MGM-Loews, Paramount, Fox, RKO, Warner Brothers) operated factory-like production studios *and also* each controlled distribution and exhibition of motion pictures in different regions of the American-Canadian market. Control of exhibition was accomplished through a combination of devices. Each of the "majors" owned and operated key "first-run" theaters in the cities in the portion of the American-Canadian market where they were in charge. They also regulated the distribution of films produced by all of themselves to maximize their exhibition profits through timing the "clearance" between "runs" of their films by the first-run and independently owned theaters in their chosen market areas. "Block booking" and other coercive practices forced the independent theaters to market whatever films the major producer-distributors chose to release for exhibition. The production capacity of the majors was insufficient to supply the theaters with films. Three other large production companies which did their own distribution but did not themselves own theaters (Columbia, Universal, and United Artists) enjoyed terms about as favorable as those of the majors for marketing their films as well as the certainty that their films would be profitably exhibited. Lying outside of the eight production companies in question was a fringe of Independents (e.g., Republic, Monogram) and B film producers who made Western and action films at low budgets. This outer fringe of producers were at the mercy of the six major integrated chains for the possibility of getting their films distributed and exhibited, and for the terms they would have to accept.

If one looks at the industry structure of that period as a whole, clearly effective control was exercised at the point of distribution where the identity and terms for exhibiting films were determined. At its peak level of growth, during World War II, the vertically integrated majors effectively controlled the market for the 18,413 theaters in the United States although they owned and operated only 3137 strategically located theaters. The remainder, some 83 percent of all theaters were "independents," completely dependent on the majors for their films. This structure obviously excluded foreign films from general theatrical exhibition. The five major producers which owned theater chains received 73 percent of the *total* film rentals paid by all theaters in the United States in 1943–1944. The other producer-distributors (Universal, Columbia, and United Artists) received 22 percent. The best measure of the dominance of the eight giant oligopolists is the 94 percent of total film rentals which they received (Conant, 1960, pp. 44–49).

This was the monopolistic structure which was broken up by the application of the Sherman and Clayton Antitrust laws in the United States in 1948.[18] By that decision the majors were forced to sell all their theater holdings. And the local theater monopolies which had existed were attacked by requiring diversity of ownership of the theaters previously held by the majors, as well as by prohibition of the use of the "run," "clearance," block booking, and other monopoly practices. The result of this was to restructure the industry in the United States. Of course the United States antitrust action had no effect in Canada. And the vertical control established over Canadian feature film production, distribution, and exhibition by the majors (of which Paramount which happened to have staked out the Canadian market as part of its share of the combined United States-Canadian market) has never been disturbed by the Canadian government.

Some feature films with Canadian themes were produced in Canada before 1922—notably those by Ernest Shipman based on novels by Ralph

---

[18] *United States v. Paramount Pictures*, 334 U.S. 131.

Connor—which were commercially successful in the laissez-faire period in which films were exhibited from wherever they could be obtained most profitably, be it Canada, the United States, or England. But the community of commercial interest between Canadian, American, and British businessmen who struggled to control the Canadian film industry in that period produced a structure controlled by the Paramount vertical monopoly. Its control over Canadian motion pictures was the outcome of the most conspicuous struggle in Canadian film industry development. It took place between the Allen theatrical chain (which had been built up in Canada by an American family beginning in 1906) and its rivals. Chief of these was the Paramount group led by Adolph Zukor, backed by Kuhn Loeb and Company, investment bankers in New York and represented in Canada by a Canadian. At its peak the Allen chain operated 56 theaters (mostly in Canada though some were in the United States) which for defensive purposes (to ensure a reliable flow of "star" products) affiliated with First National—an American independent theater cooperative. The Paramount subsidiary, Famous Players Canadian Corporation Limited, chartered in Canada in 1920, purchased the Allen theaters in 1923 and with the British-owned Odeon theaters later cooperating, effectively monopolized Canadian film distribution and exhibition. Necessarily this prevented the development of a Canadian film production industry. There was one serious government challenge to the foreign-controlled monopoly of Canada's film industry when, in 1931 under the Combines Investigation Act, suit was brought in the Canadian courts only to have the charges summarily dismissed in 1932.

The United States states that 102 film-producing countries use quotas or other discriminatory methods of ensuring that their own films will have access to their own theaters (Crean, 1976, p. 104). Canada has never done that. Why not? Because of the political power used by the American industry. Susan Crean, in *Who's Afraid of Canadian Culture?* presents the historical pattern of political domination which has frustrated all attempts to develop a viable Canadian film production industry, with the saving if partly inhibited exception of French Canada where popular support has nourished a significant indigenous film production capability. The stakes, even in revenue terms, are high. Canada in 1975 was Hollywood's most valuable customer, returning $54.5 million to the United States for the producers there. This is not the full measure of United States profits however, for the difference between $54.5 million and the more than $200 million box office receipts in Canada in 1975 was mostly revenues received by foreigners and spent—or retained as surplus reinvested in Canadian cable TV or Canadian hockey teams or a mini-conglomerate, Agra Industries, Ltd., operating a vegetable oil refinery, soft drink production and distribution of paperbacks and magazines in Saskatoon, Saskatchewan.[19]

The basis in Canada of the vertical monopolies' control is 80 to 90 percent ownership of film distribution and in 1972 outright ownership of 44 percent of the theaters by Famous Players and 19 percent by Odeon. According to the president of Famous Players,

> It's been a historical fact that major distributors align themselves with either one circuit or the other. People like Paramount, Warner Brothers, and United Artists will play 100 percent Famous, and people like Columbia and two-thirds Universal and one-third Fox would play Odeon. . . . it was agreed, I understand, (in the) early forties how the breakdown worked when Odeon was first formed (quoted in Crean, 1976, pp. 84–85).

Ownership of as many as 63 percent of the theaters, when these are the most strategically located and blessed with "first-run" privileges confers effective control over what will be screened by the remainder of the more than 1400 theaters in Canada. This control is exerted in two ways: through the films available to the "independent" theaters; and through the invaluable "word-of-mouth" advertising created by publicity and the reputation films achieve in the first-run theaters. The practice of *block booking* is general when a monopolist, such as the United States industry, controls distribution of films.[20] This means that in order to get a particularly popular picture an independent theater is obliged also to buy less popular American pictures.

The implicit policy of the Canadian government has been consistently to accept the dominant presence of United States films and their industry. But as remarked earlier, the role of comprador is uneasy; to placate the natives, explanations and pseudo solutions for continuing the subservient role are called for in the interest of face-saving for the ruling elite. At times the explanations echo the National Policy of the 1870s which sold out Canadian natural resources for "direct investment." Thus, in 1926, the head of the Canadian Motion Picture Bureau wrote:

> We are attempting at all times, as Canadians, to induce American capital and manufacturing interests to come to Canada and establish branch-plant factories. I look on the American film as a branch factory idea insofar as it affects Canada. American motion picture producers should be encouraged to

---

[19] The Financial Post Corporation Service, CUSIP no. 135440, 17 February, 1978, especially p. 5.

[20] It is perfectly legal in the United States for the entire motion picture industry to act like a monopolist in dealing with foreign countries. The Webb-Pomerene Act, 1918, exempted such behavior from the United States antitrust laws. And Canada appears impotent to enforce its anticombines legislation to prevent such behavior.

establish production branches in Canada and make films designed especially for British Empire consumption. I believe that really worth-while American producers would be glad to make typically Canadian pictures if they can secure the right cooperation, assistance and technical advice (Ray Peck, quoted by Crean, 1976, p. 75).

Half a century later the same siren song of United States money was heard from the Ontario minister of industry and tourism as he headed for Hollywood:

My selling point will be that Ontario not only has gorgeous scenery and exciting cities to entice Hollywood filmmakers, but that we want to encourage co-production—that is, United States money combined with Canadian talent (Claude Bennett, 1975, quoted by Crean, 1976, p. 93).

In the years immediately following World War II, United States cultural imperialism was pushing films hard as part of the "free flow of information." Canada, like Britain and many other countries was suffering from balance of payments problems and needed to conserve foreign exchange reserves. Britain imposed a 75 percent duty on all imported films and settled the resulting dispute with the United States by setting an annual limit of $17 million of profits which American film companies could withdraw from Britain (as against earnings of $60 million). In 1947 the Canadian government imposed import restrictions on many United States goods, but left films off the list at a time when about $20 million were being taken in film profits to the United States each year (Crean, 1976, p. 77).

In response to a CCF proposal in 1947–1948 for a protective tariff on films, linked with use of the resulting tax revenue to stimulate a Canadian film industry, C. D. Howe promoted a counter proposal from Hollywood, the "Canadian Cooperation Project," which became Canadian government policy until 1958. Under it, the industry could export its profits and in exchange offered a melange of public relations: Hollywood would make a film on Canada's trade-dollar problem. There would be more complete coverage of Canadian news in the film newsreels. National Film Board films would be released in the United States. A short film on Canada would be made by Hollywood. Radio recordings praising Canada would be made by film stars. Film sent to Canada would be more carefully selected. And Canadian "sequences" would be introduced in Hollywood features. To further make their point, the Liberal government from 1948 to at least 1975 helped United States companies further to take their profits out of Canada by giving them a special 5 percent "relief" on the statutory 15 percent withholding tax on exported profits (Crean, 1976, pp. 78–80).

What has Canada done affirmatively in motion pictures? The National Film Board was created in 1939 and impressed with the policy of realistic documentary production by John Grierson. Initially, it was an

effective instrument of propaganda production in the interest of pros-
ecuting World War II and as such was intimately associated with the
American (Office of War Information) and British propaganda machines.
After 1945 its documentaries and abstract art films won innumerable international awards and created the illusion externally that Canada had a
film production industry. In reality, the NFB has been fenced off from
feature film production both by the terms of its federal funding and by the
same obstacle which has defeated indigenous commercial film production: inability to get distribution and exhibition with the necessary
publicity. As a result, the NFB in the 1940s and 1950s had little domestic
popular significance as film producers. It did, however, train several
generations of film producers, directors, writers, cameramen, and
editors, most of whom joined the "brain drain" of actors and actresses
southward. Conspicuous among the latter were Mary Pickford, Walter
Huston, Raymond Massey, Walter Pidgeon, Beatrice Lillie, Jeanette
MacDonald, Lorne Greene, Raymond Burr, Glenn Ford.

The French unit of the NFB, created in 1959 under Pierre Juneau,
was the springboard for the struggle for a domestic feature film production capability as part of the assertion of French-Canadian nationalism.
Six or more Québec producer-directors produced feature films which
more than recovered their costs at box offices where Québécois could see
feature films which reflected their own culture and its problems during
the "Quiet Revolution" and afterward. As a result of strong pressures
from both French and English producers connected with the NFB, the
Canadian government established the Canadian Film Development Corporation (CFDC) in 1968 to stimulate domestic feature film production
by partial government funding. Initially a revolving fund of $10 million
(increased to $20 million a year later) was created. Upon application up
to 50 percent of the film budget could be provided by CFDC (up to 60
percent for low budget films). By 1974 feature films in French and
English were winning awards at international film festivals. But by that
time, the struggle had bogged down. Private Canadian investors were no
longer willing to join in CFDC ventures and many recognized Canadian
directors sought work in Hollywood. Susan Crean (1976, p. 72) says:

> It was a clear sign that trouble was on the way when Canadian films
> originally failed to get adequate distribution through the movie theatres.
> After seven years, 20 million tax dollars and 150 films, only 6 percent of the
> Canadian theatregoing public were actually seeing any of the CFDC-backed
> films. . . . When film-makers tried to distribute their films, they discovered
> that the Canadian distribution and exhibition systems were closed circuits.
> Even with a market worth $200 million a year, Canada could not support its
> own cinema in 1975 because the structure of distribution and exhibition tied
> tightly with the United States industry, did not permit it.

Significant of the bureaucratic bias of the Canadian Broadcasting Corporation toward the United States film is the fact that by 1974 only 2 of the 112 CFDC films then available had been shown on CBC (Crean, 1976, p. 110).

The struggle for an indigenous feature film industry broadened and clarified the issues. In 1973 the Council of Canadian Film Makers (CCFM) was formed by seven unions and the British Columbia film industry representing some 8000 people. Borrowing from the practice of 102 other countries, it proposed the use of a quota on imported films and a tax on box office sales to support distribution and exhibition of Canadian films. It proceeded to lobby the parliamentary committee on film, the secretary of state, and the CFDC. In response, the Canadian government has used every conceivable device to avoid the necessary steps toward establishing the conditions in which a domestic feature film industry would develop. A series of secretaries of state in the 1970s pleaded with the United States industry to grant even token distribution and exhibition for Canadian films. United States investment as co-producers of Canadian films has been sought by CFDC—a "prescription for a branch-plant film industry," as Susan Crean calls it. "Voluntary quotas" were proposed by the United States industry and the secretary of state in 1975—and in practice disregarded by the American-controlled distributors. Fast tax writeoffs of capital investment have been offered investors in film productions which can be certified as "Canadian." A promoter's brochure in 1978 illustrates this device for branch-plant film production. The film was "Hank"—a story about a young girl (American star) who wins a fight to preserve wild horses from being slaughtered for dog food (a recent American conservation issue). Six "points" were necessary for the project to qualify as "Canadian" in addition to its being filmed in Canada, the producer being technically a Canadian, and 75 percent of the production budget spent in Canada. The six points were earned by Canadians' being the director, editor, director of photography, and composer of the sound track. But the writer and both the male and female leads were to be American. The financial soundness of the project rested on distribution agreements for NBC TV network showing, and a contract with Time/Life Films, Ltd., for pay TV and TV syndication rights worldwide. The Chemical Bank of New York was the banker for the project. No Canadian distribution was mentioned.

Meanwhile, evidence of wide popular support for the CCFM is the public interest in indigenous Canadian feature films:

> Film festivals in Canada began to assume considerable importance. . . . A six-hour marathon of Canadian films at the St. Lawrence Centre, Toronto in October, 1973 turned away an overflow audience. The Festival of Nonexistent Canadian Films at the University of Western Ontario in London in

January 1973 likewise attracted an overflow audience. Ten thousand turned up to see Canadian movies at a festival at the University of Saskatchewan in Saskatoon in January 1975. That same month, about 1,200 appeared in downtown Toronto in the middle of a snowstorm to see the NFB's premier screening of Robin Spry's *Action*, a documentary on the October Crisis of 1970 (Crean, 1976, p. 83).

A compromise on the policy issue is impossible—and both the United States industry and the CCFM know it. Yet the Canadian government continues its 60-year evasion of the issue. The reason that compromise is impossible may be put thus: (1) Canada could produce feature films with plot, location, actors, directors, cameramen, and producers who have something to say which is distinctively Canadian. Most of such films would have to be produced at budgets which could be recovered from exhibition of the films in Canada, although some of them would be exhibited abroad. Distribution and exhibition of the films would have to be assured in Canada. This would be a viable policy if supported with quotas on imported films and box office levies. (2) Alternatively, Canada could produce films aimed explicitly at the foreign (i.e., American) market. Such films would imitate the plots and values common in American-made films. Their budgets would need to be commensurate with those of the typical American film, i.e., much higher than for type (1). Moreover, there is no assurance that Canadian films of type (2) would receive reasonable exposure at the hands of American film distributors in the United States. (If it is impossible to get Canadian-made films distributed in Canada by United States distributors, why should anyone expect better treatment when they are offered to the United States?) If the Canadian ruling elite were serious about giving a realistic base to the idealist rhetoric about the need to use communications to strengthen Canadian identity, actions to make possible the creation of a Canadian feature film production capability through taking effective control over the Canadian film industry away from the United States would be a logical step. It would then need to be supplemented with import quotas and box office levies to subsidize the domestic film production industry—practices common around the world.

This chapter has analyzed print and film media development in Canada. Apart from daily newspapers which flourish in monopolistic, Canadian-owned, splendor in Canada, we have found the print media and film stifled by the consistent policy of the Canadian government and ruling class of preferring accommodation to first British and later American capital and business organization to any significant indigenous development of these industries. The next chapter examines the development of Canadian telecommunications.

MEDIA OF CANADIAN CULTURAL SUBMISSION II: TELECOMMUNICATIONS

The preceding chapter has shown how the press, periodical, book, and film industries in Canada are all tributary to United States markets albeit in different forms. The press and periodicals are dominated by the United States media which specialize in producing audiences for advertisers to buy to market mass-produced consumer goods. The book and film industries are dominated in structurally different ways, but the end effect is the same. In this chapter we examine the telecommunications industries in Canada.

From the beginning, telecommunications in Canada were organized to take advantage of its resources for the benefit of English and American capitalists. The first objective was to link Montreal to Halifax and the latter to New York in order to send news dispatches dropped from transatlantic vessels at Halifax to the markets of New York and Montreal. In 1847, telegraph lines were pushed eastward from Québec City and north from Maine into New Brunswick, connecting to the line from Québec the next year. Also in 1847, connections were established between Buffalo and Toronto (Marshall et al., 1936, pp. 123–124). By 1850, the line backed by the Associated Press of New York opened service north to Halifax. The first major "trust" among the early TNCs was Western Union Telegraph Company. It extended its system into Canada in the 1850s, buying the Montreal Telegraph Company. In the 1850s it also penetrated British Columbia several hundred miles, preparatory to establishing between Alaska and Siberia a link with Russian Imperial Telegraph. After the successful inauguration of the transatlantic cable in 1866, it maintained its service in British Columbia while abandoning the plan for the Alaska-Siberian link. In 1881, it bought the American Union Telegraph Company which, with its subsidiary, the Dominion Telegraph Company, operated extensively in Ontario and Quebec. It consolidated its Canadian holdings in the Great Northwestern Telegraph Company, part of which system was the telegraph service of the Canadian Northern Railways.

When the Canadian National Railways were created in 1923 the telegraph lines of the Canadian Northern, Grand Trunk, Great Northwestern, and some government lines were consolidated in the Canadian National Telegraphs. In 1927 and 1929 Western Union sold its remaining land lines in the Maritimes to Canadian National Telegraph, except for the 1185 miles which it still owns linking its Nova Scotia and Newfoundland cable terminals with its land lines in the United States (Marshall et al., 1936, pp. 125–126).

By 1856 English and American promotors of the transatlantic cable had extended telegraph service to link St. Johns, Newfoundland, with both Canada and the United States, thus avoiding construction of some 1500 miles of submarine cable-laying. The first attempt was temporarily successful in 1856 and in the 20 days the cable worked congratulatory messages were exchanged between the Queen and the President (no mention was made of Canada).[1] In 1866, a third try succeeded, and Canada was permanently established as a way station for submarine telegraphs. A second cable linked France with Nova Scotia in 1869. Before 1900 12 transatlantic cables landed in Canada. In 1894 the "Colonial Conference at Ottawa" considered imperial communications policy. All the existing lines to India and Australia passed through non-British territory and would be vulnerable in event of war. Accordingly, the Dominion of Canada invited bids for construction of a cable from British Columbia to Australia (Bright, 1898, p. 149). Such a cable called the *Red Cable* was laid in 1902.

Canadian participation in submarine cable activity, whether through providing cable-head landings in the Maritimes or in relation to the Alaskan project of the 1860s or the British cable from Canada to Australia, was as a passive agent of the British empire. Geopolitical strategy considered cables as a decisive element in empire, to which shipping, coaling stations, consular offices, and branch banking were subordinate.[2] The daring thrust of Western Union through British Columbia to link up via Alaska with the Russian telegraph system across the Bering Sea was part of a joint maneuver by British and American capital. On the

---

[1] A good source on early cables is Bright (1898, p. 36).

[2] Tribolet (1929). The reference to shipping, coaling stations, etc., is based on Elihu Root, quoted at p. 43.

British side, the trans-Russian telegraph line had been built by the Great Northern Telegraph Company, Limited, a Danish company with major investment and control in Great Britain. The Russian Czar had "large interests in the line across Russia" (Tribolet, 1929, p. 72). This enterprise built the transcontinental line and connected with the British network of Asiatic cables serving India, Indochina, China, Japan, and Australia controlled by the Eastern Cable Company (English). The control of the Asian network (especially service to and in China) was the strategic object of both the British and American policy, though each schemed to control the other, beginning in the 1850s.[3]

The ultimate outcome of the strategic struggle for world dominance in electronic communication facilities was not resolved until after World War II when the principal aspect of the contradiction was transformed by the American empire eating up the British. By that time Canada's telecommunications system (as well as its print and film media) had already been brought under American control. It is to Canada's internal telecommunications system that we next turn our attention.

Under the British North America Act two major telephone companies have been chartered by the federal Canadian government: Bell Telephone Company of Canada, and British Columbia Telephone Company, as branch plants of giant United States TNCs. Bell was chartered in 1880. Its wholly owned subsidiary, Northern Electric, has manufactured equipment and provided supplies to the telephone operating companies of Bell Canada since 1892. Both were tied to the parent operating/holding company (American Telephone and Telegraph Company) and its United States-based counterpart to Northern Electric, Western Electric Company. The means of control were stock ownership and a triangular structure of contracts for (1) patent licenses (between parent and operating companies), (2) manufacturing (between parent company and manufacturing subsidiaries), (3) supplies (between operating and manufacturing subsidiaries) (Daniellian, 1939, pp. 365–366).

When telegraph and telephone companies were chartered in the nineteenth century, the state might have built and operated its own telegraph and telephone facilities (as indeed was the mode adopted in Europe), or it might delegate to the chartered company the doing of the service. At that time the arts of telegraphy and telephony were distinct and separate from each other and from other industries. Canada and the United States opted for private operation. And at first the Bell company envisaged itself as having ". . . the purpose of working the entire telephone system of Canada. . . ."[4] In a study of one prairie province's telephones, I

---

[3] Tribolet (1929, chap. VI, "China") recites the scenario.
[4] Canada. House of Commons, "Proceedings of the Select Committee on Telephones" (1905, p. 404). Hereafter referred to as Mulock Committee.

found that for the development of the vast, unsettled area, such as that now occupied by Alberta, Saskatchewan, and Manitoba:

> In the 1870s and 1880s the hegemony of Anglo-Saxon Canadians on the prairies hinged on limiting United States military forces to the official border, enforcing their control of the territory as against native peoples and Metis, and preparing the transportation and communication system to accommodate a vast flood of European migrants who would occupy the land (Smythe, 1974, p. 4).

The first two of these conditions were met by the Royal Northwest Mounted Police, the third by the building of the railroads, and the fourth by the telegraph and telephone, but especially the latter. Bell Telephone of Canada had extended service as far as the prairies by the 1880s, but it never reached British Columbia. Moreover, its service was limited to the largest towns in the area and even so was inadequate as to quality and price of service as compared with small privately owned telephone companies. Bell Telephone of Canada's policy was to skim the cream from the large markets and to ignore the needs of the small town and agricultural areas. The president of the company told the Mulock Committee (Vol. I, p. 622):

> If it is a question of erecting an exchange in one large place and of giving a service needed by 1,000 people, we certainly, and quite properly, in doing that give preference to the needs of a large number rather than to a lot of farmers' lines. There is a much better return from the expenditure of money on that work than there will be from the expenditure of the same money on smaller lines. On the same principle, if a line is required from Toronto to Montreal to give a service to the businessmen, to the mercantile community of Montreal and Toronto, and on the other hand the same amount of money is required for farmers' lines that will give little or no return, on any proper business principle anyone would say: Build the long line, and give the service to the greatest number of people to whom it is of the greatest value.

Public corporations are operating the telephone services of the three prairie provinces, rather than the Bell company, because of this Bell policy which frustrated efforts to expropriate that company through Parliament.

The populist drive for public ownership of giant monopoly corporations between 1890 and 1910 in the United States (see Chapter 3) appeared also in Canada. It surfaced at hearings by a Parliamentary Committee chaired by the Postmaster General in 1905, Honorable William Mulock. Testimony by the government expert, Mr. Francis Dagger (a telephone engineer with English and American experience) found the Bell Company service unsatisfactory in four respects:

1. High rates in large cities.
2. Disproportionately high rates in cities of from 25,000 to 60,000 inhabitants.
3. High long distance rates.
4. Lack of rural communication (Mulock Committee, Vol. I, pp. 7-8).

He concluded that the state or any municipality could give service at much lower rates and earn satisfactory profits because their capital outlay would be much less than that on which the Bell Company had to earn returns—referring to the fact that one-fifth of the $5 million Canadian Bell stock had been exchanged for American Telephone and Telegraph Company patent rights which had long since expired. He proposed that the federal government take over Bell's intercity facilities and operate them within the Post Office. The operation of municipal service he proposed be licensed to provincial or local governments—the licenses to include the common law obligations of a common carrier. Rural service, he said, should be provided by rural cooperatives. Federal standards for telephone plant should be prescribed for municipal and rural service. They should also prescribe for mandatory connections between telephone systems.

Dagger's recommendations were echoed by dozens of witnesses, headed by the Union of Canadian Municipalities, and a wide representation of farm and rural users. The gist of hundreds of printed pages of their testimony was that farmers wanted telephone service but were unable to pay the rates charged by the commercial companies (mostly Bell). By doing it themselves they got service at about half the rate charged by Bell. But they were denied interconnection to the Bell lines in cities and towns, and to railroad stations under Bell contracts with both Canadian Pacific Railroad and Grand Trunk Railroad except on conditions which restricted expansion of their service areas.

The patterns of strategic defense of their monopoly privileges by the telegraph and telephone vested interests in the United States and Canada had an essential unity, although the tactics worked out somewhat differently in detail. In both cases the telegraph and telephone industries were united with monopoly capitalist corporations in achieving dominant control of the state structures in the period, 1890-1914. In both cases the telegraph and telephone industries had to face the threat of government ownership—a threat strengthened by the fact of government ownership and operation of such services in the advanced European countries—whereas heavy and light manufacturing, resource extraction and processing, and consumer goods production industries throughout the capitalist world were undisputably in the private sector. This threat was met by using their political power in governments, and through the production of public opinion by means of mass-media-produced-audience power and manipulation of the news component of the free lunch (by the editorial policy of the press and the wire service news agencies). But to ensure their industrial hegemony the telephone and telegraph industries of the United States and Canada needed to coopt the criticism of their monopolistic rate and service policies which was constantly being reproduced by the practice of those policies.

In May 1905, while the parliamentary hearings were still in process, the Honorable William Mulock abandoned the committee to attend a Pacific Cable Conference in England. No policy conclusions or recommendations came from the committee. Five months later Mulock left the government on grounds of ill health, was knighted and appointed Chief Justice of the Exchequer Court of Ontario. His successor as Postmaster General was Mr. A. B. Aylesworth, counsel for the Bell Telephone Company at the committee hearings. The view expressed by Mr. Robert Borden, Opposition leader, and by influential newspapers was that Mulock's departure and the failure of the committee to recommend legislation was a clear victory for the Bell Telephone Company (Britnell, 1934, pp. 20–21).

The Bell interests had decapitated and defeated the popular forces whch had been advocating nationalization of telephones in Canada 15 years before their similar success in the United States (see Chapter 4). They were content to abandon the politically thorny and economically less profitable potential markets west of Ontario, in favor of intensive enjoyment of their monopoly from there east. And to ensure against serious threats of government takeover in the lucrative eastern markets, the Bell interests promoted in Canada (as they did in the United States) public "regulation" of themselves. In the United States, the FCC's telephone investigation report stated:

By 1910, competition had been eliminated insofar as it threatened seriously the profits of the [Bell] system. The Bell management was sufficiently farsighted to realize that a nation-wide telephone monopoly could not be achieved in the absence of competition as insurance against extortion unless some degree of public regulation were provided. The annual reports of the American [Telephone and Telegraph] Company for the years 1908, 1911, and 1912 indicate an acceptance of public regulation as a substitute for effective competition. The hope was expressed that the State regulatory commissions would adopt the judicial attitude, would be permanent, and therefore less susceptible to public pressure (U.S. Federal Communications Commission, 1939, p. 475).

Federal regulation in the name of the Interstate Commerce Commission was obtained by the Bell System by an amendment to the Interstate Commerce Commission's duties in 1914.

In Canada the obvious "permanent" regulatory body "less susceptible to public pressure," was the federal Parliament which granted Bell Canada and B.C. Telephone their charters and periodically amended them from 1880 onward. Such statutory "regulation" was necessarily cumbersome and unhandy. In imitation of the American practice therefore, limited authority was given to permanent federal regulatory commissions beginning in 1903 when the Board of Railway Commissioners was created. Canadian Transport Commission was established in 1967 and in 1977 the Canadian Radio-television and Telecommunications Commission was given certain regulatory functions.

The regulatory functions of such commissions in Canada and the United States stemmed from a common source: the English common law on "business affected with a public interest," and more narrowly, "common carriers." It is a doctrine derived from the medieval *justum pretium* which confers a monopoly on a business enterprise engaged in what the common law found to be "common callings." In return the enterprise has the obligation to give reasonably good service to all customers, safely, without discrimination and at a fair price. In common carrier industries, the firm gets its monopoly by statute, certificate, or license. The general formula for rate regulation is that the rates approved and charged should yield sufficient revenue to cover all prudent expenses, and profits sufficient in the long run to attract the recurrently necessary input of capital to replace worn-out or obsolete plant. The assumptions of the common carrier doctrine as applied in Canada and the United States include:

It was assumed that the subject to be regulated was an enterprise, not a market or a series of markets . . . This was a crucial assumption, appropriate in the 19th Century, but obsolete now in telecommunications. . . .

It was assumed that the function of the regulatory commission was passive and negative and that the management of the regulated company had the prerogatives of planning industry development, financing it, determining the mode and content of investment in plant, procurement of equipment, supplies and services of all kinds, initiating new services and pricing them. Herein lay a grave paradox: If regulation were to be effective from the public point of view it must invade managerial prerogatives. If a commission forces management unwillingly to make an important decision will it thereafter protect management from stockholder suits alleging management's fiduciary responsibility to stockholders to use its best judgment? . . .

It was assumed that, as in a judicial proceeding, the opposing parties would be able to present their cases competently. In other words, it assumed that a sort of countervailing power existed in the regulatory setting between the industry on the one hand and the representatives of the general public on the other. The fact is that while the industry is well-equipped at expense of its customers to protect its interests before the regulatory commissions, the consumers are typically unorganized, uninformed, inadequately staffed with competent expertise, or simply unrepresented. The hope of many reformers that the staffs of the commissions would be advocates of consumers' interests have been unrealized either because the staffs shared the industry viewpoint or were subject to constraint to behave in a quasi-judicial way by their employers, the commissioners. The ombudsman function of the commissions then went unfulfilled.

The fundamental assumption is that monopoly will perform like a competitive business when regulated: [and quoting from Professor Horace M. Gray]

"It is an ingenious, though somewhat naive, synthesis whereby society can enjoy the benefits of competition by abolishing it; and avoid the evils of private monopoly by creating and legalizing it. In short, one can have monopoly and not have it at the same time. This seeming contradiction, it is assumed can be resolved by public regulation, which will function as a catalytic agent to reconcile private monopoly with the public interest."[5]

The common carrier regulatory scheme as applied in the United States and Canada has served to protect the regulated industries from effective remedial action. This conclusion and recommendations for its reform have been the subject of many critical books and articles. (Gray, 1940; Smythe, 1971; Melody, 1969; Trebing, 1969a, b; Wilcox, 1955; Lewis, 1966; Johnson, 1961; Averch and Johnson, 1962; Westfield, 1965; Posner, 1969; Stigler and Friedland, 1962).

After the defeat of the Mulock initiative, it was evident that no federal action would be forthcoming to meet the need for telephones in the three prairie provinces. Alberta and Manitoba acted promptly in 1906 to create government ownership of telephones, and Saskatchewan followed two years later. In all three provinces, the Bell interests sold their properties willingly. The crown corporations created to operate the telephone systems of those three provinces appear to have performed much more efficiently than has the Bell Telephone Company of Canada and BC Telephone Company (Babe, 1978). Moreover, because their profits have not been siphoned off to private shareholders in the United States and Canada, these profits have been available for cross-subsidizing unprofitable rural services and lightening tax burdens on their populations.

---

[5] Smythe (1970, pp. 62–65). The quotation from Professor Gray is from *Hearings* before the Antitrust Subcommittee on the Committee of the Judiciary, House of Representatives. *Monopoly Problems in Regulated Industries*, Part I, Vol. 1, 1956, pp. 76–88.

For its part the Bell Telephone Company has prospered mightily in its denser and more lucrative market. Its powerful political influence has produced a benevolent shield of policy on the part of Parliament (through regular reconsideration and amendments to its corporate charter and through the Canadian Transport Commission) with a regulatory statute effectively narrowed to the issue of whether its net income yields a reasonable return on its capital investment. As a concentration of power, it is a private government of formidable proportions. Its total revenues in 1973 were $2.1 billion, to equal which one must cumulate the total public revenues of four Canadian provinces (New Brunswick, Newfoundland, Nova Scotia, and Prince Edward Island). To equal its revenues in 1973, one would have to add the total revenues of Royal Bank of Canada to those of the Bank of Montreal. In that year its revenues were 70 percent larger than those of all Canadian Pacific operating divisions combined and lacked only 20 percent of equaling those of Imperial Oil. With about 70 percent of all telephones in Canada, Bell is a giant among pigmies. It has a commanding position within the TransCanada Telephone System— a nonorganization established in 1932 which links telephone service from the Atlantic to the Pacific Ocean.

The Bell Company successfully clings to the obsolete notion that telecommunications is a "natural monopoly" in which the monopoly firm may serve and be regulated in a distinct, discrete market structure. As a result of the vast expansion of research and development *outside* the telephone company during World War II and the post-Sputnik space race, inventions such as the transistor, wave guides, printed circuitry, communications satellites, and computers are now the common resources of a number of giant (aerospace) firms. Technically, the only remaining element of "natural monopoly" in telephones is the local switched telephone system. Transmission between cities is inherently competitive. Transmission of telephone messages, TV programs, computer data, and private line services has been for some time an area where competition by different entities using satellites and microwave relay is feasible and desirable. So also is the installation of specialized user networks which need interconnection with the switched public telephone network. The Bell Telephone Company rejects or resists such interconnection and it uses its monopoly market (the switched public telephone network) to produce profits with which it cross-subsidizes its services designed to kill off competitors in the specialized user network markets.[6]

---

[6] The "Seven-Way Cost Study" conducted by Dr. William Melody for the Federal Communications Commission found that when costs and investment were fully allocated, the net operating revenues as percent of net investment for the interstate services of American Telephone and Telegraph Company in the United States were: Message toll telephone, 10.0

In similar fashion, under Bell leadership the Canadian telephone industry has fended off the threat of an alternative mode of conducting telephony—cable TV. The Bell company is prohibited by charter provisions from holding cable TV or broadcast licenses. Secure in its legal monopoly of the use of streets for telephone facilities, the telephone companies have used their economic and political power to impose heavy costs on cable TV companies while denying them the possibility of owning the cables which they are permitted to pay for and use—attached to telephone poles (Babe, 1975).

In yet another imitation of American practice, the device of a privately controlled monopoly corporation to own and operate communications satellites was borrowed from the United States experience with COMSAT when TELESAT CANADA was formed in the early 1970s. Essentially created to broaden the market for telecommunications equipment for the benefit of equipment manufacturers (conspicuously Hughes Aircraft Corporation and RCA, aerospace giants), the ANIK satellites have been promoted on the specious argument that they would serve the need for "development" of the indigenous peoples in Canada's north country. No such development has been planned or undertaken. The satellites are substantially unused by the telephone and telegraph common carriers who own effective controlling interests in TELESAT CANADA and prefer to enjoy the profits to be made from building and operating their microwave transmission systems (see Melody, 1979).

The telephone monopoly corporations have been less successful in coping with the problem of data processing. That pioneer in computer technique, International Business Machines (IBM), has grown to be a giant TNC rivaling in revenues ATT itself, with its operations spread through dozens of countries. Worse, still, from the telephone company standpoint has been the competitive nature of the computer business, with many companies offering a bewildering array of services both "on-line" and "store-and-forward." Moreover, equipment in the computer services is made obsolete every five to seven years by more powerful and complex innovations, as compared with a cycle of 20 or more years for telephones. The techniques of computerized data processing and telephony are inextricably intermixed. Every electronic switching system installed by the telephone companies to operate their switched public networks is a computer. And the use of computers requires telephone channel connections except for occasional isolated computers. *Teleprocessing* of information is

---

percent, Wide Area Telephone Service, 10.1 percent, Telephone Grade Private Line, 4.7 percent, Teletypewriter Exchange Service, 2.9 percent, Telegraph Grade Private Line, 1.4 percent, TELPAK, 0.3 percent. All other, 1.1 percent, and total, 7.5 percent. Quoted in Smythe (1970, p. 124).

the trend in the data-processing industry. And telephone companies are in the process of converting their analog systems to accommodate digital data transmission, switching, and connections with computers.

Computers have posed basic problems of privacy in all manner of contexts and in all countries touched by them. A contradiction exists between privacy (whether personal, institutional, or national) and access to computerized data banks. Without ready electronic access, the efficiency of computers is crippled; yet the definition and enforcement of restrictions on access in the interest of privacy is extraordinarily difficult of determination. At another level computers challenge vested common carrier interests in telecommunications markets. Computers, cable-TV systems and communications satellites can provide telephone and broadcast services as an alternative system to conventional telephone and over-the-air broadcasting stations and networks. For Canada, with 80 percent of its computer market controlled by United States transnational corporations, considerations of national hegemony necessarily are in contradiction with an ideological preference for competitive rather than monopolistic enterprise.[7] Pioneering studies of policy issues have been done by the Department of Communications, but as yet the essential policy issues have not been settled. Meanwhile the privacy issue becomes regularly more exacerbated. As early as 1970, the accounting records of the Bank of Canada were in a data bank in the United States as also are the insurance and credit card records of individual Canadians. For that matter, the *local* flight reservations of Hungarian Airlines and Bulgarian Airlines are "banked" in a computer in Atlanta, Georgia, USA.

The "vertical" ownership relation between telephone operating companies and telephone equipment manufacturing subsidiaries is another monopoly hangover from the nineteenth century which wastes resources, inflates the cost of telephone service to the public, and nurtures inefficiency in the industry. Northern Electric Company (with total net sales of $423 million of telecommunications equipment in 1969) supplies 75 percent of the Canadian telecommunications equipment market. After an exhaustive study of the anticompetitive aspects of the vertical control by Bell Canada of Northern Electric, the Director of Investigation and Research, Combines Investigation Act, concluded that in the 1960s:

. . . Bell Canada exerted a pervasive influence over its unregulated subsidiary in a manner which tended to impair the ability of Northern Electric to perform effectively and efficiently. At the same time, Bell Canada main-

---

[7] Although already somewhat outdated, the analysis of computers in the Canada. Department of Communications *Instant World* (1971b, chap. 5, 15), is comprehensive and still valid in principle. The 80 percent figure is from p. 166.

tained the subsidiary's dominant position in the telecommunication market by following policies which foreclosed large parts of the telecommunication equipment market to all suppliers except Northern Electric. . . . As well, Northern Electric's innovative performance was weakened by early control of product innovation by AT&T and resistance by Bell Canada to develop independent research and development facilities (Canada. Director of Investigation and Research, 1976, pp. 8–9).

In conclusion the report said: In 1973 the then president of Northern Electric stated that Northern Electric had been an economic colony of ATT for too long. The findings of this inquiry would suggest that Northern Electric has also been an economic colony of Bell Canada for too long. . . .(p. 11).

Typical of the colonial mentality perpetuated by such a dependent relationship are the following remarks quoted in the Director's *Report* (1976, p. 120) from a Northern Electric internal report:

The Bell-ATT relationship. . . . It inhibits the creativity of N.E. technical personnel because they cannot keep abreast of outside technical developments. It also means that N.E. cannot work on designs which fit Canadian needs. Bell's reliance on ATT suggests to N.E. managers that Bell does not yet have full confidence in N.E. R&D. "The Bell engineers frequently pack our prototypes in their briefcases and run down to AT&T to get the dear kind spirits there to tell them whether the product is any good."

The pernicious situation in which even the nominal (if not casual) regulation of the operating telephone company is frustrated by the padding of expense and capital accounts through payments to the subsidiary company which manufactures equipment and purchases on behalf of the operating company *with no regulation at all* should be evident. Dr. William H. Melody testified before the Restrictive Trade Practices Commission:

There is no basis on which it can be demonstrated that vertical integration is more efficient than competition in the telecommunications equipment market. A major cost of vertical integration is the loss of any independent test (market or non-market) for judging the efficiency of that internal relationship, closed from an open market test or public scrutiny. . . .

If the vertical integration relationship is efficient, it will prevail in the face of open information and active competitive bidding. If the market is opened, the in-house manufacturer should still win all the business. . . .

In fact, of course, no manufacturer in telecommunications will be the most efficient supplier of everything. The competitive market will result in a distribution of sales among the various manufacturers in accordance with their respective efficiencies and specializations on different types of equipment and along different product lines. The *Report* provides ample ground for implementing public policy in that direction (Melody and Smythe, 1977, pp. 9–10).

What has been said here about the relationship of ATT to Bell Canada and Northern Electric may be echoed in principle regarding British Columbia Telephone Company and its ownership by foreign interests as well as its practice of purchasing almost all its equipment from affiliated companies. Like Bell Canada, B.C. Telephone Company was incorporated by Dominion charter, in 1916. Having completed acquisition of Okanagan Telephone Company in 1966, it now dominates telephone activity in British Columbia. In 1926, B.C. Telephone Company was acquired by majority stock purchase by Anglo-Canadian Telephone Company, which, despite its name is a holding company operating no telephones. Quebec-Telephones with revenues about one-sixth as large as B.C. Telephone is Anglo-Canadian's other telephone carrier in Canada. Control of Anglo-Canadian in turn was merged by Theodore Gary and Company with General Telephone and Electronics, a TNC headquartered in New York, which currently controls more than 170 subsidiary companies, including the telephone company serving the Dominican Republic. As part of the same merger transactions, B.C. Telephone found itself with a group of affiliated telephone equipment manufacturing corporations (Automatic Electric, Lenkurt Electric, and Phillips Cables). The total telecommunications equipment sales of those GTE manufacturing subsidiaries amounted in 1969 to $95 million—almost one-fourth the volume of Northern Electric.

Two questions concern us regarding B.C. Telephone Company. One, the extent of equipment purchases by B.C. Telephone from its sister companies and the effect of these purchases on price and quality of telephone service. From 1970 to 1974, B.C. Telephone purchased 82 percent of its telecommunications hardware from Automatic Electric and Lenkurt. Given the absence of competition in the Canadian telecommunications market (with both Bell and B.C. Telephone forced to buy from their manufacturing affiliates), and given the absence of information on cost of manufacture, it is impossible to determine how much the accounts of the operating telephone company are overcharged. Regarding quality of service, however, it is clear that B.C. Telephone's customers are using switching equipment which was obsolete when it was purchased from Automatic Electric (Canada. Dept. of Communications, 1975). The second question is whether the relationships between B.C. Telephone and its manufacturing and supply affiliates negate the purpose of public regulation to produce reasonable rates for telephone service. It must be recalled that until now *only common carriers* have been under such regulatory mandate. GTE owns only about half of the stock of B.C. Telephone. But it owns all the stock of the *unregulated* manufacturing and supply affiliates from which B.C. Telephone buys its hardware and telephone directories. The Department of Communications (1975, p. 5) found that:

The return on owner's equity in the unregulated affiliates has been significantly greater than that yielded on either the overall investment in the Canadian communications equipment manufacturing industry or on the average of all industries in Canada.

Regarding Dominion Directories, the GTE producer of telephone directories for B.C. Telephone Company, the Department of Communications (1975, p. 34) found that "The annual rate of return on owner's invested capital in Dominion is very high, averaging about 83 percent over the period 1969 to 1974 and exceeding 100 percent in 1973." The rip-off of consumers practiced by B.C. Telephone under GTE control is a crude example of the violation of the principles which Dr. Melody stated to the Restrictive Trade Practices Commission.

The telecommunications manufacturing industry in Canada, as stated, is dominated by two integrated giants: Bell Canada–Northern Electric and the GTE complex. There are other companies and other telecommunications products than those used by telephone operating companies. The larger nonintegrated companies include RCA, Ltd., Collins Radio, Ltd., Canadian General Electric, Canadian Westinghouse (all subsidiaries of United States TNCs) plus Canadian Marconi, Philips Electronics Industries, and Canada Wire and Cable. These foreign-owned firms tend to import product designs and to pursue production and marketing policies determined abroad. As a *Telecommission* report put it,

> The small businesses in telecommunications manufacturing tend to be Canadian owned and to be engaged with specialties, for example, Central Dynamics and McCurdy Radio Industries Ltd., produce audio and video studio equipment and Spilsbury and Tindall Sales Ltd. produce certain types of radio communications equipment. These companies generally create their own designs (Canada. Dept of Communications, 1971a, p. 8).

Fundamental to telecommunications since the invention of radio communication is the management of the electromagnetic spectrum.[8] Originally developed as an aid to marine navigation, and the transmission of news to and from ships, control of the use of the radio spectrum is an absolute necessity on a global and national scale for two reasons: Such control is necessary if the terms and conditions of radio spectrum use are to permit tolerable use by many users. And secondly, such control is necessary for governmental functions, especially military functions (see Chapter 4 and Appendix).

Canada appears to have been one of the first nations to formalize national policy on radio allocation, adopting a Wireless Telegraph Act in 1905—possibly because Marconi, supported by British capital, depended

---

[8] For a historical analysis of such management on the global level see Codding (1952).

on Canadian cooperation and subsidy of $80,000 in his pioneering trans-Atlantic transmission of radio telegraph signals from England to New-foundland. From 1909 to 1930, radiotelegraph service was provided to shipping in the North Atlantic from Cape Race, the most easterly radio station in North America (Canada. Dept. of Communications, 1971b). During World War I, radio operations in Canada were taken over by the navy (as in the United States). In the United States immediately after the war the United States Navy acted to create an American-owned monopoly for the use of radio (see Chapter 4).

Canada was generous in allowing extraterritorial use of its territory for American radiotelegraph stations. Large United States newspapers (New York *Times*, Philadelphia *Public Ledger*, *Chicago Tribune*) built a station at Halifax to exchange news with circuits connecting with the British Post Office in England in December 1921. In 1924 they extended their circuits from the Halifax station to Italy. Until then, these newspapers which were the nucleus of the specialized news common carrier, Press Wireless, a few years later, had no stations in the United States but used Western Union Telegraph land line wires from Halifax to American cities. Parliament was very obliging when

> In 1927, the committee organized a corporation, under a Dominion of Canada charter, called the News Traffic Board, Ltd., which owned and operated its radio properties in the Halifax district (Herring and Gross, 1936, p. 89).

The administration of the regulation of the radio spectrum in Canada grew up as a very junior partner in its "continental management" by the United States increasingly after World War I. Military use of radio is its highest-priority use in every nation and the effective subordination of the Canadian to the American military after World War I (see Chapter 5), inevitably influenced the spectrum allocation process in Canada to harmonize it with American policy. And with the development of knowledge and equipment to use the radio spectrum, the organizational integration of the American and Canadian spectrum allocation policy has steadily become more intricately textured. As late as 1920, civilian uses of radio in Canada were limited essentially to three classes: broadcast, amateur, and other (including ship, transoceanic, air). In light of the state of the art at that time the usable part of the spectrum lay below 3 MHz. To administer the national allocation process, Canada had first located responsibility for it in the Department of Public Works (1900), then in the Department of Marine and Fisheries (1909), in the Department of Naval Service (1914), back to the Department of Marine and Fisheries (1922), and later to the Department of Transport, and in 1969 to the Department of Communications.

Obviously with the intimate and casual relationship which existed between the government regulatory arm for radio spectrum management and the manufacturing and operating segments of telecommunications, close linkages organizationally would develop between the public and private sectors. In the United States, planning for postwar hegemony began in the radio spectrum when exemptions were granted under the antitrust laws to permit the formation in 1943 of the Radio Technical Planning Board to develop recommendations regarding radio frequency allocation (standards, bands appropriate to particular services, and plans for locating radio frequency assignments geographically taking into account the engineering standards). In an earlier work I analyzed the process by which private and public sectors had been integrated regarding the vastly expanded range of services and regions of the radio spectrum for which equipment and knowledge permitted the use of the spectrum in the United States between 1943 and 1947. At that time the RTPB represented no less than 19 trade associations of telecommunications manufacturers and users. It worked through 13 panels (Smythe, 1977). In 1948, the RTPB was replaced by the Joint Technical Advisory Board with a similar organization.

It should also be obvious that because Canada's telecommunications infrastructure consists almost entirely of enterprises owned or controlled by United States corporations, Canada would find it logical to adopt an array of industry advisory organizations occupied by the branch plants of the American corporations which mirrored those already established in the United States. And this is what happened in the 1940s and 1950s.

The enormous expenditures for military uses of radio in World War I and II were the engine which powered the exploration of the radio spectrum and the equipment with which to use it. Civilian uses of radio have been a by-product or spinoff from the military funded research and development. It is not surprising then to find that the same corporations which conducted the research and development for the military emerged in peacetime with the capacity to determine the kinds of civilian radio services which they in fact would innovate. We find historically that after both World wars new segments of the radio spectrum were allocated for civilian services after 1945 especially for TV, FM broadcasting, and mobile radiotelephone. In the 1920s the region from 2 to 30 MHz was thus opened up; in the 1930s, from 30 to 200 MHz; in the late 1940s, the region from 200 MHz to 10GHz. As a result of the space race after Sputnik in 1957 enormous funds were devoted to R & D for use of radio as part of missiles, satellites, and space vehicles by the military. It must be remembered that *every* controlled space craft and missile is equipped with communications and is in a sense a communications satellite. The by-product was the spinoff of civilian uses of satellites for communications, remote sensing, navigational aids, etc. In consequence the history of radio frequency allocation planning at the level of the International Telecommunications Union, world regions, and within them, nations, is marked by the "congestion" associated with the interference caused by these cyclical surges of innovation of spectrum-associated services. Every couple of decades these "congestion" pressures lead to major changes in the assignments of services to bands of frequencies by the ITU, as a result of which a new surge of spinoff development of spectrum use can take place.

The Atlantic City plenipotentiary conference of the ITU (1947) was one such major reorganization of frequency planning. As early as the 1920s the United States had considered predominance in radio communication as being on a par with leadership in oil and shipping as bases for imperial expansion.[9] By 1945 the United States held a major share of world radio frequency assignments. In the portions of the spectrum most suitable for long-distance communication, 4 to 20 MHz, more than half the world's supply of "yardstick channels" was registered for United States use, of which 911 out of a world supply of 1200 were in the 4 to 10 MHz regions.[10] This recalls the top priority given control of information by Secretary of State John Foster Dulles (Chapter 1). Clearly, the "free flow of information" doctrine which was basic to United States foreign policy after World War II would rest on continuation of United States hegemony in radio communication among the nations of the world. The ITU had been completely under the control of the advanced countries until the 1947 conference when the Soviet Union and its Eastern bloc allies refused to yield to American domination (Smythe, 1957, pp. 81–101). But with a clear majority of votes in its pocket the United States continued to dominate ITU decisions until at the Geneva Extraordinary Radio Conference in 1963 some Third World nations, as well as the Soviet bloc, were heard in opposition (Schiller, 1969, p. 132). That conference dealt favorably with American demands for frequency assignments to accommodate American commercial communications satellite development (COMSAT). In the next ten years a tide of resistance to the "free flow of information" doctrine emerged from Third World nations in the ITU (especially at the World Administrative Radio Conference on Direct Broadcast Satellites in 1977). In UNESCO a declaration modifying the old UNESCO-UN policy on "free flow" by the addition of assertions of

---

[9] United States Senate, Committee on Interstate Commerce, *Hearings* on Section 6, 71st Congress, 1st Session, pp. 319, 1089. Testimony of Owen D. Young and Captain S. C. Hooper.

[10] United States Senate, Subcommittee of the Committee on Interstate Commerce, *Hearings* pursuant to S. Res. 187, 78th Congress, Extended by S. Res. 24, 79th Congress, 1st Session, Part 1, pp. 110–114. Testimony of Admiral Joseph R. Redman.

cultural autonomy for nations on the receiving end of the one-way flow was adopted in 1978. (See Appendix for further analysis of the political economy of the radio spectrum.)

Canada has conducted its frequency allocation processes in ways strictly compatible with those of the United States and has been a steadfast supporter of the American policy of cultural imperialism in radio matters at all times in the proceedings of ITU and UNESCO. In the 1979 World Administrative Radio Conference (ITU), Canada advanced an "elaborate multilateral coordination process . . ." as an alternative to the planning of the use of the geostationary orbit, the objective of the Nonaligned nations. This was a trial balloon, supported by the United States to block the Nonaligned group (Rutkowski, 1979, p. 12).

As we have noted (see Chapter 4, 5, and 6) the monopoly-capitalist development of the mass media in Canada no less than in the United States set the stage for the innovation of radio broadcasting as a new and supplementary means of producing audiences to market things and ideas to themselves.

Because telecommunications covers all electronic means of communication and increasingly is concerned with computer data, its scope includes a major share of information production and transmission, using the term *information* in the broad sense used by Norbert Wiener (1950, p. 17): what passes between human beings and between them and their environment. It will be recalled (Chapter 1) that the production and processing of information in the more limited sense in which information is defined to include advertising, mass media content of all kinds, package design, accounting records of all kinds, etc., has risen to become 46.2 percent of United States gross national product in 1967. We may close this chapter by referring to what J. Voge might call his *law of information/ subsistence substitution.* His summary of a startling paper, "Economics, Information and Communications," says:

> Statistics gathered by Machlup and Porat, primarily in the USA, indicate that information activities have grown much faster than general economic growth. Taking dollars at their 1958 value the US gross national product per worker is today about $10,000 of which about half represents information activities; at the end of the last century the figures were about $2,500 of which only 12.5% (a little over $300) was for information activities.
>
> One should not be surprised by this trend. The number of workers (manufacturers and distributors) in the information field has increased in proportion to the national product. Their actual productivity has remained constant. *It is normal that the volume of information tends to increase in proportion to the square of the number of the speakers.* C. Northcote Parkinson made this law famous by applying it to bureaucracy; but it is relevant to any activity that involves information.

A maximum level of "maturity," in terms of economic growth, must theoretically be reached when information activities make up 50% of the total national product (which I call the quantum of information). This point will be reached soon in the USA and within a few years in the other leading industrialised countries. *At this stage, to increase the American national product per worker from the existing $10,000 to $12 to 16,000, it would be necessary to raise the information quantum from 50% to about 70%. In this case, the part of GNP made up of physical production would decrease from $5,000 to about $4,000. It is unlikely a society would willingly forego such material wealth in exchange for something—information—that was already considered to be in superabundance.*[11]

The phenomenon which he predicts is already observable in the advanced capitalist countries where food, energy, textiles, building materials become increasingly scarce and expensive while advertising, packaging, and the whole range of record-keeping activities continue to proliferate. At some point the choice will have to be made, not only between missiles and butter, but between information and butter. The fantastic inertial momentum which pushes information production higher and higher, however, comes from profit-seeking institutions which may be counted on to delay remedial steps to bring our process for answering the "what to produce?" question into better balance. M. Voge may be said to have contributed immensely to the study of the ecology of information.

The electronic mass media of communications are to telecommunications as is the portion of the iceberg above water to that which is below. On the foundation laid in this chapter, we move in Chapter 8 to consider radio and television.

---

[11] Voge, M. paper given at International Institute of Communications Conference, 1978, Dubrovnik. M. Voge is Le Directeur Délégue pour les Relations Internationales, Direction Générale des Télécommunications, Secretariat d'Etat aux Postes et Télécommunications, Paris. (Emphasis added.)

MEDIA OF CANADIAN
CULTURAL SUBMISSION III:
BROADCASTING

In regard to radio and television broadcasting, the same tributary relationships to the United States exist that we have observed in the press, periodicals, books, film, and telecommunications industries. As against the perennially reproduced needs and interests of the Canadian people in living their own lives *in their own way* (regularly hailed by national slogans proclaiming the elusive Canadian identity), the operational rule of the Canadian bourgeoisie and of governments for Canadian media in English-speaking Canada has been in reality: "If it is uniquely Canadian, it cannot be much good—unless it will sell in the international (United States) market."

RADIO BROADCASTING

It was argued in Chapter 1 that the capitalist system's mass media were invented and innovated in order to legitimize and direct the development of that social system. In this respect the mass media became a major type of institution, comparable with the educational institutions. Unlike the educational institutions which directly affect mostly children and young people and then only part time, the mass media exercise their role as to all age groups 365 days a year. The electronic media necessarily use the radio spectrum and are therefore dependent on the national state in an inescapable way which distinguishes them from the print and film media. Radio broadcasting, when it was innovated, was treated by every country except the United States and Canada as requiring state control and administration, parallel in a sense to the educational system. Although there were variations in the institutional patterns devised, the British Broadcasting Corporation model was predominant: a state corporation with a certain insulation from the current political scene, financed directly by listener fees, with no advertising, and a program policy which mirrored the upper- and middle-class values in the country. The purpose of such systems was to produce audiences which would be better informed and better assimilated to the bourgeois culture of their society. (Radio broadcasting in the Soviet Union was a state monopoly used to serve the ideological line of the ruling Communist party—a partial exception to this generalization.) The success of such a radio broadcasting policy would be embodied in the reproduction of the kind of people and kind of society which existed before World War I—a class society with class consciousness and recognizable class struggle.

The struggle which shaped the new institutions for conducting broadcasting (aural and television) in both the United States and Canada was between the power of monopoly capitalism on the one hand and a tacit united front of liberal and conservative elements from the churches, trade unions (in Canada more so than in the United States), voluntary community groups (e.g., parent-teachers, home and school groups, etc.), concerned teachers at all levels of educational institutions, professional critics of the arts (e.g., Gilbert Seldes), etc. The principal contradiction in broadcasting became one over the adoption of the BBC or the commercial model. It existed simultaneously with, and intersected the principal contradiction of Canadian nationalism as an expression of the real needs of the Canadian people vs. the forces and relations embodied in monopoly capitalism. This latter and all-encompassing contradiction involved the issue of hegemony (what interests should be in control) at the local, provincial, and national levels in Canada. Subordinate to the *principal contradiction in broadcasting* have been innumerable other contradictions, e.g., the struggle between local and high-power radio stations, between radio broadcasting and the press over broadcast policy especially regarding advertising, between over-the-air television stations and cable television, between cable television and telephone companies, etc.[1]

---

[1] Broadcasting in Canada has been a history of struggles—between two great railway systems; between railway and telephone transmission interests; between provincial and federal authorities as to jurisdiction; between small community and large regional privately

In the sixty years of development of the American model of broadcasting both in the United States and Canada, the forces in the principal contradiction in broadcasting which represented the "public" side won occasional minor tactical victories (e.g., when resistance to the vulgarity of advertising briefly achieved certain standards of "public service"). In the United States the struggle which produced the Federal Communications Commission "Blue Book" (*Public Service Responsibilities of Broadcast Licensees*, 1944) was such. So too was the struggle which gave birth to the Canadian Broadcasting Corporation. But such tactical victories were only delaying actions. And the revolutionary forces of monopoly capitalism, working both sides of the street (i.e., through the propaganda of the commodity "deed" as well as through the propaganda of the advertisements and free lunch), began each tactical surge toward more commercial domination where the last one had been stopped. By the working of Gresham's Law, mass-produced fare specifically designed to optimize the efficiency of the marketing system progressively drove out of circulation public service fare.

Having achieved cultural hegemony north of the Rio Grande by 1945, monopoly capitalism acted on the strategic advantages it then enjoyed on the world scene and beginning in the early fifties innovated the commercial model of broadcasting using television as the battering ram which it had developed in the United States in Canada, the United Kingdom, Australia, and other Commonwealth and non-Commonwealth countries. In doing so it took advantage of the systemic blind spot which the ideology of capitalism had embedded in the consciousness of bourgeois society. Because it had *seemed* that the publication of news was the principal product and purpose of nineteenth century newspapers (whereas in reality it had always been the production of audiences disposed to accept a certain ideology), it *seemed* as if the important aspect of broadcasting was the program content serving John Stuart Mill's conception of a "free marketplace of ideas." Possessive individualism and pluralism thus masked the fact that what was now to be produced was collective action by audience members in the service of the ideology of corporate capitalism. That bourgeois and Marxist intellectuals alike were victims of this blind spot made the task of monopoly capitalism infinitely easier because its left and left-liberal "progressive" opponents were effectively disarmed ideo-

---

owned stations for a share of limited revenues; between hucksters and the intellectuals; between artists demanding adequate remuneration for their talent and stations occasionally struggling to make ends meet but occasionally ready to take any and every advantage of talent; between aspiring amateurs and trained professionals; between various program elements, regions and language groups seeking places in the sun as well as their share of available dollars; between bureaucracy and creativity, and, encompassing all these, between public and private broadcasting (Weir, 1965, p. 449).

logically. The flexibility of pluralist ideology is illustrated by advertisers who argue seriously that advertising, being the voice of the legal "person" of a corporation, is protected by the right to free speech in Anglo Saxon law (e.g., by the First Amendment to the United States Constitution).

Radio broadcasting in its first decade in the United States and Canada was fumbling toward a viable institutional arrangement. The giant monopoly corporations whose patent agreements at the close of World War I made possible their innovation of radio broadcasting were by no means agreed as to the form it should take.[2] ATT intended to monopolize broadcasting through building and operating stations and permitting community program groups to use them—for a price—a model based on the public pay station telephone.[3] RCA, however, preferred to exploit its radio patent position by licensing a large number of manufacturers to produce radio transmitters and receivers. ATT built and operated the first New York radio station, and offered the first North American network broadcasts. RCA's policy prevailed by 1925 when ATT sold out its interest in broadcasting. The way was clear for the licensed manufacturers (and RCA itself) which built stations and used music and other entertainment as the lure to get audiences to buy receivers. Newspaper publishers, scenting a rival for audience production to sell to advertisers, built more stations than any other industrial class of station owners and shortly formed an association to prevent the flow of news to radio stations. The economic base of radio broadcasting, American-style, was to be advertising.

The public side of the struggle to determine the nature of broadcasting however, was strongly represented by the educators. In June, 1922, of a total of 382 broadcast stations, educational institutions operated 79, followed by 69 operated by newspapers with the remainder a scattering of municipal, labor and commercial enterprises. In 1927 when the Federal Radio Commission was formed, the majority of the 732 broadcast stations were not selling time and 90 of them were operated by educational institutions. Less than a hundred stations were network affiliates (Barnouw, 1966, p. 98, 209).

But how was competitive enterprise to be reconciled with the fact that the number of possible radio broadcast station frequency assignments was limited by the nature of the radio spectrum? Coolidge's Secretary of Commerce, Herbert Hoover, presided over "think sessions" by American businessmen in annual conferences from 1922 to 1925 as they wrestled with this contradiction. The Radio Act of 1912 which he administered had not foreseen radio broadcasting and provided him no guidance. By

---

[2] See Chapter 4 for the description of the agreements resolving the patent impasse.
[3] This was as late as 1923, see Daniellian (1939, pp. 123–124).

1925 there were some 600 radio broadcast stations in the United States, when Canada had 34. Under existing international regulations, 95 channels were available for both countries. Under repeated urging from Canada, the United States agreed to allow Canada the exclusive use of six of these plus shared use of 11 other channels. Following the logic of his ideology, the president of Zenith Radio Corporation "jumped" his Chicago station to a channel allocated to Canada and was supported in doing so by the United States courts. Hoover thereupon abandoned his efforts to rationalize the licensing of radio stations and referred the problem to Congress. In 1927, the United States Radio Act of that year resolved the impasse, institutionalizing a new contradiction: that between public service and profits. Private commercial radio stations would be licensed by a regulatory commission (the Federal Radio Commission, succeeded by the Federal Communications Commission in 1934) for terms of no longer than five years. Competition for licenses through promises of performance, and performance itself in the case of renewal of licenses, would result in the licensing of the applicant best qualified to serve the "public interest" (undefined). In legal theory the licensee acquired no title to his frequency assignment and if he sold the station no value could be attached to the license. In practice, the values of licenses have been capitalized in such transactions. There would be no program "censorship" by the commission; if a station sold air time to one candidate for political office it must sell air time to the candidate's rivals. This was the model which Canadian broadcasters would later struggle successfully to achieve in Canada.

Before it could be successfully implanted in the United States, however, the educational radio stations had to be substantially eliminated. And Consciousness Industry used the Federal Radio Commission to this end. According to E. Pendleton Herring,

> While talking in terms of the public interest, convenience and necessity, the Commission actually chose to further the ends of the commercial broadcasters. They form the substantive content of public interest as interpreted by the Radio Commission (Herring, p. 173).

Of a total of 95 educational stations licensed between 1927 and 1932, only 33 were still on the air by 1933. The tactics used to get rid of educational stations included forced reduction in power, forced share-time relationships with commercial stations, and repeated changes of frequency. The Carnegie Corporation and John D. Rockefeller, Jr. even organized a nationwide committee to lobby locally for the proposition that commercial broadcasters would provide free time for education (Barnouw, 1966, p. 261–262).

Canada, which had been involved in Marconi's first transoceanic radio transmissions, was notably indecisive in establishing institutional arrangements for radio broadcasting. The first Canadian broadcast station was set up by Canadian Marconi in 1920, and physicist A. S. Eve in presenting the first over-the-air demonstration of radio broadcasting to the Royal Society of Canada observed that it was one of "Some Great War Inventions" (Peers, 1969, p. 5). Apart from set manufacturers, the innovators of radio broadcasting in Canada were mostly big city newspapers, churches, and the Canadian National Railways. Under regulations by the Department of Marine, the licensing agent, "direct advertising" was forbidden between 6:30 and 11:00 PM in 1922. Indeed express permission was required before direct advertising might be broadcast and then "such permission will only be granted in special cases," as late as 1929 (Weir, 1965, p. 25). A year later, apparently following the American example, it encouraged nondirect (i.e., institutional) advertising without restriction. The record is replete with disavowals of advertising—or anyway offensive advertising—on radio in Canada (Sir Henry Thornton of CNR rejected "an atmospheric billboard") as in the United States.[4] At the same time in Canada radio listeners' fees were established at $1.00 per annum by the Department of Marine in 1922.

The relatively small number of Canadian radio broadcast stations in the 1920s were typically low power, with irregular transmissions. Their service was especially poor to Canadian rural areas, where 40 percent of the receivers were located (Peers, 1969, p. 21). Not surprisingly under the existing conditions, "From the beginning, Canadians listened to American stations more than to their own"—especially to programs from NBC (from 1926) and CBS (the next year) (Peers, 1969, p. 20). So scarce were Canadian radio frequency assignments that for years *phantom* stations operated. (Broadcasters who did not own the station they used.) In such cases the phantom station, using its own call letters, broadcast from a station whose facilities it contracted for—a practice resembling the "pay station" model which ATT had wanted to establish in the United States. The program structure of stations was unstandardized: clock hours and their subdivisions did not rule programs which were mostly music. News was virtually excluded from radio for ten years, by action of the Canadian newspapers beginning in 1926.

The entrance of the CNR—a Crown corporation, albeit one primarily concerned with railroads—into radio broadcasting in the mid-1920s provided a prototype of what CBC would later do. On a one-time basis it

---

[4] See Barnouw (1966) for similarly efulgent proclamations from Herbert Hoover, David Sarnoff, etc.

broadcast the first network program in Canada in December 1923. The following year it planned a transcontinental network of stations with its own key stations in Montreal, Moncton, and Vancouver. Indicative of Canada's dependency on the United States is that until July 1931 any transcontinental radio network broadcast used telephone circuits in the United States between Detroit and Seattle. Regular CNR network operation began in December 1929 with ambitious cultural programs. It broadcast the Toronto Symphony Orchestra a year before CBS began its broadcasts of the New York Symphony Orchestra. Although the express reason for the CNR's broadcast activity was to encourage tourism, its integrative cultural purpose was also evident. The private stations were not threatened (or regulated) by it and found it a profitable source of programs and advertising revenues.

The procrastinating posture of the Canadian government regarding the sort of broadcast policy it would adopt continued until the end of the 1920s. Britain had obtained the benefit of two royal commission reports in 1923 and 1925. And the United States had crystallized its policy with the Radio Act of 1927. Finally in 1928 the Canadian Aird Royal Commission was created. Fittingly enough for a conservative capitalist country the issue which provoked its appointment was religious: controversies over attacks by radio stations operated by fundamentalist sects against the denominations dominated by middle-class Protestants and the Roman Catholics. The Aird Commission was obviously impressed by the growing penetration of the American radio networks into Canada (by 1932 four leading Canadian stations—two in Montreal and two in Toronto were affiliated with United States networks, and NBC was known to have a plan to extend its network coverage into Canada). Its report emphasized the public (i.e., educational) import of radio broadcasting and therefore recommended that *all* broadcasting in Canada should be owned and operated by a Crown corporation, with provincial control of programs broadcast within it. In this respect it was consistent with the BBC pattern.

But contrary to widespread misinterpretation of its report, the Aird Commission did *not* propose that the broadcast system be financed entirely from listener fees and therefore free of advertising. It recommended that three sources of revenue be used: listener fees, indirect advertising, and if necessary, subsidy by the federal government. And it expected advertising to yield one-fourth of total revenues. The hope that advertising could be limited to indirect (i.e., institutional) advertising was either naive or hypocritical, no more than a pious wish. From this time on, Canadian broadcast policy, like that in the United States, contained within it the contradictory forces standing for established and publicly determined values on the one hand and the policy of Consciousness Industry on the other. In this respect the Aird report differed fundamentally from the BBC model which excluded all advertising and financed itself through listener fees. It proposed a Crown corporation which would internalize the struggle between public service and profit. As one of its members, Dr. Augustin Frigon, was to say in 1932, ". . . you cannot mix up the interests of the man who wants to make money out of the equipment and the man who wants to render service to his country"(Weir, 1965, p. 111). Yet this contradiction has been central to the Canadian policy since then.

The period, 1930 to 1936, witnessed a struggle between the popular forces in Canada fighting for public service broadcasting and those seeking private profit. And because the basic pattern of later Canadian radio and television policy was established in that struggle it deserves careful attention. The popular forces were organized around the Canadian Radio League, led by two young Canadians, Graham Spry and Alan Plaunt, both from establishment backgrounds, but possessed of liberal, nationalistic zeal. They found enthusiastic support from trade unions (the All-Canadian Congress of Labour and the Trades and Labour Congress), the churches (United Church, Roman Catholic, and Anglican), farm groups (the United Farmers of Alberta and Saskatchewan), the Canadian Legion, principal women's organizations (National Council of Women, Catholic Women's League, IODE, Federation of Canadian Women, Hadassah of Canada), educational leaders (Universities Conference, Royal Society of Canada), senior officers of the banks (Royal, Bank of Commerce, Bank of Nova Scotia, Imperial Bank of Canada), and insurance company executives. In the political sector their supporters included two former Prime Ministers (Borden and Meighen), a future Prime Minister (Louis St. Laurent), Sir John Aird, Vincent Massey, and George Wrong. As if to validate vulgar determinist theory, a substantial number of newspapers that did not own radio stations supported the Canadian Radio League, including two owned by the Southam family.

Opposed to implementation of the Aird report was a long list of large corporations, prominent among which were branch plants of the United States TNCs (Swift Canadian, Quaker Oats, The Borden Company, Pepsodent Company, Philco, Canadian National Carbon, Wm. Wrigley Company, Robert Simpson Company, Imperial Tobacco, Dominion Stores, Rogers Majestic), large private radio stations, four major newspapers, the Canadian Manufacturers Association, and the CPR. This last was very active in organizing the opposition. Graham Spry is quoted as saying in March 1931:

> The opposition to a Canadian Radio Broadcasting Company is now coming from three sources, one, R. W. Ashcroft [manager of the *Telegram* station in Toronto] and the private stations owners, publicly; two, from the American radio group by quiet methods and by visitors appearing in Toronto and Montreal to praise the American system and damn the British; three, from the

Canadian Pacific Railway through newspapers, and radio papers circulating in Canada, under its influence, through the Canadian Broadcasters Association, through quiet methods known to them but becoming obvious to us; and through the personal intervention of E. W. Beatty [president of the CPR] by conversation with our people and by correspondence (quoted in Peers, 1969, p. 72).

The focus of the first battle was the parliamentary committee in 1932 which was considering radio legislation.

Specifically, how did the two forces differ? The Canadian Radio League at that time had retreated from the Aird Commission position in favor of public ownership of *all* radio stations and proposed publicly owned high-power stations operating a network to feed free programs to local commercial stations. Whereas the Aird Commission would have eliminated all but indirect advertising, the CRL would allow up to 5 percent of time for advertising for both public and private stations. The CPR proposed that there be created a Canadian Broadcasting Company in which railways would participate along with other interests as shareholders. The company would acquire key stations to form a network. It would carry advertising but the CPR wanted it to receive a portion of the license fees at the beginning at least. This "Canadian Broadcasting Company" and the private stations would be regulated by a radio commission to exercise general control over broadcasting, advertising, policy on controversial broadcasts, etc. It was a proposal obviously modeled on the American precedent. The CNR by that time was cutting back its radio service and looked forward to selling wire service to whatever network would emerge.

Considerable public heat was generated around the hearings of the 1932 parliamentary committee, as well as an incredible amount of lobbying. Graham Spry's testimony was clearly the climax of the hearings. As part of a comprehensive and careful analysis of the facts and the legislation, his testimony is summarized by Peers as follows:

. . . Spry quoted Judge Robinson, former chairman of the Federal Radio Commission, on the growth of monopoly in American broadcasting, and also three senators on the "radio trust." He suggested that one group in North America (the group associated with RCA) "controls the greatest agencies of public entertainment, popular education and communication, the manufacture of the equipment of these services, and allied arts and industries." Then he described the American connections of witnesses appearing before the Committee in opposition to the Aird Report: CKGW; CFRB; the Radio Manufacturers Association "representing Canadian radio factories in which sixty percent of the capital, according to the Bureau of Statistics, is American . . . Station CKNC, of the Canadian National Carbon Company, a subsidiary of the National Carbon Company of the United States." Spry noted that "there has also been present, without intervening, a counsel of the National Broadcasting Company, before this Committee, who is reporting to Mr. Aylesworth" [President of NBC].

"Why are the American interests so interested in the Canadian situation? The reason is clear. In the first place, the American chains have regarded Canada as part of their field and consider Canada as in a state of radio tutelage, without talent, resources or capacity to establish a third chain on this continent. . . . In the second place, if such a Canadian non-commercial chain were constructed, it would seriously weaken the whole advertising basis of American broadcasting. The question before this Committee is whether Canada is to establish a chain that is owned and operated and controlled by Canadians, or whether it is to be owned and operated by commercial organizations, associated or controlled by American interests. The question is, the State or the United States" (Peers, 1969, pp. 90–91).

This probably was the high point of Canadian national consciousness. The Report of the Parliamentary Commission followed in most respects the position taken by the popular forces of the CRL. Its provisions, when enacted in law in 1932, created a Canadian Radio Broadcasting Commission with a mandate to build a national system. The spine of the system would be a chain of high-power stations, probably five 50 KW, one 10 KW, two 5 KW, six lower-power stations, and a number of 100 w stations. The public network would feed programs to local private stations for community purposes. Financing should be self-sustaining from listener license fees and advertising, the latter limited to 5 percent of each program period, but unlike the Aird recommendation, the finances were not under the control of CRBC, being allocated by the government. Administration of the whole system would be by a nonpartisan commission of three. Its regulatory power was comprehensive. It should regulate all broadcasting; could lease, buy, or expropriate any or all existing private stations, control the issue and cancelation of licenses, prohibit private networks, and subject to parliamentary approval, take over all broadcasting in Canada. The 1932 act seemed consistent with the Aird Commission report: a national system, possibly entirely publicly owned. Three weaknesses distinguished it from the BBC. First, it encapsulated within itself the irreconcilable contradictory forces of public services and the production of audiences for advertisers. Second, it did not forthrightly order the expropriation of the private stations. By deferring this action and leaving discretion to a regulatory agency, it left the door open for the private, commercial lobby to work on both future legislatures and the administrative agency to reverse the effect of the intended policy. Third, the CRBC did not have budgetary autonomy and was dependent for funds on whatever pressure groups dominated the Canadian government.

The CRBC was a far cry from the BBC, but it would have been unthinkable that the parallel forces favoring public broadcasting in the

United States should have attained as much. But the popular forces—social democratic, social gospel, liberal, and reformist as they were—in Canada had what those in the United States lacked: a nationalist issue and national institutions which, whatever their weaknesses, were potential tools of the Canadian people. Although the victorious CRL could not have succeeded in this effort without the overt support of much of the ruling class (including newspapers whose self-interest was seen to be served by it), the effort drew broad support from the working class of European-derived Canadians. The interests of indigenous peoples of Canada were not considered. It was a sweeping victory for the CRL and its dedicated and able leaders, Spry and Plaunt. But it was ominous that this exercise in Canadian nationalism, based as it was in the superstructural concerns with education and bourgeois culture, was mounted successfully at the very time when United States capitalism was consolidating its control of Canadian resources (see Chapter 5).

The immediate sequel was anticlimactic. The government took a negative, reluctant approach to the administration of the 1932 act. Frank Peers, in his careful study of the period, put it well: "Canadian public authority was most reluctant to interfere with private initiative or with property values" (Peers, 1969, p. 116). Even if the disposition of the Conservative government had been favorable, the act would have been extremely difficult to administer successfully. In essential ways it had created the CRBC as merely another government department. The CRBC was required to recruit its unique type of staff through civil service procedures. Its revenues (from license fees and advertising) were channeled through the Consolidated Revenue Fund of the government, to be released through Treasury Board and government procedures. It had no power to borrow money. No statutory provision was made for the commissioners to use senior officers who would bear responsibility for operational details, which were effectively made the business not only of the commissioners but the minister of marine, the cabinet, and Parliament as well. Moreover it appears that in the selection of the first three Commissioners, the government chose men lacking in administrative experience. In the resulting policy situation from 1932 to 1936, the public service component in the CRBC was slighted and restrained, while the never-ending lobbying pressures of the private sector were supported.

The establishment of a nationwide chain of radio stations, the creation of a program-producing organization and facilities, the establishment of engineering standards and frequency allocation policy, the regulations as to advertising and controversial issues broadcasting, the negotiations with telecommunications carriers for wire-line networks—all added up to a monumental task which would require generous financial support. The Aird Commission had estimated a budget of $2.5 million a year, and the CRL, taking account of depression-reduced prices, estimated the budget needed in 1933–34 at $1.5 million. But while taking in license fees $1,290,000 in 1932–33, the government allowed the CRBC only $150,000 in that year and $1 million in 1933–34. The policy of fiscal deprivation for public service purposes thus established was a bipartisan policy which still exists.

In the event, the CRBC moved timidly in building its own stations. Apart from acquiring the CNR stations, it built only two 1 KW stations (Québec and Windsor) and began building a 5 KW station in Vancouver in its four years, and developed a chain of 8 stations, several of which were leased, while the number of private stations grew to 72. The reversal of the spirit of the act is shown by the CRBC's having to *pay* the high-power private stations (affiliated with United States networks) in Toronto and Montreal to broadcast its network programs; in 1934–35 payments to such politically powerful stations accounted for 18 percent of CRBC expenditures (Peers, 1969, p. 134).

Despite its handicaps the CRBC managed to broadcast two and a half hours of national network programs each evening, plus Sunday afternoons, and regional programs by Autumn 1933. By 1936 it had generated a considerable volume of programs superior to those available from the private sector. Network news programs for the first time provided Canadians with an alternative to the local preoccupations of the newspapers' "free lunch." Special events (commemoration of Jacques Cartier's landing in Canada, the Silver Jubilee of King George V, the installation of a new Governor-General) contributed to national consciousness. Dramatized historical events programs, weekly talks, and a regular service broadcast to the North, "Northern Messenger," had a similar effect. Its program policy inevitably raised in acute form the issue of bilingualism. Even French introductory announcements in programs irritated politically powerful prairie figures whose lobbying for the private sector unquestioningly identified Canada with American culture. At the same time the predominance of English-language programing on the CRBC network irritated Francophone Canada which correctly perceived the Anglo-American erosion of its culture. With all its internal contradictions, CRBC programing made substantial progress toward national coverage. By 1936, 60 percent of the population were within the effective service areas in the daytime, and 49 percent at night (because of skywave interference, mostly from American and Mexican stations).

Nowhere was the struggle in broadcasting's principal contradiction more evident in this period than in the actions and words of the government. Prime Minister Bennett's speeches gave ample recognition (lip service though it was mostly) to the public service forces supporting the legislative purpose of the act. But in 1934, he was persuading parliamentary supporters of the private sector to allow the CRBC one more year to "adjust its affairs" (Peers, 1969, p. 146). In 1935 a plot of 27 Conservative members sought to take advantage of the prime minister's absence from the country to authorize power increases to 50 KW for three prairie private stations while limiting the life of CRBC to two months. The acting prime minister, however, faltered and Prime Minister Bennett, returning home, denounced the "sinister conspiracy" and persuaded his party to a six-months extension to "let another parliament decide whether it [CRBC] should be abolished or its powers modified" (Peers, 1969, pp. 153–154). In the same debates the minister responsible for the CRBC praised it because the private stations were being allowed to carry advertising ". . . for as much as 15 percent of their time" despite the statutory limit of 5 percent (Peers, 1969, p. 155). Peers (1969, p. 161) remarks:

> In 1932 the broadcasters themselves had urged the limitations on advertising which the commission attempted to enforce. This did not prevent them from appearing at the 1934 committee to complain that these restrictions were putting them out of business; their complaints then led to a speedy relaxation of the regulations.

From the standpoint of the private sector of broadcasting, great progress was made under the CRBC. They had survived intact or with higher power than before. Advertising standards had proved to be readily relaxable as the public adjusted its taste to ever-more intrusive advertising. It is interesting that the CRBC had also positively assisted them. Between 1933 and 1935 the number of private stations which met CRBC's technical standards rose from 12 to 52 because "the Commission with its competent engineering staff, was of definite help by way of advice and assistance" (Weir, 1965, p. 185). And structurally the private sector was strengthened in this period by the formation in 1934 of the Canadian Newspaper Radio Association (of newspaper-owned radio stations). It included stations owned by the Southam and Sifton newspapers which in 1932 had supported the CRL. From this point on, the majority of Canadian newspapers supported commercial rather than public service broadcasting.

How should the crucial first four years of public broadcasting be assessed? The interlocked forces of private stations, advertising agencies, advertisers, and newspapers, backed by an increasing fraction of the Canadian ruling class had the initiative and improved on their opportunities. While Canadian nationalistic rhetoric was a powerful tool of the advocates of public service broadcasting, the principal contradiction was tilting in favor of Consciousness Industry. Peers is correct when he observes that even if somehow the CRBC had been given the budget and authority necessary to produce and broadcast a full national service as envisioned by Aird:

> . . . it could not have won the majority of listeners for Canadian programs. American advertisers were not only appealing to popular tastes but creating a popular culture which was continental in scope (Peers, 1969, p. 157).

Inevitably the split between the United States–oriented Anglo-Canadian and the Francophone communities was painfully obvious. It seems that the dominant classes and institutions were capable of emotional nationalism on the idealistic level while acting realistically in the patterns set by United States Consciousness Industry.

Against the backdrop of analysis of the period 1932–1936, we consider the Canadian Broadcasting Corporation and its policies in radio broadcasting in the years 1936–1953—what has been called *the golden age* of CBC radio. In 1936 a new Liberal government used a parliamentary committee to provide all interests opportunity to state their positions. The advertising agencies, advertisers, and private broadcasters all lobbied hard for what was to become a 30-year campaign: regulation by a government agency (in this case the Department of Marine) and reduction of public broadcasting to a program-producing-and-distributing organization. Mr. Plaunt, for the CRL, conducted a skillful campaign for reaffirmation of the CRL's 1932 program. After a surprisingly low-key struggle, the committee report and ensuing act *did* reaffirm the policy originally stated by the Aird Commission.

There was created a new body—the Canadian Broadcasting Corporation—headed by a board of nine members, a manager, and an assistant manager, and with a larger measure of organizational autonomy than the CRBC had enjoyed. License fees and other revenues would be automatically available to the CBC and it could borrow money and hire staff free of civil service procedures. "The principle of complete nationalization of radio broadcasting in Canada" was reaffirmed. Until such a condition existed, full cooperation between the CBC and private stations under the plenary regulatory power of the former was to exist. Coverage should be increased either by establishing new CBC stations or adding private stations to the network. Technical regulation was vested in the Department of Marine (as Aird had proposed) but that minister should obtain the recommendation of the CBC before licensing a broadcast station. Political broadcasts should be allocated equitably between the parties, with open sponsorship, with no dramatization and no political broadcasts on election day or the two immediately preceding days. The government appointed a competent Board, with a brilliant chairman, and the CBC chose a competent manager and assistant manager. After four years of fumbling, the public service policy was to be given a reasonable chance of success. Or so it seemed and in a sense was. But the tactics and pressures which had been demonstrated earlier were to continue.

The bipartisan tight restraint on CBC station construction was pursued staunchly by C. D. Howe, Minister of Marine—who believed that the willingness of Americans to invest so much money in Canada was the best possible indicator of progress (Newman, 1975, p. 327). The Board proposed a construction program, phased over three years, which would yield 13 CBC stations plus relay stations in British Columbia, northern Ontario, and northern Québec, calculated to provide service to 84 percent of the population. The capital cost was $2,200,000. In the first of a series of hard personal confrontations with Howe, which may be taken as typical, the Board understood him to respond that, regardless of their statutory mandate; (1) CBC should become only a program-production organization; (2) improvement of broadcast facilities should be left to private capital; (3) public opinion did not support public ownership of broadcast facilities; (4) complaints from Saskatchewan and the Maritimes should be disregarded because those areas were receiving all the CBC service which their geographical and economic position warranted (Peers, 1969, pp. 202–203). The Board stood firm and won the first round. Between 1936 and 1938 the total wattage of CBC stations increased from 14,200 to 112,200 watts, while private stations increased from 64,000 to 69,000 watts (Weir, 1965, p. 216). By the latter date, network coverage had risen to 78 percent; when the new stations in Saskatchewan and the Maritimes were operative, it would rise to 84 percent. Howe disagreed with this plan and before he approved the financing for the Saskatchewan station, the Board had threatened resignation and a broadcast to give the reasons for it. As Weir (1965, pp. 217–218) says of this recurrent problem:

> The Minister's opposition, although based on principle, coincided with pressures from other sources anxious to stop the Corporation in its tracks. At that time, a powerful group within the Liberal Party was also seeking higher power for another station on the Prairies.

The CBC Board even on occasion went on the offensive. Thus in 1939, Chairman Brockington, in speaking to the Parliamentary Committee said:

> Anybody who occupies the public domain enjoys a franchise that is in the nature of a public utility. The principle of public utility ownership is that it shall be highly regulated and that there shall be limitations on its profits with surplus profits going back for the improvement of the public service. . . . Now the CBC does not want, and I am sure nobody else wants, to prohibit private radio stations making a reasonable profit. But I think the essential interests of the community demand that there shall be no profiteering in private radio. I am going to suggest for the consideration of this Committee some legislation whereby the profits of holders of a franchise be-

ing part of the public domain should be limited rather than increased (Weir, 1965, p. 220).

It would be tedious to recount every round in the struggle over funds for capital expansion. So successful were the opponents of public broadcasting that it was not until the mid-1960s that CBC coverage with its own stations met the Aird Commission recommendations 35 years late—by which time its coverage had effectively shrunk because of increased noise from the large numbers of United States and Canadian private stations, power tools, household gadgets, etc. High-power public broadcasting from publicly owned stations was another Canadian dream aborted.

Because of its chronic impoverishment, CBC became perforce an invaluable ally of Consciousness Industry in making possible production of nationwide audiences which otherwise would have been unattainable for sale to advertisers. CBC was seeking both to build nationwide audiences through its network and to serve them as many hours a day as possible. In 1936 it had produced about 6 hours a day of network programs; by 1938 this had risen to 16 or more; in later years the hours of service increased further. But CBC's operating budget forbade programing these many hours *with its own* productions if program quality was to be at all competitive with that offered by private stations. As Weir (1965, pp. 224–225) puts it:

> Canadian branches of American-owned enterprises could reach the most concentrated population centres and the most profitable areas of Canada at very little additional cost. Many American sponsors were ready to extend their coverage over the less densely settled areas of Canada, provided it could be done at reasonable additional cost. The task ahead of the CBC was to induce these advertisers to extend their programs across the country and share in the programming of the entire network, instead of confining their coverage to only parts of one or two regions.

> Commercials were important in the network schedule, not only for revenue alone but perhaps even more for the hours they filled with popular audience-building programs. This relieved the Corporation of the obligation of filling a great deal of time with what, in many cases, due to the CBC's limited budget, must inevitably have been mediocre production.

Whereas the CRBC had confined its sponsored radio programs to its owned and operated *stations*, CBC began with a policy of carrying sponsored *network* programs. CBC introduced a system of regional discounts, by which sponsors were given station time for progressively smaller prices the further from the center of the lucrative markets one moved out. This was a system never employed by the American networks. Together with regional discounts, CBC negotiated tremendous reductions in wire-line charges for network transmission of commercial sponsors' programs. For radio this meant that when a nationwide audience was produced for advertisers, CBC just about broke even; when less than the entire network was used, CBC earned a small surplus on the program. In either case the advertiser reached a broader audience market than a private network would have produced. The same regional discount plan was later used by CBC for television, but there it involved heavy subsidies by CBC (and tax-payers) to the lucky advertisers. In radio the private stations got half of their published network rates and CBC absorbed all discounts and agency commissions of 15 percent. In addition, the private stations received the full CBC sustaining service free of charge and were obliged to broadcast certain important public service programs. CBC treated the private stations more generously than did United States networks which paid affiliates nothing for the first 16 hours of commercial network programs per month and for the next 25 hours only 25 percent of the station's network rates. In dollar terms CBC paid stations 54 percent more than did the United States networks (Weir, 1965, pp. 227–228).

These arrangements between the CBC, the advertisers, and the private stations distressed Canadian newspaper and magazine publishers who resented the "diversion" of advertising revenues from themselves. The CBC response was: help us raise the listener fee from $2.00 to $3.00 and we will not need nor seek so much advertising revenue. As the CBC general manager advised C. D. Howe in 1937, the newspapers were prepared to support the $3.00 license fee. The venality of the press was evident from an article in *Marketing:*

> A constructive suggestion was made that if the CBC would seek to secure its needed additional revenue by increasing the license fee on radio sets, the press would stand back of it and help the public realize that such increase was just and necessary; otherwise the press would have to consider the advisability of revealing what the CBC is doing in flooding Canada with United States programs (quoted in Peers, 1969, pp. 214–215).

In fact many newspapers attacked the increase in fees *and* the alleged flood of United States programs, especially the *Globe and Mail*, the *Montreal Gazette*, and the *Montreal Star*.

Thanks to the astuteness of the Board and management of CBC and to the dedication of the people they employed, CBC programing *did* perform a nation-building role. In 1938 the CBC Drama Department was formed. During the next four years it considered more than a thousand plays a year of which about 350 were broadcast—none of them commercially sponsored. Possibly the most significant feature of CBC programing, however, was its work for farmers and fishermen:

The first CBC programs of special interest to farmers were instituted in Quebec on April 11, 1938, with "Reveil Rural" which has continued ever since. In 1939, the English Farm Department was started. . . . On a regional basis, it was soon furnishing the latest market prices and information, including daily fifteen minute serials on farm life and problems. Later it began "Farm Forum" which has not only persisted here but has spread to many other countries around the world. The Farm Department has given continuous encouragement to the co-operative movement, and has recruited a large number of extremely able young men. . . . It keeps in daily—almost hourly—contact with every movement of importance in today's agricultural world (Weir, 1965, p. 268).

During World War II, CBC's own National News Service was established, and radio was imaginatively used in all aspects of the war effort. High bourgeois culture was amply celebrated in music, grand opera, literature, poetry, and theater. CBC maintained its own symphony orchestra and grand opera troupe and encouraged the development of Canadian talent—singers, instrumentalists, comedians, etc., through competitions conducted over the air. Canadian talent in drama was cultivated.

During the year 1948–49, three hundred plays were presented, 92 percent by Canadian authors. There were sixty from Vancouver, forty-seven from Winnipeg, sixty-five from Montreal, twenty-five from Halifax, and 103 from Toronto. These figures do not include the many productions of "CBC Sunday Night" or any on the commercial programs (Weir, 1965, p. 274).

Especially for the intellectual elite from 1947 on, Wednesday night's programs were cleared of all commercial matter and devoted to ". . . a varied diet for the discriminating listener, free from interruption": plays, poetry, and music. Public service programing also included a much-used school broadcast schedule and special events of national significance. Regarded as a whole, CBC's public service radio programing between 1936 and the mid-1950s was at least comparable to that of BBC and state-operated radio service in Europe. Nothing resembling it came from the United States commercial system and it would not have happened in Canada if left to the private sector. In addition, of course, CBC programed the most highly regarded commercial programs derived from the United States—comedy, variety, musical, and dramatic. The French CBC network was even more successful than the English. All in all, CBC radio from 1936 to the mid-1950s was a battlefield on which the Canadian people made progress toward cultural hegemony, only to find their never-achieved economic hegemony limiting the extent and duration of their cultural offensive.

It is indicative of the strength of the private sector influence on radio that it was equally effective through both the Liberal and Conservative parties from the time of the Aird report (1930) to 1946 when the Conservative party began a consistent policy of open and complete support for the private sector. In that 16-year period the Liberal party created the Aird Commission and the CBC in 1936. The Conservative government established the CRBC (1932) and acquiesced in the establishment of public service broadcasting in the CBC (1936). In both parties the lobby for high-power private stations effectively enforced the tight rein on CBC financing which marked the whole period of radio, 1932 to the mid-1950s. The ruling class in Canada thus followed a bipartisan policy which sought to encourage both public service and commercial broadcasting in the unstable setting of the CRBC and the CBC. But during World War II, private radio prospered even more than did newspapers in terms of profits, and newspaper publishers joined forces with non-newspaper-owned private stations to press ever harder for "freedom" from "regulation" by their "competitor," the CBC. In reality, the CBC was notoriously lax in enforcing its regulations for the private stations and, as noted, had greatly increased the revenues of the latter by the terms on which it supplied them with both sponsored and unsponsored programs.

TELEVISION BROADCASTING

The advent of television destroyed the uneasy compromise between public service and private profit which had been the basis of the CBC's unique program performance. If Canada had seriously intended to protect its culture from total domination by United States Consciousness Industry, drastic measures would have been employed. Instead of adopting the same technical standards for television as were used in the United States, Canada would have adopted different and superior standards (French, British, or German). At the gateway points (e.g., Toronto, Montreal, Vancouver) selected United States programs would be transcoded from the United States standards to the Canadian for broadcast in Canada. European countries have done such transcoding through the Eurovision network when it is deemed in the national interest to import television programs. Total CBC ownership of all television stations would have been mandatory. The financial base of CBC would have been federally funded budgets for five- to ten-year periods. Through prohibition of the importation or production of television sets designed on United States standards, the viewing of United States television programs received directly from United States stations would have been prevented. When the technique of cable television developed in the United States, Canada would have restricted cable television operations to those employed by CBC to improve reception in big cities. All these measures were adopted by some European countries. None of them was considered worthy of discussion nor adopted in Canada. The integration of Canada's culture and ruling class with that of the United States by the end of World War II had progressed so far as to make such protective measures laughably impossible. United States dominated Consciousness Industry did quietly in Canada beginning in 1948 what it did more controversially in Britain, Australia, New Zealand, and elsewhere in the 1950s: penetrate and ultimately take over the public service institutional model which had been adopted (largely on the BBC model) for radio broadcasting.

The initiative to innovate television in Canada came from the electronics industry, mostly United States branch plants, eager to develop a market for receivers and station equipment. Thus far the pattern followed the precedent of radio in the 1920s. Television—as compared with radio—required many times the capital investment, and many times the operating expenses during the initial promotional period before it could become a sufficiently productive medium for advertisers to pay back the get-started costs, let alone provide the anticipated profits. In the postwar period:

> Soon the manufacturers of television equipment began to press Ottawa to open up the Canadian market by providing a program service that would ensure the nation-wide purchase of sets (Weir, 1965, p. 256).

In the United States the television industry had to provide the capital to build the network facilities and to provide the initial program service (free lunch) which would induce people to buy television receivers. In Canada the capital for both purposes was to be put up by the taxpayers. C. D. Howe was happy to oblige.

The tight fiscal rein on CBC was replaced by the spur. Abruptly, in March 1949, the government directed the CBC to establish television production centers in Montreal and Toronto as quickly as possible and to limit private television stations to one per market. A loan of $4 million was given it. The listener-viewer license fee was abandoned in 1953 and henceforth the CBC would be directly dependent on the government for annual grants and on advertising revenue. The first two CBC stations began broadcasting in 1952. The same year it was ordered to extend television nationally, with six of its own stations. Of these three were in relatively small markets (Halifax, Winnipeg, and Ottawa). The remainder of the country ws to be served by private stations (including the capitals of five of the ten provinces). From 1952 to 1961 no CBC stations were built; only private. And to give all possible advantage to private stations, CBC station construction budgets were severely limited. In Toronto the government prevented the CBC from spending enough to build its antenna on the best site. The result was to restrict its service area and provide an argument for a nearby private station to be built (Weir, 1965, p. 258). Again the government pressed the CBC for speed:

> There was again the sense of extreme urgency. CBC staff and facilities were driven to the utmost limits to build stations and studios, to secure equipment, to recruit and train additional staff, both technical and production, to produce a schedule of programs and assist private stations to get under way (Weir, 1965, p. 260).

So efficiently and hastily did CBC work that according to the president of the Electronics Industry of Canada the market for new sets was saturated within five years—almost twice the rate of expansion achieved in the United States (Weir, 1965, p. 261). In Canada, as in the United States, the first few years of television were its "golden age" in programing terms. For this there were several reasons. In order to optimize the attractiveness of the free lunch, networks and stations spent liberally on program development. And given the opportunity to experiment before the strictures of advertising sponsorship took control of most programing, the talents of Canadians and Americans had large scope for creativity.

From the innovation of television on, the public service aspects of the Canadian broadcasting system steadily deteriorated. The famed Massey Royal Commission (1949–1951) (Canada. Royal Commission on National Development, 1951, p. 46) totally misread the lessons of broadcasting history. Dismissing the ". . . vexed question of lines and frames which has affected the development of television in Europe" as a trivial technical issue, it blandly stated that standards do ". . . not constitute a problem on this continent where it may be assumed that all countries will adopt the established system of the United States." What Lynn Trainor later said of color television standards applies equally to monochrome:

> It appears evident that in the matter of colour television, as in so many other technical matters affecting Canadians, an inferior system was adopted primarily on the grounds of compatibility with American systems. This example is particularly disconcerting because the superior SECAM III system would have provided a natural barrier to the flood of American television programming and a natural encouragement to economic and cultural exchange with France. . . . Even when technology and economics favour an independent Canadian cultural stance, the Americanization of Canada persists.[5]

The decision to adopt American standards, according to J. A. Ouimet, Chief Engineer of CBC (1950, p. 173):

---

[5] Trainor (1970, pp. 246–247). Evidence of the inferiority of the American system was elicited by parliamentary question. See House of Commons, *Debates*, June 7, 1961, pp. 1250–1251.

. . . was decided a year or so ago by the Department of Transport, after consultation with the CBC, RMA, ACB, and others interested. . . . [This] will enable Canadians to tune in directly to American stations, if they live near enough to the border to be able to receive them. . . . Any other standards would have erected a television curtain between Canada and the United States, and, although Canadians will always insist on an adequate amount of Canadian programmes, I do not believe they would like any standard which would automatically exclude anything else.

The RMA, of course, was the Radio Manufacturers Association, which is dominated by branch plants of United States electronic TNCs (see Chapter 7). The ACB was the Association of Private Canadian Broadcasters. The issue was settled bureaucratically with no parliamentary or other public consideration.

As far as the Massey Commission is concerned, its majority report echoes the Aird Commission and a long list of parliamentary committees in stating the obvious: that Canada should have a national broadcast service which met the Canadian people's needs for national and cultural identity. But by 1951 these had become pious platitudes; the popular constituency to press them (the CRL, for instance) had long lost its coherence and zeal.

Consciousness Industry in Canada, powered by the private sector in television, was clearly in control. And it got its way by changing and exploiting the one national system of broadcasting to its own ends which focused on television. One thrust was directed to over-the-air broadcasting. Structurally, the 30-odd year campaign to free itself from CBC "regulation" was achieved as soon as the Progressive Conservative government took office in 1957 for the first time since 1936, under Diefenbaker. Rather than to regulate a national system, in Diefenbaker's words, his newly created Board of Broadcast Governors was to regulate "the public and private systems." The B.B.G., patterned on the American FCC, relieved the CBC of regulatory responsibility and devoted its attention to protecting the interests of the private sector. Its policy was reflected when the chairman of the BBG told the Canadian Association of Advertisers in 1961 how research could help them:

First, there is evidence that a substantial part of the audience uses the commercial time segments to withdraw from the screen and to do other things. Is this deliberate withdrawal necessary? How much attention has been given to ways and means of introducing the commercial message so as to reduce withdrawals or to circumvent it?

Second, it is clear that a large part of the audience can remain in front of the screen without any part of the commercial message registering. Half an hour later, or less, they could not tell you what they had seen or heard. How is this kind of escape possible? Can anything be done to correct it?

Third, how far is it true that the people who constitute the audience merely accept advertising on sufferance, and place no reliance on it? What difference would it make if a serious effort were made to increase the credibility of advertising messages?

Fourth, there is a strong reason to believe that some part of the audience finds some part of the commercials positively offensive. How is this related to the general attitude to all advertising? Is it necessary to offend even some of the audience? If not, what are the more acceptable alternatives?[6]

The meaning of the structural change became apparent in practice in the controversy over whether the CBC or the commercial television network should telecast the championship game in professional football, the Grey Cup, in 1962. The occasion was fitting, for not only is professional football a favorite free lunch, highly prized by advertisers, it is also a sport conducted mostly by imported players from the United States. The BBG tried to force the CBC into a subordinate role to the private network in broadcasting the game. The CBC asserted its superior right to broadcast such a nation-building spectacle. The outcome was an agreement as between equal powers of the CBC and the private network to govern forevermore the telecasting of the Grey Cup. The Canadian system was henceforth to be a dual system in its formal aspect, thus totally abandoning the "one national system" concept.

The exploitation of the facade of a public broadcasting service took many forms, of which I single out advertising and commercial networking. The Liberal government's Royal Commission of 1956 (Fowler Commission) recommended that the CBC actively seek advertising revenue in competition with the private stations. This advice which became CBC policy was reinforced by parliamentary commissions in 1959 and 1961 (under Progressive Conservative governments), and by the parliamentary committee (Fowler again) of 1965: the latter setting a goal of advertising at 25 percent of total revenue requirements. The results were predictable as far as program policy was concerned.

I have described how the CBC found it necessary in radio to induce advertisers to undertake network broadcasts by a system of regional incentive prices and remarked that financially CBC about broke even on such stimulated national network sponsored programs. Television's production costs were so much higher than radio's that, if Canadian commercial network programs were to be broadcast (and advertising revenues ob-

---

[6] Quoted appreciatively by Firestone (1967, p. 71). The passage quoted is from "How the Media can be Made More Effective Advertising Vehicles," Address by Dr. Andrew Stewart to the Association of Canadian Advertisers, Toronto, May 2, 1961, pp. 11–12.

tained), CBC was forced to subsidize such commercial program costs. In 1959 CBC had to bear 57 percent of production cost of Canadian productions for *commercial* programs; since then, the percentage has risen (Weir, 1965, p. 388). Although ultimately this was a taxpayers' subsidy to commercial advertising, CBC budgets have been limited. Therefore economic pressure is heavy on CBC to rely on imported United States programs. The result is that CBC programing has become dominated by commercial policy values. In its submission to the 1965 Fowler Committee, the CBC said:

> Even the most attractive and saleable Canadian programming apart from NHL Hockey cannot be sold to national advertisers unless it is offered as part of an American-Canadian deal. The situation presented on the English network precludes even a modest change in the program balance without the grave risk of jeopardizing most, if not all, our evening sales opportunities and thereby our important commercial revenue. The evening schedule as a whole has to be saleable if most of its constituent parts are to be sold. To partially unsell the evening schedule might well create a stampede of advertisers away from the remaining programs for lack of ancillary support of a mass character and for lack of inexpensive American programming to maintain a low cost per thousand on a multiple purchase by an advertiser. *It is impossible to exaggerate the degree to which the present commercial preoccupations and responsibilities of CBC television determine the character, quality and balance of CBC programming.* Without drastic relief from this situation it is literally impossible to plan a major improvement in the present program service in the evening hours.[7]

Truly, as Weir says, commercial pressures are ". . . persistent and inexorable and those who have never been in the business have no idea how insidious and compelling they can be in the face of tightening budgets (Weir, 1965, p. 312). The Fowler Commission recommendation (1957) that CBC budgets be established in five-year terms was intended to insulate CBC from incessant niggling by the private sector (it was never taken seriously by Parliament). But its recommendation that such budgets be tied to a percentage of "Personal Expenditures on Consumer Goods and Services" was a rational expression of the function of the CBC for Consciousness Industry.

There remain to be considered the regulations on advertising and Canadian content of the BBG and its successor, the Canadian Radio and Television Commission. The BBG regulations limiting advertising time

---

[7] Quoted in Weir, E. Austin, "Some Observations on Canadian Broadcasting and the White Paper, 1966", Appendix 15. Canadian House of Commons Standing Committee on Broadcasting, Films and Assistance to the Arts, *Minutes and Proceedings.* Ottawa: Queen's Printer, January 31, 1967, p. 1790. Emphasis added.

were more lax than previous CBC regulations. Even more lax limits were set for programs with "Canadian content." The regulations of Canadian content have been a facade. The CBC's programs have consistently exceeded them. And the private station programs have complied with them in ways which reproduce in Canada the United States commercial television policy. Again, to quote Weir (1965, p. 379):

> Private television is falling into the same general pattern as radio—news, sports, weather, local church and other similar pickups; quizzes and prize contests, with prizes contributed by groups of sponsors; one-man interviews, a few network shows, but very, very little that could be considered creative or requiring any marked production efforts.

The second thrust of Consciousness Industry to reshape the Canadian broadcasting system focused on cable television. Originating in the United States as a means of improving and extending television services to viewers whose location deprived them of signal reception (because of mountains, distance, or urban interference), cable television found its earliest and largest growth potential in Canada. The high proportion of Canadians living within 200 miles of the American border were the target for this thrust and they responded eagerly to the prospect of receiving more (mostly American) television programing than their antennas could bring them.

Why should Canadians want more United States TV programing? Basically for the same reasons they have learned to want United States radio broadcasting, films, magazines, mass production paperbacks, and comic books. As the preceding analysis has shown, Anglophone Canadians have been substantially assimilated to American cultural values of all kinds, after their first dependency on Britain weakened. Several centuries of dependence on Britain and later the United States has given most Canadian people a feeling that their country is inferior in most ways to the imperial way of life. It must be remembered that Canadian views of American life are those of the colonial. More specifically, the economies of scale make possible and necessary in the United States Consciousness Industry the production of media material with a degree of technical virtuosity, glitter, and glamor which indigenous Canadian productions can imitate only weakly. This is especially true of TV as to which there is a specific factor. In Canada there is only one network (CBC) which offers Canadian-produced entertainment programs, excluding sports and contest programs. If Canadians can have access to United States TV broadcasts (either via cable or over the air), they get three United States network services as well. At any given hour a choice of one of four program services offers an attractive possibility. One could speculate that perhaps the more egalitarian values imbedded in United States cultural productions (exemplified in references to the First and Fifth amendments to the United States Constitution) are also attractive to Canadians, accustomed to a more authoritarian constitutional system and living in a more hierarchically class-structured society than the Americans. The whole question has not been studied with the care it deserves. It is notable that the Québécois have sustained a much larger audience for indigenous TV and radio programs than have Anglophone Canadians and that there is a close relation between rising Québécois national consciousness and their CBC programs (see below).

By 1977, 74.1 percent of Canadian television households could subscribe to cable television and 50.1 percent of them did. No other country comes close to such penetration. In the United States at that time 20 percent of all United States television households subscribed to cable television.

The subversion of Canadian broadcast policy by cable television was a logical extension of the commercial policy which took control of Canadian broadcast policy in the 1950s. Market forces, unhampered by government or royal commissions, simply moved in. Neither the CBC nor the Board of Broadcast Governors licensed or regulated cable television in its formative stages. Instead the Department of Transport routinely licensed it as it would have mobile radio. It did not grant exclusive licenses for given areas. Only when protests of private television over-the-air stations about loss of revenue to cable competitors stirred it did the government "freeze" new licenses of cable television in 1964 while it considered what to do about it. By that time a very substantial vested interest had been created of which a large proportion was owned in the United States. When the BBG began to regulate cable it was facing 314 operating cable systems which earned $22.1 million in revenues and served 8 percent of Canadian households in 1967. United States companies owned $150 million worth of those cable properties.

In 1968, almost 20 years after cable television appeared on the horizon, the new Broadcasting Act which created the Canadian Radio Television Commission gave it responsibility to regulate cable companies as integral parts of the Canadian broadcasting system. By then cable television had diverted a substantial share of television audiences and revenues from over-the-air Canadian stations. The amount of such diversion has increased since then.

Apart from reducing United States ownership of cable and over-the-air stations systems to no more than 20 percent, CRTC's policy since 1968 has been to contain the damage which cable television does to over-the-air television stations in Canada, to protect interests of cable companies to whom it assigned market monopolies, to "referee" complaints by users against the cable systems, and to encourage the development of "community channels" for noncommercial uses. It forced the reduction in foreign ownership between 1969 and 1972. A series of measures has been employed to limit the number of United States television signals provided by the cable systems (and thereby to protect the audiences produced by Canadian over-the-air television stations):

1. Priorities were established for the types of television station programs which a cable television system might transmit. Preference was given to stations owned by CBC and private stations serving the area in question, including educational programs if requested by provincial authorities. If these priorities are accommodated there is no limit to the number of United States station services which may be picked up by the "head end," provided that no microwave system is employed to bring in such signals. If microwave facilities are needed to bring in United States signals, they are limited to no more than three.

2. Simultaneous program deletion and substitution was required if two channels on a cable system were carrying the same program at the same time, to the effect that both channels would carry the program as broadcast by the station service with the higher priority. The intent is to protect the advertising revenue of high-priority Canadian stations.

3. Closely linked with (2) is permission to delete commercials from signals received from United States stations and to replace them with Canadian advertising, subject to station-cable system agreement and CRTC approval. The intent is to permit the Canadian station to sell the spot announcement time for the substituted commercials; the cable system was not allowed to sell announcements.

As would be expected with the market-forces approach to cable television, the cable television industry is dominated by a few very large enterprises. Of 274 enterprises operating cable systems in 1973, six served 50 percent of all cable subscribers. Seventeen enterprises served 72 percent. As measured by revenues ($133 million in 1974), or net profit before taxes ($30 million in 1974), the cable television industry is large by Canadian standards and earns in revenues about one dollar for every three earned by the private over-the-air television broadcasters and approximately one dollar in net profits before taxes for every two earned by the television broadcasters.

Observation of CRTC policy regarding cable television suggests that as in the case of over-the-air broadcasting, the federal regulatory agencies established since 1958 consider the welfare of the regulated industry first. In this regard one recalls that Harold Ickes (Secretary of the Interior under F. D. Roosevelt) defined a bureaucrat as a government officer who thinks twice before preferring the private to the public interest. With the disappearance of effective political forces supporting public service broadcasting in Canada shortly after World War II, by this definition Canada's regulation of broadcasting has not been *bureaucratic.*

Two aspects of cable television development in Canada are fuzzy. One is the future of "wired city" type interactive services, including the presently inchoate "local channel" television services. The other is the future institutional shape of cable television itself: a regulated public utility monopoly, or competitive free enterprise. The two aspects are interdependent because both rest on the uncertainty which surrounds the exploitation of the techniques for broad band and digital communications and satellites. If Canada (and the United States of course) were starting afresh from where they were in respect to broad band digital techniques in the early 1960s it would have been sensible to base the switched public telephone network on the cable technique and satellites. The immense accumulated economic and political power of the telephone industry has thwarted this possiblity. It has also treated cable television with hostility —using its monopoly power to deny use of its pole lines and conduits except on punitive terms which the cable companies can accept only because of their own enormously profitable operations. (Typically the telephone company charges the cable company for stringing the latter's cable on its telephone poles, then charges the cable company an annual rental for use of the poles, and after termination of a short contract, typically ten years, the cable belong to the telephone company.)

Fuzziness regarding the future interactive services which are quite feasible technically using cable television arises from the uncertainties regarding institutional arrangements which might be worked out. For instance, shopping via cable television and credit card would involve institutional arrangements which would deeply affect the operations of retail establishments. Banking services via cable television would require analogous arrangements between banks and cable companies, with analogous rearranging of banking facilities and practices. And so on through the long list of *possible* features of the wired city which may or may not ever come into being.

The ultimate institutional form or forms of cable television would depend on whether and how these specialized services develop. It is possible to envisage a situation in which providing the hardware service of cable television is a public utility whose customers are enterprises engaged in providing wired city sorts of services to different markets. The frequent comments by CRTC disavowing any "public utility" status for cable television systems appear as deficient in understanding of these possibilities as they are in understanding that under the public utility rubric it is quite possible to avoid undesired cross-subsidization if the regulatory agency chooses instead to exercise close supervision and full-cost pricing.

Community channels face the necessity to develop new institutional arrangements analogous to those required for the wired city specialized services. But for them, the "interfaces" yet to be arranged before the utopian goals of enthusiasts for such channels can be realized are in the realm primarily of social, educational, even political institutions at the local level. How are people to reorient the ideology and practices of possessive individualism in their role as workers for Consciousness Industry in order to build viable local institutions to take advantage of the possibilities of community channels? They cannot expect the cable television companies to exert much initiative in this regard for those companies are geared strictly for their own profit-making roles in Consciousness Industry. What gestures they make (a small studio, some camera equipment) are only tokens which they provide in order to comply with the letter if not the spirit of CRTC regulations.

What happened to radio broadcasting since 1953 was common to both Canada and to the United States a few years earlier. Nationwide mass audiences ceased to be produced by the radio industry as television demonstrated its superior cost per thousand efficiency in marketing goods and services. And radio broadcasting became a vehicle for spot advertisements at the local level. Meanwhile, the unique advantage of radio for producing audiences of automobile drivers, and for incidental listening (while preparing and eating meals, doing household chores, etc.) was capitalized. Deprived of its national advertisers, the radio networks of CBC found their role shrunken and they quickly disappeared. And in the mid-1970s CBC abandoned efforts to sell advertising on radio. From that point on, Canada's "dual" radio system consisted of material produced, as President Johnson (1977, p. 58) of CBC said of CBC programing in 1977 for ". . . its central purpose of distinctive and distinguished programing," and an enormous flood of spot announcements, news snippets, and popular music produced by a growing number of private commercial AM and FM stations. The casual observer has trouble distinguishing Canadian from American private radio broadcasting in recent years. It is not so obvious that Canadian private radio broadcasting is extemely profitable—more profitable than American. A recent study done for the CRTC found the following principal differences between the Canadian and American radio industries:

(1) The radio industry [as a whole] is more profitable in Canada than in the United States.
(2) The average revenue per station is higher in Canada than in the United States.
(3) Radio revenues as a share of the GNP are approximately twice as much in Canada as in the United States.
(4) Radio advertising rates are lower in Canada than in the United States.

(5) FM revenues are becoming relatively and absolutely more and more important in both Canada and the United States.

(6) Revenue growth, net profit growth and average profitability over the period 1965 to 1976 have all been higher in Canada than in the United States.

(7) The United States radio industry appears to operate in a more competitive environment than its Canadian counterpart and its profitability is more sensitive to the general economic growth rate.

(8) AM radio in both countries seems to be a mature industry, in that its share of GNP is stable or declining.

(9) FM radio in both countries is growing faster than AM. However, it is currently both more independent of AM and more important in terms of market shares in the United States than in Canada (Watson et al, 1978).

But not all radio stations in Canada are equally profitable: local stations commonly are not very profitable, but high-power stations are extremely profitable. With good cause big business in the private sector in radio no less than television in Canada has effectively and profitably won the struggle which began in the 1920s for broadcasting on the United States model.

CBC plays a continually diminishing role in Canadian broadcasting to Anglophone Canadians, as judged by audience production. Its English television program service produced only 29.3 percent of the prime evening hour audience in 1971 and 22.9 percent in 1975. (The remainder of 100 percent was produced by programs originating from private Canadian and American stations south of the border.) Its English radio service produced only 7.0 percent of the evening audience in 1971 and 7.8 percent in 1975. Significantly, CBC's French television service produced 45.7 percent of the audience in 1971 and 46.8 percent in 1975; the CBC French radio share of audience rose from 10.6 percent in 1971 to 12.5 percent in 1975. Not only did CBC's French service produce substantially larger audiences than CBC's English service for both television and radio, but the CBC French shares were rising while the English shares were declining or staying constant.[8] This probably shows that the political consciousness of Francophone audiences and program production staff has been higher in terms of cultural autonomy than that of the Anglophones, and has been rising. Even so, the shares for the television audience reflect the fact that the data are for evening service and therefore include audiences for CBC's heavy importation of United States programs, especially for the English service. Clearly the trend is for Anglophone CBC in-

---

[8] In the case of television the audience shares reported relate to a total which includes cable television audiences as well as over-the-air audiences. The shares include audiences to CBC distributed programs received from affiliated private stations. (Data from CBC Research Division.)

digenous programming to become a Canadian counterpart of the United States NET-PBS as far as audience size is concerned.

Although Canadian broadcasting, like the newspapers, has been astonishingly profitable as Senator Davey said, the integration of Canada into the incessant process of United States dominated Consciousness Industry (which they have deliberately struggled for since the 1920s) is not without its self-limiting aspects. The increased penetration of Canada by television signals from south of the border via cable television has fragmented the audience and reduced profits from over-the-air television stations and networks. The CRTC has attempted to protect private station profitability by permitting the substitution of Canadian advertisements for American advertisements deleted by the cable systems from the over-the-air signals received from south of the border. In effect "electronic gateways" are being built for whole provinces and regions. Significantly what is being done to protect Canadian advertisers and stations was not done to protect Canada's cultural hegemony as a corollary of adopting incompatible standards for television in the 1940s. But the problem of protecting Canadian television station profits can hardly be solved so simply. The CRTC estimated in 1971 that between $24 million and $30 million annually was lost to the Canadian broadcasting system because United States border stations are used by United States based multinational corporations to advertise directly across the border. And Canadian companies also spent between $12 and $15 million on advertising to Canada from United States border stations. The total was between $36 and $45 million.[9] The recent policy of disallowing such advertising expenses for income tax purposes affects only those Canadian advertisers, of which there are relatively few, who operate independently of TNCs. Advertisers dependent on TNCs can avoid such penalties by handling such cross-border advertising out of their parent company's offices in other countries.

Most Canadian viewing is of United States-produced programs which reach Canadian viewers from Canadian over-the-air and cable systems and directly from United States terrestrial TV stations. And the efforts of CRTC to protect the Canadian stations and cable systems just described have been problematic enough. With the recent American use of communications satellites to relay program material between American cable systems and terrestrial broadcast stations for distribution domestically, however, a new serious threat faces the Canadian stations and cable systems. Ground stations capable of receiving signals directly from the American satellites were first used in remote mining and oil-

---

[9] CRTC, "The Integration of Cable Television in the Canadian Broadcasting System," Public Announcement, 26 February, 1971.

producing communities in Canada's far North. Box Office TV programs thus received are then carried by cable to homes. Such ground stations are inexpensive to build and operate. They are also illegal under present Canadian law. Their use has spread in the denser population near the American border, adding a new fragmenting force to those previously existing. As this is written, it is estimated that 10,000 of them are in use. And their unit cost has fallen to the range, $1,000 to $3,000. The government of British Columbia in 1980 openly defied the federal government to try to stop their spread.

Against this incessant and massive flood of imported TV programs, the policy of protecting Canadian content or even Canadian private broadcasters recalls the futility of King Canute's command to the sea. In all respects this flood is powered by possessive individualism. With insignificant exceptions, public service broadcasting for the masses of Canadians now exists only at a token level.

As against this one-way flow of American Consciousness Industry audience production by all the mass media to Canada, the only available processes for the struggle for Canadian hegemony are those of the Canadian institutions of representative government in a formally autonomous nation. French Canada is acting through such processes. In political-economic and cultural terms it is increasingly difficult to find any other significant real differences between Canada and, for instance, the Pacific Coast states of the United States which also have their own unique history and identity while being part of the American system.

9

REALISM IN ARTS AND SCIENCES

Chapter 1 emphasized that the mass media of communication under monopoly capitalism have a crucial agenda-setting function which directs the attention of people to priority issues of vital importance to the capitalist system. Chapter 2 developed the concept of the audience as the principal product of the mass media and Consciousness Industry in the core areas of capitalism. In Chapters 3 and 4, I traced the dynamic process by which the capitalist system invented the mass media that became essential to the success of the giant corporations. These corporations, having achieved hegemony in the core areas of monopoly capitalism, depend upon the mass media production of audiences to market consumer goods and services, political candidates, and public policies. Chapter 5 briefly analyzed the politico-economic basis of the dependency of Canada on first Britain and then the United States. The dependent development in Canada of the press, book publishing, cinema, telecommunications, radio and television broadcasting was the subject of Chapters 6, 7, and 8. At this point it is necessary to examine the artistic component of the process we are considering. Science which is dealt with sketchily here will be analyzed further in Chapter 10.

Culture, I understand (with the anthropologists) to be all that people use and value in their daily lives. And it always exists in a context of social relations. "Whoever says culture also says administration whether they want to or not," said T. W. Adorno (1972, p. 123, quoted in Kellner, 1978, p. 54). It is to be sharply distinguished from "Official Culture"— certain "leisure time" pursuits which the upper classes have arbitrarily defined as culture. *Art*, I understand to be that aspect of peoples' practices and thoughts which illuminates them with the qualities of love, hate, wonder, humor, critical insight, zest, indignation, rage, malice, etc. The media of art are various: words, sounds, and material objects including tools. Neither art nor ideas drop from outer space: both grow out of the real world in which our material lives and immaterial consciousness have their being. Art, like science, arises from the dialectical process of life and comments on it with a range of styles from irony and subtle understatement to the manifestly urgent. Like science, art grows out of, is nourished and spread by, the social formations in which people live, and in turn contributes to changing them. Both art and science provide identity and cohesion to the social formations from which they arise. Both existed before modern capitalism and will outlive it. Art, like science and our daily lives, has been capitalized by monopoly capitalism for the sake of the bottom line. Art and science have been used in the interest of cultural domination to help set an agenda by which people tend to live, conforming them to social systems resting on hierarchical privilege, economic strength and military power.

In only one chapter it is impossible to deal with all aspects of the arts and science in theory and practice in Canada and the United States, much less in other older cultures. Nevertheless, a major part of this chapter will be devoted to analysis of the systemic background which is a necessary basis for even a little analysis of the arts in Canada.

The advent of socialist societies embracing some 30 percent of the world's population in the twentieth century has raised the question, what have been the essential features of the arts and sciences for the capitalist system? The controversy over "socialist realism" in the arts which began in the Soviet Union in the first decade after the 1917 Revolution was an overture to a policy debate which will continue for at least several centuries. This is because historically, the capitalist system cultivated distinctive characteristic features of the arts and sciences. Just as those features were different from those of the culture of Medieval Europe and those of Imperial China, so they may be expected to differ from those of future socialist societies. At issue here is the question, what aspects of the art of ancient Greece or of ancient China, of medieval Europe, of modern nationalism are universal and timeless, and what aspects are specific to the class cultures which produced them? In what respects may socialist art be different?

It is too early to tell in detail. But we are a century or so late in understanding the necessary contribution which the institutional system of art and science, developed in the Western World, made to the development of the modern capitalist system since the Renaissance, i.e., the rule of capitalist realism. This chapter is a modest attempt to identify and analyze those unique features and that contribution in Canada and the capitalist core area.

The context of the arts and sciences in any social system is the cultural realism of that system. *Cultural realism* means the central values of the system as expressed in its artifacts, practices, and institutions. These central values may be thought of as the rationalization which informs and is implicit in the relations of the components of the system.

The urgency of addressing the problems of cultural realism for artists and scientists arises from two major "fronts" in the world today. The first and historically unprecedented front is the emergence of socialism in, chronologically, the Soviet Union, Eastern Europe, China, North Korea, Cuba, and Indochina. The second is the accelerated penetration by developed capitalist nations' cultures in the so-called less-developed parts of the world. In the former case, the core of the problem is: How to decide what new elements of culture are required immediately to build socialist humanity and which elements of the culture of capitalism should be rejected, which transformed, and which accepted into the cultural realism of socialism. In the latter case, the core of the problem is to determine the basis for admitting or rejecting alien and often destructive cultural artifacts, services, and values in favor of preserving and transforming traditional styles of life and the accompanying material artifacts. In fact the two major fronts have overlapping problems. For the socialist nations face the problem of screening (the second case) and in some less-developed and presently nonsocialist nations there is the problem of making the cultural transition *directly* to socialism (the first case) while also concentrating on the screening problems. (The issue of cultural screens is dealt with in Chapter 10.)

A major barrier to directing appropriate talents of artists and scientists to solving these problems is that there is inadequate understanding of how their systems have served to develop capitalist realism. Before artists and scientists can build socialist realism they should be aware of how capitalist realism trained them to serve it.

I: WHAT DO WE KNOW ABOUT THE SYSTEMIC ORIGINS OF CAPITALIST REALISM?

Science and art inevitably arise out of human life, social and individual. Both science and art have tactical and strategic levels of existence. At the tactical level, art and science have in common the ordinary human problem-solving procedure: Define the problem (or job), study it, try to do it, review or evaluate the results. The respective methods, at the tactical level, differ but there is a large degree of overlap between them. At the strategic, or institutional level the systems of art and science have structural similarities. Both are cumulative and self-renewing. Both are embodied in associations which have their own institutional inertia, being themselves political organisms like any institutions. Both depend for their existence on the extant social power structure and hence inevitably respond to such logistical support with mixtures of accommodation and resistance. Further, art and science at both the tactical and strategic levels are inescapably political in nature. In both it is necessary to choose the problems or concepts to be dealt with, and the methods to be employed in relation to them. Such choices arise out of, and are conditioned by, the ongoing social structure of power relationships, and hence have political significance by reason of the choices made. Following the completion of the artistic or scientific exercises such choices have consequences for the social power structure. Apart from the political bias imparted by the choice of problem and method, there is the further political bias arising from the lure of effective opportunity for the scientist and artist to "do his/her thing." The availability of funds to support scientific research, of financial support whether from patrons or the market for artists, and the availability of recognition, honors, etc., combine to impart a bias in favor of the sources of such support and recognition. All of this process *does* appear, whether one considers capitalist or socialist systems.

1. What central values are fundamental to the growth of capitalist realism in art and science over the past 700 years? How do art and science relate to the ideology of modern capitalism? There are three central values in capitalist realism.

a. People and world are natural systems.   They are to be thought of as perpetual motion machines. They are susceptible to rational understanding. This was the fundamental view of man and the world held in modern times. And it applied to both art and science in Europe through the fifteenth century. Only in the sixteenth century and afterward was art held to be autonomous from science and learning (Hauser, 1957, Vol. 2, p. 75).

Being natural systems, man and world might be manipulated if one learned how the system functioned. The Copernical mechanical model of the world, according to Hauser (1957, Vol. 2, p. 183), manifested itself in the Baroque art of the sixteenth century:

> The whole of the art of the baroque is full of this shudder, full of the echo of the infinite spaces and the interrelatedness of all being. The world of art in its totality becomes the symbol of the universe as a uniform organism alive in all its parts. Each of these parts points, like the heavenly bodies, to an infinite, unbroken continuity; each part contains the law governing the whole; in each the same power, the same spirit is at work.

If man and nature are essentially machines, technique is the key to understanding them. Beginning with the Renaissance it is obvious that technique becomes the central issue for art in capitalist realism. All the conventions of art (e.g., perspective) are rationalized (Hauser, 1957, Vol. 2, pp. 16, 64). In contrast with the Middle Ages when art was based on an objective "What," art in the Renaissance and after was based on a subjective "How" (Hauser, 1957, Vol. 2, p. 70). The reciprocal of the technical preoccupation was the view of the individual as unlimitedly manipulable. Madison Avenue's cynical view of the individual as infinitely plastic when properly conditioned was already held in the Baroque artistic salons of France in the seventeenth century when it could be said of the individual ". . . stripped of all extraordinary qualities, he attains an average, handy, easily manageable size" (Hauser, 1957, Vol. 2, p. 204).

For science, the mechanical view of people and the world seemed to be true—at least as the fruit of physical science had a spectacular payoff. The notion of science as the means of "conquering" nature which sanctioned the rape of the world's natural resources for the benefit and profit of business was fundamental to all our later "technology" and was taken over by Marxist socialism in the Soviet Union and elsewhere (Leiss, 1972). As applied to people as social beings it inevitabley took the form of "scientism": A mechanical view of men and women with implicit denial of the reality of their consciousness, and their apparently disorderly political behavior. Parallel to the trends in art, the science of man likewise took a manipulable view of people and looked for technique to control their behavior. Positivism has been a necessary feature of capitalist realism. Hobbes's theory of knowledge anticipated it in its rejection of metaphysics and its insistence on semantic precision. His psychology anticipated the mechanistic shape of behaviorism. His political philosophy rationalized a mechanically conceived society in which authoritarianism ensured the successful manipulation of the common man. Spinoza considered man's actions and desires "in exactly the same manner as though I were concerned with lines, planes and solids."

In the eighteenth century, Adam Smith, Joseph Townsend, and the Physiocrats developed systems of economic thought in which atomic individualism was the basic assumption about human beings. The mechanics of hedonism and the ideological rationale for consumerism—the basis of Madison Avenue—were refined by the utilitarian system of Bentham and James Mill in the nineteenth century. The positivism of Saint Simon and August Comte envisioned society as manipulative, mechanical, rationalized technocracy with intellectuals like themselves running it. Herbert Spencer, William Graham Summer, and Ludwiz Gumplowicz happily incorporated Darwinism into similar scientific systems of methods and theory.

Psychology became positivistic with the associationism of Hume and Hartley long before the behaviorism of Watson, Hull, and Skinner developed the "S-R" school which regards people essentially as robots. Behavioral science is the cross-disciplinary unity of those (such as Lasswell) who would reduce the social sciences to the means by which people are treated as conditioned and manipulated animals.

Communications theory and research—which might be expected to be applicable to art—fall mostly into the behavioristic category of science which takes a Newtonian mechanical view of life. Bernard Berelson (1956, pp. 304–305), speaking approvingly of a quarter century of work in public opinion research said:

> . . . the field has become technical and quantitative, a-theoretical, segmentalized and particularized, specialized and institutionalized, "modernized," and "groupized"—in short, as a characteristic behavioural science, Americanized. Twenty-five years ago and earlier, prominent writers as part of their general concern with the nature and functioning of society, learnedly studied public opinion not "for itself" but in broad historical, theoretical, and philosophical terms and wrote treatises. Today teams of technicians do research projects on specific subjects and report findings. Twenty years ago the study of public opinion was part of scholarship. Today, it is part of science.

Such has been the systemic view of people as part of nature in capitalist realism for the arts and sciences.

b. Science and art are pure—i.e., value-free and nonpolitical. They are therefore ecumenical in the sense that they are universal, timeless, and benign. This metaphysical concept is unique to capitalist realism.

In the sciences, this notion developed only in the nineteenth century when science became formally institutionalized in academies, societies, and universities and when access to the ranks of scientists was effectively opened to young people from social classes below the controlling bourgeois power structure. In the earlier centuries of the Renaissance and Enlightenment, scientists were more closely knit to the ruling group and did not deceive themselves as to the political nature of their scientific activities. Francis Bacon put it candidly:

> The roads to human power and to human knowledge lie close together and are nearly the same; nevertheless, on account of the pernicious and inveterate habit of dwelling on abstractions, it is safer to begin and raise the sciences from those foundations which have relation to practice and let the active part be the seal which prints and determines the contemplative counterpart (quoted in Bernal, 1939, p. 6).

Before the nineteenth century, scientists understood that the Platonic idealist notion that science was concerned with pure thought was self-contradictory. As Bernal (1939, pp. 5–6) says:

> If the contemplation of the universe for its own sake were the function of science as we know it now it would never have existed, for the most elementary reading of the history of science shows that both the drive which led to scientific discoveries and the means by which those discoveries were made were material needs and material instruments.

As far as the political consequences of science are concerned, it is unnecessary to do more than refer to the overseas period of imperial conquest from the fifteenth to twentieth centuries which was made possible and efficient thanks to the scientific solution of transportation-and-weapons-related problems (including the astronomical contributions of Galileo, Copernicus, and Newton which were essential to modern navigation), to the development of the textile industry in Western Europe in the eighteenth and nineteenth centuries (made possible by the chemical scientists), and to the development of nuclear power within living memory.

Social science, however, was heir to the naive notion of science's "apoliticality" developed in the nineteenth century. When he faces the area of political life, the capitalist behavioral scientist has, as Floyd Matson (1964, p. 70) says, three choices each of which is allegedly value-free and apolitical:

> First, he may choose to concentrate upon those mechanical and peripheral details of the political process which can be readily manipulated by the quantitative methods of sampling, scaling, testing, and content-analyzing— such matters as electoral statistics and mass media research ("who says what to whom through which channel"). Second, the behaviouralist may take up his measuring rods and push on into the central areas of politics, ignoring their ambiguity and trivializing their content; in the words of Hans Morgenthau: he "can try to quantify phenomena which in their aspect relevant to political science are not susceptible to quantification, and by doing so obscure and distort what political science ought to know." Finally, the behavioural scientist may abandon political realities altogether and retire to the heights of pure Method—with the vague intention of some day returning to the world when the master formulas have been computed and the tests for statistical significance are in.

I say "allegedly value-free and apolitical" because any commitment of resources, whether material or personal, in the context of the real world obviously has a dialectical political consequence: Either in some fashion to support or to change the ongoing social system, or to clarify or obfuscate political issues, or both. Behaviorism and logical positivism have provided a rationale for conservative, conformist, and escapist activity by scientists. By limiting knowledge to the perceptually verifiable, they have made it socially respectable for intellectuals to find busywork, to make comfortable careers for themselves by the ready rewards for "counting" more and more about less and less. By treating the individual as an isolated atom, they provide a model for the academic world which coincides ideologically with the model of free-enterprise capitalism. The advent of foundation-supported scientific research, and "think tanks" supported by the military and TNCs, adapted the market structure of science to that of monopoly capitalism between 1920 and the 1960s.

To say this is not to say that one should be antiscience, that one opposes the use of mathematical and statistical tools, or that one would throw out the baby with the bath. I welcome mathematical and statistical tools. But I want them to be used to attack questions which are stated correctly, i.e., that they used to pursue questions framed in a realistic policy context. Far from being value-free and nonpolitical in its application around the world, the great bulk of what passes for social science today is culture-bound and highly political in its consequences both in its home country and in other nations.

The alienation of art and artists from the collective concerns of mankind was one of the necessary but most tragic consequences of capitalist realism. In the Renaissance, artists ". . . lost the connection between artistic forms and extra artistic purposes, a simply and absolutely unproblematical reality taken for granted in the Middle Ages" (Hauser, 1957, Vol. 2, p. 84). Subordination to the ruling classes during the Renaissance confronted artists and humanists with the twin dangers of bohemianism or servility and they succumbed to both. If the artist does not adopt a servile role openly:

> He abstains from all political activity, in order not to tie himself down, but by his passivity he only confirms the holders of power. This is the real "trahison des clercs," the betrayal of the intellectual values by the intelligentsia, not the politicization of the spirit for which it has been blamed in recent times. The humanist loses touch with reality, he becomes a romantic who calls his estrangement from the world aloofness, his social indifference intellectual freedom, his bohemian way of thinking moral sovereignty (Hauser, 1957, Vol. 2, p. 83).

The result in terms of allegedly nonpolitical art has been the "art for art's sake" rationalization of political escapism which at the same time is a deformed protest against capitalism. And because technique is the politically safest and most attractive feature of modern capitalism "art for art's sake" tends to center on technique. As early as the fifteenth century in the self-governng city republics of Italy this phenomenon is found (Hauser, 1957, Vol. 2, p. 42). And the Rococo period in the eighteenth century provides a genre of *l'art pour l'art* said to be perhaps more spontaneous and genuine than that of the nineteenth century (Hauser, 1957, Vol. 3, p. 34). Given the social context, it was inevitable that as early as 1719 Dubos would stress that the purpose of art is not to "teach," but to "move" and that the only adequate attitude to take to it was one not of reason but of "feeling." He thus provided the basis for the conditioning by popular culture, especially advertising, which today is so blatant.

Such escapist tendencies were inevitable, given the shift from *belief* to *sensation* as the basis of art which fifteenth-century art in Italian city states made. "Pure pleasure," "feeling," "manifest sensations" for the individual were its epistemological foundation, as Lauro Martines says in his *Power and Imagination: City States in Renaissance Italy* (1979, pp. 248–265):

> The advancing edge of change in art, the vanguard vision was in the imitation of everyday reality. . . . In the fifteenth century, the portrait was the attempt *par excellence* to capture the face of contemporary reality; it was a pragmatic coming to terms with actual appearance and surfaces. It depended upon a vision of things that did not, however, come forth in isolation. The vision was related directly to the new domineering view of reality; it was related to the growing concentration of wealth and power, which went to enhance the self-confidence of the upper-class groups. . . . The attendant view of reality—as glimpsed, for example, in militant humanism—was poised, optimistic, and imperious. . . . Nature, as that which is looked upon every day, was deemed benign by the groups at the top (Martines, 1979, p. 258).

The rationale which undergirds the apology for the alienation of the arts and artists from political activity now rests on a series of fictions. One is that in the Renaissance there was a universal appreciation of art and that art had uniformly high quality. A second was that the art of the High Renaissance at least was a timelessly valid and eternally human art. As we note later, the very *system* of the five Fine Arts was premised on just such an absolute, timeless, spaceless judgment. The economics of the art market reinforced these fictions. Because "old masters" exist in limited supply, the risk to dealers in handling them is less than with living artists whose productive potential is uncertain, and therefore the market prefers to deal in the former. What we look back on as Renaissance art was produced on order for the rising bourgeois class by artists who depended on its members, as Martines (1979, Chapters 11 and 13) demonstrates in analyzing humanism and the arts. It was their art; it was not the popular art of the lower classes. The socially approved art was "the jealously guarded possession of a highbrow and Latinized elite" (Hauser, 1957, Vol. 2, p. 51). Nor, in reality was Renaissance art timelessly valid:

> Its art is just as time-conditioned, just as limited and transitory, with its own standards of value and criteria of beauty, as the art of any other period (Hauser, 1957, Vol. 2, p. 93).

c. Individualism, private property and market organization are systemic necessities for the arts and sciences. The notion of the dignity of the individual when linked with its ideological counterpart, private property, became the foundation of the Renaissance, of modern capitalism, and of Protestantism. The class character of Renaissance humanism was crisply stated by Marsilio Ficino in his *Platonic Theology on the Immortality of Souls* (1482):

> But the arts of this type, although they mould the matter of the universe and command the animals, and thus imitate God, the creator of nature, are nevertheless inferior to those arts which imitating the heavenly kingdom undertake the responsibility of human government. Single animals scarcely suffice for the care of themselves or briefly of their offspring. *But man alone so abounds in perfection that he rules himself first, which no beasts do, then governs his family, administers the state, rules peoples and commands the entire world.* And as though born for ruling he is entirely impatient of servitude (quoted in Martines, 1979, p. 217, emphasis added).

Concluding his analysis of humanism in Renaissance city states, Martines (1979, p. 217) says:

> However general the heroic view of man's dignity, however, much it purported to depend upon a notion of human potentiality, none came closer to realization of the ideal than the men with the resources for learning, culture, patronage, and the *trained* capacity for enjoyment of the world's goods. This is so obvious that it seems trivial, yet in surveying the age, historians constantly suppose, like the humanists themselves, that the heroic vision spoke for all men. Not at all. It spoke for an elite, and to ignore this is both to get the Renaissance wrong and to show that we do not see the forces and social interests that lie behind our own values.

Acquisitiveness, competition, and dependence on the market mechanism became the operational mode for capitalist realism. The arts and science both embraced these institutional innovations, though with somewhat differing manifestations and consequences.

Possibly the most obvious feature of the capitalist system for the arts was the systematic cultivation of possessive individualism. The commoditization of art objects fitted them into the class structure appropriately along with all other commodities. Like all commodities, the production of art commodities became separated from their "consumption" by institutionalized markets, replete with critics able to appraise (and shill for) the art products, middlemen, and brokers, and in time, a myriad of specialized trade journals.

Just as individualism became the ideological hallmark of production in business enterprise in trade and industry, so in the arts the doctrine of individualism took the quintessential form of genius. The system provided for the division of artists into the geniuses (or "stars") and the much larger number consigned to "Grub Street." Capitalism made art a commodity identified with the bourgeois class ("high art"). And aesthetics became the area of knowledge in which knowledgeable amateurs among the bourgeoisie and their philosophers provided the rationale for their behavior in the art markets, be they concert halls, opera houses, or art galleries.

The notion of the artist as genius helped to "depoliticalize" art for the common person by making a myth about the exclusive capacity of alienated geniuses to produce "high art," and the analogous capacity of the "refined" bourgeois consumers to appreciate it. The Greeks never had this myth.

The artist-as-genius was also a useful concept to the capitalist system because it served to justify the "star" system. Based on that multifaceted notion of personality (or character), the star as genius could receive and seem to deserve unusually high income. We find that early in the Renaissance (fifteenth century) star artists (e.g., Michelangelo) received very high income from their work. In interesting analogy to physical capital goods, the mere capacity for reputed work of genius became the basis for income: the creation of new markets (as compared to the Middle Ages) in the *uncompleted* sketches or drawings of prints or sculptures. The star precedent set in the fifteenth century was duly followed in music, literature, poetry, architecture, sculpture, and of course, by the motion picture, radio, TV, and press.

When art became a commodity, as market dependence required, its main market was the elite upper class, for only they would have the amateur's expertise (rationalized in aesthetics) to discriminate properly in such a market (as well as the ability to pay the price). The result was that the typical art market product would have the quality of high art, i.e., the best. The policy of "competition in publicity and scarcity" which Veblen identified as the systemic principle underlying Consciousness Industry's Civilian Sales Effort (chapter 3) had been developed for bourgeois art centuries earlier—if only for handicraft production for small markets of the upper class.

The pleasure in art of the upper class would thus be ensured, and the propaganda results of having a system which produced high art would be maximized. Never before the Renaissance was the pleasure principle made the basis of a massive system of culture such as modern capitalism. Its incorporation as the basis of modern aesthetics later on justified the application of the pleasure principle throughout the system (in popular culture, in personal attitudes, in family relations, etc.). For this reason the capitalist system focused on analysis of the arts its interest in developing theories of feeling, sensitivity, and beauty—the net effect of which was to glorify the cult of the personality and of pleasure. Out of this process came typical capitalist market phenomena for art, including the notion of intellectual private property in the commodities produced. Throughout, this side of the rationale for capitalist realism in the arts combined Machiavellian cynical amorality in acquisitiveness and the expression of individual creativity, within limits of what the market would take.

If aesthetics is a "buyers' guide" to art, rather than a theory to which producers pay attention, as artists tell me, the buyers of capitalist art are rather less protected by the system than are the buyers of durable consumer's goods in the United States: at least manufacturers *care* a little what the Consumer's Union product ratings say about their products. The class-specific origin of aesthetics is worthy of more attention than critical scholars (including Marxists) have given it. For Lukacs and other European Marxists aesthetics appear to be above politics rather than to have had a clear bourgeois origin (see, for example, Sanches Vasquez, 1973) and their concern is to distinguish art which is "true" (i.e., eternally and everywhere valid) from that which is ephemeral (Lukacs, 1964).

The rationale for capitalist realism for science relied on individualism and private property much as for the arts. But the role of the market was less significant in science than for the arts. Leaving aside the commercial market for books and journals, the major dependence of scientists has been on employment by industry, governments, and universities. Being part of the ruling class they have thus dealt with the tensions between influences toward servility and intellectual freedom without all the major confusions introduced into art by market phenomena.

2. What was the nature of the process of institution-building for capitalist realism in the arts? It was part of the historical process by which modern capitalism and the modern nation-state emerged from the medieval/feudal system in Western Europe. Capitalist realism in art matters, like policy on science, lay close to the seat of power. What concerns us in this analysis of its processual character is that city states and later nation-states used their power and resources quite openly to develop styles and structures for the arts which would serve the capitalist system realistically.

Art academies, combining the functions of teaching, production, and debate were created by the state for the development of standards, styles, and skills in the arts, first in Florence and Genoa in the sixteenth century, then in France, England, and the Low Countries a little later. The very *identity* of the fine arts was the subject of debates lasting over three centuries. These nationally conducted debates in the sixteenth to eighteenth centuries concerned the evaluation of ancient and medieval cultural forms and traditions and their transformation in the interest of capitalist realism. These debates served to develop the ideology of modern capitalism, but seen in retrospect, the objective was to rationalize the status of the five "major arts" as clearly separated by common characteristics from the crafts, sciences, and other human activities. One such debate, running from the sixteenth century to the eighteenth and crossing national boundaries, was on the supposed parallel between painting and poetry. A second concerned the parallel between painting and sculpture. Approaching the matter from a different viewpoint, a running debate for several centuries on what may be called "the amateur tradition" concerned the basis for selecting artistic activities most compatible with the pleasure of the individual. In Castiglione's *Courtier* (1561),

> The exercise, as well as the appreciation of poetry, music and painting are grouped together as pursuits appropriate for the courtier, the gentleman or the prince. . . . The occupation with these "fine arts" is not clearly marked off from fencing, horse-riding, classical learning, the collecting of coins and medals and of natural curiosities or other equally worthy activities (Kristeller, 1970, p. 127).

Others disagreed. Conrad Gesner (1548), placed

> . . . poetry between rhetoric and arithmetic; music between geometry and astronomy; and lists architecture, sculpture and painting scattered among the mechanical arts such as transportation, clothmaking, alchemy, trade, agriculture and the like (Kristeller, 1970, p. 128).

Under the disciplined system of French academies the debate hardened into what came to be known as the *Querelle des Anciens et Modernes* from 1675–1700. A systematic comparison between the achievements of antiquity and of modern times in all areas of human endeavor and a classification of all knowledge and culture was undertaken. This in turn fed into activities of the Encyclopedists and resulted in the cultural fertility of the late eighteenth century in France, as well as the production of the *Encyclopedia* which literally defined all existing knowledge in modern capitalistic bourgeois terms.

The debates about which arts deserved priority continued and reached their conclusion in the *Encyclopedia* with the rationalization of the selection of painting, sculpture, architecture, music, and poetry as the "fine arts."[1] Almost simultaneously and in the same milieu, Immanuel Kant (1764) in his *Critique of Judgement* provided the definitive formal philosophical theory of beauty and the arts. With Kant, the system of fine arts for capitalist realism may be said to have been completed.

The similarity between this process and that used to initiate socialist realism in the twentieth century is remarkable. The role of the state and the dominant class in establishing policy and prescribing practice for

---

[1] Kristeller (1970) traces the debates in detail.

socialist art have been decried by the capitalist art establishment and its sympathizers within the new socialist states. Yet the conservative line in socialist states extolls the "freedom" of the artistic genius to produce for an art market as if it were a universal and timeless characteristic of art. It must be remembered that for capitalist realism (1) the development of high art was directly the result of state intervention in the interest of the dominant class; (2) new class-linked institutions were created by the state to conduct the development; (3) the process took a long time—at least three centuries. A similar process is in prospect for socialist realism.

In pursuing a closer analysis of the arts and science in Canada and the United States a series of massive contradictions confronts us. If, as noted in the beginning of this chapter, the only scientific definition of culture embraces all of people's artifacts and values, the grossest contradiction is that between this conception of culture and that given us by our class society. That upper class equates culture with the fine arts (enlarged to include the performing arts of opera, the dance, and the theater) and with its own "sensibilities." Even so fine a book as Susan Crean's *Who's Afraid of Canadian Culture* begins with the same definition of culture which I have adopted and then is constrained to deal with the arts as embodied *only* in the media, education, and the fine and performing arts. It will be helpful to diagram the contradictions which unfold upon analysis:

Figure 1: The Arts and Their Divisions

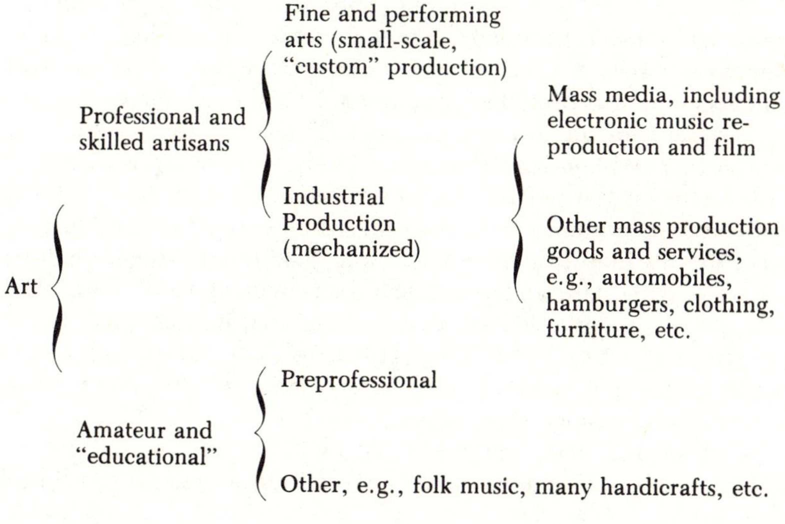

Art
- Professional and skilled artisans
  - Fine and performing arts (small-scale, "custom" production)
  - Industrial Production (mechanized)
    - Mass media, including electronic music reproduction and film
    - Other mass production goods and services, e.g., automobiles, hamburgers, clothing, furniture, etc.
- Amateur and "educational"
  - Preprofessional
  - Other, e.g., folk music, many handicrafts, etc.

Conventional literature on art will be found to focus on the profession-alized fine and performing arts, with perhaps a somewhat condescending acknowledgement that the mass media of communications are a related nether region which may serve to somehow "broaden the audience" for official art. Thus we find Baumol and Bowen (1966, p. 247) in their careful study of the performing arts for the 20th Century Fund saying:

> The vitality of live performance in the United States is undoubtedly desirable from an aesthetic standpoint, and is absolutely essential if for no other reason than to provide new material and trained personnel for the insatiable mass media.

Of course, the distinction should not be between "live" and nonlive per-formances but between small-scale and mass production because both the performing and other fine arts (e.g., painting, sculpture) practice small-scale "custom-made" productions rather than mass production.

Canadian policy for the fine arts early manifested its readiness to employ the state as agent for the elite class which ran the country. Sup-ported originally by bourgeois artists and private community organiza-tion, the Canadian National Gallery was formed in 1880 and formalized by legislation in 1913. In the United States, with its antipathy toward state intervention in the arts, traceable to the antiaristocratic policy ex-hibited in its Declaration of Independence (1776) and Constitution (1789), the fine arts remained a matter of private support down to 1937 when the National Gallery was created by Congress (although financed privately). Although donations to the arts were made deductible by in-dividuals for income tax purposes in the United States in 1917, direct federal support began only during the Cold War when the state depart-ment began the practice which still continues of sending performing arts groups and other art abroad ". . . as a weapon of ideological warfare" (Baumol and Bowen, 1966, p. 357). If it works abroad it should work at home seems to have been the logic, and in 1965 the first federal budget for direct support of the arts was adopted. The activities for which grants were authorized confirms the broad interpretation given in Figure 1: music (instrumental and vocal), dance, drama, folk art, creative writing, architecture and allied fields, painting, sculpture, photography, graphic and craft arts, industrial design, costume and fashion design, motion pic-tures, TV, radio, tape and sound recording (Baumol and Bowen, 1966, p. 359). In the preparation of elite opinion for this decisive step, the Rockefeller Brothers Fund report (1965, p. 11) cited as precedents the creation of the British Arts Council after World War II, and the creation of the Canada Council some ten years earlier.

One of the acute contradictions within Official Culture arises because, although deemed vital for the capitalist system, it is incurably a small business with a narrow audience both in numbers and in its "demographics." In Canada where audience research is less developed than in the United States we must content ourselves with Susan Crean's (1976, p. 122) estimate that for opera and ballet (the acme of Official Culture) the audience is between 1 and 2 percent of the population. For the United States, Baumol and Bowen conclude from a sophisticated empirical analysis that the unduplicated individuals attending drama, orchestral music, opera, and dance in 1963–1964 was about 2 percent of the population. This audience emphatically represents an elite. Baumol and Bowen (1966, pp. 96–97) conclude that the first characteristic

> . . . is the remarkable consistency of the composition of audiences from art form to art form, from city to city and from one performance to another.
>
> Second, the audience is drawn from an extremely narrow segment of the American population. In the main, it consists of persons who are extraordinarily well educated, whose incomes are very high, who are predominantly in the professions, and who are in their late youth or early middle age. . . .
>
> When professional performances are given free of charge or with carefully set low prices, the audience is drawn from a consistently wider cross section of the population. But even here there are no easy and overwhelming victories—in these audiences the number of blue collar workers is almost always under 10 percent and the number of professionals is always well over 50 percent, over 50 percent of the males have completed college; . . .

Their studies of English audiences showed the same audience characteristics.

In 1978 Dimaggio and Useem published a reanalysis of 268 studies of audiences for the fine and performing arts in the United States of which 80 percent had been made after 1971. As they summarize these studies, ". . . the social composition of the audience is far more elite than the general public, and the center of the audience is more elite than its periphery. Education, and to a lesser degree, income are good predictors not only of who consumes the arts but of the intensity of their consumption." Between 1965 and 1975 the scale of this elite activity expanded greatly: major professional dance companies, from 10 to 51; professional opera companies, from 23 to 45; professional orchestras, from 58 to 105; and resident nonprofit professional theaters, from 25 to 101. Government funding also rose dramatically: federal from $2.5 million annually to more than $149 million; state from $1.7 million annually to more than $55 million. The authors, however, found that during the period 1960 to 1977 no significant changes had taken place in the audience "demographics." Blue- and white-collar workers and ethnic minorities were insignificantly included in the audiences. "There are no signs that the democratization of arts funding is bringing a democratization of arts consumption" (Dimaggio and Useem, 1978, pp. 180, 192, 195).

Baumol and Bowen's (1966, p. 276) analysis of elasticity of demand shows that the box office demand for the performing arts is markedly inelastic. Moreover, after price increases the immediate reduction in demand disappears. The policy problem of whether to present "classics" or innovative modern program content contains a severe contradiction. Audience taste in the performing arts prefers ritualistic repetition of familiar classic works, whereas elite class interest in the industrial consequences requires steady infusion of innovative material (Baumol and Bowen, 1966, pp. 254-257).

Why should these fine arts be so conservative in form and content? They rest on the "star" system (for composers, choreographers, painters, etc., and their products likewise have the character of "stars") and as noted, stars as monopolies have been central to the official culture of capitalism since the Renaissance. As a badge of membership in the international capitalist system, each nation's official culture is linked into the international market for stars in the arts. The main reason for the rigid adherence to traditional grand opera works was given by the Rockefeller Brothers Fund report (1965, p. 29) as ". . . every musically developed country must have its national custodian of the classical repertory to maintain standards of performance and give young artists a focus for their aspirations."

Susan Crean makes it evident that since the creation of the Canada Council, the policy of official culture in the fine arts has been to cultivate the standards and productions which would meet the market test in New York, London, or Paris. But what is less recognized is that United States fine arts are still in important respects linked to European standards and products. Thus in what may be the most delicately cherished of the fine arts—ballet dance—the proportion of performances by "American groups" between 1954 and 1964 never rose above 50 percent and the median year percentage was 30 (Baumol and Bowen, 1966, p. 435). That the dance draws an extremely small audience was shown by Baumol and Bowen (1966, p. 95) who estimated the total number of individuals attending one or more dance performances in a year at 326,000. This was half the number attending grand opera, and a fourth the number attending the 25 major orchestras.

Structurally, the "boom" in fine and performing arts in Canada and the United States since the mid-1950s involved the bureaucratization and to a limited extent the professionalization of the organizations specializing in arts production and exhibition. In taking hegemony of arts organizations away from local groups among whom artists were founding members, Canadians are on the same course as their American counterparts. Thus, in considering the fact that artists had frequently created arts organizations in that country, the Rockefeller Brothers Fund report (1965, pp. 152-153) brushes aside the possibility that artists might have a dominating influence in the new generation of community and state arts boards which has arisen there. Rather it proposes that the new boards prepare for a ". . . smooth transition" when the founding artistic leadership departs. The (Massey) Royal Commission on National Development in the Arts, Letters and Sciences (1951, p. 375), after an exhaustive and sensitive investigation of Canada's arts, sciences and humanities, in 1951 followed the model of the Arts Council of Britain (1945) and of Richelieu several centuries earlier—in recommending the creation of a national council for the arts, funded by government, ". . . to increase the accessibility of the fine arts . . . to improve the standard of execution of the fine arts." The Canada Council was overlaid on a complex structure of voluntary arts organizations at the local and provincial levels in which the management was in the hands mostly of local elite with a fair admixture of creative artists. But as Susan Crean (1976, p. 151) remarks,

> In our lifetime, arts organizations have pushed artists aside, assuming all of the responsibility for selecting, presenting, interpreting and defining art and doing it in such a way that artists do not have to be present or even alive. [And further, she says (1976, p. 11):] It is a matter of public record that the same people who direct politics, business and industry sit on the governing boards of ballet companies, museums and the CBC in their spare time. They form a small and self-perpetuating coterie that manipulates culture, that is Official Culture, as surely as it directs the economy.

A crucial, if subtle, change was made in implementing the Massey Commission recommendation for creation of the Canada Council. The Massey Commission (Canada. Royal Commission on National Development, 1951, p. 381) had recommended that it should advance the arts, letters, humanities, and social sciences in Canada by means of

> The encouragement of *Canadian* music, drama and ballet (through the appropriate voluntary organizations and in cooperation with the Canadian Broadcasting Corporation and the National Film Board) by such means as the underwriting of tours, the commissioning of music for events of national importance, and the establishment of awards to young people of promise whose talents have been revealed in national festivals of music, drama, or the ballet (emphasis added).

When, however, the Canada Council was created, the enabling act deleted "Canadian" as qualifying artistic work and substituted "persons in Canada" to be recipients of the awards for work in the arts, humanities, and social sciences. Given the ideology of the elite class in Canada, it is therefore not surprising to find that the policy for guiding the development of Canadian art should be directed to the international market for stars which exists in the United States and other capitalist countries. What Susan Crean (1976, p. 4) says about painting is equally applicable to the other fine arts:

> With some exceptions (the Musée d'Art Contemporain in Montreal and the Vancouver Art Gallery) the aspiration of most Canadian galleries is to join the international "main stream" and leave the "provincial" national scene behind.

The monopoly which "professionalism" has in Canadian official culture, and the definition of such professionalism as work by an artist who can "make it" in New York (or perhaps London or Paris) is nowhere more stultifying than for the Canadian indigenous peoples. The Canadian art establishment treats them as Indian artists, whose work stereotypically should be lodged in a museum along with tomahawks. Indian artists confront a contradiction if they elect to compete with white artists because the individualistic values in the international bourgeois art market conflict with the collective values of the traditional art of the indigenous peoples. A few get some recognition in the international market; most are screened out because they are Indians.[2]

As with all branches of art (in the sense of the schema in Figure 1), the principal concern of the entrepreneurs is to produce *audiences*. This pervasive principle, the theory of which is the burden of Chapter 2, is as obviously true of the small-scale custom production of the fine and performing arts as it is of mass production. And we find the Rockefeller Brothers Fund report (1965, p. 5) saying, "Perhaps most important of all, both the creative artist and the performing artist need an intelligent and understanding audience." Audience education, moreover, is ". . . of crucial importance for increasing public support for all arts organizations and for providing another element of stability" (p. 100). Baumol and Bowen (1966, p. 257) say ". . . the desirability of increased audiences will be accepted as an article of faith by all those who believe in the importance of the arts for society." And their research is evidence of the application of science to audience building. Among the devices recommended are advertising of fine and performing arts events in the mass media, direct mail advertising to lists of people with the desired demographic characteristics, special children's performances, reduced-price tickets for students, and reduced-rate series tickets (a block-booking device), ticket-selling competitions with free vacations in tourist spots as prizes, and fund drives (women's auxiliaries), sales of baked goods, and organized benefit performances.

Such fund drives build captive audiences by enlisting women. Au-

---

[2] A symposium of interviews with indigenous Canadian artists, "Native Art," in *The Native Perspective* (1978, pp. 31–90).

dience promotion is also the object of flexibility in ticket-pricing by which it is urged that weeknight tickets be priced lower than Friday and Saturday night tickets, and the differential between matinee and evening ticket prices widened. Baumol and Bowen's (1966, pp. 249–257, 279–282) statistical analysis of demand led to the conclusion that lower prices would attract a younger audience, more students and teachers, and lower-income patrons. In Canada, the "hard sell" techniques of the 1960s and 1970s duplicated the American practice. And "audience development programs" became the basis of justifying the public budgets which would merchandise international star artists to the "uncultured" masses of the middle- and blue-collar classes while retaining the values of international upper class art.

The focus of the mobilization of private and state concern and resources just described is of course the professional "creative artist." Yet capitalist realism has always expected its professional artists to live on part-time, inadequate incomes. Composers, playwrights, and choreographers typically are unable to live on their earnings from those activities, depending on teaching income (composers), free-lance writing, acting, public relations (playwrights). Of these three groups, choreographers are worst off. The typical actors and actresses, authors, and artists are unable to depend on performing income for a living, beset as it is with unemployment and irregular earnings. Most piece out low annual incomes by other employment and income of spouses. It is striking, however, that small proportions get very high incomes (the stars). Thus, Baumol and Bowen report (1966, p. 106) that in the mid-1960s 10 percent of male actors, 8 percent of male authors, and 6 percent of male artists and art teachers received incomes as high as the top 9 percent of *all* male professional-technical occupations in the United States ($15,000 or more). And while almost zero percent of women in all professional-technical occupations earned $15,000 or more, 9 percent of actresses, 6 percent of female authors, and 1 percent of female artists and art teachers did. Comparable information on Canadian creative talent in the fine arts is lacking, but it is probable that the percentage receiving high incomes in Canada is much smaller than in the United States for that is where almost all Canadian stars are to be found. Crean (1976, pp. 158–159) quotes Jack Chambers:

> The prevailing myths that do most harm to artists are those which extol his genius and in the same breath underscore his inability to agree with his fellow artists, his incapacity to organize for his own good, his carelessness and unconcern for others. These myths, which are by definition fictitious, provide the unthinking public, and the unthinking artists as well, with a ready-made image that flatters while keeping him vulnerable to predators. It is in the interest of the middleman, the nonartists, the commercial dealer and institutional administrator for whom the artist is a meal ticket that those myths originate and circulate.

This is not new: the systematic cultivation of a pool of unemployed creative people in the fine arts, frequently stereotyped as "bohemian," has been a feature of high culture under capitalism for at least four centuries. In the second half of the twentieth century, however, creative people as a class have struggled through union and other professional organizations to obtain higher income, better working conditions, and a voice in determining the nature of their work. The type of repression they meet is illustrated by a quotation from G. Hamilton Southam, Director General, National Arts Centre in Canada:

> I don't believe that artists have anything to do with politics; the artists who get mixed up in politics are usually second-class artists . . . the great ones have nothing to do with politics, nothing to do with unions, nothing to do with campaigns (Crean, 1976, pp. 171–172).

Despite the low incomes typically paid creative talent in the fine arts, arts organizations chronically show operating deficits ranging from 46 percent of operating expenses for 25 major symphony orchestras in the United States and 45 percent of ten opera companies other than the Metropolitan to 24 percent for the New York City Ballet and 15 percent for 14 regional theaters. In Canada deficits average 45 percent for the performing arts and between 75 and 92 percent for museums. As Baumol and Bowen demonstrate this is no temporary phenomenon. It has been characteristic of the fine arts since the Industrial Revolution and occurs because the small-scale, unmechanized production of the fine arts is very "labor intensive." That is, the possibilities of cost reduction from capital investment in machinery are virtually nil, while increases in productivity in physical goods production (and some service industries) take place regularly as a result of increased capital investment in machinery. Meanwhile workers in the fine arts must share in the results of the increases in productivity elsewhere through income increases, modest though the latter may be. The result is ever-increasing deficits.

To distribute the burden of the subsidies, all the audience-building techniques of Consciousness Industry are being applied to the fine arts. And scientific management tries to isolate the creative artists from the policy-making process. Meanwhile the dominant class in Canada and the United States ruthlessly abandon (for the fine and performing arts) the doctrine of consumer sovereignty and openly seek maximum contributions from private corporations and the state to meet present deficits and the larger deficits which forced expansion of the productions of the fine arts will entail. Baumol and Bowen (1966, p. 382) in concluding their Twentieth Century Fund study list four benefits from this policy:

1.   "Prestige conferred on a nation by its performing arts," quoting George London, as testifying that the arts were being used as "a potent propaganda weapon of the Cold War";

2.   The stimulation of revenues from tourism, restaurants, and the creation of a community environment to which a transnational corporation will be able to bring its professional-techno-bureaucrats and reduce their turnover;

3.   Anticipated but unspecifiable benefits to future genera-tions from preservation now of the Fine Arts;

4.   The educational effect on the young now.

In our Figure 1, the other "wing" of professionals and artisans in the arts was their incorporation in industrial mass production of goods and services. And here we may distinguish (1) the mass media, including elec-tronic music reproduction; (2) other mass production of goods and ser-vices, especially consumer goods and services.

The mass media content has been the object of what a large literature in sociology has considered "mass culture" in the past 40 years in North America. This literature generally approaches the object ahistorically and without regard to the politico-economic context in which mass media con-tent has been produced (Rosenberg and White, 1964, 1971; Larrabee and Meyersohn, 1958; Gans, 1974). True, in a sense the mass media have replaced the role of the theater, vaudeville stage, circuses, and carnivals, and the reading of popular literature in providing what the system calls "entertainment," as well as that of the competitive local newspaper in providing "news." Certainly the mechanization of the production of entertainment and news has fantastically multiplied its availability. An orchestral performance on television reaches an audience of perhaps 20 million instead of 2500 in a concert hall—an increase of productivity by a factor of about 8000. And a major athletic event may be seen by 60 million as compared to perhaps 1000 in the bleachers at a local "big game"—an increase by a factor of about 60,000. But to say, as some do, that the mass media event satisfies "higher critical standards than its pre-cursors" (Baumol and Bowen, 1966, p. 246) is to miss the crucial differ-ence between the present and earlier periods.

Common to the industrial production of all cultural goods under monopoly capitalism (mass media products and consumer goods and ser-vices) from the standpoint of art is that the state and practice of the art are ruled by a phalanx of constraints in the interest of profit-maximization (including capital gains) for the dominant giant enterprises responsible but not accountable for the other consequences of their actions. The master chef of the TNC who determines the quality and quantity of the meat to be made into the hamburger, the machine tool operator who cuts the prototype for the stove on which the hamburger is to be cooked, the writer who draws the story-board for the 30-second TV spot announcement to advertise the hamburger, the actress who performs in the spot announcement, the musician who composes the score for the sound track of the spot announcement, the clown who publicizes the TNC's hamburger near the elementary school, all these and innumerable other ancillary artistic activities are under clear policy direction by Consciousness Industry. So also with the art of the advertising director of the TNC in selecting the particular program material (the free lunch) which will be appropriate to the purpose of the particular spot announcement. These decisions in turn generate the constraints passed through the management of the program-producing enterprises (TV station and program-producing companies) to the "talent" which produces, writes, casts, acts in, prepares musical score for, edits film or videotape of, and synthesizes film, music, and sound track in a single final production of the free lunch designed to help sell the hamburger. In all these activities the artist working with the industrial arts is constrained by policies which are *scientifically* determined to be most efficient.

This is not the place to do justice to the history of the artists and of the institutions through which they work in the struggles between dominant and oppressed classes. It is a history which began with the first formation of class societies. The persons who conducted the religious rituals of the first theocratic communities were maintaining the existing class relations. And all congregate assemblies, whether labeled "entertainment," religion, sports, industry, or warfare, inevitably perform acts of support or subversion of existing class relations. So also with the institutions and persons engaged in the representational arts of painting, drawing, sculpture, poetry, literature, radio, cinema, and television. Possibly the clearest example of the success of capitalist realism in controlling the ideological aspect of all the arts is the lack of awareness by professional artists of the long tradition of class struggle of which they are heirs. I have found no general treatments of this history; only fragmentary, unconnected bits of the process seem to have been analyzed (Boswell, 1932; Carlson, 1966; Harbage, 1941; Leith, 1965; Lough, 1957; McKechnie, 1969; Mander and Mitchenson, 1965; Mayer, 1969; Rosenfeld, 1960). But here I must be content to note the fact of systemic constraints on the artistic potential of people in the core areas of monopoly capitalism. As the executive vice president and general manager of the Newspaper Advertising Bureau in New York, Leo Bogart (1976, p. 109) says:

> Changes in the media, with all their tremendous consequences for the flow of information and the character of public taste, are not made by popular request. They do not reflect the "democracy of the marketplace." Rather they

result from the decisions made either directly by advertising buyers [of audiences] or by media managements anticipating advertiser demand; they are decisions made by the numbers.

The broad front of the struggle lies precisely between Consciousness Industry on the one hand, and on the other, people with what Thorstein Veblen (1899) called the "instinct of workmanship."

The monopoly-capitalist system continually produces new markets (audiences, generically) to consume new products, especially service commodities. Before our very eyes literally, since 1948, it has created a series of markets to serve which especially trained professional artists are required: the sports markets. In rough chronological order specialized sports markets were created for baseball (more than doubling the number of teams in the American "major leagues"), boxing and "wrestling," bowling, American-style football, basketball, ice hockey, tennis, skiing, and currently emerging in the USA and Canada, soccer football. In the early years of TV it is arguable that boxing, "wrestling," bowling, and baseball contributed as much to TV's growth and profitability as it did for theirs. In their professional form each of these sports requires of its labor force that in addition to being competent athletes, they be performers with audience-building capacity for showmanship (including stereotypes as "bad" and "good" guys), calculated and permitted displays of pseudo-spontaneous violence, etc. Moreover, in an almost incestuous way, the system has attempted to erect new sports on the basis of the old by creating competitions between star performers from the various "old" sports in skills *other* than those in which they reached stardom.

An extremely complex structure of interlocking markets has developed for sports-related services, which is diagramed in Figure 2. First in importance, because it can produce the audience out of the people, are the mass media. With their acknowledged expertise and close ties with advertisers, the media are the catalysts and organizers of major market innovations. The advertisers are the next most important factors in creating new market commodities. The power to attract audiences either in stadia or to media resides, for the sports free lunch, with professional performers and the businessmen who specialize in managing athletic talent. These entrepreneurs historically appear to have been involved in gambling.[3] And gambling on sports events is a major industry in its own right. Publicly owned stadia with mass capacity have been an essential component in the sports market complex for the dual purpose of placing the capital cost on taxpayers and enlisting "civic" support for the local "team." The

---

[3] For the origin of the National Baseball League in 1876 by gamblers who needed to rationalize the season's games, see, Kampf (1977), and Hoch (1972).

Figure 2: Sports-Related Markets and Institutions

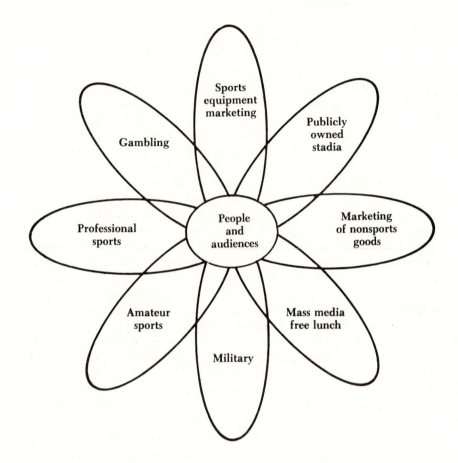

patronage of military-nationalist influence has been a consistent support for innovation in sports, originating in the last two decades of the nineteenth century in identical movements to improve physical fitness and instill discipline in major capitalist nations. The last of the intersecting institutions in the complex is absolutely essential to the future development of professional sport talent and audiences: amateur (or as it might be more properly called, preprofessional) sports. People available to be produced as audiences are the common base for all these intersecting institutional activities.

This sketchy survey of the political economy of the arts in monopoly capitalism concludes with the amateur and educational phase of the arts. And here we may divide them into two tendencies, the frankly preprofessional, and the I-just-want-to-do-it. When we turn to considering amateurism in the fine arts, the amazing fact emerges that the professional fine arts, at least in the performing arts sector is like the tip of an iceberg as related to amateur activity in those fine and performing arts. Thus in the United States in 1965, 99.5 percent of the 40,000 theatrical groups were amateur, 99 percent of the 754 opera groups were amateur, and 96.2 percent of the 1401 symphony orchestras were amateur, as were 97 percent of the 200 dance groups (Rockefeller Brothers Fund, 1965, pp. 13–14). Chorus singing is a performing art in which it is estimated millions of Americans participate through uncounted organizations. Data are not at hand regarding painting, sculpture, and poetry, but the amateur substratum in those fine arts may be assumed to be proportionately larger than the professionals. Quite apart from both the pre-professionals and amateurs in the fine and performing arts, there remains the vast range of artistic activity for which there is *no* professional cachet and which is condescendingly referred to as "hobbies." Here we may begin an open-ended list with hunting, fishing, cooking, winemaking, woodworking, metalworking, weaving, knitting, gardening, ceramics, etc. Presently these arts are stimulated and organized as a result of efforts to develop markets for materials, tools, and techniques by the "do-it-yourself" elements of Consciousness Industry—often served by specialized magazines. To the extent that this broad range of artistic activities is caught up in the process of audience-production, it embodies a significant contradiction. Such amateur artistic activities often have a stance critical of the policies of Consciousness Industry. For example, hobbyists in cooking typically view their hobby as rejecting standardized fast foods provided by Consciousness Industry.

What are the consequences of the system of capitalist realism as it concerns culture, arts, and communications?

1. The very long period of time over which capitalist realism developed imparted to those living in it the impression of timelessness and universality. For those living in it, minor controversies within the system (naturalism vs. impressionism, new directions in cinematic art, etc.) might be analogized to the significance of a movement within living memory of a few feet in the extension of a glacier over the northern Great Plains in Canada in the last glacial age. But it must be remembered that the task faced by the builders of capitalist realism was no less grandiose than the time scale of the effort: How to revise the knowledge and ways of thinking of a thousand years after the breakup of the Roman Empire.

2. The fine arts provide cultural legitimation for the capitalist system and for their own lives for the middle-class people able to enjoy the fruits of the system.

3.   The fine arts are an adornment for capitalism and effective advertising as a means of ideological warfare in the world community. The consequence would be mitigated to the extent that socialist realism engaged the attention and respect of artists and other intellectuals throughout the world.

4.   The arts in general (including not only the fine arts but other arts lower in the pecking order) provide the spark of novelty which is incorporated in the planning, production, and marketing of all consumer goods and services under capitalism by means of design, packaging, and advertising thus contributing to the planned obsolescence which makes the consumership system function.

5.   The fine arts in Canada have been administered in the interest of continuing Canada's dependence on the United States through the cooptation of professional talent to the metropolitan core art market and discouraging other aspirations of the artists. But for the amateur artists, i.e., those whose raison d'etre is not constrained by the values of that international market, the opportunities to express a Canadian resistance to colonial domination are ever-present. For those artists and artisans engaged in the production of mass media materials, and for that larger number perennially subject to deskilling in the practice of the industrial arts, the protection of their creative integrity depends upon their developing common means of resistance to Canadian domination in the interest of compradors responsible to foreign TNCs. The role of art in Canada is dialectical. On the one hand, the "fine arts," as Gail Dexter (1970, p. 165) says are propaganda for capitalism, American style. They have value

. . . only to that class of people which profits from the mystification of life experience: to that class of people which equates a marginal artistic license with human freedom; to that class of people for which real life struggles are either irrelevant or dangerous. The art of the imperialist bourgeoisie therefore presents unity where real life presents class struggle. . . .

On the other hand, Canadian artists and artisans serve the cause of the bulk of the Canadian people when they organize and struggle for indigenous values.

One of the objectives of this chapter has been to demystify the class conception of art and the artist. The prevalent mystification has been found to be embodied in capitalist realism in the arts. It has been noted that this capitalist realism also mystifies science, but attention in Chapter 9 has been focused on the demystification of the arts. In Chapter 10 I undertake the demystification of science as embodied in the propagandistic concept, technology, and go on to discuss *cultural screens*—the means by which nations protect and nurture their own culture.

10

ON "TECHNOLOGY" AND COMMODITIES AS PROPAGANDA; NEEDS AND CULTURAL SCREENS

The bourgeoisie cannot exist without constantly revolutionizing the instruments of production and thereby the relations of production, and with them, the whole relations of society (Marx, Karl, and Engels, Frederick, *The Communist Manifesto*)

"Technology" may rival "free flow of information" as the propaganda term most valuable for monopoly capitalism in the last century. It is said to offer us all kinds of "good" *or* "bad" things. And when bad things come to pass, more technology in turn will cure them, *if* we use it to produce more good things, and not more bad things. And so on. Canadian communications *technology* is said to be responsible for our cultural dependence on the United States. Humanity's ecological crisis will be the result of technology. Developing nations need not high technology but intermediate technology. Catastrophic world war, if it comes, is the result of our use of technology. Think tanks like the Hudson Institute prosper by predicting future technologies which in some way reflect the fancied strengths and weaknesses of the present. China is welcomed into the orbit of American technology by people and institutions which backed a 20-year boycott of that country; and China shocks many of its left-liberal friends at the same time—because of its welcome to Coca Cola and other Western technology.

What *do* we mean by *technology?* Let us test the question against the proposition that the technology of privately owned automobiles is the chief cause of atmospheric pollution in North America. Science is often linked with statements about technology so let us begin with that. The connection lies in the decision (or perhaps merely the possibility) to apply scientific knowledge in some practical way, e.g., to the production of a vehicle powered by an internal combustion engine. Both the knowledge and the practical use of it arise out of the concrete social reality of a class society as described in Chapter 9. But at its junction with science, "technology" is an abstract thing. Such an abstract possibility produces none of the pollution of the urban atmosphere caused by private automobiles. Clearly science alone is *not* what is referred to by technology.

Perhaps "technology" refers to science plus research and development. Broadly speaking, R & D involves work which proceeds in two opposite directions: (a) experimental work which embodies the results of new scientific knowledge and proceeds to answer the question: if we put this new knowledge to work, what practical results will it have?; (b) experimental work which proceeds from known practical problems toward new solutions based on new knowledge and which answers the question: can we find a practical solution to a certain practical problem, given that we can now apply some new scientific discoveries? This is the state in which work on electric automobiles has been for some years. In this possible meaning of *technology* we may speak of it properly as the search for an optimum *technique* for doing something. That something will arise out of and reinforce the dominant class interests in a society—when it is put into general use. The terminology of capitalism has now for about a century obscured the fact that the R & D applications of knowledge are forms of *art*—a fact well understood by the ancient Greeks. Until near the end of the nineteenth century, people customarily referred to the *industrial arts* to mean what we here call *technique*. And patent law under capitalism still retains the term when it relates patent rights to improvements "in the state of the art." Instead we substituted the term *invention* to refer to the results of R & D. By now it should be generally recognized that not all R & D results in inventions which are put into general use. To continue our illustration both the steam- and electric-powered engines were invented for automobiles by the early 1900s. But R & D work on the gasoline-powered automobile did not cause atmospheric pollution.

The most common meaning of *technology* in Western capitalism is the *full implementation* in practice of some invention which has emerged from the R & D stage. And by *full implementation* I mean, to use the example of the internal-combustion-powered private automobile, the production of the automobile and of all its parts, the production of highways on which to drive it, the production of an organization for selling, servicing, and repairing automobiles, and for distributing the fuel, oil, replacement parts, and accessories for the automobile, the organization and facilities appropriate to off-street parking, and similarly for industries like the trailer industry which depends on the automobile. E. G. Mesthene of Harvard University's Program on Technology (quoted in McDermott, 1972, p. 152) defines *technology* as ". . . the organization of knowledge for practical purposes. . . ." In a recent Canadian book, Wallace Gagne (1976, p. 9) defines it ". . . to refer both to the physical means of production and to the norms and values which organize and direct that productive system." And Jacques Ellul (1963, p. 10) defines "technique," which he prefers to use in place of "technology," as "the new and specific *milieu* in which man is required to exist, one which has supplanted the old *milieu*, viz., that of nature."

The first point to be made regarding technology is that when experts choose to define it, *technology* is defined as meaning the same thing as *modern civilization,* or *modern capitalism* or any other term descriptive of the totality of our social order. I return to this point later. But first there is the amazing fact that most writers on it never define it. I made a modest search in some dozens of books (out of the thousands published in the past century with *technology* as a central theme) for definitions of the term. What I learned was that hardly any of these authors ever troubles to define the term technology. Is it so obvious that it doesn't need definition? Then *why use it instead of one of its better-defined synonyms such as "modern society" or modern capitalism?* After all it was not socialism which developed the factory system with its smog or the automobile, but capitalism. Is it possible that unconsciously for the most part intellectuals have wanted to have their cake and eat it at the same time? If "technology" can be blamed for the ills of our social order, then the responsibility is displaced. A convenient scapegoat has been found, labeled, and criticized. But the social order rolls on, protected to some extent against serious criticism by the smoke screen of the controversy over—technology. David Sarnoff, president of RCA, once responded to critics of radio programing: "Do you blame the plumber for what goes through the pipes?" When one looks at the evils of "technology" it seems that the only full cure is to abandon the whole social order and return to nature. Yet all institutions in the social order resist such nonsensical advice.

It should have been self-evident that to analyze technology as if it were synonymous with modern society raises fundamental questions which are as old as social organization. Because science is inevitably incorporated somehow into the analysis, our knowledge of the origin of life is involved in analyzing technology, and we are diverted to debating cosmology. Also the specter of determinism—"technological" or economic—is to be found either openly debated or smuggled into the discourse between the lines. I suppose that if one were to pursue the issue through the vast literature on technology, one will find that the problems of "technology" have been connected with predestination, original sin, and assorted theological issues which otherwise no longer occupy the center stage of debate.

In short, only by stretching technology to include everything concerning humanity through all prehistory and history could it be said to be *autonomous*, and then only at risk in metaphysical debate about the origin of the universe. It is a fantastically elastic diversionary *cul de sac*. It is a red herring and we should begin to substitute "industrial arts" for it. Then the inescapable political nature of the essence of the term *technology* becomes evident. As David F. Noble (1977, pp. 33–35) remarks:

> Modern technology, as the mode of production specific to advanced industrial capitalism, was both a product and a medium of capitalist development. So too, therefore, was the engineer who personified modern technology. In his work he was guided as much by the imperatives that propelled the economic system as by the logic and laws of science. The capitalist, in order to survive, had to accumulate capital at a rate equal to or greater than that of competitors. And since his capital was derived ultimately from the surplus product of human labor, he was compelled to assume complete command over the production process in order to maximize productivity and efficiently extract this product from those who labored for him. It was for this reason that mechanical devices and scientific methods were introduced into the workshop. . . . If some economist drew a distinction between technology and capitalism, that distinction collapsed in the person of the engineer and in his work, engineering.
>
> Even in his strictly technical work the engineer bought to his task the spirit of the capitalist. His design of machinery, for example, was guided as much by the capitalist need to minimize both the cost and the autonomy of skilled labor as by the desire to harness most efficiently the potentials of matter and energy. The technical and capitalist aspects of the engineer's work were reverse sides of the same coin, modern technology. As such they were rarely if ever distinguishable: technical demands defined the capitalist possibilities only insofar as capitalist demands defined the technical possibilities. The technical work of the engineer was little more than the scientific extension of capitalist enterprise; it was through his efforts that science was transformed into capital. "The symbol of our monetary unit, the dollar," Henry Towne wrote in 1886, "is almost as frequently conjoined to the figures of an engineer's calculations as are the symbols indicating feet, minutes, pounds or gallons." "The dollar," he later told Purdue engineering students, "is the final term in every engineering equation." . . . The economic inspiration inherent in technical work, of course, did not altogether rule out the possibility of conflict between the demands of technological superiority and of market expedience. When such conflict did arise, however, there was never any doubt about the outcome. The president of the Stevens Institute Alumni Association, for example, was unequivocal on this point, and his address to students in 1896 had no trace of ambiguity: "The financial side of engineering is always the most important; the sooner the young engineer recedes from

the idea that simply because he is a professional man, the position is paramount, the better it will be for him. He must always be subservient to those who represent the money invested in the enterprise."[1]

Technology is *not* an independent autonomous force.

As Chapters 3 and 4 have shown, the organization and policies of Consciousness Industry were quite rationally developed to rationalize the mass production of consumer goods in the period, 1880s to 1950s. This was when the various mass media institutions were "invented" by the monopoly-capitalist system to serve its purposes by mass producing people in audiences who would market such mass-produced goods to themselves. We have seen in Chapters 5–8 how the people of Canada and the United States have been converted over time to the lifestyles, consumption habits, and values which are central to Consciousness Industry. The process was one of interaction between consciousness and material forces.

A striking example of how the needs of monopoly capitalism to pursue its goal of developing a technology efficient in producing audiences to market consumer goods to themselves were met is that of the fate of broadcast facsimile (see Chapter 4). It is significant that the FCC approved the standards and rules for operating *both* television and facsimile broadcasting in those years. But while necessary for innovation such approval did not result in the innovation of either as technology. Either of the two modes of broadcasting was equally feasible as a technical and regulatory matter. They implied alternative institutional modes either of which could have been developed. But not *both* for their implications were mutually exclusive at that time.[2]

The development of TV technology, with all its later technical additions (videotape, porta-paks, cable TV, pay TV, etc.), was thus the result of the policies of Consciousness Industry. It was *not* determined by machines, or science, or any autonomous force mysteriously emanating from our origins in primordial ooze or original sin.

Any society must address itself to the satisfaction of the needs of its population. The agenda for satisfying such needs in traditional (i.e., precapitalist) societies gives prime place to institutions for meeting the needs of people for activities in which commodities are marginal or absent. Sexual activities, child-rearing, making and enjoying the subtleties of communities, healing, consoling, learning, artistic, religious needs are in this

---

[1] My only criticism of Noble's treatment of technology is that he never defines *technology*; does not use it in quotation marks nor acknowledge its values as a propaganda weapon for capitalism.

[2] See Lessing, Lawrence, *Man of High Fidelity* (1956) for analysis of corporate politics which promoted television and suppressed innovation of FM and facsimile.

category. (The overthrow of the Shah of Iran in 1979 by a population organized around the religious and ethnic focus of such needs was an example of their power unforeseen by the Central Intelligence Agency and monopoly capitalism.) These activities and the institutions built to satisfy such needs over millennia—the family, the clan, religious organizations, etc.—are precisely those which Consciousness Industry has invaded and capitalized through the commodity route.

To satisfy the needs which require commodities, any society necessarily has also to provide answers to three basic questions concerning the commodities it needs: (1) *What* goods to produce with its limited human and natural resources? This question divides into two others. (a) *What* goods to produce for primarily common or public use (e.g., schools, railroads, ships, communication facilities)? (b) What goods to produce primarily for private use (e.g., clothing, private automobiles, etc.)? (2) *For whom* and on what terms to produce the goods it chooses to produce (e.g., primarily for its dominating or elite class or primarily for everyone)? (3) *How* to produce the goods it chooses to produce and on what terms to distribute them to those for whom they were produced (e.g., what organization and industrial arts to employ, how to distribute authority in the production and distribution of commodities)?

Are these questions economic or political? In all societies they are treated as questions to be answered at the level of the state. They are clothed with the symbols and handled through the institutions of the dominant social classes and the communication institutions in the society are programed to legitimize the modes chosen to answer the three questions. In theocratic states, they appear to be treated in religious or ethical terms, as is true of many traditional societies in recent times. Following the development of modern capitalism some three to four centuries ago, the dominant capitalist class and its economists insisted that its chosen instruments, the market and capitalist organizations (most recently the giant corporation, often a TNC), should determine the answers to these three questions. Within the bounds set by the market and corporate practice, the mystified and mystifying term *technology* has served to shield from effective criticism the rather obvious and crude practices which are the reality. Because the capitalist class has controlled the state apparatus under capitalism, and because the policies of the state are inescapably political, it follows that the answers given these questions by capitalist markets and organization are politically sanctioned. That is, they are the outcome of power struggles (for wealth and prestige) within the body politic. Economic theory under capitalism attempted to justify and provide the rationalizations which explain how such markets and organizations function. And because such rationalizations *assume* the immutably natural character of the exercise, critical treatment of such questions has been systemically removed from the rhetorical scope of capitalist politics. Analyses such as this which question the alleged *apolitical* character of these questions and of all capitalist economic jargon thus sound strange.

Politics, then, is *always* in command; and the choice of what politics—the support of a given class-dominated pattern of life or of an alternative and more egalitarian pattern—is made consciously or unconsciously by everyone in the society.

As was pointed out in Chapters 1 and 9, the fact that more than one-third of the human race now lives in countries which are trying in various ways to achieve the more egalitarian objectives of socialism gives us the first opportunity ever to understand the difficulties we face in considering how to free ourselves from the undesirable characteristics of monopoly capitalism. Who will decide the kind of development a presently dominated people will pursue? And who will benefit *most* from the kind decided upon: the process currently focuses on the issues *what* is to be produced, *for whom*, and *how*, questions in their political setting.

WHAT IS TO BE PRODUCED?

The first question then, *What* is to be produced? There are two types of consumer goods (end products): those which are sold for *private* use (automobiles, for example), and those which are for *public* use (schools, for example). The productive effort and organization under capitalism which is devoted to private use is referred to as the *private* sector, that for public use as the *public* sector. Monopoly capitalism has devoted its command of resources to the private sector so successfully that we tend to identify it with the whole question of "what is to be produced." Our consumer goods are all in this sector. As designed, packaged, and sold, they are very attractive, especially to those people who have not up to now been able to buy such things. The list is long and glittering and may be extended by reference to the mass media: private automobiles, one-way TV, family-sized refrigerators, washing machines, vacuum cleaners, air conditioners, electric kitchen utensils, cosmetics, soap, drugs, soft and alcoholic drinks, trademarked "breakfast foods," "junk food," stylish clothes and shoes, personal hygiene items (deodorants, shampoos, toothpaste, etc.), media products such as phonograph records, and tapes, sports equipment, etc. All such consumer goods have certain characteristics in common.

1. They appeal to and cultivate in their users individual selfishness because the basis of their design, packaging, and sales appeal is to individual insecurities and potentials for aggression or exploitation (including the "I'm OK, you're not OK" relationship between individuals, sexes and races). They are all teaching machines.

2.   They are aimed at the middle, working, and upper class; the poor are *not* the expected users of them (except as sold to them secondhand or as charitable gifts from the better off). Collectively they obscure the unadvertised fact that monopoly capitalism does not serve the poor people who, measured by their ability to buy a "minimum health and decency" budget, number between one-third and 40 percent of the population of the wealthy capitalist core nations such as the United States, Canada, and the United Kingdom.

3.   They provide TNCs with their vast profits.

4.   They collectively account for the environmental pollution the responsibility for which is shifted from monopoly capitalism to technology, and thus avoided.

5.   Their intrinsic use value is far below their exchange value, under capitalism. Slack-filled packages, shoddy workmanship, calculated built-in obsolescence with short useful lives—these characterize the output of the private sector. They are conceived and produced by Consciousness Industry usually as embodying images: consumable salable images. A genuinely mysterious mixture of use values and insubstantial images characterizes most of them. Here one confronts subtle distinctions. There is of course still a quantum of objective use value in most of them. Meat from animals, fattened with steroids and antibiotics, packaged with artificial coloring, still has nutritive value even if also elements not calculated to enhance the consumer's health. A camera, fragile and soon to be obsolescent, does take pictures. Especially in luxury commodities, substantial materials well hand-crafted provide residual examples of use values often with styling which is minimally pretentious. But nevertheless, a systemic bias exploits the profit potential of illusion in most mass-produced consumer goods. And the stylistic features of such goods (and their packaging) is very attractive to peoples in both peripheral and core countries who have never had enough to eat, wear, and who cannot otherwise enjoy the commodities of Consciousness Industry. Such commodities are powerful propaganda for the capitalist system and when imported into, or imitated within, countries now trying to go through the transitional stage to socialism they exert strong ideological pressure in favor of reproducing the capitalist system. The juridical title to ownership of the means of producing consumer goods in the name of workers and peasants, as distinct from private ownership of the means of production is a necessary but insufficient basis for building socialism. The sufficient basis of socialism will be found in finding systemically different answers to the questions, what, for whom, and how consumer goods are to be produced. As yet the process of determining these questions in ways ap-

propriate to socialism has not yet been tackled on a large scale anywhere.

6. Because of the waste inherent in the apparently endless expansion of the production of private goods, they absorb the great bulk of natural and human resources which the capitalist core extracts and uses. They engorge the private sector and starve the public sector.

Is my argument that all commodities—producers' and consumers' goods—are *intrinsically* and *permanently* carriers of capitalist ideology? By no means. Instead I submit that all commodities to some degree embody a contradiction between opposite ideological qualities: tendencies toward their use primarily for private profit, and tendencies toward their use for individual (and collective) welfare. Again, let us divide one into two. Producers' goods conceived and built to apply power obviously contribute to general (and individual) welfare by relieving direct labor of dangerous and irksome drudgery. But they also are conceived and built to damage welfare (although producing profits) by producing weaponry both nuclear and conventional, as well as by the ecological damage which even nonmilitary machines produce as side effects of their operations. Secondly, as to consumer goods, I argue that they too have a similar internal contradiction embodied in them. To greater or lesser degree in the case of individual commodities, then, it appears that they are damaged. As has been argued throughout this book, that new commodity produced by monopoly capitalism—the audience—is produced as damaged people.

The foregoing argument leads to the conclusion that until the twentieth century the great burst of technical inventiveness occurring in the preceding three centuries necessarily resulted in industrial arts and consumer goods in which the internal capitalist ideological component has dominated the welfare component. The lopsided emphasis on goods production by the "private sector" also foreclosed the possibilities of devoting more of this great burst of technical inventiveness to the production of public rather than private goods. So *the aggregate* of possible goods production has been damaged by the neglect of the welfare component for the capitalist world economy as a whole. In the brief period since the Russian Revolution in 1917, the socialist states have not yet had time to generate industrial arts and consumer goods in which the welfare component generally is dominant. Uncritical borrowing of techniques for producing both producers' and consumers' goods from capitalist countries by the socialist countries postpones the development of industrial arts and consumption goods which would be more appropriate to socialism than those they borrow. This is, of course, especially and crucially true of the borrowing from Consciousness Industry of "scientific management" techniques for producing both physical commodities and audiences.

In 1971–72, I studied the relation of ideology to communications and culture in both Hungary and China. In Hungary I was told by a senior officer of the state that within five years it would have twice as many private automobiles as it then did. I pointed out that even then the atmospheric pollution in Budapest was dangerous, that a superhighway had been built from Budapest to Lake Balaton on which TNC-owned gas stations provided gasoline, and asked him whether the socialist road for Hungary figuratively had as its goal a Cadillac for every peasant and worker. His response was an angry glare and from that point the interview deteriorated rapidly. In China it appeared that because of the policies followed for the preceding twenty years the formerly hungry, ill-clad, ill-housed, and chronically diseased bulk of the Chinese population were approaching the point where the physiologically necessary goods and services would be available in adequate supply and at low cost to everyone. I asked whether private or public consumer goods would get the highest priority once everyone had enough food, enough simple warm clothing, enough simple housing, enough health care—in short, "After Bicycles, What?" At that time in China, politics was said everywhere to be in command, and a key slogan was that China would take the "socialist road" rather than the "capitalist road" taken by the Soviet Union. At the same time, it was emphasized that China lagged behind the West and must "catch up." I remarked that there was a serious contradiction here: could the industrial arts in a China pursuing the socialist road be measured against the accomplishments of those in capitalism? Conceding that such comparison might be possible in terms of capability to produce some producers' goods, it did not seem possible for consumer goods, where the roads fork with the capitalist road specializing on private consumer goods and the socialist road on public consumer goods. The test of the socialist road would be: does a particular commodity serve the masses of people collectively or as individuals?

I illustrated my point with the example of two-way TV. In conversations with revolutionary committees running TV stations I was told that at that time China had only a few million TV sets and few TV stations but that they planned for a truly nationwide TV system. I asked them if the plan was to adopt the one-way TV system capitalism had developed to make possible the production of audiences which would market commodities to themselves. I said that it was an implicitly authoritarian system in which influence was transmitted from the top down; no electronic response capability was built into it. When capitalism "invented" one-way TV it would have been equally possible to have designed a two-way system in which each TV receiver would have a video response capability, the responses to which could be broadcast in turn. I pointed out that in China the existing TV receivers were located in public places (commune meeting halls, factory recreation centers, etc.) rather than in homes and that for receivers in such places large-screen sets with video feedback facilities would be economically feasible.

My hosts asked me why I thought it desirable in China for the TV system to be two-way. I replied that customarily and especially during the Cultural Revolution the Chinese people made much use of *tatzupao* (big character posters pasted on walls or signboards) in which they expressed their opinions freely. A two-way TV system would be an electronic *tatzupao* system and would aid the discussion of matters of comon concern at the community level. Now when China was still not committed to a Western style one-way TV system, China could design a TV industrial art which would serve its ideological purposes rather than adopt uncritically a capitalist industrial art for TV which embodies capitalist ideology. Substantially the same conversation took place in Shanghai, Nanking, Beijing, Wuhan, and Kwangchow and in every instance the suggestion was received with interest, and the comment that they would think about it. The response from University of Peking economists and philosophers, however, was essentially that "technology" was universal and politically neutral; that socialism could use one-way TV without ideological danger because of social ownership of the equipment. In my opinion this was un-critical adoption of vulgarized Marxism derived from Soviet Marxists. The Chinese have proceded to innovate one-way TV.

A second illustration is the possibility of "moving sidewalks" as a social commodity which would largely solve transportation problems in the central areas of cities. Derived from science fiction and practice in large airports, it envisages multiple horizontal escalators moving at higher speeds as one stepped from the sidewalk toward the center of the street. Powered by electricity, it seems to offer fairly rapid transportation (on an individual basis rather than the "batch" basis of trains, buses, or trolley cars) plus avoidance of the problems of pollution and parking which private automobiles involve.

The design of communities and dwellings is a third example which il-lustrates how capitalism inevitably turns both community and dwelling into commodities. An example of one kind of community as commodity may be La Jolla, California. During the daytime hours the elegant shops on the downtown streets are matched by well-dressed people who park their very expensive automobiles hubcap to hubcap on the streets. It is a busy scene. At night the streets are deserted except for the occasional eating place and the lone cinema theater. One could shoot a machine gun down the street and rarely hit anyone. But at night if one drives along the elite residential street next to the ocean cliffs one passes a succession of elegant forts. Those homes are surrounded by walls, electrified with burglar alarms, patroled by guard dogs, and typically valued at at upward of half a million dollars apiece. Their inhabitants live very private lives. Frequently the flickering blue light from TV screens is reflected from the walls to the street. This is the elite paradigm which epitomizes what the English architect, Martin Pawley (1974, p. 16) says:

> One by one the familiar consumer durables of the twentieth century—led by the dwelling itself—have stopped off what were once enormous and necessary areas of social contact between members of the family and between families.

And as W. Russell Ellis (1976, p. 109) remarks:

> The process Pawley traces out is that in which consumer goods come to stand for community, family, neighbourhood, and the like through the agency of advertising. The "stopping off" of inter- and intra-familiar relations is an outcome in which advertised images of product-attached relations become preferrable to the reality; where consumption of images of consumption becomes preferred social action.

Monopoly capitalism also produces a complete community commodity where housing tract development features a lot or home as part of a package including shopping mall, recreational facilities (swimming pool, tennis court, etc.). Analogous "retirement" complexes provide a comparable community package for elderly people able to pay the stiff price; for those unable to pay that price the nursing home, or cheap apartment or hotel room in city centers offer "parking places" where the elders unwanted by the nuclear family waste away until death.

These are negative examples of what dwelling and community facilities might *not* mean if they were considered as social goods rather than private commodities. No one knows until the priority for dwelling and community facilities is high on the agenda of a society on the socialist road what the possibilities and limits might be to such public goods. Certainly that most stultified of the professions, architecture, could have a renaissance under such conditions; under monopoly capitalism architects are reduced to nonentities by the contradiction between the fact that their art centers on facilities for community while their practice is confined to designing marketable community commodities.

To summarize the significance of the policy on *what* commodities to produce, it should be obvious that the type and choice of commodities to be produced, as well as their specific character, will embody the ideological aspirations of the society making the choices and will result in teaching those aspirations to the young and their parents. For every consumer commodity is itself a material incentive—either toward individualism or toward collective welfare. Every commodity is in a sense a "teaching machine."

FOR WHOM AND HOW TO PRODUCE?

To the extent that the process of answering the "what to produce" question is raised consciously in a society, it will also raise the issues inherent in the processes for answering the "for whom" and "how" questions. For indeed the three processes are closely interactive. In every society today the three processes are central to the struggle between dominators and dominated. And in all societies today hierarchy is the major operative principle employed in providing answers to all three questions. Downward flowing authority from boss to worker is the model, as much in civilian economic organization as in military. In capitalism the ultimate authority comes from the owners of private property—a well-recognized class formation. In socialist countries the ultimate authority comes from the Communist Party, standing as proxy for the workers and peasants— another class formation. In capitalism the forms of representative government obscure the fact of class domination. In socialist countries the forms and substance of democratic centralism and the mass line fall short of providing adequate democratic participation in collective decision making from the grass roots upward through the hierarchy. Both technoprofessional workers and elites unconsciously or consciously are authoritarian in both capitalist and socialist countries. The authoritarian power of hierarchy in North America was revealed in startling and unmistakable terms by Stanley Milgram's research (1974) which found that most Americans would carry an experiment to the point of electrocuting a man when directed to do so by a scientist who assumed responsibility for the consequences. There is no evident reason to doubt that a similar subordination to downward-flowing authority is characteristic of socialist societies today.

What does, however, distinguish class domination in the socialist from that in the capitalist societies is the formal commitment of the former to Marxist theory which holds that class struggle is part of an historical process, that democratic participation by workers and peasants in the process of deciding the answers to the *what, for whom,* and *how* questions is a goal to be struggled for. The nature of the process for answering these questions in the socialist countries is acutely problematic because of uncertainty in applying Marx's theories. He had expected that the transition to socialism would take place first in the highly industrialized capitalist countries of Western Europe. What happened was that the first socialist revolution was in Russia—then a backward, semifeudal, industrially undeveloped country. And the second great socialist revolution was in China—then in a similar state. Must such countries experience the development of the "productive forces" through essentially the same growth process that England and France experienced *before* they can change the "relations of production" from capitalist to socialist, i.e., decisively eliminate the exploitation of the masses by a small ruling class? "Automatic" Marxists answer affirmatively, but Mao Zedong regarded this as the "capitalist road" and a betrayal of Marxism. In his view such a policy condemned the masses to a very long period of quasi-capitalist domination, regimentation, and exploitation in the service of a techno-bureaucratic elite *before* a genuine socialist revolution could initiate socialist policies; meanwhile such socialist nations on the "capitalist road" would behave as social imperialists, competing with monopoly capitalist imperialism in their relations with Third World nations.

The heavy propaganda in and from the Soviet Union extolling the "Scientific and Technological Revolution" seems to support Mao's interpretation. Teleological determinism by "science and technology" pervades this literature. For example, speaking of "the scientific and technological revolution," Vice-president of the U.S.S.R. Academy of Sciences Millionshchikov (1972, p. 26) says:

> Its role stems from the dialectical nature of the changes in the material life of society. Indeed, on the one hand, the results of the scientific and technological revolution are too attractive not to be sought after. On the other hand, participation in scientific and technological progress inevitably brings in its train a conflict between all-pervading scientific ideas of the world and the unreasonable, outmoded and unjust social institutions of a society based on exploitation.

Essentially the Soviet line on science and "technology" is the same as that of the capitalist nations: science and technology are autonomous and worldwide in their scope. The juridical base of public ownership of capital goods, in their view, distinguishes their practice from capitalism. That their practice involves taking knowledge as private property, useful to secure professional and bureaucratic positions of privilege also seems obvious.[3]

Is it not possible for a country like China to develop an autonomous socialist system without having to run through the same experience as the advanced capitalist countries (exploitation and alienation of people, pollution of the environment, etc.)? Is it not possible that federations of countries in Africa, the West Indies, Latin America, Southeast Asia, etc., might also by-pass the "technological trap" of capitalism?

Class struggle *within* socialist societies, indeed within the Communist parties, is the core of the process toward socialism and the key to understanding the conflict between capitalist and socialist "roads." There is reason to believe that such class struggle goes on in the Soviet Union and

---

[3] For example, *Man, Science, Technology* (1973) argues lengthily the case for technology which this chapter seeks to expose as essentially propaganda for a capitalist view of science and technology.

other Eastern European socialist countries, but it is currently denied by the ruling technobureaucratic elites in power. In China, however, since the onset of the Great Proletarian Cultural Revolution in the early 1960s, class struggle over the issue of hierarchical authoritarian power has been acknowledged. Indeed, Chairman Mao Zedong's target in stimulating that Cultural Revolution was the senior level of the hierarchy in both the Party and state where he charged "capitalist roaders" were in power; his personal *tatzupao* was headed "Bombard the Headquarters." The problem of changing the "relations of production" to eliminate downward-flowing, self-interested authority is one which will require a long time to cure. For example, Chairman Mao said on many occasions that it would require not one cultural revolutionary struggle to gain that goal but many, stretching perhaps over the next century or longer. In the long sweep of human evolution, so deeply established an institution may well resist that long, even when class struggle actively seeks to overthrow it.

Let us sum up the preceding analysis. I have argued that under the disguise of *technology* is the reality of class-dominated societies developing their politically responsive interests in scientific inquiry and applying the results of such inquiry in their own material interest through specific forms of the industrial arts. Arguments for the alleged "autonomy" of technology are current versions of age-old searches for divine essences. And when the usual implicit meaning of technology as coextensive with modern society or modern industrialism, or more naively, as "modernism" is examined, it turns out we are talking about the real processes by which capitalism has answered the questions what is to be produced, for whom and how. The current spate of books, articles, and conferences about technology is therefore a conscious or unconscious attempt to shift the responsibility for the consequences of modern monopoly capitalism to a meaningless scapegoat. The alleged autonomy of "technology" has been especially useful in concealing the real differences between a system which pathologically overextends the private sector's production of private consumer goods on the one hand, and the process of two-line struggle which is under way in the socialist countries, on the other hand.

The argument others make that technology is responsible for our society's ills is therefore a highly political one. And at the same time "technology" is credited with making possible the cornucopia of consumer goods produced by Consciousness Industry. In short, capitalism is not responsible for the ills of technology, but claims credit for its consumer goods and consumer culture. It is the cure for all of capitalism's ills. This is pie in the sky. As McDermott (1972, p. 151) says:

> If religion was formerly the opiate of the masses, then surely technology is the opiate of the educated public today, or at least of its favorite authors. No

other single subject is so universally invested with high hopes for the improvement of mankind generally and of Americans in particular. The content of these millenial hopes varies somewhat from author to author, though with considerable overlap. A representative but by no means complete list of these promises and their prophets would include: An end to poverty and the inauguration of permanent prosperity (Leon Keyserling), universal equality of opportunity (Zbigniew Brzezinski), a radical increase in individual freedom (Edward Shils), the replacement of work by leisure for most of mankind (Robert Theobald), fresh water for desert dwellers (Lyndon Baines Johnson), permanent but harmless social revolution (Walt Rostow), the final come-uppance of Mao Tse-tung and all his ilk (same prophet), the triumph of wisdom over power (John Kenneth Galbraith), and lest we forget, the end of ideology (Daniel Bell).

CULTURAL SCREENS

Chapter 9 argued that nations and ideological systems, such as capitalism and socialism, have overall policies called *cultural realism*, meaning the central values of the system as expressed in its artifacts, practices, and institutional policies. Collectively they are the rationalizations which provide coherence to the people, things, and institutional policies of a country or ideological system. I now speak of *cultural screens*. They are the aspects of a national culture or ideological system which serve to protect its cultural realism against disruptive intrusion. They have been with us for millennia. What do they consist of? Language, religious and mythical beliefs and customs, together with border control of the movement of people and things, are elements of cultural screens which have been practiced since human beings formed extended communities. If the idea of cultural screens, and the necessity for them, is today novel or strange, that shows how far modern capitalism has undermined them in its ceaseless quest for profits.

The worldwide expansion of the capitalist system since about the sixteenth century necessarily involved the systemic penetration and liquidation of the cultural screens of traditional societies in Africa, the North and South American continents, India, east Asia, Australia, Imperial China and Japan, Indochina and the islands of Oceania. The mechanisms of penetration were simple: It began with trade and military conquest. Once the traditional societies were brought within the capitalist web of commodity markets (including the market for slaves), the acquisition of *formal* empire followed inevitably. Thus in modern times the Portuguese, Spanish, Dutch, English, French, Germans and Americans progressively blanketed the traditional societies with their names, economic penetration, and military might. In light of the emphasis on free trade, free flow of information, relatively free migration, free flow of tourism, free flow of capital, etc., which has dominated imperial policies since mid-nineteenth century, it is important now to recall how the cultural screens erected by each of the rising empires in the preceding three or four centuries prescribed in detail the controls which were imposed on trade, the flow of information, tourism, capital movements, etc., in order to protect themselves. *Mercantilism* was the name given to the English system of cultural screens in that period but each of the expanding capitalist countries had its own system. It is not so important to describe the mercantilist system in detail as it is to direct attention to its unquestioned need for such cultural screens in the formative stages of development of capitalist empires. And to point out that in the subjugated colonies of those empires, the cultural screen of the mother country was imposed on the colonies, if necessary by "gunboat diplomacy."

By the middle of the nineteenth century, the system seemed substantially stabilized and the dominating empire—the British—led the way in relaxing its controls. They were no longer providing benefits in excess of costs because it then appeared that the empire would be better served by a policy of free trade, free movement of people and capital, etc. The imperial system had imposed its own system of cultural realism on the traditional societies. Thereafter the worldwide system of markets and imperial control of capital could mobilize colonial peoples and their resources through the international division of labor, specialization, and professionalization without the need for detailed controls by prescription.

The world system of *formal* capitalist empire began to crumble as a consequence of the interimperialist World War I and the resulting Russian Revolution. World War II and the subsequent Chinese Revolution signaled the end of formal capitalist empire. Meanwhile the forces of United States capitalism, strengthened by its participation in both World wars took over the role of organizing capitalist empire on a world basis. The United States empire did not rest on gunboat diplomacy alone although the United States certainly used its military might. But the United States empire relied increasingly on the "free flow of information," capital, and the activities of the several hundred TNCs around the world. Thus, the chairman of one TNC said in 1977:

> The multinational tends to look at the world as a single source of supply serving a single market. Its normal modus operandi is to rationalize world demand and world supply as efficiently as possible—as if there were no national boundaries, as if there were no uneconomic national aspirations. Multinationals tend to operate as though the world accepts the concept of true interdependence, and as though there are no forces impeding the most

efficient development of the world's resources to most economically satisfy the world's increasing needs.[4]

The chairman of another revealed the ideological role of technology:

> As we head into what is apparently to be a period of heightened nationalism, the official role of the United States government will become less effective in many countries, and in some it will be quite unwelcome. The quiet, unofficial operations of the anational [sic] corporation, I submit, are made to order for this kind of situation. They are in fact most effective when they are unofficial. The grass-roots, people to people kinds of relationships that grow out of the teaching situations, *when know-how is passed on from person to person on the job*, are a much better international cement than the best kind of diplomacy. . . . Allow us in the anational corporations to teach those in the lesser developed countries our technologies, so that they can share our abundance, and not simply be envious of it (Gerstacker, 1972, emphasis added).

Speaking of TNCs relations with the Soviet Union, but in terms equally applicable to China, the chairman of a third giant corporation said:

> The potential market is enormous. Substantial imports of capital and consumer goods, as well as agricultural commodities will be needed for some time to fill gaps in current Soviet production. Over the long run, imports of entire factories, fertilizer plants, petroleum and natural gas facilities, power generating systems, transport and distribution systems, high-technology hardware and software in non-military areas, and managerial know-how, will be needed to spur industrial modernization. . . . I am confident there will be other constructive effects, as the Soviet economy modernizes and adjusts itself to wider world influences. Person to person contacts between East and West will broaden at all levels of both societies, labor as well as administration, management and bureaucracy. Some of the insulation which isolates the entire Soviet society will have to peel away. *The Soviet economy will begin to interact with—and integrate into—the dynamic technological revolution that is under way in the west. Pressures will build on the Soviet system to "consumerize" it in the direction of Western models* (Kendall, 1978, emphasis added).

The United States, as the leading agent of Consciousness Industry, using the hegemonic power it and its allies possessed in the United Nations, UNESCO, the ITU, etc., after 1945, used all its economic, diplomatic, intelligence agency resources to advance and protect the markets from which it profits outside its own borders. Canada acts as a subimperial center in this United States–dominated system. The system of cultural domination which emerged after 1945 is analyzed and described

---

[4] Malott, Robert H., Chairman and President, FMC Corporation, before the Chicago Business Publication Association, Chicago, Illinois, 7 February, 1977.

in Herbert I. Schiller's *Mass Communications and American Empire* (1969), *The Mind Managers* (1973), and *Communication and Cultural Domination* (1976).

As we turn now to consider the measures which dominated countries take to protect themselves, it is necessary to dispose of conventional bogeymen with which Western governments and intellectuals try to discredit such defensive measures. *Censorship* is a dirty word which free-flow proponents use for this purpose. It is a relic of the struggles of the rising capitalist class to free itself from repression by the landed feudal power of monarchies in Western Europe in the seventeenth to nineteenth centuries. It is embedded in capitalist ideology because the Crown then arbitrarily interfered with the efforts of the capitalist class to use the printing press and the stage to express its views. Censorship continues today to refer to the exercise by governments, whether elected by representative democratic processes or not, of their power to determine policy in matters concerning the mass media, the fine arts, and popular culture—in the extreme case as it relates to pornography.

The act of modern censorship is essentially a decision as to what is to be mass produced in the cultural area. So long as current cultural production is in the hands of privately owned giant corporations, *they* must also make decisions as to what is to be mass produced in the cultural area and what will not be produced. Because in monopoly capitalism, privately owned giant corporations are regarded as legal persons, we are accustomed to yield them the same privileges to which natural persons are entitled. It is as accurate therefore to refer to corporate decision making in the cultural area as being *censorship* as it is to refer to government decision making by that pejorative term. The choice is between decision making by public or private governments. In the modern corporation-dominated state, *government* really refers to organizations which make decisions from which ordinary citizens have no effective appeal or redress. The issue should be the merits of the decision rather than whether public or private government makes it. In a real sense, the monopoly-capitalist corporations censored the possibility of facsimile broadcasting. The gas company which sponsored the TV program on Nazi concentration camps censored the word "gas" from the script where the final solution was applied.

Advocates of cultural screens are also accused of fostering xenophobia, cultural stagnation, and the perpetuation of repressive superstition by "dictators" or national oligarchies. Schiller (1976, p. 84ff) deals at length with these arguments. As he says, elements struggling for cultural liberation and screens should oppose repressive authority and domination whether it is exercised from within or outside a country. The dynamics of the class struggle in neocolonial countries characteristically exhibit the process by which new layers of former compradors seize power when the external imperial force is nominally removed and seek to continue to use repressive measures against the bulk of the population of peasants and city dwellers until they in turn are removed by struggle.

Cultural screens are thus a name for a dialectical struggle over the terms of national development—the interests of which class it should serve. Cultural screens simultaneously involve the issue of whether science, the fine arts, commodities, and the techniques for producing them are everywhere good and deserving of free access to every country. The extension of capitalism for many centuries through a worldwide structure of markets has rested on the arguments for division of labor on an international scale. For the foreseeable future humanity is committed to *some* division of labor on an international scale, with the consequent necessity for international trade in raw materials, partially processed goods, capital equipment (hardware and software), and consumer commodities. But the controversies involved in cultural liberation for peoples previously dominated from outside their countries relate to precisely what goods, equipment, and consumer commmodities should be imported, and the terms on which production within a country should be *designed* for export to other countries. The principle seems clear: there must be critical analysis of the implications and probable consequences of such foreign trade and appropriate actions taken before it is allowed to occur if the interests of cultural liberation and autonomy are to be served. No simple, dogmatic rules are relevant, for the process of cultural screening is a crossroads where issues, material and nonmaterial values, and plans are caught up in myriad ways through class struggles.

National liberation movements, increasing awareness and determination to preserve national values from extinction, and growing demands for a new international economic order and a new international information order have produced since the late 1960s the as yet small beginnings of efforts to regain cultural, political, and economic hegemony on the part of a growing body of nonaligned nations. As Herbert I. Schiller (1978) says:

> Initially noticeable in some mild and tentative statements expressed at UNESCO meetings at the end of the 1960s and subsequent years, the first full blown statement of resistance to cultural colonization was registered at the Algiers Conference of the Heads of State of the Non-Aligned Countries in September, 1973. There, the chiefs of some 75 member nations declared:
>
> > "It is an established fact that the activities of imperialism are not confined solely to the political and economic fields, but also cover the cultural and social fields, thus imposing an alien ideological domination over the peoples of the developing world.
> >
> > "The Heads of State or Government of Non-Aligned Countries accord-

ingly stress the need to reaffirm national cultural identity and eliminate the harmful consequences of the colonial era, so that their national culture and tradition will be preserved.

"They consider that the cultural alienation and imported civilization imposed by imperialism and colonialism should be countered by a repersonalization and by constant and determined recourse to the people's own social and cultural values which define it as a sovereign people, master of its own resources, so that every people can exercise effective control over all its national wealth and strive for its economic development under conditions ensuring respect for its sovereignty and authenticity, and peace and genuine international cooperation."[5]

Countries which are trying to liberate themselves from the domination of Consciousness Industry have made significant progress at the UN, UNESCO, International Telecommunications Union—organizations in which each country has an equal vote, and in which a clear majority is now held by Nonaligned, Third World, and socialist countries. Communications satellites were an application of the industrial arts (spun off from the military space race) which concerned the socialist and Nonaligned countries beginning in 1959 when the UN General Assembly set up a committee to study their implications. By 1972 UNESCO adopted a resolution to the effect that *prior* agreement is necessary between the states concerned before direct broadcast satellites may beam programs into countries. The UN General Assembly supported this resolution by a vote of 102 to 1 (the United States casting the latter; Canada abstaining). A second initiative concerned the "free flow of information" doctrine itself. When UNESCO was established, the United States succeeded in embedding this doctrine in its charter and subsequently UNESCO activities promoted the movement of equipment and software to Third World countries effectively supporting the dominating role of Consciousness Industry. Beginning in the late 1960s a frontal attack was levied against the "free flow" doctrine. In 1972 the Soviet Union introduced in the UNESCO General Assembly a resolution which struck at the roots of the "free flow"—it called for state responsibility for the activities of its mass media.

In 1974 UNESCO published the statistical study by Kaarle Nordenstreng and Tapio Varis, *Television Traffic—a One-Way Street?* which documented the proposition that the industrialized capitalist countries exported much more TV programing to the Third World and socialist countries than they received from them. President Kekkonen (1973) of Finland

---

[5] The passage quoted from the Algiers Conference is from Singham and Tran van Dinh (1976).

in commenting on it at a UNESCO symposium correctly traced the "free flow" doctrine to the ideology of laissez-faire capitalism and noted the current tendency for UNESCO and the UN to move in the direction of encouraging instead a "balanced flow." Three years later at the General Assembly of UNESCO at Nairobi, pro and anti free-flow forces collided with great heat over essentially the Soviet proposal of four years earlier—without resolving the conflict. But for the next five-year program,

> It was generally agreed that the highest priority should be given to measures aiming at reducing the communication gap existing between the developed and the developing countries and at achieving a freer and more balanced international flow of information. . . . (Quoted in International Commission for the Study of Communication Problems, 1978, p. 12).

The organizing vehicle for much of the work on cultural screens has been the conferences of the Nonaligned countries. Concretely, the development of national, regional, and Nonaligned countries news agencies was undertaken by those countries with help from UNESCO, beginning about 1974. Based on the radio-telegraph system and experienced news agency staff of TANJUG (the Yugoslavian news agency), the agency has grown rapidly. By January 1977, more than 40 news agencies were working through it and in that period 16 new national news agencies were formed in Nonaligned countries. In quick succession, meetings of the Nonaligned nations in Lima (1975), Tunis (1976), New Delhi, and Colombo (also in 1976) worked out a constitution for the Nonaligned Press Agencies Pool and established

> . . . an Information Coordination Council which would oversee such terms as the promotion of cooperation in information questions; compilations of statistics on information issues; promotion of further pooling arrangements in television, film, radio, photography, books, etc.; linkages of research and training agencies in the field of information; promotion of cultural contacts, and formulation of a common approach with a view to evolving an international code on the functioning and use of satellite communications, etc. (Quoted by Schiller, 1978).

Surrounding and stimulating these official conferences has been a constant stream of seminars, conferences, books, and articles.

The postponed "declaration" on the free flow was considered at the 1978 UNESCO General Assembly. The outcome was an ambiguous compromise between the capitalist core countries and the nonaligned and Soviet bloc countries. It affirmed the Third World countries' demand for a "free flow *and a wider and better balanced dissemination of information.*" It was a considerable victory for them to have Article IX:

In the spirit of this declaration, it is for the international community to contribute to the creation of the conditions for a free flow and wider and more balanced dissemination of information, and the conditions for the protection, in the exercise of their functions, of journalists and other agents of the mass media. UNESCO is well placed to make a valuable contribution in this respect.[6]

Sweden had voiced the dissatisfaction of the capitalist core countries in objecting to the implicit assumption in the declaration that states or "the international community" had *any* responsibility for the operation of the mass media! The declaration served the propaganda purposes of the Western powers in many respects (e.g. in the emphasis on the exercise of freedom of opinion, expression and information in strengthening peace and international understanding), yet on balance the declaration established both a precedent and substantive provisions which favor the Third World nations.

At the Nairobi UNESCO General Conference, following the contentious debate on the declaration, it was generally agreed that "a review should be undertaken of the totality of the problems of communication in modern society." Such was the task given by the Director General to an International Commission for the Study of Communication Problems, headed by Sean MacBride and including representative members from the diverse economic and social systems around the world. The conclusions in that Commission's report some two years later, covered the same issues debated in producing the Nairobi declaration and, it may be argued, reflected the same positions taken during those debates. (International Commission for the Study of Communication Problems, 1980). But the impact of the Commission's work is not to be judged by such a superficial critical evaluation. Nearly 100 reports by as many specialists drawn from all parts of the world were commissioned and published by the Commission as part of its work program. These reports represent a commitment to the study of the extremely complex problems confronting humanity which are rooted in communications practice and theory by widely diverse social systems. Moreover, the confrontations which appear to have taken place during the Commission's work, necessarily involved a learning process for the groups involved.

Of all the conclusions by the Commission, it is directly relevant to the issue of cultural screens to note that it recommended (*sup. cit.*, p. 259–60):

---

[6] *Intermedia*, Vol. 7, No. 1, January 1979, p. 10.

Establishment of national cultural policies, which should foster cultural identity and creativity, and involve the media in these tasks. Such policies should also contain guidelines for safeguarding national cultural development while promoting knowledge of other cultures. It is in relation to others that each culture enhances its own identity.

Communication and cultural policies should ensure that creative artists and various grass-roots groups can make their voices heard through the media. The innovative uses of film, television or radio by people of different cultures should be studied. Such experiments constitute a basis for continuing cultural dialogue, which could be furthered by agreements between countries and through international support.

Introduction of guidelines with respect to advertising content and the values and attitudes it fosters, in accordance with national standards and practices. Such guidelines should be consistent with national development policies and efforts to preserve cultural identity. Particular attention should be given to the impact on children and adolescents. In this connection, various mechanisms such as complaint boards or consumer review committees might be established to afford the public the possibility of reacting against advertising which they feel inappropriate.

While yielding ground slowly and reluctantly on the rhetorical front the United States position in this struggle has offered, as an inducement to the Third World nations, easier access to communications "technology," particularly communications satellites and more training of their journalists, which would increase rather than decrease their dependence on the capitalist core.

Just as domination of the UN General Assembly and UNESCO by the United States and its allies has begun to crumble, so also with the International Telecommunications Union. The basis of frequency allocation policy by that organization, dominated by capitalist core countries until the 1970s, was a pragmatic, first-come-first-served basis, in which frequency bands would be allocated by the ITU to particular classes of users, and the various nations would "notify" the ITU Frequency Registration Board of their intention to use particular frequency assignments. By 1977, of the 153 member nations of ITU, 85 were nonaligned or developing nations. And at the 1977 World Administrative Radio Conference on Broadcasting Satellites, the ITU made specific frequency assignments at specific orbital locations for coverage of prescribed service areas on the ground for Regions 1 and 3 even though not all—or even many—of them will be occupied in the near future. Region 2 is the Americas where, because of the opposition of the United States, Canada, and Brazil, the old first-come-first-served policy was continued. The World Administrative Radio Conference held in September 1979 considered all radio frequency allocations. At it the nonaligned nations pressed vigorously the "positive planning" approach. The relatively poor countries are now waging their struggle for equality of treatment in the use of humanity's common property, the radio spectrum (Probst, 1977; Gould and Reinhart, 1977; Rutkowski, A.M., 1979). (See Appendix A.)

The foregoing developments show the capacity of Third World and socialist countries to struggle for recognition of their rights to autonomous development, but it must be recognized that such achievements are significant mostly in terms of international diplomacy, public opinion, and international law. What has happened at the national level? At the level of national policy, cultural screens have been erected in most countries to protect the national autonomy of mass media institutions. The print media have been protected by various methods of regulation and support for a century or more in the interest of national autonomy.

> Those regulations which are widely used are as follows: (1) prohibition of overflow advertising; (2) national control of distribution with priority rights given to national publications; (3) discrimination against foreign publications through customs duties, foreign exchange regulations, special taxes, quotas, and required price differentials; and (4) requirements that all publishing firms, including newspapers, be owned and managed by nationals. It has been felt that these defensive approaches are inadequate by themselves to insure that a national press and publishing industry will flourish. The giant firms, like Luce Publications, can still play a dominant role. Therefore, states have granted positive assistance to national publications through the following programmes: (1) special postal rates for magazines and newspapers; (2) enforcement of anticombines legislation; (3) special tax concessions to struggling publications; (4) regulation of advertising even to the extent of taxation and distribution controls; (5) other indirect subsidies, such as free transportation, telephone and telegraph services; and (6) direct public subsidy to cultural publications. Within the constrictions of the private enterprise economy, these programmes would go a long way towards developing a publications industry in Canada (Warnock, 1970a, p. 129).

No such screens were adopted or considered to protect the Canadian print media.

Most countries protect their cinema theater audiences from unlimited influence from imported films through import quotas often linked with box office taxes the proceeds of which are used to support their domestic film productions. According to United States complaints against such "interference" with the "free flow" of its cultural influence, 102 countries follow this practice. But, as shown in Chapter 6, Canada does not.

As noted in Chapter 8, most countries protected their autonomy in regard to radio broadcasting by creating public entities to provide radio broadcasting service which contained no advertising—largely on the BBC model. But when TV was innovated, it was linked with advertising of consumer goods and services from capitalist Consciousness Industry shortly after World War II. The combination rapidly converted most "free world" broadcasting—both TV and radio—to the United States model, thus punching great holes in the national screens protecting national autonomy. As stated, at the rhetorical level, the sanction which the United States had built into the UN and UNESCO charters for this one-way flow of TV and radio influence, has been blunted. But at the operative level, not much progress has been made in reestablishing limits to domination by Consciousness Industry via TV-radio and advertising. Canada appears helpless to rescue control of programing by TV-radio. Canadian viewing of *Canadian* TV and Canadian listening to *Canadian* radio programing remains at a level statistically comparable to the use of educational TV and radio in the United States—an insignificant figure probably in the neighborhood of 8 to 10 percent; a level similar to the proportion of Canadian theater patrons who see Canadian films (6 percent).

As concerns imports of consumer goods, such national cultural screens as exist for the most part take the form of import tariffs, quotas, and embargoes which had their origin in the desire to protect domestic producers against competition and were a traditional feature of mercantilist policies. Such customs regulations lacked the prior critical analysis which is essential for cultural screens. Although such import tariffs, quotas, and embargoes may on occasion serve to screen out alien political influence embodied in the commodities, this result is accidental. Behind national screens—or the lack of them—today is the scarcity of effective class formations dedicated to self-reliant, indigenous development as opposed to acceptance of the distortions and deformations in institutions and policies which accompany subordination of the countries to the policies of TNCs (whether based in capitalist or socialist countries) (Barnet and Mueller, 1974; Magdoff, 1978).

The situation of China offers a case study on the issue of the politics of "technology" and consumer goods which is significant because almost one-third of the world population lives there. Isolated by a 28-year embargo by the United States and its allies and by a 10-year breach in relations with the USSR, China was forced to adopt policies aimed at national self-sufficiency. The Great Proletarian Cultural Revolution between about 1963 and 1972 had mobilized people in all China's institutions to pursue the development of unique socialist institutions and policies rather than to depend on the capitalist or the socialist countries for its development model. To many observers it seemed to be a process which was succeeding in that course (Robinson, 1969; Bettelheim, 1974; Wheelwright and McFarlane, 1970).

In 1971 when China took its seat in UNESCO, its ambassador Huang Chen said:

> We stand for the normal growth of cultural, scientific and educational exchanges and cooperation among the peoples of all countries so as to increase their mutual understanding and friendship. We hold that progressive cultures of all nations, regardless of the length of their history, have their respective characteristics and merits, which should be the cultural nourishment of other peoples and serve as examples in their cultural development. There can be mutual assimilation and overcoming of one's own shortcomings by learning from the strong points of others. *Of course, this assimilation is by no means uncritical eclecticism. An analysis should be made of foreign cultures. Even their progressive elements should be appropriately adapted to the specific domestic conditions according to the needs of the people and conveyed through national forms before they can answer the purpose of serving the people at home. It is inadvisable to the development of national cultures to have blind faith in foreign things and transplant them in toto.*[7]

The italicized portion of Huang Chen's statement clearly assumed that there would be critical appraisal of foreign cultural materials and practices *prior* to their introduction in China. Would the *what* to produce question be answered increasingly by innovating historically unprecedented public goods more than the private goods which capitalism had already overdeveloped? For consumer goods there is no "socialist road" to be found in the productive experience of capitalism—unless, of course, the socialist road is defined as tailing along behind capitalism in offering everyone the illusory possibility of owning a Ford automobile, or a Cadillac. Did the Chinese in fact establish a deliberate critical screening practice in the early 1970s?

What did appear after 1971 caused consternation among those who had thought China was firmly on the road to autonomous socialist development. At first it was a trickle of imports (e.g., Boeing aircraft, a communications satellite ground station, chemical plants, etc.). But with the opening of full access to capitalist technology, the trickle became a flood.

"Modernization" became the dominant policy after the death of Mao Zedong and the elimination of the "Gang of Four." Whereas Mao Zedong had excoriated the Soviet technobureaucratic revisionism with its "goulash communism," the policy identified with Deng Xiaoping is one of adapting China's economy to the modes of capitalism. Gone is the em-

---

[7] Huang, Chen, Head of the Delegation of the People's Republic of China, Speaking to the 17th Session of the UNESCO General Conference, 25 October, 1972 (emphasis added).

phasis on the politics of socialist relations being in command; in its place are the politics of capitalist-style production, efficiency, and profits. In late 1978, Deng Xiaoping (1978, p. 6) told the 9th National Trade Union Congress that a "faster pace" of modernization was necessary:

> Speeding up the tempo of economic development requires much greater specialization of enterprises, a far higher technical level of all workers and staff members, conscientious training and evaluation, far better economic accounting in enterprises, and much higher labour productivity and rate of profit in proportion to the funds. Therefore, major transformations are required on various economic fronts not only in regard to technique, but in regards to systems and oranization as well.

Economic incentives are emphasized: production bonuses, cash awards to individuals for inventions, and a concerted drive to speed up workers on the "model" worker principle (reminiscent of the Stakhanovite movement in the USSR) are being implemented. And

> Leading comrades and comrades in charge of Party work and political work must have a democratic style of work, listen earnestly to the opinions of scientists and technicians, actively back their rationalization proposals and inventions, encourage them to be bold in pondering on and raising problems and solving them. In the academic field, the policy of "letting a hundred flowers blossom, letting a hundred schools of thought contend" must be implemented in real earnest and different viewpoints and schools must be allowed to freely contend (On Policy Toward Intellectuals, 1979, p. 15).

At the same time, major efforts to strengthen the Chinese legal system and methods of democratic control of senior Party and public officials are under way.

The issue of the political (or ideological) character of science and "technology" with which we are concerned here is raised sharply by the aggressive search for capitalist scientific knowledge, industrial arts, and know-how which the post-Mao regime is pursuing. Technicians have been invited to visit China from Japan, West Germany, France, the United States, Switzerland, Sweden, Denmark, Finland, Holland, Austria, Canada, Spain, and Britain. Observers' groups have investigated "world advanced science and technology"; Chinese exhibitions on an expanded scale have facilitated export contracts and deals by which foreign technique become available to China (Wang, 1979, p. 24). The volume of foreign trade rose in 1978 to all-time high levels. Chinese rationalizations for its very rapidly increased scale of importation of capitalist technology frequently repeat Mao Zedong's and Zhou Enlai's advice to learn from foreigners their "good points," while screening out their "bad points." But there is a conspicuous absence of reference to any process for systematic critical screening of foreign "science and technology" to this end. Meanwhile criticism is addressed to cultural isolationism in which the arguments for internationalism are advanced uncritically under captions such as "Is It Safe to Keep People in a 'Safe'?"[8]

There is increasing evidence that it is the "software" component in technology which the Chinese are most eager to import and adopt. Thus, the Communique of the Third Plenary Session of the 11th Central Committee reports that China is adopting a number of major new economic measures, among which first place is given to "conscientiously transforming the system and methods of economic management."[9] And to cite just one example reported, we are told that in installing 13 large imported chemical fertilizer plants:

> Through earnestly learning the advanced foreign techniques and methods of management, the cadres, technicians and workers of the seven plants already in production mastered the necessary technical and management expertise within a relatively short time (Why China Imports Technology and Equipment, 1978, p. 11).

The argument is repeatedly made in different forms that undiscriminating imitation of foreign technology is urgently necessary if China is to "catch up" with capitalist achievements. For example, Lenin is quoted (from 1920) in support of the statement that "science and technology have no class nature" (Why China Imports Technology and Equipment, 1978, p. 12). And again:

> Lenin once worked out a very interesting formula in an outline he made when preparing the article "Immediate Tasks of the Soviet Government." The formula is:

> "The readiness to absorb things good and foreign: Soviet government plus good order on the Prussian railways plus American technology and trusts plus national education in the United States, etc., equals the sum total equals socialism."

Has China uncritically adopted the policies of Consciousness Industry? Whatever might be the undisclosed cultural screening in the case of producer's goods, such as fertilizer plants, it seems incredible that any cultural screening would pass China's new policies regarding consumer product design, packaging, trademarks, and advertising. An article by a spokesman in January 1979 said:

> Now our foreign trade firms are willing to arrange for production of export items according to the buyer's design, using the buyer's materials, parts, machines and trademark (Wang, 1979, p. 25).

---

[8] *Beijing Review*, No. 4, January 26, 1979, p. 7.
[9] *Beijing Review*, No. 52, December 29, 1978, p. 11.

From this practice can come only (1) learning how to operate Consciousness Industry (monopoly capitalist model) and (2) exporting the surplus value of Chinese labor in exactly the way Singapore, Taiwan, Hong Kong, and other countries exploited by TNCs export the surplus value of their labor forces. The same may be said about China's vastly expanded catering to foreign tourists. China was visited in 1978 by more than 100,000 tourists (other than overseas Chinese), three times as many as in 1977, and equal to the total for the previous 14 years. The "achievements" in this industry seem lacking in any ideological protective screening:

> Various steps have been taken to boost China's infant tourist industry since the beginning of 1978. For instance, some 100 cities and places including those of historical interest have been thrown open to foreign tourists, customs formalities simplified and new hotels in more than 30 cities built or planned. Transport services have been improved, e.g., special trains now run between Beijing, the capital, and the Great Wall and there are now more buses and cars for tourists. The state has also signed agreements of cooperation on tourism with a number of countries.
>
> Negotiations are now going on with foreign businessmen to use foreign funds to build hotels. Hunting, skiing, mountaineering, and other outdoor sports activities will be included in the list of tourist activities for 1979. In pastoral areas, foreign visitors will be able to stay in herdsmen's felt tents.
>
> The young industry is growing, attracting visitors from all over the world, and many problems and shortcomings remain to be overcome, such as inadequate or poor facilities, management and transport services and the lack of qualified interpreters. But every effort is being made to overcome these, and fast (China's Tourist Service, 1979, p. 38).

Even more weighty evidence that China seems to be joining Consciousness Industry in its international activities is the advertisement on the back cover of *Beijing Review* for February 16, 1979:

DO YOU WANT TO DO MORE BUSINESS?

Consult us. We can help. It's our business to promote your business.

We handle commercial advertisements for foreign manufacturers and traders as well as Chinese export organizations.

We can design and print trade labels, catalogues, brochures and so on for you.

We arrange exhibitions for you in Shanghai and provide mannequins, display stands, and other equipment.

We will be pleased to assist you in China and abroad.

Write now for particulars.

Shanghai Advertising Corporation. Address: 97 Yuan Ming Yuan Road, Shanghai, China. Cable Address: 'ADVERCORP' Shanghai.

The argument of this book rests on the analysis developed in Chapters 1–4 of the way in which monopoly capitalism came into existence through applying "scientific management" on the job front, and "scientific marketing" on the consumer front, where people work to market the output of Consciousness Industry to themselves. Lenin's writings within three years after the Bolshevik Revolution reflected the dire straits in which the Soviet Union found itself when, exhausted by civil war and repelling foreign invasions, it was forced to take any expedient opportunity to save itself. These measures in no way represent principled Marxist theory on how to build a socialist society once national security had been established, such as China 30 years after its revolution might well create and apply. For understandable reasons, Lenin never analyzed the demand management aspects of monopoly capitalism, nor the political implications of scientific management at the job front. Because he did not do so does not mean that they are not the real, dynamic strength of the monopoly-capitalist system.

No socialist justification can be found for competing in market research, product- and package design, mass media advertising techniques with Western Consciousness Industry. Nor for joining the activities of Consciousness Industry in developing the tourist industry with its inevitable ideological training of Chinese peasants and workers for capitalist practice. Nor for effectively reinstituting enclaves on Chinese soil where TNCs may use Chinese labor to produce Consciousness Industry's products for core market profits. The best that could be said for China's recent policy on foreign trade and "technology" is that it will increase the possibilities of a favorable balance of trade. But it should be noted that this indiscriminate welcoming of capitalist technology will further develop a technobureaucratic elite within China. Assuming as I do that Mao Zedong correctly predicted the zigs and zags of China's struggles toward socialism, it seems obvious that the fuel is being accumulated which will power a later phase of class struggle taking off from where the Cultural Revolution ended. Meanwhile China may well call the Soviet Union *hegemonist* (as it does) but may not call it *revisionist* (which, having turned toward the capitalist road itself, it no longer does).

> Khrushchev's "communism" takes the United States for its model. Imitation of the methods of management of U.S. capitalism and the bourgeois way of life has been raised by Khrushchev to the level of state policy. . . . He wants to copy the United States in the sphere of industry as well as that of agriculture and in particular to imitate the profit motive of United States capitalist enterprises (On Khrushchev's Phoney Communism, 1964, pp. 84–85).

This is the apparent direction of current Chinese policy.

It must be understood in context however. A two-line struggle is active in China—and has been for more than 40 years. The people who identified with Chairman Mao's development policy—which emphasized self-sufficiency, decentralization of industry, reduction of differences based on rural and urban living, between manual and mental labor, and deemphasis on experts—are very much alive and struggling. Currently the ground on which struggle is most obvious is the issue of increasing the democratic aspects of democratic centralism and the mass line, as well as reform of the legal system and the courts. Sometime in the next few years, there probably will be a fundamental transformation of the present economic policy. A second great Proletarian Cultural Revolution in the foreseeable future is possible, and this time with safeguards against the bureaucratic abuses of the Gang of Four.

11

ON CONVENTIONAL AND CRITICAL
THEORY OF COMMUNICATIONS

The preceding chapters have dealt with the structure and policy of mass communication as it relates to Consciousness Industry and people. It is necessary now to examine both conventional and critical theories of communications in order to lay a basis for considering consciousness.

THE ESTABLISHMENT THEORY OF COMMUNICATION

Because the crucial phase of the production of consciousness under monopoly capitalism is the interface between the mass media and audience members, it is necessary to examine theory about what happens at that interface. The conventional theoretical treatment of that interface is unilinear—the message moves from the tube to the audience. This is entirely consistent with the notion that the transmission of news, entertainment, and "education" is the principal product of the mass media. In this view the role of advertising is incidental to the principal product; it is transmitted by the media in order to finance the production of the principal product: the message of the program (the free lunch). As indicated in Chapter 2, messages, entertainment, education, etc., are subjective mental entities and all deal with superficial appearances. So also is Marshall McLuhan's combination of these entities with technique in, e.g., his slogan, "the medium is the message." Historically, before the advent of mass media it was true that the principal product of the newspaper and magazine appeared to be the news, entertainment, and information in it. This has been an unreal and idealistic view of the mass media for about a century in the core of capitalism. Its perpetuation in industry practice serves the interest of the media and the advertiser by concealing the fact that the principal product of the mass media is the audience. How have the social sciences treated this problem?

Economists have avoided recognizing and dealing with the reality of the audience commodity (see Chapter 2). Neoclassical economic theorists ignore the existence of mass media, advertising, demand management by Consciousness Industry, and the very fact of the audience commodity. Marxist economists and institutional economists either ignore the whole problem (Lenin) or like Galbraith, Boulding, and Baran and Sweezy recognize the existence of the mass media and the reality of demand management but stop short of recognizing the audience commodity.

Sociologists and psychologists, however, have produced thousands of research studies in what has been called *communication research* which do recognize the audience if only inadequately. In the Western world communication research grew out of the propaganda activities of the United States government during World War I and the need of advertisers and the mass media for tax-supported university research which would provide them with the techniques of market research. During World War II, the United States government again funded elaborate research in this area (Hovland et al., 1949, Vol. 3). Between the wars, in the late 1930s it was given impetus by a seminar organized by the Rockefeller Foundation.

These studies have four characteristics:

1. They concern only the content and effects of the *free lunch*—the editorial material which appears between advertisements in the mass media. They assume that the question, "What are the effects of the mass media?" is formally equivalent to the question, "What are the effects of the news, entertainment, and information which appear between the advertisements in the mass media?" By omitting advertising from their research they divert attention *away from* the principal intended object of the mass media, to produce and market to advertisers the means to complete the marketing of consumer goods and services. In this way, they naturally protect from investigation the blind spot: the audience, and its work.

2. They take the free lunch "message" as *the object* of which the effects are to be studied. The model for their research was the paradigm formulated by Harold Lasswell (1948), "Who says what to whom through what channels with what effect?" It is a one-way flow of *messages*, from Consciousness Industry to members of the audience. The studies begin by defining audiences in *terms of the types of messages addressed to them* (e.g., soap operas, acts of violence in pro-

grams, etc.), rather than beginning with people in audiences as commodities, doing a particular kind of work.

     3. For the most part this communications research has relied on stimulus-response learning theory—the type of psychological theory associated with J. B. Watson (1924), C. L. Hull (1943), and B. F. Skinner (1949, 1957). Watson (1924, p. 40) put the bias of the theory plainly:

> The interest of the behaviourist is more than the interest of a spectator; he wants to control man's reactions as physical scientists want to control and manipulate other natural phenomena.

There were significant exceptions in which alternative theoretical tools were used, but they serve by contrast to highlight the dominance of the "Engineering of Consent" motive so brashly proclaimed by Bernays (1947) who openly advocated manipulation in his public relations work.

     4. They all assume that mass communication takes place in a *stable* social system such as that dominated by monopoly capitalism in the 25 years after World War II. As the contradictions in that social system progressively signaled the breakdowns of that stability (national liberation movements in Cuba, Vietnam, Congo, Chile, Panama, Iran, etc., and domestic civil rights struggles), the assumed context of conventional theory became increasingly unreal. Lacking recognition of movements of people to change the existing social system, mass communication theory became increasingly irrelevant except to give surface plausibility to the establishment's tactical measures (e.g., technical aid for use of United States hardware and software in peripheral countries). All these characteristics have combined to distort and invert the study by "communication research" of the interface between people and Consciousness Industry.

A review of conventional communications research will be useful for several reasons. It shows the extent, substance, and limits of such socially uncritical research. And it provides a contrasting basis for the development of some critical, realistic theory of how mass communication works. In the nature of behavioristic research, studies proliferate, become ever more specialized and almost defy synthesized generalization. We owe gratitude therefore to Joseph T. Klapper (1960) who published a careful analysis based on reanalyzing more than a thousand such research studies. His analysis was stringently critical and cautious. If we bear firmly in mind that he was summarizing studies of the effect of the free lunch and not the whole message (including its advertising component), and further

the bias of behavioristic theory on which the studies were based, his conclusions are useful:

      1.   Mass communications *ordinarily* does not serve as a
necessary and sufficient cause of audience effects, but rather functions
among and through a nexus of mediating factors and influences.

      2.   These mediating factors are such that they typically
render mass communications a contributory agent, but not the sole
cause, in a process of reinforcing the existing conditions. (Regardless of
the condition in question—be it the vote intentions of audience
members, their tendency toward or away from delinquent behaviour,
or their general orientation toward life and its problems—and
regardless of whether the effect in question be social or individual, the
media are more likely to reinforce than to change.)

      3.   On such occasions as mass communication does func-
tion in the service of change, one of two conditions is likely to exist.
Either:

      (a) The mediating factors will be found to be inopera-
             tive and the effect of the media will be found to be
             direct; or

      (b) The mediating factors, which normally favour re-
             inforcement, will be found to be themselves im-
             pelling toward change.

      4.   There are certain residual situations in which mass
communication seems to produce direct effects, or directly and of itself
to serve certain psychophysical functions.

      5.   The efficacy of mass communication, either as a con-
tributory agent or as an agent of direct effect, is affected by various
aspects of the media and communications themselves or of the communication situation (including, for example, aspects of textual
organization, the nature of the source and medium, the existing
climate of public opinion, and the like) (Klapper, 1960, pp. 7–8).

It may be helpful to the development of a *non*-message-based theory of
the effects of the mass media to repeat his summary findings regarding the
major role played by the "mediating factors," with brief notes identifying
the kinds of issues or problems to which the underlying studies were
addressed:

The fact that persuasive mass communication serves more often as an
agent of reinforcement than of conversion seems to be due, at least in
part, to the way in which its influence is mediated by certain extra-
communication factors and conditions. Among these are:

(a) *Predispositions and the derived processes of selective exposure, selective perception and selective retention.* People tend to expose themselves selectively to communications in accord with their existing views and to avoid exposure to unsympathetic communications. If exposed to unsympathetic material, they not infrequently distort (i.e., selectively perceive) its meaning so as to bring it into accord with their existing views. People also tend selectively to retain sympathetic material better than unsympathetic material. Although these phenomena are extremely common, they are rarely if ever experienced by all persons in any communication situation.[1]

(b) *The group, and the norms of groups, to which the audience member belongs.* Predispositions which reflect norms of groups to which the audience member belongs seem especially resistant to change (initiated by mass media). It has been proposed that resistance is particularly high if the norms are currently salient, and among people who particularly value their group membership, but research findings on these two points are inconclusive. Groups themselves may facilitate reinforcement in various other ways. They often increase selective exposure. They also provide arenas for interpersonal dissemination of the content of sympathetic communications, for the exercise of opinion leadership, and for discussion which may render the norms more salient or conspicuous.[2]

(c) *Interpersonal dissemination of communication content.* Such dissemination seems more likely to occur among people who share pertinent opinions on the topic in question. It thus seems likely to increase the native potential of the communication for reinforcement without similarly increasing its potential for conversion.[3]

(d) *Opinion leadership.* People have been shown to be more crucially influenced in many matters by [local] "opinion leaders" than they are by mass communications. Such opinion leaders are typically "super-normative" members of the same group as their followers, but are more exposed to mass communications and thus serve as transmission agents or interpreters. Although most studies of opinion leadership have to date focussed on the leaders' role in produc-

---

[1] Citing studies of presidential elections, war bond purchasing, blood donation, attitude toward the United Nations, antismoking campaigns, acceptance of "other" ethnic cultures, metamorphosis of rumors, stereotyping in regard to prejudice, propaganda against the Soviet Union.

[2] Citing studies of presidential election campaigns; stimuli against norms of boy scouts and Roman Catholics; teenager peer groups in response to film stars and popular music.

[3] Citing studies of small group behavior by Festinger and others, and studies of presidential election campaigns.

254 DEPENDENCY ROAD: COMMUNICATION, CAPITALISM, CONSCIOUSNESS & CANADA

ing change, there is good reason to postulate that they frequently exercise their influence in favour of constancy and reinforcement.[4]

(e)   *The nature of commercial mass media in a free enterprise society.* It has been held that in order to avoid offending any significant portion of their necessarily vast and varied audience, the media were perforce reduced to espousing only such attitudes as were already virtually universal. Content analyses of entertainment fare prevalent in the 1940s and early 1950s bore out these allegations. A resulting sanctification of the status quo—a social and individual reinforcing effect—was widely alleged but never scientifically demonstrated. Some current media material *seems* less orthodox and more daring. No research has identified the effects of such material, and, in any case, it apparently remains the exception rather than the rule. Mass media probably still function predominantly, if less consistently, as socially reinforcing agents, and the economic character of the media and of this society may well render such a situation inevitable (Klapper, 1960, pp. 49–51, emphasis in original).

The salience of individuals and of informal as well as formal associative institutions in the production of consciousness and their potential resistance to domination is evident.

How does market research relate to the behavioral studies of message-identified audience power? How did Klapper deal with the two-way relation between the research on the effects of the "free lunch" and market research? Here we are at the psychologists' and sociologists' mutual frontier with the blind spot.

Klapper tried to exclude consideration of the two-way relation of free lunch audience research and market research. In his preface he states:

> No attempt is made to deal with the effects of the media as instruments of consumer advertising. Not only is much of that vast research privileged, but the lion's share presents findings which can be regarded as valid only in reference to the specific situation researched and which are in general too precisely "applied" to be particularly useful for this more basically oriented volume. By the same token, the findings of the research which are cited in this volume cannot be assumed to be generalizable to the effects of consumer advertising. The goals of such advertising and the psychological significance to the audience members of the decisions involved are often quite unlike the goals and decisions involved in the kind of persuasive communications here discussed (Klapper, 1960, pp. x–xi).

---

[4] Citing studies of personal influence, presidential election campaigns, public issues, food purchasing habits, habits of dress, selection of movies to attend, how farmers adopt new farming practices, how physicians adopt new drugs.

The reasons given for this decision are unconvincing. The specific, applied nature of market research puts it on the same footing as the vast number of nonmarket research studies which he *did* reanalyze. True, most market research is not published, yet Klapper was obviously familiar enough with it to flatly distinguish its goals from those of the free lunch research with which he did deal. It is arguable that, as he says, his findings regarding free lunch research should not be *mechanically* carried over into the market research area. But as we know, there is a two-way interpenetration between research in the two areas. Market researchers come from academic institutions and take the knowledge of free lunch research with them and market researchers draw on academic research. Moreover, despite his announced intention to exclude crossing the line between them, in several places he does cross it. And in a number of other respects his findings are obviously transferable between the two research areas. It is useful, then, to reverse Klapper's position and to say: in principle all his findings are applicable to some degree to market research.

Before dealing with a critical theoretical approach to the interface of Consciousness Industry and people, critical theorists ought to be familiar with the tools of manipulation which the mass media possess, as seen from the perspective of an establishment theorist. There follows an extensive summary of these tools, considering the advertising and free lunch messages as one inextricably entwined "message" type. What are these tools?

1. *The advantage of being first.* To the extent that the mass media present *new* issues they have immense power to create the kind of opinion they wish to create on such issues. The importance of the agenda-setting function of the mass media (emphasized in Chapter 1) is here supported by Klapper. After reviewing much experimental and small group research, he concludes that the media:

> . . . are extremely effective in creating opinions on matters about which the audience is *unlikely* to have pre-existing opinions. Communications on such topics have been found capable of "inoculating" audience members, i.e., of rendering them more resistant to later communications or experiences suggesting a contrary view. . . . To the degree that the issue is really "new," the communication is unlikely to run afoul of unsympathetic predispositions, unsympathetic group norms, or unsympathetic opinion leaders (Klapper, 1960, pp. 60–61, emphasis in original).

"They wouldn't print if if it wasn't so" is a twin of "they shouldn't print it if it isn't so" in popular consciousness in the core area. It is assumed that the media are *responsible* in the role of agenda setting for society. Klapper agrees with Lazarsfeld and Merton when they say:

> The mass media *confer* status on public issues, persons, organizations and social movements. . . . The mass media bestow prestige and enhance the

authority of individuals by *legitimizing their status*. . . . The operation of this status conferral function may be witnessed most vividly in the advertising patterns of testimonials to a product by "prominent"people. . . . Such testimonials not only enhance the prestige of the product but also reflect prestige on the person who provides the testimonial (Klapper, 1960, pp. 104–105, emphasis in original).

2. *Conversion.* Klapper finds communications research shows mass media do produce "conversion" (switching sides on an issue) although on a much smaller scale than "reinforcement." Conversion appears most likely when the nexus of mediating factors is either inoperative (leaving the mass media as the sole agent of change) or impelling toward conversion itself. Two of his elaborations on this conclusion seem pertinent to our interest in the effects of the total message of the mass media. He concludes that

> Persons under cross-pressures have been found to be peculiarly susceptible to conversion, to be unstable in opinion and thus susceptible to reconversion, and to tend on occasion to lose interest in the issue altogether (Klapper, 1960, p. 96).
> And that: Persons who are required to parrot—and, even more, those who are required to supplement—the arguments of a communication with which they initially disagree often tend to accept the arguments. . . . These findings offer a partial explanation of the persuasive efficiency of "brainwashing" (Klapper, 1960, p. 96).

Conversion also appears in the "bandwagon effect." Studies in the laboratory and in the field have demonstrated that switching sides in order to be on what is generally perceived to be the winning side is common in campaigns, although small minorities facing defeat may dig in their heels even harder (Klapper, 1960, pp. 125–127).

The two kinds of effects—that from the capacity to *initiate* opinion on a mass scale on new issues and that from the capacity to *convert* people's attitudes from one side to the other of an issue—would seem mutually reenforcing perhaps in a multiplicative rather than additive fashion. The effect of inducing people to hum advertising jingles would seem consistent with the finding that "parroting" arguments with which one disagrees results in conversion.

3. *Canalization.* Can existing audience needs be effectively mobilized by the mass media? New needs?

> Social scientists, public relations experts and the like have commonly observed that persons are far more amenable to having their existing needs implemented than they are to developing entirely new needs. Communication research generally confirms this view, strongly suggesting that persuasion is more likely to be effective when it can make the opinion or behaviour it

espouses appear to the audience to be a mode of satisfying their existing needs. . . .

The efficacy of advertising with which, however, we are not here primarily concerned, is believed by some observers to be largely due to its almost exclusive concern with such canalization. Even before the days of formalized motivation research which in effect identifies semi-conscious or unconscious consumer needs and suggests modes of partially sating them, Lazarsfeld and Merton (1948) observed that:

"Advertising is typically directed toward the canalizing of pre-existing behavior patterns or attitudes. It seldom seeks to instill new attitudes or to create significantly new behaviour patterns" (Klapper, 1960, pp. 120–121).

The creation of new needs requires manipulation of people's existing goals. Kurt Lewin called it appeals to the "life space" of the audience, and:

. . . Joseph Goebbels suggests that existing audience attitudes may be directed toward new objects by the use of words which are associated with existing attitudes; such symbol transference is, of course, part of the conscious or unconscious stock in trade of virtually all successful propagandists (Klapper, 1960, p. 12).

For bourgeois theorists, the needs which advertisers cultivate in order to sell commodities as remedies are in Klapper's terms "boundless" and to canalize them is to provide the audience with the means of heightening them.

4. One side vs. both sides. More persuasion is accomplished via mass media if "both sides" *seem* to be presented, *if the audience is better educated,* but in the case of the less educated, one-sided presentation is more effective. The use of this device is obviously tricky for a truly balanced "both sides" presentation produces no effect at all while an obviously fraudulent "both sides" has a counterproductive effect. Product advertisers seem to avoid use of this device in general, but recent advertising which presents comparisons of one brand with another in terms of some specifications and price may employ it.

5. Explicitness vs. implicitness. According to Klapper:

Research evidence strongly indicates that persuasion is likely to be more effective if the communication draws explicit conclusions rather than allowing the audience members to draw the conclusions themselves. . . . Action in accord with the recommendations of the communication likewise seems to become more probable as the suggestion for action becomes more explicit.

And he cites G. Wiebe, who had had extensive market research experience, as arguing that ". . . it is easier to sell commodities over television than it is to sell good citizenship because specific action may be more easily suggested and action outlets more easily provided (Klapper, 1960, pp. 116–117).

6. Threats.   In light of the common observation that advertising often employs threats, it is significant that Klapper says after reviewing extensive research literature that:

> Communications which evoke extreme fear are *less* likely to persuade the audience to take precautionary actions than communications which do not so strongly emphasize the threat (Klapper, 1960, p. 131, emphasis in original).

7.   Repetition

Belief that repetition in itself helps to make persuasion successful is manifested by current advertising techniques, often asserted by public opinion experts, and, to a lesser extent, attested by communications research. A campaign designed to improve the public's attitude toward the oil industry, for example (1954) was found to have produced the greatest attitude changes in regard to those points of view which were most often reasserted (Klapper, 1960, p. 119).

But repetition *with variations* is more effective than straight repetition because it minimizes audience irritation. Here Klapper mentions the experience of Joseph Goebbels as well as numerous studies.

8.   Opinion leaders, group norms, and interpersonal strata of dissemination.   We have earlier examined the mediating role of these institutions in estimating the limits on the capacity of the mass media to produce attitudes which favor or oppose change. The other side of that coin is the immense multiplication of media effects when the media are orchestrated *together*, in the same direction, with opinion leaders, group norms, and interpersonal strata of dissemination. That such campaigns do take place is common knowledge. The Cold War rested on a turnabout in popular attitudes toward the Soviet Union between VE Day in 1945 and 1952. It was a campaign by the capitalist system in the core area. In it popular acceptance of the Soviet Union as a wartime ally (which itself had been a reversal of public opinion from prewar hostility in which media management of news had been deliberately practiced to that end) was reversed by hysteria. This switch was produced by the media in cooperation with United States government leaders, plus Churchill and Prime Minister King, using spy scares, atomic secrets, the trials of the Rosenbergs and Hiss, and the anti-communist "inquisition" in which Richard Nixon and Senator Joseph McCarthy earned their public fame. I. F. Stone (1952) documented the campaign for the Korean War. The public relations campaign which built the legend of J. Edgar Hoover and the FBI has been analyzed (Lowenthal, 1950). The campaign by the military-industrial complex to maintain the arms race has been analyzed in many books (for example, Cook, 1962; Schiller and Phillips, 1976). And of course, the campaign against the Peoples Republic of China which denied it access to the United Nations and effectively quarantined it economically and culturally from 1950 to 1972 rested on the systematic misinformation program of the capitalist system in the core area which Felix Greene (1964) called the "Curtain of Ignorance." In the private sector many campaigns of this character have been exposed. Examples are that of the United States Chamber of Commerce and the National Association of Manufacturers for the hegemony of monopoly capitalism within the American state by James W. Prothro (1954), and that of American Telephone and Telegraph Company to discredit public ownership of telephones and secure the kind of state regulatory machinery which it favored, by N. R. Daniellian (1939). Readers may extend the examples.

9. *Order, emphasis, and organization of the message; the technical factors.* Here, in the present state of public knowledge, is an unassessed collection of essentially technical factors which perhaps represent a "black box" of undetermined manipulative potential. Klapper (1960, pp. 122–123) speaks of hundreds of studies, which would require a large staff and years of work to reanalyze, and which he was unable to synthesize. He refers to

> . . . an almost endless list of variables related to the organization of content and to techniques of presentation. Included among such variables are the number of topics treated; the position (first, last or intermediate) of the topic, and the order of arguments (strong before weak, or weak before strong); the form of the presentation (monologue versus dialogue, documentary with "visuals" versus straightforward presentation, etc.); clearly defined organization versus poorly defined organization; and a host of technical matters pertaining to size of print, position of pictures, radio montages, television camera angles, duration of shots and the like.

Klapper's analysis of the effectiveness of the tools employed to produce audiences to market commodities was limited to the perspective of stimulus-response administrative theory. That theoretical stream was discredited by about 1960 but was substantially continued under the name of *diffusion* theory by Rogers and others.[5] Meanwhile functional theory of uses and gratifications was developed to study the uses which individuals made of mass media content.

The functional study of uses and gratifications of media material had been a major contributor to understanding the relation of consciousness to media, beginning with the studies of radio soap operas and political campaigns in the 1940s and 1950s, by Paul Lazarsfeld, Robert Merton, Herta Herzog, and others. Those studies rejected the S-R paradigm and centered their research on the analysis of content and radio listeners to determine

---

[5] Rogers (1962) borrowed the name from the work of anthropologists, particularly A. L. Kroeber, and revised it as a form of administrative theory.

what uses were made of the content. These early studies showed that soap operas performed a number of functions for listeners:

1. The stimulation of imagination
2. The provision of vicarious social interaction—substituting fantasy social relations for real ones
3. Provision of a common ground for social intercourse of a superficial kind—material for conversation and group interests, e.g., movie fan clubs, popular music peer groups
4. Provision of emotional release—a chance to cry, vicarious participation in happy marriages, consolation for the listener's own troubles, identification with a successful hero, etc.
5. Provision for relaxation
6. The school of life function—sources of information and advice on how to meet real-life problems (Klapper, 1960, pp. 173–177).

It was one thing to recognize that people used media content for certain types of gratifications. But what do such patterns of uses of media material mean?

Escape? Educators, media critics, religious bodies, etc., have regularly denounced each of the mass media in turn as containing "escapist" material which they thought people used in antisocial ways while industry and media defend it as mere "entertainment."[6] Klapper (1960, p. 196) concludes an analysis of seven studies as indicating that:

> The weight of the findings, in short, tends to support the view that escapist media material is not so likely to *create* the kind of orientation which its fans seem to possess, as to be *used* by persons who are already so oriented.

He hastens to add that this is not to exonerate the media, using the analogy to morphine: you can't blame morphine for a person's becoming a drug addict, but if no morphine were available the drug addict might well have found a better solution for his problems.

Escape is a slippery concept. It is applied indiscriminately to media content, to the drives which lead to audience exposure, to the social context of exposure, and to the psychological process of "consumption" of mass media fare. Reviewing many functional studies of escape, Katz and Foulkes (1962, p. 381) conclude:

> . . . there is impressive evidence that alienation or deprivation are associated with increased exposure to particular media or particular kinds of media content. However, . . . if mass media exposure is sought for relief from, or compensation for, inadequacies in certain of an individual's social roles, that does not mean necessarily, that positive feedback is impossible for the roles in

---

[6] Although this criticism long predated these, see Siepmann (1948) and Seldes (1950).

question. It certainly does not mean that such feedback is impossible for other of the individual's roles.

As to mass media content, for example, news, "educational" programs, etc., which are not usually termed escapist content, may serve that function on occasion. Similarly with the social context of media consumption. The very fact of attending to a medium implies cutting oneself off from other roles. Concern with the consequences of media use is at the root of criticism of escape. As Katz and Foulkes (1962, p. 385) say:

> . . . an individual operates at many levels and . . . a given pattern of exposure can contribute functionally at one level and dysfunctionally at another. The same behavior that causes an individual to withdraw from social and political participation may contribute to the success of his performance at work the next day.

Escape, however, is an answer which refers only to individuals, not to the larger social formations.

Social apathy? Granting that functional analysis may have given a realistic response to the "escape" criticism of the mass media, it must be emphasized that treatment of that issue has been confined to *individuals* and *the short run*. Moreover, the consequences of escape, as observed by Katz and Foulkes include the "dysfunctional." Looking at the audience-as-a-whole in the existing social order, Paul Lazarsfeld and Robert Merton asserted flatly in 1948 that the mass media have a "narcotizing dysfunction." As far as I am aware, nothing in the literature of sociology and social psychology since then has developed a macrotheory of how the media work in that way *in the long run*. To be sure, Klapper (1960, p. 199) does link the mass media to the production of apathy but at the level of individuals:

> . . . It may be said that two highly pertinent points are reasonably well established by the literature. In the first place, mass communication is not so likely to produce great attitude or personality changes as it is to reinforce existing orientations. In the second place, escapist fare does seem to feed and exercise the asocial orientation of persons who are already socially apathetic. Putting the two points together, it would seem logical to suppose that escapist fare is likely to reconfirm the social apathy of the apathetic, but unlikely to quench the fires of the socially active and ardent.

And in the book's concluding chapter, he warns against the social psychologists':

> . . . tendency to go overboard in blindly minimizing the effects and potentialities of mass communications. Mass media of communication possess various characteristics and capabilities distinct from those of peer groups or opinion leaders. They are after all, media of *mass* communication, which

daily address tremendous cross-sections of the population with a single voice (Klapper, 1960, p. 252, emphasis in original).

He also reminds us that the research he had summarized was based on laboratory or naturalistic situations "within" a relatively stable society." In times of "massive political upheaval or in situations of actual or imminent social unrest" mass communications ". . . would appear to be capable of molding or 'canalizing' the predispositions into specific channels and so producing an active revolutionary movement" (Klapper, 1960, pp. 252–253)—or counterrevolutionary movement. In the 1980s with America's empire showing signs of breakup, the difference between the reality situation and the unreality of the commodity messages (both the physical commodities and the media images) of monopoly capitalism becomes sharper and more disruptive to the system.

In the two decades since the Klapper, and Katz and Foulkes review of the literature on needs and gratifications research, studies of media-related needs have proliferated and spread from the core area to Europe and other areas. One can agree with Katz, Blumler, and Gurevitch (1937–74, p. 521) in their review of this literature that ". . . media researchers ought to be studying human needs to discover how much the media do or do not contribute to their creation and satisfaction." However, all the studies reported on there *and* the theoretical perspective of the authors limit their conception of media content to the free lunch. By common tacit consent, the message they are interested in studying is that content which *seems* to be the principal product of the mass media. Moreover the needs as studied seem always to find their satisfaction or dissatisfaction in terms of individuals' actions in an assumed stable politico-economic context.

To pose the object of needs and gratification research as the authors did in the passage quoted and to simultaneously *reduce* the problem to that of free lunch audience relations is on a par with a situation in which a doctor performed a surgical operation to cure stomach ulcers while never noticing that the patient also was suffering from severe circulatory disease. The same criticism may be made of the monumental pile of communications research dealing with effects of violence in television programs on children. The damage done by damaged *commodities*, including the continuous production of audiences as damaged commodities, permeates the whole core society. To continue the medical metaphor, to study and try to remedy policy regarding "violence" in television programs (for adults and children) without noticing the injury done by damaged commodities as a necessary corollary informing all commercial media content and the real world of commodities is to identify a minor fraction of the patient's symptoms as the effective cause of his sickness.[7] Or, to mix the metaphors, to try to bail out a swamped boat with a teaspoon.

APPROACH TO A CRITICAL THEORY OF COMMUNICATION

A realistic theory (as opposed to the idealistic theory of establishment theorists) must begin with people, not messages nor media. Because there is little or no awareness of the significance of the audience commodity under monopoly capitalism in the core area what follows is advanced in a tentative and exploratory way.

An approach to a critical theory of communication should begin with recognition of how audience power is produced in real time. Audience power, looked at where it is conceived through the businessman's eyes, is equivalent to markets—whether it be markets for homogenous package goods, for durables such as television receivers in the 1940s or for political candidates. In order for a TNC to embark on production of a commodity, it must first be satisfied that a demand (i.e., audience power) may be produced to guarantee realization of surplus value from the marketing of some commodity, profitably fabricated. Far from the impetus lying with either the message or the medium, it lies in the possibility of audiences paying with money, time, and energy for the production, use, and discarding of the proposed product. The real sequence is no prospective profit, no audience, no message, no medium, no production of the commodity. The primacy of audiences in the sequence is undeniable and would hardly need mentioning if the process had not been so elaborately misrepresented and mystified for so long.

The audience thus defines the mass media. As the necessary means to the marketing of consumer goods it beckons them into existence. As the marketing agent, audience power is the commodity *par excellence*, for through it all markets for consumer goods in turn were and are beckoned into existence. As Bill Livant (1979b) remarks, presently we know very little about this strange commodity, the audience. On the one hand, audiences are not social groups in the sense that older voluntary associations, such as work, recreational, religious, etc., formations, are groups. Audiences almost never meet together. And on the other hand, audiences are not merely statistical aggregates. They manifest themselves collectively in

---

[7] See Ontario Royal Commission on Violence in the Communications Industry, *Approaches, Conclusions and Recommendations*, Vol. 1 (undated, 1978?); and for a summary of the United States Surgeon General's *Report* by the Scientific Advisory Committee on Television and Social Behavior and its task force studies, see Bogart (1972–73).

the rush to buy gold and silver, etc., as hedges against inflation, in lining up to buy 9:00 AM "specials" at the local department store, in conversations over lunch buckets about Archie Bunker, etc. There is some commonality and interaction involved in being members of an audience as their effect on teenager peer groups in relation to hit records indicates.

It would be a great mistake, however, to think of the face which audiences address to the business world (which might be called their private face) as if it were all there is to audiences. They have another face which might be called their *public face*. Presently we know almost nothing about this public face of the audience except that it exists and that it is concerned with the uniquely human aspects of life. In short we know that it is or may be involved in the defenses and strategic offenses which humanity can address to the formation that produced the species of organization known as the audience—monopoly capitalism. The political economy of the audience is yet to be explored and analyzed and it will be.

A basic element in a realistic theory of the interface between audiences and the mass media will involve analysis of the role of audiences produced by the media *in the total strategic plan of the advertiser for creating a profitable market for each specific commodity*. Such an element in the theoretical structure will deal with the relation between the way audiences receive the mix of advertising and free lunch from the mass media and the context of actions and relations in which such materials are processed. And here perhaps the figure of speech of the relation of the wave crest to the supporting movement of water in the ocean may be helpful. It seems that audience work is performed so effectively and cheaply for advertisers because advertising is like the wave crest—very visible and quite capable of giving you a ducking if you are in its path when it breaks, but dependent upon a massive and complex moving substructure. This metaphor helps us to see that audience work begins long before the mass media program-*cum*-advertisement appears on the tube face, and continues long afterward.

Audience work begins early in childhood, typified by two paradigmatic situations. In the core area for some two decades or more the child at the crawling-starting-to-talk stage looks at TV and listens to radio in the home. The question usually arises, "Mommy, the TV just said that brand X of bread was the 'best' bread; but at breakfast time the TV said that brand A was the 'best' bread; which is right?" From a logical positivistic point of view and with the assumption that it is desirable that young children learn to be commodity consumers, research has studied this children's work, but from an uncritical "socializing" standpoint. The first assumption made by the authors of one series of such studies is:

> Consumption for children is as legitimate an activity as it is unavoidable. Efforts would seem to be better spent on preparing children for *efficacious in-*

teraction with the marketplace than on protecting them from the multiple
influences on product preferences and purchasing which are indigenous to
childhood (Ward et al., 1977, p. 12, emphasis added).

Some of the conclusions of such research are significant from a critical
standpoint. It is known, for example, that advertisers have sought to influence family expenditures by making children into their agents to press
parents to buy certain products. The authors find that such pressures are
more effective with "low socio-economic" mothers than with middle- or
upper-status mothers. And while about half of the children in each age
group are given money to spend regularly:

> More low-status mothers than high-status mothers simply give money to their
> children, and lower-income children have more spending money than mid-
> dle and upper-income children up to the sixth grade. . . . (Ward et al., 1977,
> pp. 180–181).

It is reassuring for advertisers to be told that the implications of this
research are that:

> The major [controversial] issues concern particular practices in marketing
> stimuli and children's net impressions of products as a function of exposure to
> advertising. Our data suggest that marketing efforts to children should be
> geared to their level of cognitive ability in order to insure that they can fairly
> evaluate promotional activities designed to influence them. Marketers who
> take such steps demonstrate responsiveness to current public-policy concerns.
> *Moreover, one could argue that systematic improvements in advertising to*
> *children may ultimately contribute to the emergence of more efficacious, less*
> *skeptical consumers—a very positive outcome for marketers* (lWard et al.,
> 1977, p. 189, emphasis added).

The second archetypical situation is the supermarket where the in-
fant rides in the seat of the shopping cart as its mother perambulates
through the aisles, monitoring the mother's use of her "shopping list" and
impulse-buying behavior until they reach the cash register where the
child learns how much of family income is spent. I am unaware of
research into the learning by the child of how to do audience work in this
practical aspect of real life.

It is obvious that as children, teenagers, and adults, audience
members come to the TV tube with rich past experience with commodities-in-general. They have observed and evaluated old and new
models of products on the street, in the homes of friends and peer group
members, and on the persons of people they see at the job front, the
school, and in all other social relationships (including transportation
vehicles). They will also have discussed with family members, friends,
and strangers the merits and demerits of the old and new models in any of
a thousand different social contexts. That Henry Ford enjoyed an expand-

ing and enthusiastic market for the black Model T automobile *in the absence of any advertising program at all* in the early years illustrates the substance and power of the wave's substructure minus the wave crest of advertising. As Gerry Mander would say, this illustrates the point that people will beckon the product into existence with no advertising, no free lunch. I suggest that this constant process of direct experience with commodities and the emulative habits nurtured by possessive individualist lifestyles goes on constantly. It blends into all aspects of audiences' lives all the time. And advertisers get this enormous volume of audience work (creation of consumer consciousness) *as a bonus* even before their programs and advertising hit the television tube.

The process of innovating genuinely new durable consumer goods illustrates the point. When TV was being innovated in the core area in the 1940s and early 1950s, the demonstration effect—not media advertising—was the principal means of producing markets (audiences) for TV receiving equipment. Taverns, bars, and other public places were used to show the public what TV could be, with sports events (baseball games, Friday Night Fights, etc.) and variety shows (e.g., Ed Sullivan) as the initial free lunch. From its inception in 1945 the TV broadcast industry had to produce and broadcast programs at a loss because the number of TV receivers in public hands was so small that audience sales to advertisers could produce only trivial revenues. Accumulated operating losses built up to high levels for the TV networks and initial affiliated stations, which were paid for out of accumulated capital from radio broadcasting. That was the period, referred to by Charles Siepmann at the time as TV's *Golden Age*, when creative artists were encouraged to explore the program possibilities of the new medium with freedom from tight advertiser constraints. In this way the first two purposes of new product advertising were accomplished, i.e., to establish in popular consciousness (1) the need for the new service, (2) the knowledge that a generic new commodity was available to satisfy that need. Simultaneously, media advertising was used to advance the sales of each of the national brands of TV receivers.

Consciousness Industry is pragmatic about planning campaigns for such innovations. When the first mass-produced automobiles relying on electricity rather than the internal combustion engine will be innovated, there will be no problem of establishing in popular consciousness awareness of the need for such a commodity. Nor will the forthcoming availability of the generic new commodity require paid-for advertising. The rising price and shortages of gasoline will already have accomplished the first and second purposes of advertising. The demonstration of available electric cars and the promotion of one or another brand will complete the innovation process simultaneously and at little promotional/advertising cost *because of audiences' previous work on the product.* There is already waiting in the newsrooms of the mass media a high place on the daily news agenda for the headlines and stories about the first electric-powered automobiles of modern design to make a nonstop round trip between Manhattan and Washington, the first to drive between New York and Chicago, etc. Being part of the free lunch, this will cost advertisers nothing. All that remains for advertising to do in such a case is use audiences to choose between the competitive brand names and prices of the product available "from your local dealer."

The preceding discussion leads to these conclusions. Advertising via the mass media must be viewed as an integral part of a broad campaign to establish a market for a "new" commodity or a "new" model of an old commodity, and to maintain the markets for existing commodities. The audience/market formation of people is an aspect of a lifelong process of learning about, and coping with, commodities of which the events on the tube face and in the audience while attending to the tube face are but a brief moment. People's preparation over time—their readiness to recognize and internalize a "need" for the commodity being offered is always the basic and indispensable condition for their motion to serve in a specific audience. In this way again we see the primacy of people in the universal audience over the medium and the message. An essential feature of this realistic theory of communications is the location of people and audiences in their real historical context. This book exemplifies an attempt to provide a critical theoretical analysis of such a context.

This contextual setting is absolutely necessary if we are to assess realistically the relation of what happens at and following the encounter of people with the mass media "at the face of the tube." It was demonstrated abundantly in Chapters 1 to 8 that the audience is the principal product of the mass media. My argument is that the audience is a new social institution with two faces: the "private" face which serves as market and marketing agent for Consciousness Industry, and the "public" face which struggles for the non-commodity goals of life through various institutions (the family, church, union, etc.). And everyone in the core area has both a private and a public face. Now we can see that *everyone in the core area is in the audience all the time* because collectively *everyone* is engaged in producing and selling commodities-in-general. As Bill Livant (1979b) says:

> The penetration of market relations into the watching and listening of audiences is uneven and not yet worldwide. But it is a fact in the United States. U.S. TV shows us precisely the formation of a *single general market* in the activities of the audience.
>
> Consequently it is no longer true that someone who has not seen or heard a particular message is not in the audience. He *is* in it. *He is a member of the*

audience who hasn't seen or heard the message. The failure to see this point stems from our message-based definition of the audience. When the members of the audience are in a market of the audience, there is a qualitative change in the way meanings are generated. Whereas previously the problem for members of the audience was accepting or rejecting *the message*, the problem is now one of *accepting* or *resisting the market* [all commodity relations as presently existing in the core area].

We are now beginning to grasp a critical theory of communications, rooted in the lives of people. It is certain to be more useful in explaining how communications relate to consciousness than the establishment theories, which are all idealistic in their preconceptions and analytical concepts.

I am aware of a considerable body of theoretical work stemming from the Frankfurt School, of which that of William Leiss (1976) is an example. For a variety of methodological and substantive reasons which I have summarized in my Introduction, I do not find them particularly helpful. It was to be expected that bourgeois social scientists would grasp the notion of images and emphasize them in analyzing mass communication (Boorstin, 1962). So also have some Marxists (e.g., de Bord (1970). I mistrust such analysis because it seems static—ahistorical and tending to ignore the movement of the principal contradiction: people vs. capital.

There is also a line of realistic critical studies of policy and structures of communications institutions and their broader politico-economic context. Herbert Schiller (1969, 1973, 1976) and Armand Mattelart (1979) have made path-breaking studies of this sort. There is a series of bibliographies, *Marxism and the Mass Media: Towards a Basic Bibliography*, edited by Seth Siegelaub. Journals devoted to critical analysis of communications exist in a number of countries, e.g., *Media, Culture and Society* in England. The International Association for Mass Communication Research has a political economy section with a very active group concerned with critical theory of communications, living and working in countries as widespread as Scandinavia, Western Europe, the Soviet bloc, India, Australia, Latin America, the United States, and Canada. A common criticism to which many in this line of work are subject is that they are economistic or "automatic Marxist."

My previous work has been mostly concerned with critical analysis of policies and structures affecting communications and has in large measure deserved the criticism "economistic" (but not "automatic Marxist"). Such work has tended to emphasize the power of capital through the policies and structures of capitalist communications, while slighting the resistance which people conduct to protect themselves against domination by capital. Nevertheless, it is arguable that knowledge of the process by which one is dominated is necessary before the consciousness of the dominated is prepared to go on the offensive. The work on this line has served to describe and anatomize the process of domination *and thus clear the way* for work on the other factor in the principal contradiction: people. This book may be criticized as economistic. It seems possible, even probable, however, that the emphasis here on the analysis of the audience as an institution may help initiate a new and more complete series of theory-building attempts which will comprehend more validly than what has been produced until now the dialectical process which contains the principal contradiction. Such is the momentum of work on the critical analysis of communications that one might expect to find this book regarded as quite immature within a few years.

With this background of theory we may approach the relation of communication to consciousness in Chapter 12.

12

ON CONSCIOUSNESS

All fixed, fast frozen relations, with their train of ancient and venerable prejudices and opinions, are swept away, all new-formed ones become antiquated before they can ossify. All that is solid melts into air, all that is holy is profaned, and man is at last compelled to face with sober senses his real conditions of life, and his relations with his kind (Marx, K., and Engels, F., *The Communist Manifesto*)

We have been analyzing the institutional processes characteristic of monopoly capitalism in the heart of its core area—the United States with its Canadian connection—with special attention to the cluster of industries called *Consciousness Industry*, led by the mass media of communication. Because of the power and demonstrated effectiveness of that system, the overall impression given the reader is that of a dominant, *irresistible* social formation acting on *passive* people as individuals and in their customary institutional relationships (family, school, church, labor union, "cultural" groupings, government, etc.). True, people are subject to relentless pressures from Consciousness Industry; they are besieged with an avalanche of consumer goods and services; they are themselves produced as (audience) commodities; they reproduce their own lives and energies as damaged and in commodity form. But people are by no means passive or powerless. People do resist the powerful and manifold pressures of capital as best they can. There is a dependable quantum of individual and group resistance, reproduced every day, arising out of people's innate capacity and need for love, respect, communal relations, and creativity. That is, the principal contradiction in the core area (as in the whole world)

270

is that between people and capital. And presently people are the principal aspect of that contradiction. This chapter is devoted to analysis of that contradiction from the standpoint of consciousness and its potentials.

Consciousness is the total awareness of life which people have. It includes their understanding of themselves as individuals and of their relations with other individuals in a variety of forms of organization, as well as with their natural environment. Consciousness is a dynamic process. It grows and decays with the interaction of doing (or practice) and cognition over the life cycle of the individual in the family and other social formations. It draws on emotions, ideas, instincts, memory, and all of the sensory apparatus. It is evident in our culture (as defined in Chapter 9). It seems focused at the "interface" between matter and spirit. As Karl Marx said,

> From the start, "spirit" is afflicted with the curse of being burdened with matter which here makes its appearance in the form of agitated layers of sound, in short, of language. Language is as old as consciousness, *language is practical consciousness* that exists also for other men, and for that reason alone it really exists for me personally as well. Language, like consciousness, only arises from the need, the necessity, of intercourse with other men. . . . Consciousness is, therefore, from the very beginning a social product, and remains so as long as men exist at all (Marx and Engels, 1970, pp. 50–51, emphasis added).

Consciousness, like language, is both retentive and intentional. Community and communications exist because people share emotions, ideas, and joint undertakings. *Ideology* for me means the system of beliefs, attitudes, and ideas which support or tend to transform a larger social enterprise—a political-economic system, be it capitalist or socialist. For example, the ideology of capitalism rests on (1) possessive individualism, (2) hierarchical organization headed by professionals/experts, (3) relativism and pluralism in values, linked to an alleged apolitical character of art, science, and "technology," (4) a theory that change is linear and the result of technical manipulation of the secrets of a mechanical universe. A dominant class must constantly produce public opinion in order to maintain its control of a politico-economic system; and a dominated class can make a successful revolution only when it has first created public opinion to support it.[1]

Where does consciousness come from? It does not come from outer space—from the realm of pure thoughts or essences. It comes from real

---

[1] Capitalists would agree that "To overthrow political power, it is always necessary first of all to create public opinion, to do work in the ideological sphere. This is true for the revolutionary class as well as for the counter-revolutionary class." Mao Zedong, *Speech at the 10th Plenum*, 1962.

life experience—from people's interaction with each other and with their environment. The core area of monopoly capitalism—the United States and Canada—has been fertile in producing books and movements which advocate the possibility of "consciousness raising" through individual or collective reliance on inspirational sources, be they religious or mystical in nature. There is a rich history of these efforts in the nineteenth century (with such utopian "community" efforts as Oneida, Brook Farm, etc.), and the protest movement of the 1960s produced a large literature and many sporadic efforts to establish small communities and individual "consciousness raising" devoted to this objective. This idealistic approach simply does not "work" as a practical matter because the politico-economic system within which these efforts are minuscule dissenting elements has too much power for them to survive. Indeed that system need not do anything special to crush them; it simply allows its multifaceted inertial power to pass them by. When they become mass in character and seem to threaten the system as did the "counterculture" of the 1960s, the capitalist system merely coopts the rhetoric, the dress, the costume jewelry, the hair styles, and the music of the protesters and uses them to provide a spark of daring-yet-safe novelty to the output of Consciousness Industry.

For the mainstream of scholarship and social science in the United States and Canada, investigation of consciousness is simply not on the agenda for serious inquiry. The pervasive influence of logical positivism and pragmatism regards it as pure speculation. In effect the prevailing view of institutions and collective consciousness in the core area is to look at them with X-ray eyes, seeing only individuals and small "peer groups" in them. In conversation with David Riesman, I once urged the proposition that the presidents of American Telephone and Telegraph Company and Columbia Broadcasting System, for example, wielded by virtue of their official positions, power vastly greater than ordinary citizens. His reply: "What you don't recognize, Dallas, is that they are as much prisoners of their peer groups as you and I are of ours."

Marxist scholars in the core area continue to be fixated on the need to deal with consciousness in terms of the dichotomy between the economic base and an ideology-producing superstructure. This tendency which pervades the European scene, e.g., in the work of Althusser (1965), has some residual validity as applied in the real world in Europe. There the nineteenth-century class structure stubbornly persists, if only in gradually attenuating form under the onslaught of mid-Atlantic style Consciousness Industry. What escapes the attention of adherents of the base-superstructure paradigm is the fact of uneven development of capital in the realm of culture and consciousness.

In the North American core area the distinction between base and superstructure has disappeared. And its disappearance follows the penetration of international capital formations (TNCs) in Europe, Third World countries, and socialist countries which admit their activities.

The development of a realistic, critical theory about communications and consciousness under capitalism in the core area is presently at or near a threshold where it is necessary to avoid both the shoals of idealism and logical positivism while also avoiding the rocky cliffs of slavish dependency on archaic notions borrowed from Europe.

Possibly a good way to approach that threshold is to raise the question is there class consciousness under monopoly capitalism in the core area? Ollman (1971, p. 205) defines *class consciousness* as that of social units based on:

1. People's relation to the mode of production;
2. Similar economic conditions and interests;
3. Consciousness of those interests;
4. The existence of a group-wide political organization;
5. Cultural affinity and a common antagonism for opposing groups.

It is important to note that *all* of these relations are required. There is *no* revolutionary class consciousness in the United States and Canada by these criteria. The class formations brought with them by the migrants from the United Kingdom were substantially eroded by the conquest of a vast and rich continent and the massacre of the indigenous people, driven by the ethic of possessive individualism and the lure of the rich resources taken from the original inhabitants. What remained of the class structure brought from Europe was decisively homogenized by Conciousness Industry, as indicated in Chapters 3–8. For a century now, a dominant capitalist power formation of which the decisive portion is monopoly corporations, led by an assault force of Consciousness Industry TNCs has controlled the American and Canadian states. The great majority of the population works most of the time and lives in fear of unemployment.

Although there is no general revolutionary class consciousness in the United States and Canada there is considerable spontaneous class consciousness which appears in the struggles between poor and rich or between advantaged and disadvantaged blocs of people in the core area. In this sense there is an undeveloped guerrilla struggle in the United States and Canada.

The formations of that population which display this spontaneous class behavior are ethnic groups, conspicuously the Québécois, and the Blacks, Chicanos, Puerto Ricans. To this list might be added the indigenous people if and when their political cohesion matures. Two other segments are distinguishable in terms of *some* of the criteria, both age-based. One of these is the aged, defined as over sixty-five, a group comprising 11 percent of the United States population in 1977 and destined to grow in size and impoverishment, caught between inflation in the cost of living and inadequate pension/relief incomes. The larger is the youth class (16 percent between ages fourteen and twenty-one in 1977). This formation over its lifetime has been a prime target of Consciousness Industry. The process was easy. The propaganda of clothes, music, hair styles, psychedelic and narcotic drugs, working through peer groups, formed this age group into audiences, working diligently to market goods to themselves and to acquire commodity characteristics as persons. But if denied employment or incomes sufficient to permit them to marry and obtain housing, this group has the potential of resistance to the system—a resistance with tendencies both to left and right. The women's movement may in time be added to this list when its consciousness matures.

By no stretch of imagination can any or all of these present or incipient formations meet the requirements of Marxist specification, nineteenth-century style, for classes with class consciousness. But they are the only approximations in the core area of capitalism. And all of them exist in contradictory relations with monopoly capitalism.

But first, how was the nineteenth-century class structure of Europe, which had been transplanted to the United States and Canada earlier, transformed to its present condition in those countries? By the process by which capitalism destroyed its relatively competitive structure and transformed itself into monopoly capitalism of which Consciousness Industry is the mainstay. As was shown in Chapters 2–4, the application of science to both the job front and the home front transformed both work places and in so doing distributed the earlier ideological-instruction role of the old "superstructure" in substantial measure into the work place where people are paid for working and the home where they work but are not paid. In terms of the old contradiction between infrastructure and superstructure, the mass media are simultaneously in the superstructure and engaged indispensably in the last stage of infrastructural production where audiences are produced and consumed in the production of demand and its satisfaction by purchases of consumer goods. The result of this transformation is *not* to eliminate the contradiction between people and capital, but to intensify it by *generalizing* it. No longer are *only* wage earners in daily confrontation with capitalist industry, and then *only* at their job front; now they and their nonemployed spouses and dependents confront it 24 hours a day.

How was this process connected to the similar transformation taking place in Europe today? Possibly the experience with radio and television broadcasting policy provides a clue to the answer, in class terms. Radio broadcasting on the BBC model in Europe and elsewhere, *except in*

North America, was a continuation of nineteenth-century, premonopoly capitalist policy. It was quite consistent with classical class struggle and class consciousness. Between 1920 and 1945 there was a struggle in both the United States and Canada over whether to adopt a similar policy, as is related in Chapter 8.

In the United States the forces of conservatism (using the term in its European class sense) were weak and fought a rearguard retreating action for "public service" in broadcasting. In Canada the struggle was clearer. In Canada the creation of the CBC was the high point of the struggle for Canadian nationalism precisely because to achieve it there was a mobilization of Canadian national capital, allied with social democracy and the social gospel forces of the church. The objective of this united front was to approximate as closely as possible the BBC model in which audiences would be produced to accept the prevailing bourgeois ideology, supporting the old liberal class structure. Opposed to this premonopoly capitalist formation were the forces of the TNCs supporting a system in which broadcasters would produce audiences for the use of advertisers. As noted in Chapter 8, the victory for the CBC was immediately and chronically eroded by the quiet political influence of the Consciousness Industry forces even before 1945. With the coming of television, the substance of the original purpose of the CBC was decisively eliminated and the private sector enjoyed a quicker penetration of commercial television in Canada than it had experienced in the United States. With a time-lag of no more than several years, the same TNCs mounted the successful assault on the BBC monopoly in the United Kingdom. There followed in turn analogous struggles in Australia and New Zealand with similar outcomes. Following a long series of similar victories in the smaller and weaker European nations (e.g., Finland) and in the former colonies of the European powers in Africa and Asia, the monopoly-capitalist forces returned to transform the state monopoly broadcasting structures of France and Italy in their own interest. In Canada the struggle against commercial broadcasting was in no way expressive of proletarian class consciousness. And probably this was true for each of the other countries with this experience. The procommercial forces based their campaigns on the essential ideological foundation of capitalism, individualism, and they won handily.

If further evidence is needed to make the point, consider the distribution of advertising expenditures. Between 1950 and 1979, advertising expenditures in the United States increased more than sevenfold; those in the rest of the world increased by 26-fold (in current dollars). In 1950, 78 percent of total advertising expenditures took place in the United States; in 1979, only 51 percent (Anderson, 1979, p. 25).

Granted that consciousness is a product of real life experiences how do the mass media of communications relate to its production? In Chapter 11 we developed the beginning of a realistic, historically oriented theory of how the mass media fit into the process of consciousness production and reproduction. The role of people in audiences was seen to be paramount in that process. And people in audiences were said to relate to the process in two ways: with their "private" face where they cope with the marketing of consumer goods and services, and with their "public" face where they reproduce their own labor power and social relations. Let us pick up the argument at this point, again thinking of people confronting the media "at the tube face."

The mass media and advertising are both *less* important and *more* important in the sense of unilaterally manipulating people and determining consciousness than most textbooks and critics have shown. The findings of Klapper regarding the *major* role played by the "mediating nexus" of opinion leaders, community institutions, etc., in producing "effects" of the "message" from the mass media are correct. The people in that mediating nexus, it must be remembered, are audiences working—not merely a cog in a downwardly administered machine. Such people are in the generalized audience; whether they receive the "message" favorably or not will serve to accelerate and amplify the "effect" of the "message," or to brake it and turn it off.

But the mass media and advertisers are simultaneously *more* important in their capacity to conduct campaigns of all kinds than most of the textbooks and critics have argued. This is because of the immense advantage of having the first word, of the simple fact that the media must go through the process of making a selection (agenda) of possible topics to be considered (in their advertisements as well as their free lunch), of the power of their use of canalization, conversion, and other tools of manipulation. In their capacity as agenda setters, surveying the total scene, as designers and producers of the free lunch with whatever manipulative devices they find useful, and as the constant producers of the audience product, they serve as sentinels and surrogates for the monopoly-capitalist system which created the audience form as its most efficient protagonist, and prospectively as its most protean antagonist.

I remarked that the audience has not only a face turned toward the tumultuous flood of commodities to be privately owned, but also a face turned toward human development. How to elaborate this? We know from Chapter 9, but pay little attention to activity by amateurs in the arts, handicrafts, and hobbies which engages far more of the energies of the population in the core area than do the fine and performing arts. We should also recognize that "public service," "community" work—work with crippled children, work with the aged, and charity work of community groups ranging from Home and School Organizations, "Brownies," boy scouts, etc., to the churches—expresses the public face of the audience. It is currently fashionable among intellectuals to "put down" such audience work as ineffectual, but it ought to be taken as part of the audience's drive for humanity.

Conspicuous among such groups are the hundreds of local groups of Americans which have developed a broadcast-reform movement since the 1940s. They are integrated into national organizations such as the National Black Media Coalition, ACT (Action for Children's Television), and AIM (Accuracy in Media) and as subsidiaries of the National Organization of Women and the Gray Panthers. They do research on mass media and present petitions to broadcast stations and testimony before regulatory bodies and Congressional committees concerning policies and laws for the media in the interests of children, women, the elderly, homosexuals, and the public in general. Everett C. Parker and the Office of Communications of the United Church of Christ have been pioneers in organizing public opinion and using the courts, legislative and administrative organs to protect the interests of people as against capital. This broadcast reform movement has made significant improvements in broadcast programs and employment practices, especially since the WLBT-TV, Jackson, Mississippi case in 1964 in which the legal standing of the public before the FCC in broadcast licensing proceedings was established for the first time.

As regards public commodities (as distinct from private consumer's goods), there is little to be said in the core area. As was pointed out in Chapter 10, durable public goods creation is systemically sabotaged by monopoly capitalism.

Is it possible to give examples of the results of unselfish *effort* by audiences? Several examples of trends in popular consciousness in the United States may be given.

A so-called white backlash was proclaimed by "law and order" candidates (especially Richard Nixon) in the elections of 1968 as a result of the frequent and widespread rioting by Blacks in many American cities between 1964 and 1968. Consequently it was assumed by the media and politicians that racial integration had lost much of its previous support from whites. A study by Gwen Bellisfield (1972–73) analyzed annual public opinion poll questions on attitudes toward integration in schools and housing for the years 1963–1968.

> We found that support for integration in both housing and schools increased during the six-year study period in the population as a whole, in the urban and rural areas, among males and females, in the South and outside the South, and in all age and education groups. . . . We concluded from these findings that the twenty-year trend noted by Paul Sheatsley in 1963 toward greater acceptance by whites of racial integration was neither halted nor

reversed during the period of widespread urban disturbances in the 1960s in the United States population as a whole or in the subgroups examined. . . .

A possibility which remained to be examined is that groups closest in times and places to riots may have reduced their support of racial integration after the riots occurred even though the population as a whole and other subgroups examined did not.

The metropolitan areas where rioting took place were matched with metropolitan areas where no rioting had taken place and the polling data were retabulated. The results showed that even in the riot areas immediately following the riots, support for integration *increased*, although the size of the increase in support was smaller than in nonriot areas and in the riot areas during years in which no riot occurred. The author concluded:

Although segments of the population voted for "law-and-order" candidates, and public opinion polls showed increased support for stricter law enforcement . . . the twenty-year trend noted in 1963 by Paul Sheatsley toward greater acceptance of racial integration was neither halted nor reversed by the heightened violence. The occurrence of a riot, to be sure, appears to have slowed down the increase in acceptance of integration in that riot area and year. The surprising finding, however, is not that acceptance of integration seems to have increased more slowly in riot areas immediately following a riot there, but that it increased at all in these times and places.

The second example is drawn from testimony by the heads of all major public opinion polling organizations in the United States.[2] Invited to tell the Joint Economic Committee of the United States Congress the state of public opinion, these men revealed the current consciousness in terms which correspond to the analysis of this book. Lou Harris said:

We find that a significant majority of 67 percent of the public criticizes the leadership of the country for "not understanding that the people do not want more quantity of nearly anything but want better quality of just about everything they possess." This matter of quality is a crucial one. A majority of 53 percent of the public feels that the quality of most of the products and services it consumes has deteriorated in the past 10 years, as indeed has the quality of life, in the minds of the people themselves.

This matter of quality rather than quantity is important for it signals the important impact that the energy crunch has had on the American people. . . . Make no mistake about it, the public is prepared to cut back on a whole host of physical goods which we have automatically assumed everyone wanted in greater and greater quantity. The fact that as 6 percent of the world's population we consume an estimated 40 percent of the world's raw materials is beginning to dawn on the American people. And I am

[2] Joint Economic Committee, Congress of the United States, 94th Cong., 1st Sess., Part 2, 30 October, 1975.

prepared to say that in the next five years you are going to see a flattening out of absolute demand in this country for the vast majority of physical goods that we have come to depend on for our economic livelihood. And I might add, Mr. Chairman, most economists count on this as a basis for economic growth. This would include such items as washing machines, cars, television sets, appliances of all kinds, and even housing.

Later, in colloquy with the committee, he said that his organization had pursued the quality of life question at least four times:

It is very practical. It isn't just water pollution, Mr. Long. It is the product safety that Senator Humphrey talked about; it is employee safety; it is, and you get a high score on this, the people want to see employment of minorities and other people who have had less privilege.

The head of the Gallup Poll confirmed the point made by Harris and added:

Another thing with respect to spending, in August of 1972 we found only 9 percent were in favor of increased defense spending while 40 percent felt that the level should be kept where it was, 37 percent felt that it should be reduced, and another 5 percent felt that defense spending should be ended altogether. So there is a very clear pattern here of people wanting defense spending cuts.

The president of Peter D. Hart Research Associates testified:

The American public is deeply dissatisfied with the current performance of the economy; that there is a widespread disbelief in the ability of the "fine-tuning" approach which currently dominates official policy to produce a real and viable recovery; and, most important, that the *public has come to doubt and mistrust the basic institutional arrangement between the Government and the private sector which has shaped the face of our economic system for the last 40 years.* . . .

All of the President's statistics and all of the President's men cannot put confidence back in the economy again. To expect some spontaneous turnabout in public attitudes without a fundamental shift in who decides economic policy and who benefits from it is to seriously misunderstand the mood of the Nation.

This lack of confidence regarding the prospects for a full recovery stems from the public's fundamental convictions that neither the close relationship between the Federal Government and the Nation's big corporations, nor the leadership of the Government and corporations, any longer works to protect the interest of the average person. Again let me cite just a few figures which demonstrate these observations.

Fully 58 percent of the public feel that "public officials in Washington are dominated by the country's big corporations."

Antitrust laws, a major weapon in the public's arsenal against the imperfections in the private sector, are regarded by almost two-thirds of the people as doing an inadequate job. . . .

By a margin of 57 to 35 percent, a majority of the public feels that "both the Democratic and Republican parties are more in favor of big business than the average worker."

Thus, both government and the political parties are more than a little suspect; and this suspicion, we find, is even more pronounced when we turn to an examination of public attitudes toward the leadership being put forth by the private sector. Here we find:

By a margin of 72 to 24 percent, 3 to 1, the public feels that "profits are the major goal of business even if it means unemployment and inflation." Sixty-one percent of our citizens are of the opinion that "there is a conspiracy among big corporations to set prices as high as possible." Just one American in four gives business a positive mark insofar as "really caring about the individual" is concerned. By a margin of 54 to 31 percent, the public believes than an American multinational corporation, given the choice to sign a contract with a foreign country which would be profitable for the corporation but harmful to the interests of the United States, would sign such a contract. (Emphasis added.)

Tending to confirm my assertion that anticapitalist attitudes do not follow nineteenth-century class lines in the core area is Hart's statement:

When asked to rate the health of the American economy, fully 55 percent of the public rated the performance of the economy as below average or poor, while a scant 10 percent evaluated the economy's present performance as either above average or excellent. *Significantly, this negativism was not confined to lower income citizens. Indeed, individuals coming from the highest income groups were no more likely to give the economy a clean bill of health than were those from the lowest stratum.* (Emphasis added.)

What, in the view of consciousness thus revealed, did people want to do about it all? They were reported to want to take control of their own lives in ways long subverted by Consciousness Industry. Lou Harris said:

I realize that these are quite radical findings I report here today. They are most radical of all, because they do not fit the left-right dialog that so much of our leadership is caught up in these days. Especially in economic areas. Well, Mr. Chairman, the public is fed up with that kind of left-right division as well. They want new solutions to new problems and they do not want the solutions spoon-fed to them, either. Rather, they want to participate in making them—are unafraid to receive tough, hard truths and bad news. They do not want to be treated as 12-year old consumers. There is a whole crisis in the selling area, both in business and in—I might add—politics. The hard sell, the easy handout, the easy appeal to fear—all these are perishing. In these new days, people are going to insist on economic solutions, arrived at out in the open, and will be willing to share in the sacrifices of the upside benefits of a better quality existence—offered to all people everywhere in this land. The issue is not the division of the spoils, but rather how to desperately find ways to stop spoiling life on this planet.

Specifically,

> . . . two-thirds of the American people said that, given the choice, they would prefer working in a "company in which the majority of the stock is owned by the employees, who appoint their own management to run the company's operations." Only 8 percent of the public say they would want to work for a company "owned and managed by the Government," while just 20 percent, if given the choice, would choose to work for the now-dominant form of economic organization in our society, the investor-owned and managed corporation.

And representation of consumers in local communities on the boards of companies operating in those communities was favored by a margin of 74 to 17 percent. By a majority of 56 percent (as against 26 percent opposed), the public said they would support a presidential candidate who advocated employee ownership and control of major American businesses.

Has Consciousness Industry, for all its power, failed to "capture" people's consciousness? Does this evidence mean that the monopoly-capitalist system faces a "crisis of legitimacy" in its core area? Reviewing such evidence, E. C. Ladd (1976–77, p. 550) concluded:

> When 61 percent of a populace think quite a few of their leaders are crooked and 62 percent insist that their national government is run on behalf of a few big interests, when nearly four people out of every five profess to feel that the system is so arranged that the rich fatten up and the poor suffer, when three-quarters maintain that their country is on the wrong track and the same proportion believe their government wastes a lot of money—well, it is possible to argue that the country has problems, and maybe that there is a crisis of confidence, even an incipient crisis of legitimacy.[3]

It is obvious that the reported readiness of the American people for workers' control of giant corporations, appears to come from their consciousness *without the support which a political party or movement dedicated to that objective might provide*—and therefore *now* is a utopian wish. Especially when one also recalls that the same opinion polling organizations reported that by a margin of 54 percent to 19 percent the people felt that "a free market economy was a necessary condition for personal liberty and democracy." It is fair to say, however, that the foregoing indicates that the popular consciousness in the United States in 1976 believes that the monopoly-capitalist system has failed. A sharpening of consciousness of the contradiction between people and that system has undoubtedly resulted from subsequent events: the massive collapse of the dollar, the flight to gold, other precious metals, etc., between 1976 and 1980, with the accompanying escalating price inflation. Whether this consciousness in the United States has a counterpart in Canada will be

---

[3] The author then reviews contrary evidence and concludes it is premature to consider existence of a constitutional crisis.

discussed later. It will be useful, however, to approach the Canadian scene after considering the communications aspects of the situation of Blacks, Chicanos, and Puerto Ricans in the United States.

Consciousness, as measured by Consciousness Industry seems flat and static, except where regional or other statistical breakdowns represent various plateaus of opinion and suggest motion. If we would penetrate into the process by which consciousness is produced, it is necessary to deal with dialectical conflicts on a deeper level. True, a downward-flowing stream of authority comes out of the mass media and the producers of consumer goods and services. The free lunch of the mass media reinforces the values of the status quo hourly, as our review of the research by Klapper, Katz, et al. demonstrates. In fact communications theorists have long conceded that ideological propaganda can affect audience members' consciousness profoundly, under conditions of substantial monopoly control of media content (Klapper, 1949; Lazarsfeld and Merton, 1948). Looked at as a whole, the monopoly-capitalist system in its core area does have for the mass of the public an effective monopoly control of mass communication. The "little media" and occasional dissenting voices in the "free lunch," far from proving the contrary, support this conclusion by their marginal and sparse occurrence. On this point, Herbert Marcuse (1964) was correct although his reliance on psychological factors as the basis of audience manipulation was, in my opinion, wrong.

Because we find no working class (nineteenth-century type) in the core area, the closest approximations to it in the struggle against monopoly capitalism for the right to take control of their own lives with equitable participation in work and the rewards for work are such formations as the communities of the Blacks, the Chicanos, and the Puerto Ricans in the United States, the Québécois in Canada, and the North American Indians in both countries. All these groups face the monopoly-capitalist system with both their "private" and their "public" faces, as I have used the terms. All of them at their "private" face encounter Consciousness Industry. All of them are located occupationally at or near the bottom of the ladder and receive low incomes (as compared with WASPS). In 1973, the United States government reported the average family income in the country as $11,237; that of WASPS as $12,278, of Chicanos as $7908, and of Puerto Ricans as $7163. No data were reported for Blacks or Indians.[4] All of them have a higher-rate of population growth than the WASPS. Residentially, massive concentrations live in urban ghettoes in the case of the Blacks, Chicanos, and Puerto Ricans, the Indians in cities also have their ghettoes but are relatively   more dispersed than the foregoing

---

[4] United States Department of Commerce, Bureau of the Census, *Statistical Abstract*, 1978, p. 32.

because of the numbers living on reservations. For all four groups, the principal contradiction within their consciousness is that between their attachment to the total message of Consciousness Industry (including both the free lunch and the consumer goods and services) and their indoctrination in capitalist ideology on the one hand, and their desire to take a larger measure of control over their own lives through realization of their own communities on the other. But these groups differ in the character of the cultural screens which they can utilize in their struggles for autonomy as "nations."

The Blacks are the largest such formation, about 24 million people in 1973. They are the descendants of slaves brought to the United States in the two centuries before 1865 when slavery was made illegal. They were used as cheap labor and denied their rights as American citizens for about another century. They became a cohesive group in the course of the civil rights movement in the late 1950s and the 1960s. And they proved their political power possibilities in the demonstrations over civil rights and Vietnam which were major power confrontations in that period. Deprived of their own languages and community cultural traditions by their experience as slaves, they lack those tools for asserting their national aspirations.

The second largest ethnic minority with national aspirations within the United States is the Chicanos. In 1977 there were an estimated 14 million Chicanos in the country, most of them west of the Mississippi where they are the largest ethnic minority. So rapidly are they increasing (in large part because of illegal immigrants from Mexico) that if current trends continue, some 60 percent of the California population by 1990 will be Chicano (Azril, 1979). Unlike the Blacks, the Chicanos are linked by their cultural screen of a common language, religion, family and community mores. As yet there have been no major political confrontation between the Chicanos and the dominant capitalist power formations of monopoly capitalism, other than the perennial struggle to form and maintain labor unions of their own choosing.

The Puerto Rican community with some 2 million is superficially like that of the Chicanos. It has rapidly expanded in numbers in recent decades, with a cultural screen of language, religion, and community mores. Concentrated in the ghettoes of large Atlantic coastal cities, it has one element lacking in both the Black and Chicano movements. That is a homeland base for national liberation struggle outside the continental United States. They have strong personal, family, cultural, and political ties to that homeland.

The American Indian ethnic minority is the most difficult to assess. With relatively small numbers (793,000 by the 1970 census) more than half are in rural areas. They are dispersed across the country and fragmented politically and culturally. The object of genocidal war by European invaders for three centuries, the Indians found their culture demeaned and attacked, their languages unrespected, and their lands stolen. In recent decades the Indian movement has established a structure of national and regional leadership. With the help of court decisions restoring a small fraction of the control of stolen resources (e.g , fisheries in Washington, minerals in the Rocky Mountain states), they are acquiring some economic power. The Canadian Indians are in roughly the same situation.

As regards the mass media of communication, the situation of the struggles by these four ethnic groups has common characteristics. The laws aimed against discrimination in employment (themselves the result of civil rights agitation) have opened some job opportunities to their members, but only against the stern resistance of the dominant power structure. Restricted by lack of education and experience, their access to employment in the media has resulted in only marginal gains. Access to participation in producing the free lunch provided by the media has fared even worse. While there are numerous examples of enterprises owned and operated by members of these ethnic groups, they are constrained by general industry practice, and by the requirements of advertisers that they deliver audiences tailored to the same sorts of specifications needed for the marketing of consumer goods and services to the mass audiences. They also are affected by the policy of bourgeois Blacks, Chicanos, Puerto Ricans, and Indians who, in managing their enterprises, tend to adhere to Consciousness Industry's policies. As far as the media free lunch is concerned, the most that can be said for the efforts of the ethnic minorities to get significant changes in it to meet their needs is that the extremes of racist stereotyping in writing, casting, and acting (e.g., the "Stepinfetchit" caricature) have been eliminated. The phenomenal success of "Roots" in getting enormous audiences of Blacks (as well as whites) is a conspicuous exception to the general free lunch policy but until or unless its example is followed by more programs in the same vein, it serves by contrast to confirm the foregoing conclusion. Meanwhile the mass media continue to cultivate more or less racist values and white people's nationalism of a xenophobic nature, often playing off against each other the four groups in competition with ethnic aspirations of European-based nationalism (e.g., Irish, Italian, Polish).

Under the pressure of economic recession and inflation, the nationalism of the Blacks, Chicanos, Indians, and Puerto Ricans is powered by what would have been called *class conflict* before 1900. While dependent on Consciousness Industry for jobs and for its products, these ethnic groups have a dialectical relation to the mass media free lunch. News about conflict aspects of the minority group struggles tends to help them, but the practice of the mass media of excluding from the agenda the "in depth" analysis of the continuing causes and consequences of the conflicts weakens them.

Cutting across ethnic lines in the core area is sexism: the multiple contradictions focused on the repression of women. They are denied equal employment opportunity. They do unpaid domestic work (as cook, house-keeper, nursemaid, dishwasher, laundress, seamstress, practical nurse, maintenance man, dietician, gardener, and buyer of consumer goods and services). It is of the order of 100 hours per week in blue- and white-collar families and is generally "put down" by both capitalists and Marxists as unproductive. Their right to determine whether their pregnancies may be terminated legally is hotly disputed. The abuse of alcohol and drugs among them, especially in middle-class suburbia, is high and testifies to their frustration and despair.

Agitation for women's rights, which has grown over two centuries, seemed to become a broad movement when in the 1960s it flowered simul-taneously with the militancy of the youth and civil rights movements in advanced capitalist countries, especially in the core area. It underwent a series of splits, according to its principal internal contradictions. The arrogance of male chauvinism split the men in the protest movement from the women. Lack of consciousness and theoretical understanding of the differences between the problems of middle-class and nonprofessional employed women divided the movement so that the latter were alienated from it by 1971. The remaining middle-class movement further split when "feminists" expelled as too "political" the women who understood the errors being made. What remained of the middle-class feminist Woman's Liberation Movement then split between its liberal, reformist wing (fighting for equal job employment opportunities, legal abortion, etc.) and its extremist wing for whom men are the enemy. "Consciousness raising" small groups were reduced to promoting the interests of middle-class women, ignoring the range of different problems faced by ethnic minority and other nonprofessional employed women. Of course the problems facing women will not simply go away; a new future movement will learn from past mistakes.

Chief among these mistakes is lack of adequate theory and planning. It was to be expected that subjective, reductionist theories would confuse the issues. For example Millett (1970) and Firestone (1970) who reduced the mass of contradictions to power-structured relations based on sexual intercourse, could offer only female chauvinism, contraception, and clon-ing as a solution with no contextual theory of how it related to the politico-economic system in real time. Marxist-influenced theories com-pounded the theoretical confusion. Mitchell (1971) found the root of women's oppression in their exclusion from "production" and restriction to the family, seeing the family as outside the economy (except as the locus of consumption). Zaretsky (1973), misreading the history of capitalism since the 1890s, made the same wrong division as do monopoly capitalists, as one between "work" (at the job front) and "personal life" or "personal meaning" in the consumption of goods with assumed increased leisure time as the result of "a major social advance." For him, women's problems are in a psychological swamp of "subjectivity" which is somehow simultaneously to be related to "the economy." Mitchell and Zaretsky made the common error that production takes place only where people get paid for working. Although handcuffed by this wrong notion, Dixon (1975) makes the correct division as the principal contradiction for the women's movement: men and women vs. the monopoly-capitalist system. With a good analysis of the splitting of the recent women's movement, she argues cogently that women's work in the family produces labor power and thus is integral to Marxian labor theory of value. As this book argues, the work of women (and men) in the family is not only productive because it produces labor power but because it completes the process of production (marketing) for commodities-in-general. Not until these facts are recognized will the women's movement have a realistic theoretical base.

What can one say about the consciousness of most Americans below the flat level tapped by the public opinion pollsters? Since Henry Wallace's Progressive Party went down to defeat in 1948 at the start of the Cold War, no viable party alternative to the Democratic and Republican parties (equally dedicated to maintaining the politico-economic status quo) has appeared. There has been a multitude of attempts to start a party, or even a "preparty" movement since then, particularly in the late 1960s when the defeat of the establishment's hardline policy toward Vietnam was being accomplished by a united front of Blacks, Chicanos, other ethnic groups, women, university students, labor union locals, and a variety of petit bourgeois professionals. That the recent and current confused and frustrating conditions will continue indefinitely seems unlikely. The differential hardships being visited upon those already disadvantaged by inflation and recession may crystallize new political formations dedicated to serious alteration of the power structure of giant corporations interwoven with government at all levels. But whatever new political directions popular consciousness in the United States embraces, when it does, the role of the mass media will be central and crucial to the struggles then to take place. For as Chairman Mao remarked, it is first necessary to have public opinion ready to support it before a new system can be built.

What about consciousness in Canada? Direct evidence, such as that provided by congressional hearings in the United States, is not available. Canada has a much more elitist, hierarchical structure of authority than the United States and the contrast between the privileged and underprivileged is sharper in Canada. As thus modified, the process by which the

mass media influence people, analyzed earlier for the United States, probably works the same through the nexus of mediating factors in Canada
because it was built on the same ideological model. Several clues as to the
comparative consciousness in the two countries are available. Press
reports in 1979 contrast the deeply skeptical, pessimistic mood toward the
governing system of politico-economic organization in the United States
with the optimism and faith in the comparable organization in Canada. A
Canadian public opinion pollster, an advisor to ex-Prime Minister Clark,
said:

> The main difference is that although Canadians are perfectly aware we have
> serious problems, they believe that all of those problems—even inflation—
> can be solved by government. On "solvability" tests, you get amazing results.
> More than 70 percent of Canadians believe that our problems can be solved,
> wholly or partially. People even believe that their leaders are being too
> pessimistic. They believe they are ahead of their leaders, in the sense of their
> being more self-confident about Canada's resources, physical and human,
> than they think their leaders are. . . . I find no evidence of an erosion of
> belief in government as an institution in itself. There's considerable accep-
> tance of hierarchy and of elitism, but not, I'd have to say, of civil liberties, all
> of which add up to an acceptance of authority.[5]

When we examine some key indicators for 1968 and 1977 related to
consciousness, it appears that the struggle between the advantaged and
the disadvantaged may be sharper in Canada than in the United States.

	Relative Levels (percent)			
	Canada		United States	
	1968	1977	1968	1977
Cost of Living Index	100	178	100	174
Corporate Profits	100	301	100	194
Wages and Salaries	100	307	100	225
Personal Expenditures on Consumer Goods and Services	100	288	100	226
Number of Strikes and Lockouts	100	178*	100	112*
Days of Work Lost in Strikes and Lockouts	100	177*	100	77*
Unemployment (percentage of labor force)	100	169	100	194

* Data for 1976.

Source: U.S. Statistical Abstract, *Canada Yearbook.*

---

[5] Allan Gregg, quoted by Richard Gwyn, *Vancouver Sun,* 15 September 1979.

Personal expenditures on consumer goods and services increased more rapidly in Canada than in the United States. Corporate profits, however, more than trebled in Canada while those in the United States were not quite doubling. Probably the fact that wage and salary payments in Canada also more than trebled, while those in the United States a little more than doubled, is because Canadian wage and salary levels had *previously* been lower than those in the United States. In any event their more rapid increase during the ten years in Canada is probably because of a sharper struggle between labor and capital for a larger share of the very rapid increase in profits. This inference is strengthened by noting that strikes and lockouts were 78 percent more numerous in Canada in 1976 than in 1968, whereas they increased only 12 percent in the United States. That the struggles were more bitter and prolonged is shown by the number of days of work lost because of strikes and lockouts; in Canada, that loss increased by about the same proportion that the number of strikes and lockouts did (77 percent); but the days of work lost for this cause in the United States *decreased* by 23 percent. But although Canadian workers have had to cope with higher rates of unemployment in the 1970s than in the 1960s, the increase (by 69 percent in 1977) was less than in the United States.

This all suggests that even if a nineteenth-century style class consciousness does not seem to exist in Canada any more than in the United States, the majority of the Canadian people (i.e., those who work for salaries and wages) are in fact engaged in severe struggle with the monopoly capitalists (most of whom are American branch plants, it must be remembered) for a bigger share of the fruits of their labor. At the same time, those monopoly capitalists have been retaining more rapidly growing profits, proportionately, than in the United States. These profits derive from Canadian labor power and other natural resources.

It seems fair to infer therefore that popular consciousness in Canada may be more disturbed by bread and butter issues than is that in the United States as a whole, but represses its discontent with the politico-economic system in Canada. It is quite possible for Canadian workers to fight for a larger share of the results of their labor while being content with the ideological features of the capitalist system.

A central issue in Canadian consciousness (though not salient for the Anglophones) is whether the country will continue in its present constitutional form (i.e., one country with a central government already weaker, for example, than that of the United Kingdom, France, or the United States), or change to a federation of from two to four or five autonomous countries. The issue is forced by the struggle of Québec for autonomy which produced in 1976 a provincial government dedicated to that objective and to a plebiscite on that issue.

From the conquest of New France in the eighteenth century, the French-speaking population of Canada—about one-third of the total, most of whom live in Québec—has been treated as a subordinated, exploitable portion of a single country. Recognition of the cultural identity of the Québécois only became evident during and after World War II, and then only in idealist tokenism—bilingual currency and ration books, official bilinguality in Parliament, and in the period of Trudeau's attempt to head off separatism after 1968, bilingualism in the federal administrative bureaucracy. Meanwhile Québec remained one among 10 provinces, in a politically and economically integrated confederation known as Canada.

The mode of the economic integration began with the participation of the merchants and bankers of Montreal in the Anglophone ruling class's efforts to develop what became Canada as first a British, and later an American colony. The population of Québec enjoyed the dubious benefits of being employed and served by branch plants of corporations, managed by Anglophones from Ontario, Britain, and the United States. With the growing industrialization of what had been a primarily agricultural-extractive industry economy in Québec the contradiction between the dominators and the dominated sharpened. The original Québécois clerical-merchant power structure was transformed, especially after 1945, and a persistently growing *national* consciousness developed there. It was described in a report of the Canadian (federal) Royal Commission on Bilingualism and Biculturalism (1968) as being based on culture:

> Culture is a way of being, thinking, and feeling. It is a driving force animating a significant group of individuals united by a common tongue and sharing the same customs, habits, and experiences.

With this sense of cultural nationalism, in the late 1970s, Claude Morin, the leading ideologist of the Québécois, stated the Québécois intention to seek *full political, economic, and cultural autonomy* as a nation which will form part of the North American bloc. The Québécois reject the role of an ethnic minority within a centralized Canadian state.[6] They also correctly perceive the majority of people in Canada—the Anglophone people—as being unwilling to allow the Québécois the political and economic autonomy to achieve their national goals within the present Canadian constitutional system. Short of full Québécois national autonomy in the formal political sense, the Québécois have indicated willingness to consider some alternative options of which the creation of a binational state with common central functions of tariffs, control of monetary policy, and national defense is considered to be worth negoti-

---

[6] Morin, Claude, as quoted in Laxer and Laxer (1977, p. 205).

ating for, with a less desirable alternative being unique provincial status within a confederated Canada.

What process has brought the dominant majority of Anglophone Canadians to this mature confrontation? The reader of Chapter 5 will have observed that between the 1830s and the 1860s, the Anglophone ruling class in Canada chose between economic growth through outright annexation to, or outright free trade with, the United States, and opted for the latter so long as the United States permitted it. When the "National Policy" was created after Confederation in 1867, the tariff policy induced American direct investment and produced takeovers and branch plants of American industry. Even in the period of formal British colonial status, that ruling class never seriously considered a policy of slower, indigenous development, relying on British investment capital. They also neglected to take steps to build a cultural policy patterned on small bourgeois national experience in Europe which would protect and develop a national culture which could have grown out of the Anglophone-Francophone connection within Canada. Chapters 6 and 7 revealed how blind obedience to the profit motive working through free market forces prevented the development of such indigenously conceived policies and practices in newspapers, magazines, books, films, and telecommunications as well as in other areas of popular culture.

In Chapter 8 our analysis showed that the creation of the Canadian Broadcasting Corporation was the only significant attempt to establish a mass institution which had the objective of developing an autonomous national culture. However, it contained from the start the base for its own erosion as a public agency in the original commitment to produce audiences for advertisers and was converted by Consciousness Industry into an indispensable adjunct to the profitable operation of private stations by 1948. Moreover from the start, the CBC was a ground for struggle between Anglophones and Francophones over cultural policy. With the commitment of the government to create a television industry as a northern extension of the American system, the erosion of the public function of the CBC continued until in the late 1970s its share of audience production for Canadian programs is proportionately of the order of that of the Public Broadcasting System in the United States.

Although giving abundant lip service to the abstract ideals of CBC's role in developing Canadian consciousness in the interest of national cultural autonomy, the establishment acted through its government and industrial arms to ensure that Canadian people would be produced in audience-markets for training in the service of the Consciousness Industry of the monopoly capitalist core. In Chapter 9 it was observed that in the fine and performing arts, the direction which the Massey Commission anticipated the Canada Council would take was reversed and the council has served, just as did book publishing, to meet the test of market relations centered on the metropolitan core (New York) rather than autonomous Canadian objectives.

In each of these sectors, it was noted that the Québécois managed to make book publishing, newspapers, films, and broadcasting into agencies which maintained and enriched the Québécois culture to a degree unmatched on the Anglophone side. No one should be surprised therefore to find communications agencies in Québec deeply engaged in the struggle for national survival of the Québécois while in Anglophone Canada these agencies reflect and produce indifference to, and even aggression against, the Québécois movement. The application of the War Measures Act in 1970 was forceful punishment directed at that movement, heartily supported by the Anglophone mass media and the majority of the Anglophone population. Again in 1975 Anglophone Canada made a thinly veiled racist attack on the Québécois in a campaign against the bilingualism program of the Trudeau government over the refusal of Anglophone air pilots to permit the use of French in air-ground communications at Québec airports. This was a "red-neck" emotional storm typified by a witness at an earlier Edmonton hearing of the Bilingualism and Biculturalism Commission to the effect that "If English was good enough for Jesus Christ, it is good enough for me." It is noteworthy that in the Anglophone discussion of their attitude toward the Québécois and their problem there is seldom if ever recognition of the difference between a *country* and a *nation*. Canada is indisputably a country. But it houses two nations and the numerically larger one denies the existence of the smaller and is more closely connected with the United States than it is with the Québécois.

To anyone who cares about the continued existence of Canada as a single country with the possibility of becoming a single nation it ought to be clear that the only major element in its situation which might slow down the tide of assimilation to the United States would have been an earlier accommodation of the national needs of the Québécois. This was what President de Gaulle traveled to Canada to say, but the Anglophone mass media and political leadership chose to reject and rebuff him.

It seems to be impossible to liberate Canada from the domination of the United States so long as the present ruling class in Canada remains in power. But a necessary precondition to facing the facts is understanding Canada's relation to the United States. And it certainly obscures those facts to argue, as Laxer and Laxer do in a recent book, that the basis of Canadian existence has been the ideology of liberalism and *its negation in practice* by the government (of both Liberal and Progressive Conservative parties), of employing state agencies (e.g., the railroads, Canadian Broadcasting Corporation, Air Canada) to weld the country together (Laxer and Laxer, 1977, p. 212).

True, the ideology of liberalism has been the basis of Canadian national policy, but that its negation in practice offers (as the authors imply) any basis for *expecting* Canada to reduce its future dependence on the United States is itself an idealist illusion. The practice of all capitalist countries is based on the ideology of the market place and possessive individualism. And *all* of them, especially the United States, employ state agencies when necessary to provide economically and politically desirable results, waiving ideological purity for the sake of long-run profitability. In the United States the creation of the Tennessee Valley Authority, the Atomic Energy Program, and the creation of the Communications Satellite Corporation immediately come to mind.

Even a brief analysis of the contradiction between the country of Canada and the Québécois nation cannot ignore the United States connection. What is the interest of the United States in this conflict? It clearly is to keep Canada intact as one country. Although the present Québécois nationalist movement is bourgeois, it is evident that its ultimate thrust is one of rejecting the Americanization of its culture. A sovereign Québécois nation conceivably might become another Cuba, this time not even 90 miles from the American border. The present Canadian country has been used as and is a convenient American agent in international policies. By definition the monopoly-capitalist system benefits from the prolongation of the status quo and abhors political changes in friendly states which might destabilize the existing system. Outright incorporation of Canadian provinces into the United States would be anathema to the hundreds of TNCs headquarters in the United States which would lose valuable privileges as a result (tax concessions, freedom in Canada from effective antitrust laws and from laws forbidding interlocking boards of directors, etc.).

Given the real historical process here analyzed, what is the shape of the probable strategy and tactics of people in the core area struggling to transform the monopoly-capitalist system? While the real conditions will seem very complex, the principles may run about as follows. *At any given time* (or in the short run) it seems that people in Canada and the United States may be divided in consciousness between (1) those people who are, or seem to be, satisfied with the continuation of the status quo for whatever reasons, and (2) those people who want to change it substantially.

The first group will tend to divide into three subgroups: (1A) those who are consciously resistant to substantial systemic changes and who, if faced with probable loss of their presently privileged positions would opt for right-wing systemic changes. They will commit themselves fully to those objectives. We might call them the *last ditchers*. Secondly those (1B) who, while consciously defenders of the existing system, feel they can survive the changes which they see as inevitable. We might call them the *marginal conservatives*. Thirdly, those (1C) who are anomic, presently apathetically supportive of the status quo; presently uncommitted to change and potentially capable of being mobilized for either right-wing, or left-liberal changes in the system. We might call them the *undecided*.

The second group divides into two. The first (2A) consists of those who are ready to work for changes in the status quo, but presently think that the changes most needed are such as improved quality of consumer goods, elimination of violence from the mass media, improved access to the production of the content of the mass media by minority groups, avoidance of irreversible damage to the environment by nuclear power, chemicals, etc. Moreover this group believes, correctly, that the governments and regulatory agencies in Canada and the United States could, and should, be pressed to correct such defects in the performance of the existing system. This group is to be distinguished from group (2B) because its consciousness is essentially liberal: in short, it does not feel that the changes for which it is prepared to struggle require any major changes in the ideology and structure of the status quo. We might call them the *progressives*. The second subgroup (2B) consists of those whose discontent includes but goes deeper than that of group (2A). People in this subgroup are prepared to struggle to transform the monopoly-capitalist system, believing correctly, that, as presently constituted, the changes fought for by group (2A) will not be *securely* made until the monopoly-capitalist power structure in the core area, including its leading edge, the mass media, is structurally changed. We might call them the *liberationists*.

The probable strategy and tactics of the liberation movement in the core area in the short run will take full advantage of the available institutions of representative government (elections to the legislatures, of heads of state and representation in the UN family of organizations), the opportunities to influence regulatory commissions (the CRTC and Department of Communications in Canada, the FCC, Federal Trade Commission, Antitrust Division of the Department of Justice, etc., of the United States federal government and the counterpart agencies in the 50 states) to bring about the needed reforms.

It is especially important for the liberation movement in Canada to realize the importance of using its power through the government of Canada (or of two or more "Canadas," depending on the outcome of the Separatist struggle) simply because such state or states have enormous leverage through international organizations (United Nations, etc.) as well as through international public opinion to bring pressure on the United States government. "National" liberation is a staging point in the struggle against the transnational monopoly-capitalist system which will hold high priority in the liberation struggle.

A possible (probable?) scenario of the strategies in the struggle would perhaps run as follows. The progressives and the liberationists would form a united front on a program with which they would try to win support from the undecideds and the marginal conservatives in struggles over specific issues. The last-ditchers would direct their campaign to win support from the same two groups. The liberationists would recognize during such struggles that although it would be essential to wage and win struggles over currently salient issues (e.g., ecological issues) success on such issues will not be sufficient to prevent cooptation and the emergence of new and essentially similar issues. They should not have to learn (again) that reform movements are typically accommodated to by the capitalist system which turns them to its advantage. In the course of struggle there will be a tendency toward bipolarization, i.e., movement of people into the liberationist and last-ditchers' camps. Within the liberationist-progressive united front, and especially within the liberationist group there will be struggles among left, ultra-left, and right factions and their theorists which will induce dialectical swings of strategies and tactics which will arise out of, and contribute to, the contradictions inherent in the specific circumstances. For this reason the process will be untidy and confusing, but its result will be to broaden and deepen public opinion in favor of the objectives of group (2B). Such is the logic of the present condition of the real historical process in the core area. But, of course, the specific development of such a struggle will be conditioned by the material and ideological repercussions in the United States-Canada core area of systemic struggles within the group of advanced capitalist countries, between them and the socialist countries, and between Third World countries and the superpowers.

In the advanced technical structure of core area life, communications necessarily involve equipment and technique. In Chapter 10, we analyzed *technology* and found it to be the political and social formation for work under monopoly capitalism. The question now arises, how is the communications component in the liberation movement in the core area likely to relate to technology? Is it possible that the resistance movement may produce its own technology—using technique and equipment in "new" political, social formations to work for change, even drastic change, in the dominant system? First, how vulnerable to the liberation movement is the existing dominating structure?

In the 1960s the failure of the United States to crush the Cuban and Vietnamese liberation movements represented a passing of the initiative from the dominant monopoly-capitalist power structure in the world to popular movements intent on building a better social system. And the American imperial position began to crumble as the dollar-dominated international money market collapsed beginning in 1971. OPEC, by uniting oil-producing small countries in taking control of the sale of their major resource, set off a chain reaction of structural dislocations with resulting unemployment, inflation, and hardship in the core nations, especially the United States. It also serves as a model for other small countries specialized in raw material production. The few hundred giant TNCs had become the dominant agents of monopoly capitalism as a world system, moving capital, technical knowledge, hardware, and software to exploit labor and other resources from the core to whatever country offered lowest cost and highest profit possibilities. And in return they dominated the movement of raw materials, semiprocessed, and even finished consumer goods from the peripheral countries to the core nations. This system was one in which information was the principal thing moving from the core to the periphery, and in which in exchange, real products embodying materials and labor moved from the periphery to the core. It was and is an imposing structure as a world system, but terribly vulnerable to disruption.

In the 1980s the difference between reality (e.g., oil) and image (e.g., brand names, corporate balance sheets, experts' blueprints for TNCs' operations in country X) is crucial and connected to the struggle between people and capital through communications systems, both internationally and within nations. And systems for communicating information are notoriously fragile and vulnerable. One might paraphrase Mao Zedong: the monopoly-capitalist system is not only a "paper tiger," it is an "information tiger," and more specifically an "electronic information tiger."

Information flow and processing constitute the connections which permit the system to function. I have referred to the possibility discovered by J. Voge that the increasing opportunity cost of the rising share of resources devoted to information flow and processing may become too high for the capitalist (or any other) system to tolerate (Chapter 7). This may be regarded as the systemic vulnerability to *excess* information.

The very nature of teleprocessing information (the combination of computers, data banks, and telecommunications) means that the capitalist system is vulnerable to instant and prolonged disruption. Edward W. Ploman, Director of the International Institute of Communications, summarizing reports by Simon Nora in France and a Swedish government report in 1977, says:

> The thrust of the Swedish report is that the . . . use of computerized data systems to a marked degree contributes to the increasing vulnerability of modern highly industrialized societies; that the level of vulnerability is unacceptably high; and that it will become even higher if counter-measures are not taken. The degree of vulnerability is conditioned by a number of factors. According to the report the most important are: the dependence on foreign countries; the concentration of systems; the dependence on the few trained operational staff; and the sensitive nature of certain information. Terrorist activities and other criminal actions, threats, sanctions and acts of war

become possible or are made easier through these vulnerability factors. Some also increase the effects of catastrophies and accidents.

The level of vulnerability can be seen in relation to the level of protection. The committee looked, as an example, at the telecommunications circuits that link data banks. They found that the level of protection is high in respect to technical faults; but only medium in the case of natural calamities (storms, earthquakes, fires, etc.). Even more interesting is the discovery that protection against deliberate attacks is minimal.

The analysis makes a distinction between external and internal factors. The former are aligned along a scale that starts with criminal acts. It includes attacks against the hardware; attacks against computer programmes, documentation or registered information; attacks against telecommunications systems; and attacks against the people who are crucial for the operation of the system. Further along the scale are abuses caused by political reasons. They range from threats of economic sanctions from abroad through actions by various domestic or foreign groups, to armed conflict and war.

The internal factors refer to the vulnerability of the data systems themselves. Some information—a population census, industrial information, data on health and social welfare, criminal and police records—is vulnerable for reasons of intrinsic content. Some data systems are functionally vulnerable: administrative systems in the public sector and certain data systems in commerce, industry, etc., in the private sector. Internal vulnerability is also affected by geographical and functional concentration; the increasing coordination, integration and interdependence of systems; the lack of knowledge and training among data users (sometimes resulting in unintentional errors); the low quality of computer programming; the dependence on key staff, and so on (Ploman, 1978, p. 28).

Our experience with the fragility of the system is linked thus far to the well-known Three Mile Island and other nuclear power mishaps, massive blackouts of electrical systems, and miscellaneous but substantial thefts of money through penetrating the financial data banks. Further and escalating breakdowns in the fragile information flow and processing system must be expected, increasingly on the part of political movements. It must be emphasized that the production, transmission, and reception of information in the 1980s by the monopoly-capitalist system is wholly dependent on teleprocessing data (transmission via telecommunications and processing by computers). And such use of telecommunications depends on the use of the radio spectrum, which is not private property but world property, and which is subject to regulation by the International Telecommunications Union. That organization, at the hands of capitalist states, regarded the regulation of the use of the radio spectrum as a first-come, first-served affair, with only minimal technical regulation. The increasing awareness of the importance of radio spectrum regulation by Third World nations, beginning in the 1960s, has resulted in their use of their majority position in the ITU to reverse that traditional policy. Increasingly, positive planning for the use of the radio spectrum is replacing the first-come, first-served principle. The future possibilities for use of the ITU to regulate the use of the radio spectrum may produce fundamental challenges to the viability of the information system of the monopoly-capitalist system and thus to the viability of the system as a whole. (See Appendix.)

The unauthorized public disclosure of classified information, of which the famous "Pentagon Papers" at the height of the struggle to end the Vietnam War is an example, calls our attention to a level at which political groups favoring rapid and drastic change in the status quo will increasingly use their specialized knowledge derived from their role within the system to change it. For example, members of unions and professional organizations within the media have the knowledge, opportunity, and interest to form informal networks to exchange information and plan and execute tactical and strategic initiatives to accomplish such objectives, if linked with significant political formations of people at large.

Oppressed by a downward flow of domination through hierarchically organized Consciousness Industry, popular resistance to it has been much preoccupied with forming horizontal networks to mobilize popular pressure. On the periphery of empire there was the use of "small" technology in the Algerian struggle for independence from France (in which the radio was an essential organizing tool) (Fanon, 1965, pp. 69–98) and in the revolt led by the Ayatollah Khomeini to overthrow the American puppet, the Shah of Iran, in 1978–79. In the latter, the lowly cassette recorder was an indispensable tool for organizing and conducting the revolt which overthrew a hierarchy equipped with communications satellites and a vast secret police backed by unlimited ordnance. Meanwhile, more modest experimental horizontal communications thrusts have been tried out. One proved successful during the Allende regime in Chile (Mattelart, 1979). In Lima, Peru, the Centro de Communicacion Popular has developed outside the formal schooling system, using workshops on publications, popular theater, audiovisual techniques, movies, and songs to create and present their work each week. This initiative has received UNESCO support to some extent (Aguirre-Bianchi and Hedebro, 1979, pp. 10–12). And an international symposium was conducted in Spain in 1978 to work on a general theory of such horizontal communications and "alternative media." Other examples of such attempts exist in the Netherlands, the United Kingdom, the United States and Canada, and perhaps elsewhere.

Three principal obstacles seem to block such efforts:

1.   Lack of awareness of the ideology of repression and that of liberation. It is a seductive idealist trap to suppose that communications hardware and software (be it stereophonic music, community channels on cable television, mind-altering drugs, or pay television) which has been created by Consciousness Industry offers to *individuals* a "consciousness-raising" solution to the problems of being dominated. It can contribute only further alienation and cooptation to serve the dominating system. The only viable consciousness raising through such efforts comes through individual participation in *collective* creative initiatives for liberation so that *both* individual and collective consciousness is raised.

2.   The fragmented structure of community life (especially in the core area). Attempts to use channels dedicated by cable television operators under orders from the regulatory commission in Canada for serving community needs are an example. As indicated in Chapter 8, the respective community social and educational voluntary organizations which would like to use the channel find themselves using it to speak to their respective constituencies about the same kinds of things they would talk about *in the absence of the channel.* The schedule is one of *dis*connected consecutive users of the channel. The cable system management's obligation is fulfilled when all interested and eligible groups have been accommodated in this unintegrated way. Integrated use of electronic hardware/software for horizontal communications requires control of the needed equipment.

3.   The bias of the dominator through superior expertise and control of the hardware. This obstacle, evident in the cable television situation just described, is exemplified in a larger community by the experience of many South Pacific islanders in working through PEACESAT—an organization headed by Americans in Hawaii which has been using a voice channel in an expiring communications satellite to operate an information exchange between the islands and between them and the United States, New Zealand, and Canada. The purpose ostensibly was to elevate community practice in public health, nutrition, etc. Analysis of the use of the PEACESAT network reveals that the metropolitan terminals (Honolulu and Wellington) and Caucasian participants ". . . play an overwhelmingly dominant role. . . . as compared with Pacific Island terminals and Pacific Island people" and that "PEACESAT, in acting as a major vehicle for the dissemination of Western—and predominantly United States—ideas, . . ." contributes negatively to the development of the islanders' culture (Plant, 1980). This concrete empirical study of the way the "one-way free flow of information flourishes under the guise of "technical" aid to Third World

nations may be taken to represent the net effect of all such aid, including that in the form of access to communications satellite systems.

One theoretical principle evidently applies to all efforts to establish horizontal networks of communications to resist hierarchical domination by the monopoly-capitalist system—whether the efforts are located within the core area or are in peripheral countries. Control of the means of communications is the basis of political power. Efforts by audience-commodity groups to change the terms and means of their dominated condition will fail to the extent that control of their horizontal communication network is in the hands of the dominators. The auspices and bureaucratic structures of those who initiate and activate the system will prevail. To put it positively, successful horizontal communications absolutely require that control be in the indigenous group which initiates the venture and guides it by some relevant theory of objectives and of the process by which to struggle for those objectives.

A theory for the use of horizontal communications to achieve objectives on the road to liberation from the domination of Consciousness Industry must be part of a general theory for such movements embracing the strategies and tactics just discussed. And conversely, a general theory of how the monopoly-capitalist system may be changed must comprehend how communications processes within it work, how public opinion is produced to maintain the status quo, and therefore how public opinion may be produced by the dominated to accomplish major changes in the politico-economic structure.

A general theory for working for liberation in the core area will recognize that its purposes can be achieved only by mobilizing public opinion of the population to take their own liberation. It cannot be imposed on them from above. There are no magic black boxes of communication to solve their problems. Such mobilizing efforts involve studying the needs of the people in relation to the dialectical contradictions in them and in the dominating system. The knowledge thus derived would be concentrated and a program prepared for actions based on it. This program and its supporting rationale would then be communicated to the people. The role of artists and other intellectuals in the process is in their unique contribution to the collection and analysis of the required knowledge and the creation and execution of the resulting action program. After the program has been implemented, the process continues with the study of the needs of the people, etc. An essential condition for a democratic liberation struggle is the demystification of professionals, artists, scientists, engineers, and other intellectuals. Unless "red" prevails over "expert," bourgeois class relations will be reproduced.

APPENDIX

THE ELECTRONIC INFORMATION TIGER, OR THE POLITICAL ECONOMY OF THE RADIO SPECTRUM AND THE THIRD WORLD INTEREST

The radio spectrum (more properly *electrospace* after Hinchman)[1] is to communications today as is land to crops and water to fish. It is a peculiar natural resource, one whose politico-economic and social aspects have been largely ignored by social scientists. Like all other features of the human environment, it must be looked at in its relationships with people. For at least two millenia, Western law has held that property means a relationship not a thing. There have been three kinds of property: (a) private property (the enforceable claim to deny other persons use or possession of something); (b) common property (the respective claims of society and the individual to the conditions under which something may be used by the society *and* by individuals); (c) state property (the exclusive claim by the state to use something, e.g., the military).[2] With the worsening ecological crisis, attention has shifted from private property to common property. The chief economic characteristic of common property is the tendency of individual use to impair or destroy the capacity of the resource to serve the society. What Hardin calls the "tragedy of the commons" can be avoided only by enforcing welfare criteria for individual and collective use of the resource through government policy.[3]

---

[1] Hinchman, W. R., "Use and Management of the Electrospace: A New Concept of the Radio Resource," IEEE International Conference on Communications, *Conference Record*, Boulder, Colorado, June 1969, pp. 13.1–13.5.
[2] MacPherson, C. B., *Property: Mainstream and Critical Positions*. Toronto: University of Toronto Press, 1978, chap. 1, 2.
[3] Hardin, Garrett, "The Tragedy of the Commons," *Science*, Vol. 162, 1968, pp. 1243–1248.

The radio spectrum differs from other natural resources in possessing the following characteristics either uniquely or to a greater degree:

1. The radio spectrum's original and still principal use is the act of *sharing* information between transmitter and receiver, i.e., communication. Minor uses prove the rule, e.g., radar, geodetic exploration. For no other resource is the principal function the transmission *and* retention of information or anything else.

2. For one nation or a class of user to use it, all nations and classes of users must also be able to use it. During World War II, for example, the warring nations continued to abide by the international rules set by the International Telecommunications Union which assured them substantially interference-free use of the radio spectrum. Worldwide cooperation is therefore necessary for the radio spectrum to be used by everyone. Yet, as we will note, the time may come when interference will be deliberately employed by the great majority of the world's population in order to deter antihuman behavior (such as aggressive war) by a minority.

3. It is nondepletable and self-renewing. To be sure there is interference between users (which international regulation minimizes), but this "pollution" disappears immediately the interfering transmitters cease interfering. Other natural resources are depletable and for soil, water, and air, renewal may take millions of years and mutate organic life via the food chain.

4. Measurement of rights to use the radio spectrum are probabilistic rather than discretely specifiable.

5. Because the radio spectrum is used to transmit information, and because control of the flow of information is the basis of political power, the control of the use of the radio spectrum lies close to the seat of sovereignty in the building blocks by which the world community is presently structured: nation-states. No other resource has this order of political, tactical, and strategic significance. Whenever a coup or revolution occurs, control of the radio capability is an essential measure because through it even the military is directed. At the same time the necessary joint decision making by all nations at the world level contributes to the practice of world sovereignty. The practice of world regulation of the use of the radio spectrum by the International Telecommunications Union thus substantiates the fact that by international law title to the radio spectrum rests not with individuals or nations, but in all humanity.

These characteristics combine to place the radio spectrum partly in the category of common property on a world scale, and partly in that of state property. Like no other resource, the radio spectrum is the first form of world property.

As with more familiar resources, use of the radio spectrum was developed first by the industrialized countries and served their imperial interests well. And as with other natural resources, Third World countries have an interest in redressing the present imbalance in access to the radio spectrum. As Ali Shummo, Minister of Information of the Sudan, said recently, the developed countries ". . . have 90 percent of the spectrum and 10 percent of the population. We have 90 percent of the population and 10 percent of the spectrum."[4] My purpose here is to explore the politico-economic aspects of the radio spectrum and to identify the parties to its use and their interests.

WHAT IS RADIO FREQUENCY ALLOCATION?

What is the technical character of the process of radio frequency allocation? The radio spectrum consists of the fields of magnetic and electrical force capable of transmitting electromagnetic energy in successive waves of different lengths. When these waves are generated and information is imposed on them, it is decodable within limits. The limits are set by earthly conditions which affect wave propagation provided natural and manmade noise (including undesired signals) do not create intolerable interference. The propagation characteristics depend basically on the conductivity characteristics of the environment. Surface water carries radio waves further than land, and the geological nature of the ground affects the extent of wave propagation. The electrical storms and humidity of the tropics impair effective propagation in the Low and Medium frequencies used for broadcasting in tropical zones until now. For Low, Medium, and High frequencies at night, the waves bounce back from layers in the troposphere, providing very long distance propagation; in daytime the waves go through the troposphere into outer space, leaving daytime propagation of those frequencies to ground waves alone. In the Very High, Ultra High, and still higher frequency range, propagation becomes progressively more limited to line-of-sight, producing problems where mountains or buildings block the signals or divert them into multipath reception with its "ghosting" effect. Other technical variables affect the efficiency of radio wave propagation: the type of signal modulated (amplitude, frequency, pulse-time, etc.), the width of the channel, antenna capacity both at the transmitting and receiving end, the power used in transmitting, the polarization of the signal (vertical or horizontal), the

---

[4] Quoted by Howkins, John, "The Management of the Spectrum," *Intermedia*, September 1979, p. 12.

ability of the equipment to deliver the signals in desired directions, multiplex vs. simplex capacity, etc.

In simplest terms, spectrum management is a process of three mutually determining steps:

1.   The first step is to determine that specific classes of use should be made of specific bands of frequencies, according to engineering standards which take account of the environmental and technical parameters just described. This step may be illustrated by reference to use of radio by transportation agencies. Airlines, for example, require radio frequencies for different classes of use: long-range for navigation and for long-distance communication while over oceans, etc., but also short-range for communicating between air and ground en route or at airports. This means that they must be allocated frequencies in different regions of the spectrum where the propagation conditions are appropriate to the uses to be made of the frequencies. And because aircraft and ships move around the world they must be able to use the *same* bands of frequencies *wherever* they move. The determination of specific standards is an equally important aspect of this first step because only by such carefully designed standards will maximum use (and minimum interference) result.

2.   The second step is to determine the location of transmitting and receiving stations for use in a given hemisphere, region, or country, *given* a specific frequency band, a class of use, and *given* the determined engineering standards for that particular class of radio service. For example, the determination that a certain number of television broadcast stations may be assigned to particular locations to serve a particular population.

3.   And the third step is to determine the identity of the licensee who will use the specific location for transmitter and/or receiver performing a given class of service, operating according to specific engineering standards.

That these three steps are mutually determining is obvious. Because the purpose of the process is to be found in step three, it would seem realistic to reverse the order of the steps, but for the fact that the worldwide structure of regulation of the radio spectrum forces the pressures generated at step three into a decision-making process beginning with step one.

In the near century since the art of radio was invented, this allocation process has been developed into a hierarchical institutional structure. At the top presently some 154 countries, each with one vote as members of the International Telecommunications Union (ITU), govern the allocation process, reserving to the ITU the first step listed and delegating to subordinate "conferences" and to nation-states the detailed implementation of the whole process. Enterprises which manufacture (and do research and development on) electronic equipment and each of the classes of spectrum users organized as such (e.g., aeronautical, marine, etc.) participate at each level of the process, as do trade associations which also represent them. Decisions are made through the negotiations within this dense and intricately structured human organization at irregular intervals peaking in conferences held by the ITU, called World Administrative Radio Conferences (WARC), to reconsider and revise the substance and mode of administering the radio spectrum. WARC-79, meeting in Geneva beginning September 1979 was the first such general conference in 20 years and it decisions will shape the use of the radio spectrum until at least the year 2000.

HOW DOES IT WORK? WHO BENEFITS FROM IT?

How did the process of world management of the radio spectrum come about? Who gained from it? Who loses from it? How did it contribute to the dependency of peoples living in countries peripheral to the capitalist core area on the dominant political structures in that core? The process started when Great Britain, Germany, France, the United States, and Russia began to make use of Marconi's invention of the means of transmitting information via radio in the 1890s. From the beginning the initiative was taken by the military (to communicate with naval vessels and posts on land) in the service of the imperial interests of the great powers. The contradiction in the often antagonistic cooperation which the radio spectrum imposes was recognized by the German government statement at the first international conference to regulate radio (1903) that only:

. . . the adoption of provisions aimed at the elimination of interference between stations could prevent "une guerre de tous contre tous."[5]

The military in each country shared its concerns in the radio art with business enterprises (with scientific and engineering skills and market interests in electrical systems, especially telephone and telegraph) through research and development, financial aid, and contracts to manufacture equipment. This military-industrial alliance developed knowledge, equipment, and practice in radio communications. World War I was the occasion for the first major commitment of resources to such development. By 1920 the private enterprises engaged in production and research

---

[5] Codding, G. A., *The International Telecommunications Union*. Leiden, The Netherlands: E. J. Brill, 1952, p. 85.

on radio had reached giant dimensions. And when hostilities ended, the same giant corporations developed markets for civilian commodities adapted from military to civilian use, conspicuously radio broadcasting, devices for improving wire-telephony and wire-telegraphy, radio communications for police, aviation, and nonmilitary vessels, etc. In current jargon, the civilian uses of the radio spectrum were a spinoff from war-financed research and development for military purposes. Understanding this is the key to understanding the periodic waves of development of the use of the radio spectrum which again crested after World War II, during the Cold War of the early 1950s, and after the aerospace race between the super-powers beginning about 1958. In each of these instances, intensive government expenditures for military objectives generated intensive research and development in telecommunications, all of it resting on use of the radio spectrum.

When one analyzes the pattern of comprehensive ITU allocation conferences in relation to this dynamic process, it appears that development of the radio spectrum in the period when the major industrial countries dominated the process had a "successive plateau" character. A plateau of new development would be initiated by a new ITU review and revision of allocations and standards. The effective reason for such an ITU conference would be either or both of two events: (1) the accumulation of actual interference resulting from innovations under previous frequency allocation decisions; (2) the accumulation of pressures to innovate new radio services resulting from research and development since the last previous allocation decisions. The next plateau would be established when a new ITU revision of allocations and standards responded to a new manifestation of either or both of the two events, and so on.

The boundaries and timing of the plateaus is not precise, but it appears that such a model corresponds to the progressive exploration and occupation of different regions of the radio spectrum. Thus the Low and Medium frequency region (below 3 MHz) was the plateau occupied by radio innovations between the 1890s and 1920s. Improvements in the radio art coming out of World War I *and* intolerable interference under existing radio allocation practice led to the Washington ITU Conference in 1927. In that and the 1932 Madrid Conference, radio allocations and standards were agreed to for the High frequencies (3–30 MHz). The application of fixed (i.e., common carrier), marine, aeronautical, international (propaganda) broadcasting, land mobile (e.g., police), and government (mostly military) services quickly occupied that range of frequencies, and by 1947 acute "congestion" and interference had been produced, making the 1932 frequency allocation plan and standards unsatisfactory. During World War II, with heavy government expenditures for research and development, the state of the art developed a capability to use the Very High frequencies (30–300 MHz) and in fact they were used for military purposes prior to ITU definitive allocation. Because of the war, ITU allocations and standards for those frequencies were still in the embryonic stage characterizing an unexplored "frontier" as it existed during the last prewar ITU world conference. At the 1947 Atlantic City ITU Conference, therefore, the allocations and standards applicable to the previously developed regions (Low, Medium, and High) were again rationalized, *and* ground rules were established for occupation of the Very High and Ultra High frequencies (300–3000 MHz), leaving the military to pioneer in exploring the new frontier region of the Super High frequencies (3–30 GHz). By 1959 the pressures to accommodate "congestion" in some of the VHF and UHF regions (largely stemming from rapid growth of land mobile services) and to provide SHF allocations for military and civilian uses of communications satellites resulted in an ITU conference to resolve these issues. Accordingly, the necessary allocations and standards were devised for the SHF region between 1959 and 1963, leaving the military to explore the new frontier region of the Extremely High frequencies (above 30 GHz). Since the mid-1960s the industrialized countries have experienced acute congestion in some of the previously allocated bands—particularly in the High, Very High, and Ultra High frequencies, as well as unresolved pressures on the Super High frequencies. Moreover, a qualitatively new force in the world radio spectrum management process—the demands of the Third World countries—produced an agenda of new kinds of issues requiring the 1979 WARC to take the next steps in rationalizing world management of the radio spectrum.

Before considering those issues, some qualifications on the preceding necessarily schematic analysis are appropriate.

First, the full scope of the framework of radio frequency allocation as summarized in terms of the three interactive stages of the process emerged clearly only with the Atlantic City ITU Conference in 1947. The theory and practice of radio spectrum management thus grew from the interaction of theory and practice on the pragmatically necessary contradictions; it did not spring out of a vacuum.[6] Radio allocation practice began with concern to get international agreement merely on equipment standards and procedures for using it in such ways as to minimize interference: this was the substance of the first Radio-telegraph Convention (Berlin, 1906), and the next (London, 1912). At the 1927 Washington

---

[6] For amplification, see Smythe, Dallas W., *The Structure and Policy of Electronic Communication.* Urbana: University of Illinois Press, 1957, pp. 61–63. Republished in Kittross, J. M., *Documents in American Telecommunications Policy.* New York: Arno Press, 1977, Volume 2. And see Codding, G. A., Jr., *Broadcasting Without Barriers.* Paris: Unesco, 1959.

Conference, emphasis shifted from operating procedures and equipment standards to the development of comprehensive frequency allocation (including designation of bands of frequencies for classes of users and geographical assignment of equipment location). By 1932, at the Madrid Conference, radio spectrum management was merged with the International Telegraph Union (founded in 1865) to form the International Telecommunications Union. Regional management of the spectrum, in coordination with that on a world scale, began in 1925 with formation of a European Broadcasting Union, to negotiate frequency assignments, standards, and operating procedures for radio broadcasting and a series of such conferences followed down to date. In 1937, the Inter-American Regional Broadcast Agreement (Cuba) formalized international agreement on such matters in that hemisphere which had begun with a "gentleman's agreement" between the United States and Canada in 1927. Moreover, ITU practice has used the device of worldwide conferences devoted to working out allocations for particular classes of user and particular regions of the spectrum, e.g., WARC-77 dealing with direct broadcast satellites.

A second qualification is another aspect of the first. Although the nations of the world have *never* departed from the basic "world property" concept of the right to use specific radio frequency assignments, such rights have in practice been treated as one of the most important bases of politico-economic power on a first-come, first-served policy. In the days of formal empire, a condition of participation in the ITU (and its predecessor, the International Telegraph Union) was that the imperial powers enjoyed "colonial voting." In 1927, for example, Great Britain, France, the United States, and Imperial Russia (if it had then existed) were allowed six votes each, Italy and the Netherlands had three votes each, and Belgium, Japan, and Spain, two each. The USSR was denied even one vote because it was excluded from the Conference.[7] After World War II, when formal empires were breaking up, and when the ITU became affiliated with the United Nations, for the first time the voting rule was one nation, one vote.

A more subtle basis of maintaining imperial power than voting rights was the pragmatic "priority" allowed to the country which first "notified" the ITU of its intention to use a particular radio frequency assignment (the product of stage three of the process described earlier). This principle was agreed to at the Berlin Conference in 1906. And in this regard the United States early laid the foundation for its dominance after 1945 in world telecommunications and the formal empire it has maintained. The director

---

[7] It was at the suggestion of Secretary Herbert Hoover that Germany, although no longer a colonial power, was allowed six votes for that Conference alone.

of naval communications in the United States speaking of the mid-1920s said ". . . the most important thing is to get the channels allocated so as to get them registered in the International Bureau before foreign nations did."[8] Indicative of its success in practically preempting use of the radio spectrum was the situation in 1945. In the then most congested and used portion of the spectrum, 4–20 MHz, the United States held frequency registrations, which it referred to as "permanently assigned to American stations," totaling 1699 "yardstick channels" or a little more than half of such channels *available to the world*.[9] The policy of allowing "priority" according to date of registration satisfied the expansionist drives of the capitalist system, working through nation-states. As will be seen, this policy came under frontal attack in ITU conferences by Third World countries beginning in the mid-1960s.

This policy of first-come, first-served, and priority in registration was rationalized as a purely technical approach to international radio regulation, and the ITU was hailed by the industrialized powers as a "nonpolitical" international organization. In fact, of course, this policy embodied the same ideology of possessive individualism as that which has brought the "tragedy of the commons" to general awareness as applied to other natural resources (atmospheric pollution, degradation of the ozone layer, etc.). In fact it is just that politicization of international radio spectrum regulation in the interest of the great powers which is now in conflict with the Third World's positive planning approach—one which corresponds to the assertion of a worldwide interest in the radio spectrum common property. It is a good example of the political nature of "technology."

A third qualification concerns theory about the allocation process of a unique natural resource. Neoclassical market theory, with its competitive assumptions, is clearly inapplicable to the typically monopolistic civilian radio services markets. Common property theory, as developed in fisheries and forestry can be helpful. Critical, historical, realistic analysis such as this avoids the crude tunnel vision of economic theory and is open to the theoretical requirements of the unique aspects of the radio spectrum discussed at the outset. David Ricardo's theory of rent has useful applications. In particular his distinction between the extensive and intensive margins of "cultivation" (of soil) is relevant. He defined *economic rent* as ". . . that portion of the produce of the earth which is paid to the landlord for the use of the original and indestructible powers of the

---

[8] United States Senate, Committee on Interstate Commerce, *Hearings on S. 6*, 71st Congress, 1st Session, testimony of Captain S. C. Hooper, 29 May, 1929, p. 319.
[9] United States Senate, Subcommittee of the Committee on Interstate Commerce, *Hearings Pursuant to S. Res. 187*, 79th Congress, 1st Session, Part 1, pp. 110–114.

soil."[10] Distinguishing between commercial rent (a compound of economic rent, interest, and profits on the "improvements" of land) and economic rent, he identified the extensive margin as the "last" uncultivated land to be brought under cultivation, and the intensive margin as the return from added increments of capital to the owner of land more advantageously situated which has previously been brought under cultivation. Economic rent under competitive market conditions thus is the difference between the value of the crop which is measured at the level required at the high-cost margin of cultivation, and the value of the crop produced within the extensive and intensive margins.

Applying this theory to the process of the use of the radio spectrum, one can identify the extensive margin as the "last edge" of any given plateau of radio spectrum utilization at a given point in time. The intensive margin is at previous uses of the radio spectrum (both on that plateau and plateaus earlier developed and used). We find the President's Task Force on Communications Policy making this distinction:

> By intensive spectrum use, we refer to the simultaneous compatible use of the same spectrum resources by more than one party; as contrasted with extensive spectrum use, which means use of hitherto completely unused spectrum resources.[11]

It thus appears that over time and with growth of population and industry, economic rent is generated by the use of the radio spectrum (as it is with land) and it is received by those licensed to use that limited resource productively at points within the extensive and intensive margins. This is unearned increment. If it be conceded that such unearned increment does exist and is created by the progress of society, then it is equitable for society as a whole to devise taxes or fees which will return to it part or all of this unearned increment.

Efforts to recover unearned increment from private owners of land, between 1879 and the 1930s failed of general acceptance within the capitalist system because of the ideological reverence for land as private property.[12] No such stigma attaches to taxing the unearned increment from common property. Radio frequency assignments are common prop-

---

[10] Ricardo, David, *Principles of Political Economy*. London: J. M. Dent, 1817, 1926 (Everyman edition), p. 33.

[11] Rostow, Eugene V., *The Use and Management of the Electromagnetic Spectrum*, Part 1. Washington, D. C.: United States Department of Commerce, 1969, p. 78.

[12] George, Henry, *Progress and Poverty*. San Francisco, 1879; Young, Allyn A., *The Single Tax Movement in the United States*. Princeton: Princeton University Press, 1916; Haig, Robert M., *The Exemption of Improvements from Taxation in Canada and the United States*. New York, 1915; Brown, H. G., Buttenheim, H. S., Cormick, P. H., and Hoover, C. E., *Land Value Taxation around the World*. New York: Robert Schalkenback Foundation, 1955.

erty. They are the basis of huge profits from operating television and radio broadcast stations and networks. To tax all or part of the unearned increment from use of the radio spectrum is to return to people collectively what only people collectively could produce. This may be of interest to the peoples of countries in both the capitalist core and the Third World.

A fourth qualification concerns the alleged "scarcity" of radio frequencies. We have noted that there is much idle frequency capacity because of the practice of preempting and allowing frequency assignments to be unused or underused. But apart from this there is in principle no absolute scarcity of radio frequencies. More properly speaking, the radio spectrum is a *limited* resource at any given short period of time. If the users and would-be users of the spectrum are willing to take certain types of action, these limits (consisting of intolerable interference) may be pushed back. The first type of action is to devote the necessary resources to research and development to improve practice. As an American government report stated at a time when concern over the acute congestion and "silent crisis" in radio frequency management was at its height in 1969:

> The latent communications capacity of the spectrum far exceeds any projected demand, if one is interested in paying the price or imposing technical standards which extract the price from the user.[13]

The second thing that can be and too infrequently is done is to require the removal of obsolete equipment and weakly justified classes of use from certain frequency bands. This is nothing more than compelling acceptance of accrued obsolescence. A third measure is to require organizational innovation to economize on frequency use. Operations by "undivided joint interests" are a familiar example in submarine cable communications. Creation of a single operating entity, "ARINC" was forced by the spectrum managers in the United States more than 50 years ago to operate radio communications for all the numerous, competitive American airlines which had previously *each* demanded spectrum space. And a fourth type of measure, already practiced to some extent, is "circuit discipline" in which the operating practices of *different* entities of radio spectrum users are integrated to maximize efficiency of channel use. All four of these measures are within the competence of engineers, managers, and regulatory people. The latter should be expected to apply such measures—not economists.

This is not the place to analyze how the power conferred by the use of the radio spectrum primarily by the largest industrialized countries has served their interest well in the twentieth century. Others have written

---

[13] Rostow, *sup. cit.*, p. 78.

and more will write on that topic.[14] It is clear that the core countries, of which the United States is the center, use the radio spectrum as the basis of their military, economic, and political power. Transnational Corporations (TNCs) mostly controlled there depend upon it. Those TNCs engaged in the production, sale, leasing, and operation of computers depend on it in their worldwide network of transnational data teleprocessing and storage.[15] The great bulk of international communications using the radio spectrum either flows to or from the United States.[16] In a very real sense, the capitalist politico-economic system is one which rests upon electronic communication. Broadly speaking, the net flow of communications is from the core to the peripheral countries. The flow of the fruit of other natural resources (labor and materials) is from the periphery to the core. The flow between the industrially developed countries is by no means matched by a lateral flow between Third World countries. Of course this situation is dynamic, not static. Incessantly the need of capital to expand drives the system to penetrate previously untapped markets (e.g., China presently).

At the same time the exchange of messages via teleprocessing and the radio spectrum is very fragile and vulnerable to disruption. Ploman, summarizing French and Swedish government reports says:

> The thrust of the Swedish report is that the . . . use of computerized data systems to a marked degree contributes to the increasing vulnerability of modern highly industrialized societies; that the level of vulnerability is unacceptably high; and that it will become even higher if counter-measures are not taken. The degree of vulnerability is conditioned by a number of factors. . . . The most important are: the dependence on foreign countries; the concentration of systems; the dependence on the few trained operational

---

[14] Dealing directly or to some degree with applications of the radio art: Schiller, Herbert I., *Mass Communications and American Empire*. Boston: Beacon Press, 1971; *The Mind Managers*. Boston: Beacon Press, 1973; *Communications and Cultural Domination*. White Plains, New York: International Arts and Sciences Press, 1976. Hamelink, Cees, *The Corporate Village*. Rome: IDOC International, 1977. Mattelart, Armand, *Multinational Corporations and the Control of Culture*. Brighton, England: Harvester Press, 1979. Wells, Alan, *Picture Tube Imperialism*. Maryknoll: Orbis Press, 1972. Smythe, Dallas W., *The Structure and Policy of Electronic Communication*, *sup. cit.*

[15] Schiller, Herbert I., "The Transnational Corporation and the International Flow of Information Challenges National Sovereignty", *Current Research on Peace and Violence*, Vol. 2, No. 1, 1979, pp. 1–11.

[16] As early as 1963, about 70 percent of all telephone revenues for international communications in the world derived from traffic to or from the United States, and Western Europe accounted for most of the remainder. See Reiger, S. H., Nichols, R. T., Early, I. B., and Dews, E., *Communications Satellites: Technology, Economics and System Choices*. Santa Monica: Rand, 1963, p. 66; American Telephone and Telegraph Company, *Estimated Overseas Telephone Message Traffic, 1960*. New York, October 1961. I recall seeing totals of physical flow of messages about 1963 showing more than 80 percent of world total of transnational communication as originating in, or destined to, the continental United States.

staff; and the sensitive nature of certain information. Terrorist activities and other criminal actions, threats, sanctions and acts of war become possible or are made easier through these vulnerability factors. Some also increase the effects of catastrophies and accidents.

The level of vulnerability can be seen in relation to the level of protection. The committee looked, as an example, at the telecommunication circuits that link data banks. They found that the level of protection is high in respect to technical faults; but only medium in the case of natural calamities (storms, earthquakes, fires, etc.). Even more interesting is the discovery that protection against deliberate attacks is minimal.

After discussing vulnerability to external attacks:

The internal factors refer to the vulnerability of the data systems themselves. Some information—a population census, industrial information, data on health and social welfare, criminal and police records—is vulnerable for reasons of intrinsic content. Some data systems are functionally vulnerable: administrative data systems in the public sector and certain data systems in commerce, etc., in the private sector. Internal vulnerability is also affected by geographical and functional concentration; the increasing co-ordination, integration and interdependence of the systems; the lack of knowledge and training among data users (sometimes resulting in unintentional errors); the low quality of computer programming; the dependence on key staff, and so on.[17]

Could it be, to plagiarize Mao Zedong, that monopoly capitalism has become, not a paper tiger, but an electronic information tiger?

WHAT IS THE INTEREST OF THIRD WORLD COUNTRIES IN RADIO FREQUENCY ALLOCATION?

It appears that most of the problems people in this world face are manifested to some degree in the multidimensional contradictions focused on the allocation of the radio spectrum. The principal contradiction which conditions and dominates them, however, is that between the highly industrialized countries with a tiny fraction of the world's population, and the ex- and neocolonial countries with most of the world's population. More precisely, it is between people and the system of hierarchical structures of privileged classes derived from the history of capitalism. The core area of capitalism (the United States and the market economies of Western Europe and Japan) still dominates that system, although the USSR and some of its satellites have taken on the characteristics of the core. Almost two-thirds of the 154 countries, members of the ITU, are the Third World countries: peripheral societies which broke away from nineteenth-century types of empire after two world wars and

---

[17] Ploman, Edward W., "Vulnerability in the Information Age", *Intermedia*, Vol. 6, November 1978, p. 28.

the Russian and Chinese revolutions destroyed the old empires. Varying greatly in size of population, natural resources, cultural character, and degree of commitment to goals of materialistic progress, they nevertheless share certain common interests (to different degrees):

1.   Having had their resources and labor power plundered by empire for from one to five centuries by capitalism, they share a common interest in the "terms of trade" and the composition of trade. That is, they need to rationalize their economic relations with the advanced industrial countries, by increasing the prices of the staple commodities which they export to the latter (as with the OPEC countries). Simultaneously either as individual countries or as regional blocs, they need to develop lateral trade, while reducing their dependence on the specialization dictated by capitalism (especially through transnational corporations) through the law of comparative advantage. Economic planning in the use of their resources is necessary.

2.   They all need capital for their development as independent, more rather than less autonomous countries. They need long-term loans or capital gifts *without strings*: loans tied to the obligation to buy Western technology, they are learning, defeat achievement of the first objective.

3.   An absolute requirement, if they are to develop as independent countries is that they must own, control, and operate their own communications systems. Their control of their communications system is as vital to their independence as their military capability. Even more so because foreign control of communications is a Trojan horse which can immobilize an army and produce dependency. And communications systems need not, in most cases should not, be highly sophisticated featuring computers and data banks, interactive television-videotext, etc. It is instructive to recall in that connection that the "equipment" successfully used by the Iranian people to overthrow the Shah and take control of their own destiny consisted of nothing more complex than mosques, festivals (the *takyeh*), meetings (the *doreh*), the bazaar, cassette tapes, Xerox, tape recordings, and the telephone.[18]

Fortunately for the Third World countries, they went to WARC-79 with some collective preparation through the Nonaligned Movement. Originating in their common hostility to colonialism in the 1920s, it took organizational form in a series of meetings of which the first was at Bandung in 1955. Beginning with the Algiers Conference of the nonaligned

---

[18] Mowlana, Hamid, "Technology versus Tradition: Communication in the Iranian Revolution," *Journal of Communication*, Vol. 19, No. 3, Summer 1979, pp. 107–112.

countries in 1973, work in the cultural and communications area gained momentum through many national, regional, and international conferences—governmental, nongovernmental, individual, and organizational, policy-oriented and research-oriented. Responding to its new Third World members, UNESCO beginning in the early 1970s sponsored additional conferences, and helped the Nonaligned Movement initiate its own press agency pool. Concurrently the Nonaligned Movement attacked the "Free Flow of Information" doctrine which the United States had written into the UNESCO charter and succeeded in getting it substantially modified at the 1976 Nairobi UNESCO General Conference. In preparation for WARC-79, the Nonaligned Movement held a series of conferences. At the end of one of these in Yaounde, their Telecommunications Co-ordination Committee stated that:

> . . . the participants held that a complete modification of the radio-communications regulations was necessary for the ITU so as to enable the assignments to the participating countries to be assured of appropriate legal protection. The participants reiterated the non-aligned countries' desire for equitable use of the orbit of fixed satellite services. They also examined certain problems related to technological transfer and stressed that it was necessary for non-aligned countries to work out their own telecommunications policy. They decided to form an experts group to be charged with examination of documents for common positions. . . . The Cameroonian Minister of State in charge of Post and Telecommunications, Egbe Tabi, disclosed that industrialized countries have steadily raised the prices of radio-communication equipment and stressed that it was necessary to establish a new and balanced world telecommunication order.

It was evident some years ago that the Third World countries would strike at the heart of the ITU's previous allocation policy by rejecting the "first-come, first-served" principle of making allocations of frequency bands and station assignments within them. Instead they have pressed for positive, long-range planning for the use of the radio spectrum, with reservations of frequency assignments for nations (often themselves) which are not yet ready to make use of them. In 1974 the ITU Maritime Conference agreed to a plan that allotted frequency assignments according to a mathematical principle of fairness. Similarly the 1977 WARC on direct broadcast satellites adopted:

> . . . a comprehensive plan assigning to administration in ITU Regions 1 and 3 [all the world except the Americas], individual channels (that is frequencies) and polarizations at specific orbital locations for coverage of prescribed service areas on the ground.[19]

---

[19] Gould, R. G., and Reinhart, E. E., "The 1977 WARC on Broadcasting Satellites: Spectrum Management Aspects and Implications," *IEEE Transactions on Electromagnetic Compatibility*, August 1977, p. 171.

This more ordered use of the spectrum was opposed by the United States, Canada, and Brazil, which succeeded in preventing adoption of a similar plan for Region 2.

As the Ingenieur Generale des Telecommunications, France, said in 1977, in previous WARCs the basis of allocation was essentially technical criteria, but:

Today, that kind of exclusively technical thinking is no longer possible. Economic, social and political factors must be considered alongside the technical when fixing priorities. And we must not forget the subtle principle of equity, between services; between users; and ultimately between individuals.[20]

As against this Third World thrust:

The United States State Department spoke for the industrial countries when it said that "Frequency assignments should be based on demonstrated need and the ability to use them. The concern is that fixed allotment plans which distribute frequencies and orbital space to countries or areas independently of such need or the ability to utilize may not allow the optimal utilization of the spectrum, or provide *adequate incentives for the adoption of technologies and patterns of use that conserve the spectrum.*" The U.S.S.R. takes roughly the same position.[21]

The editor of the International Institute of Communications' *Intermedia* comments, referring to the maritime and broadcast satellite plans:

The plans are crude, and the flaws are obvious. But the move towards greater management and planning, towards intervention, is likely to be irresistible, and for good reason.

It must be said that the industrial countries, who have massive resources and great skill in these matters have not really exercised either in the search for better planning. They are finding it very difficult to adjust to the new situation (a failure that is evident in most international arenas, whether the subject is raw commodities or technology). They prefer to continue, as long as possible, with their traditional methods, rather than work towards the success of the new ones. . . .

Some industrial countries, long used to squatter's rights, regard the ITU's new thrust as rather a nuisance. Some developing countries regard the ITU as the only platform where the majority can work to correct the mistakes of the past 70 years.

As telecommunications becomes more explicitly an integral component of national development, its political connotations become clearer and more

---

[20] Quoted in Howkins, John, "The Management of the Spectrum," *Intermedia*, Vol. 7, No. 5, September 1979, p. 14.

[21] *Ibid.*, p. 14. Emphasis added.

powerful. It is not possible to say that communications is central to social organization, whether of a city or a continent, and then to expect politicians to leave future development to the engineers [and businessmen]. . . . This month's WARC gains much of its potential for achievement—and for controversy—from this political awareness.[22]

Over and above their insistence on positive spectrum planning, Third World nations had a range of other probable objectives at WARC-79 and the next general ITU plenipotentiary conference in 1982. One such is to bring sensing satellites under effective control; presently the United States LANDSAT satellites invade the prerogatives of a country by sensing and mapping its mineral, crop, and other physical characteristics without its permission. They have some urgent needs for frequency assignments in the High and Very High frequencies which are needed for broadcasting in tropical countries. And probably many more of their needs will become known when WARC-79 documents become available.

Regardless of the specific substantive demands Third World countries will make in their capacity as majority members of the ITU, the assumptions underlying those demands are the best basis for anticipating future changes in radio spectrum management. As identified by an expert on the nonaligned movement, Tran Van Dinh, these bases of Third World radio spectrum policy are: (1) radio spectrum policy is an essential aspect of national sovereignty and independence; (2) prior consent is an essential feature of present radio allocation policy; (3) positive planning for use of the radio spectrum is necessary; laissez-faire is unacceptable; (4) technology, far from being politically a neutral thing, is highly ideological in nature; (5) people must always be supreme over machines and tools; (6) "foreign aid" with communications "technology" is an arm of neocolonial policy.[23]

IMPLICATIONS

The political economy of the radio spectrum deals with bundles of contradictions involved in the necessary dependence on use of the radio spectrum by all peoples, regardless of their ideological, cultural, and economic systems and interests. In its brief history to date, the ITU has been dominated by the capitalist countries. Their prime concern has been to develop and use it for military purposes with the assumption that people around the world would tolerate whatever uses the capitalist system chooses to make of the radio spectrum. It is also a fact that the use of the

---

[22] *Ibid.*, pp. 15–18.
[23] Tran Van Dinh, "The Third World and the 1979 World Administrative Radio Conference (WARC)" (Xerox), 1979.

radio spectrum depends upon people, whose property it is in a sense different from other resources.

In taking part in the process of allocating the radio spectrum, the majority of the people, through their predominantly Third World national governments, are taking the first step toward determining the ends for which the radio spectrum may be used in the future. Presently many Third World national governments are ill aware of how the radio spectrum is used or of the process for using it. WARC-79 was thus a first step in learning for many of these countries. What those governments learned will be passed on to their people, as the contradictions in their real situations will teach them.

As a majority in the ITU, Third World countries may develop new types of regulation of humanity's common property, the radio spectrum. Two hypothetical examples are obvious: (1) *Recapture of rent.* The "developed" countries now benefit disproportionately from the use of the radio spectrum (as well as other natural resources). The economic rent now siphoned off by private business from the use of the radio spectrum (conspicuously through television and radio broadcasting) is produced by the use by people of a peculiar form of world property. To recapture all or some of this economic rent and use it for the development of communications systems for the Third World countries would be manifestly just and wise. The core capitalist countries will resist paying such license fees. And the USSR representative on the MacBride Commission flatly opposed their favorable consideration.[24] (2) *Protecting nations from foreign interference in their own affairs.* The Third World countries may use their influence to eliminate the military and communications aggressions which now continue to violate the rights of people to determine their own future.

How might this happen? Consider this scenario. At some future time, the ITU, at Third World nations' insistence, adopts general policies, outlawing the use of the spectrum for aggressive military and propaganda purposes. Potential aggressor countries resist this strongly and serve notice that they will not be bound by such a constraint. Then a dictator is toppled in a peripheral Third World country, e.g., in Central America. The United States uses economic boycott, mass media content, perhaps military aid or even open intervention. Third World countries through their own collective organizations demand that the United States stop intervention. The United States continues intervention. Third World countries disrupt American use of the radio spectrum in strategically calculated steps: perhaps jamming military-used radio frequencies, communications satellite communication, etc. Certainly such a scenario is

---

[24] International Commission for the Study of Communication Problems, *Report: Many Voices, One World*, Paris, UNESCO, 1980, p. 275.

now unrealistic. But if and when it happens, it would be a milepost passed in human development: the nonviolent prevention of aggression. Given the facts of life about the conditions for using the radio spectrum, is it in principle improbable? Maybe not so improbable as those who profit by postponing it pretend.

One recalls in this connection the statement by Jean Persin, Counsellor to the Director-General of the ITU. An intensely practical engineer, Persin said:

> If it be generally admitted that, together with gravitation which is suspected of being analogous to magnetism, electro-magnetism conditions the equilibrium of the universe, we shall not be guilty of excessive fantasy in believing that, through radio, electro-magnetism may also assist in harmonizing the human world.[25]

---

[25] Persin, Jean, "On the Eve of the Seventh World Radio Conference—The ITU and the International Regulation of Radio," *Telecommunications Journal*, March 1959, p. 53.

BIBLIOGRAPHY

Adorno, T.W. "Kultur und Verwaltung," *Sociologischen Schriften*, Vol. 1, Frankfurt: Suhrkamp, 1972.

Aguirre-Bianchi, Claudio, and Hedebro, Goran. *Communication Alternatives and the New International Order in Latin America*. Stockholm: Latinameriko Institutet, 1979.

Althusser, Louis. *Reading Capital*. Paris: Maspero, 1965. (English ed., London: NLB, 1977.)

American Telephone and Telegraph Company. *Estimated Overseas Telephone Message Traffic, 1960*. New York: October 1961.

Anderson, Michael H. "An Overview of the Wide, Wide World of Advertising and the 'New World Information Order' Debate," August 1979.

Association of Universities and Colleges of Canada. *The Symons Report*. Toronto: McClelland and Stewart, 1978.

Averch, Harvey, and Johnson, Leland L. "Behavior and the Firm under Regulatory Constraint," *American Economic Review*, Vol. 52, December 1962, pp. 1052–1069.

Azril, Bacal R. "Peace Research and the Chicano Perspective: Ethnicity and the New International Division of Labor," August 1979. (Unpublished paper.)

Babe, Robert E. *Cable Television and Telecommunications in Canada*. East Lansing: Michigan State University Press, 1975.

Babe, Robert E. "Economics of Vertical Integration in the Canadian Telephone Industry," Restrictive Practices Commission, June 1978.

Baran, P.T., and Sweezy, P. *Monopoly Capital*. New York: Monthly Review, 1966.

Barnet, Richard J., and Mueller, Ronald E. *Global Reach*. New York: Simon & Schuster, 1974.

Barnouw, Erik. *The Sponsor*. New York: Oxford University Press, 1978.

Barnouw, Erik. *A Tower in Babel*. New York: Oxford University Press, 1966.

Baumol, W.J., and Bowen, W.C. *The Performing Arts*. New York: Twentieth Century Fund, 1966.

Bellisfield, Gwen. "White Attitudes toward Racial Integration and the Urban Riots of the 1960's," *Public Opinion Quarterly*, Vol. 36, Winter, 1972–3, pp. 579–584.

Berelson, Bernard. "The Study of Public Opinion," in White, Leonard D. Ed., *The State of the Social Sciences*. Chicago: University of Chicago Press, 1956.

Bernal, J.D. *The Social Function of Science*. London: Routledge and Sons, 1939.

Bernays, Edward L. "The Engineering of Consent," *Annals of the American Academy of Political and Social Science*, Vol. 250, March 1947, pp. 113–120.

Bernays, Edward L. *Public Relations*, Norman, Oklahoma: University of Oklahoma Press, 1952.

Bettelheim, Charles. *Cultural Revolution and Industrial Organization in China.* New York: Monthly Review Press, 1974.

Blank, David M. "Pleasurable Pursuits—The Changing Structure of Leisure Time Spectator Activities," National Association of Business Economists, Annual Meeting, September 1970. (Unpublished paper.)

Bliss, Michael. "Canadianizing American Business," in Lumsden, Ian, Ed., *Close the 49th Parallel, Etc.: The Americanization of Canada.* Toronto: University of Toronto Press, 1970.

Bogart, Leo. "Mass Advertising: The Message, not the Measure," *Harvard Business Review*, Vol. 54, No. 5, September–October 1976, pp. 107–116.

Bogart, Leo. "Warning: The Surgeon General has Determined that Television Violence is Moderately Dangerous to your Child's Mental Health," *Public Opinion Quarterly*, Vol. 36, Winter, 1972–73, pp. 491–521.

Boorstin, Daniel. *The Image.* New York: Atheneum, 1962.

Boswell, E. *The Restoration Court Stage.* New York: Benjamin Blom, 1932.

Boulding, K. *Economic Analysis.* New York: Harper & Row, 1955.

Brady, Robert A. *Business as a System of Power.* New York: Columbia University Press, 1943.

Braverman, Harry. *Labor and Monopoly Capital.* New York: Monthly Review Press, 1974.

Bright, Charles. *Submarine Telegraphs.* London: Lockwood, 1898. (New York: Arno, 1974.)

Britnell, G.E. Public Ownership of Telephones in the Prairie Provinces. M.A. Thesis, University of Toronto, 1934.

Brown, H.G., Buttenheim, H.S., Cormick, P.H., and Hoover, C.E. *Land Value Taxation Around the World.* New York: Robert Schalkenback Foundation, 1955.

Bryson, Lyman. *The Communication of Ideas.* New York: Harper & Row, 1948.

Canada. Department of Communications, *Description of the Canadian Telecommunications Manufacturing Industry*, Telecommission Study 2(g). Ottawa: Information Canada, 1971a.

Canada. Department of Communications, *Instant World*. Ottawa: Information Canada, 1971b.

Canada. Department of Communications. *Review of the Procurement Practices and Policies and the Intercorporate Financial Relationships of the British Columbia Telephone Company*, Ottawa, 1975.

Canada. Director of Investigation and Research, Combines Investigation Act, *The Effects of Vertical Integration on the Telecommunication Equipment Market in Canada.* Ottawa: Department of Consumer and Corporate Affairs, Bureau of Competition Policy, 1976.

Canada. House of Commons. "Proceedings of the Select Committee on Telephones,"

Appendix A., *Journal of the House of Commons*, Vol. 40, Session 1905. Ottawa: King's Printer, 1905. (Mulock Committee.)

Canada. Royal Commission on Book Publishing, *Report*, Toronto: Queen's Printer, 1972. (Rohmer Report.)

Canada. Royal Commission on Bilingualism and Biculturalism, *Report*. Ottawa: Queen's Printer, 1968.

Canada. Royal Commission on National Development in the Arts, Letters and Sciences, *Report*, Ottawa: Queen's Printer, 1951. (Massey Commission.)

Canada. Royal Commission on Publications, *Report*. Ottawa: Queen's Printer, 1961. (O'Leary Report.)

Canada. Special Senate Committee on the Mass Media, *The Uncertain Mirror*. Ottawa: Queen's Printer, 1970. (Davey Report.)

Cantril, Hadley, Gaudet, Hazel, and Herzog, Herta. *Invasion from Mars*. Princeton: Princeton University Press, 1940.

Carlson, M. *The Theatre of the French Revolution*. New York: Cornell University Press, 1966.

Catton, Bruce. *The War Lords of Washington*. New York: Harcourt Brace, 1948.

Chamberlin, E.H. *The Theory of Monopolistic Competition*. Cambridge: Harvard University Press, 1931.

Chandler, Alfred D., Jr. *Strategy and Structure*. Cambridge: M.I.T. Press, 1962.

Chase, Stuart, and Schlink, F.J. *Your Money's Worth: A Study in the Waste of the Consumer's Dollar*. New York: Macmillan, 1927.

"China's Tourist Service," *Beijing Review*, No. 2, 12 January, 1979.

Chotas, James, and Phelps, Miriam E. "Who Owns What?" In Appelbaum, Judith, Ed., *The Question of Size in the Book Industry Today*. New York: Publishers Weekly, 1978.

Codding, G.A., Jr. *Broadcasting without Barriers*. Paris: UNESCO, 1959.

Codding, G.A., Jr. *The International Telecommunications Union*. Leyden: Brill, 1952.

Commoner, Barry. *The Closing Circle*. New York: Knopf, 1971.

Conant, Michael. *Antitrust in the Motion Picture Industry*. Berkeley: University of California Press, 1960.

Cook, Earl. "The Flow of Energy in an Industrial Society," *Scientific American*, Vol. 225, No. 3, September 1973, pp. 135–144.

Cook, Fred, J. *The Warfare State*. Foreword by Bertrand Russell, New York: Macmillan, 1962.

Crean, Susan M. *Who's Afraid of Canadian Cultures?* Don Mills, Ontario: General Publishing, 1976.

Daniellian, N.R. *The A.T. & T.* New York: Vanguard, 1939.

Davey Report, see, Canada, Special Committee on Mass Media (1970).

de Bord, Guy. *The Society of the Spectacle*. Detroit: Black & Red, 1970.

de Grazia, Sebastian. *Of Time, Work and Leisure*. New York: Anchor, 1964.

Dexter, Gail. "Yes, Cultural Imperialism Too," in Lumsden, I., Ed., *Close the 49th Parallel, Etc.: The Americanization of Canada*. Toronto: University of Toronto Press, 1970.

Dimaggio, Paul, and Useem, Michael. "Cultural Democracy in a Period of Cultural Expansion: The Social Composition of Arts Audiences in the United States," *Social Problems*, Vol. 26, No. 2, December 1978, p. 179–197.

Dixon, Marlene. "Women's Liberation: Opening Chapter Two," *Canadian Dimension*, Vol. 10, No. 8, June 1975, p. 56–68.

Dorfman, Ariel, and Mattelart, Armand. *How to Read Donald Duck: Imperialist Ideology in the Disney Comic*. New York: International General, 1975.

Drache, D. "The Canadian Bourgeoisie and Its National Consciousness," in Lumsden, Ian, Ed., *Close the 49th Parallel, Etc.: The Americanization of Canada*, Toronto: University of Toronto Press, 1970.

Ellis, Kenneth. *The Post Office in the Eighteenth Century*. London: Oxford University Press, 1958.

Ellis, W. Russell. "Advertised Life: Dwelling Family and Commercial Culture in American Habitation," in Bearse, P., et al., Eds., *American Values and Habitat: A Research Agenda*. Washington: American Association for the Advancement of Science, Division of Public Sector Programs, 1976.

Ellul, Jacques. "The Technological Order," in Stover, Carl F., Ed., *The Technological Order—Proceedings of the Encyclopaedia Britannica Conference*. Detroit: Wayne State University Press, 1963.

Enzensberger, Hans Magnus. *The Consciousness Industry*. New York: Seabury Press, 1974.

Ernst and Ernst Management Consulting Services. *The Book Publishing and Manufacturing Industry in Canada: A Statistical and Economic Analysis*. Ottawa: Information Canada, 1970.

Ewen, Stuart. *Captains of Consciousness*. New York: McGraw-Hill, 1976.

Fanon, Frantz. *Studies in a Dying Colonialism*. New York: Monthly Review Press, 1965.

Firestone, O.J. *The Economic Implications of Advertising*. Toronto: Methuen, 1967.

Firestone, S. *The Dialectic of Sex*. New York: W. Morrow, 1970.

Frank, Andrew Gunder. *Latin America: Underdevelopment or Revolution*. New York: Monthly Review Press, 1969.

Friendly, Fred. *Due to Circumstances beyond Our Control*. New York: Random House, 1967.

Gagne, Wallace, Ed. *Nationalism, Technology and the Future of Canada*. Toronto: Macmillan, 1976.

Galbraith, J.K. *The New Industrial State*. Boston: Houghton Mifflin, 1967.

Gans, Herbert J. *Popular Culture and High Culture: An Analysis and Evaluation of Taste*. New York: Basic Books, 1974.

Garnham, Nicholas. "Towards a Political Economy of Culture," *NUQ*, Summer 1977, pp. 341–357.

George, Henry. *Progress and Poverty*. San Francisco: W.M. Hinton & Co., 1879.

Gerstacker, Carl A. "A New Look at Business in 1990." White House Conference on the Industrial World Ahead, Washington, D.C., February 7-9, 1972.

Gitlin, Todd. "Prime Time Ideology: The Hegemonic Process in Television Entertainment," *Social Problems*, Vol. 26, No. 3, February 1979, pp. 257-266.

Gonick, C.W. "Foreign Ownership and Political Decay," in Lumsden, Ian, Ed., *Close the 49th Parallel, Etc.: The Americanization of Canada*, Toronto: University of Toronto Press, 1970.

Goodis, Jerry. *Have I Ever Lied to You Before?* Toronto: McClelland & Stewart, 1972.

Gould, Richard, G., and Reinhart, Edward E. "The 1977 WARC on Broadcasting Satellites: Spectrum Management Aspects and Implications," *IEEE Transactions on Electromagnetic Compatibility*, August 1977, pp. 171-178.

Gray, Horace M. "The Passing of the Public Utility Concept," *Journal of Land and Public Utility Economics*, Vol. 16, 1940, pp. 8-20.

Greene, Felix. *A Curtain of Ignorance*. New York: Doubleday, 1964.

Gundy, H.P. "Development of Trade Book Publishing in Canada," Royal Commission on Book Publishing, *Background Papers*. Toronto: Queen's Printer for Ontario, 1972. (Rohmer Report, Background Papers.)

Haig, Robert M. *The Exemption of Improvements from Taxation in Canada and the United States*. New York: M.B. Brown, 1915.

Halberstam, David. "CBC: The Power and the Profits," *Atlantic*, January 1976, pp. 33-71.

Hameling, Cees. *The Corporate Village*. Rome: IDOC International, 1977.

Harbage, Alfred. *Shakespeare's Audience*. New York: Columbia University Press, 1941.

Hardin, Garrett, "The Tragedy of the Commons," *Science*, Vol. 162, 1968, pp. 1243-1248.

Hauser, Arnold. *The Social History of Art*. New York: Vintage Books, 1957.

Heiss, Charles A. *Report on Second-Class Mail to the Postmaster General*. Washington: U.S. Government Printing Office, 1946.

Herring, J.M., and Gross, G.C. *Telecommunications*. New York: McGraw-Hill, 1936.

Herring, E. Pendleton. "Politics and Radio Regulation", *Harvard Business Review*, Vol. 13, No. 2, January, 1935, pp. 167-178.

Hills, Lee. *Faximile*. New York: McGraw-Hill, 1949.

Hinchman, W.R. "Use and Management of the Electrospace: A New Concept of the Radio Resource", IEEE International Conference on Communications, *Conference Record*, Boulder, June 1969, pp. 13.1-13.5.

Hobsbawm, Eric. *The Age of Capital, 1848-1875*. London: Weidenfeld and Nicholson, 1975.

Hobsbawm, Eric. *The Age of Revolution, 1789-1849*. Cleveland: World, 1967.

Hoch, Paul. *Rip Off the Big Game*. New York: Doubleday, 1972.

Hogan, John V.K. "Facsimile and Its Future Uses," *Annals, American Academy of Political and Social Science*, Vol. 213, January 1941.

Hovland, C.I., Lumsdaine, A.A., and Sheffield, F.D. *Experiments on Mass Communication*, "Studies in Social Psychology in World War II." Princeton: University Press, 1949.

Howard, Roger, and Scott, Jack. "International Unions and the Ideology of Class Collaboration," in Teeple, Gary, Ed., *Capitalism and the National Question in Canada*. Toronto: University of Toronto Press, 1972, pp. 67–89.

Howkins, John. "The Management of Spectrum," *Intermedia*, Vol. 7, No. 5, September 1979, pp. 10–22.

Huettig, Mae. *Economic Control of the Motion Picture Industry*. Philadelphia: University of Pennsylvania Press, 1944.

Hull, C.L. *Principles of Behaviour: An Introduction to Behaviour Theory*. New York: Appleton Century, 1943.

Innis, H.A. *The Bias of Communication*. Toronto: University of Toronto Press, 1951.

Innis, H.A. *The Cod Fisheries: The History of an International Economy*. Toronto: University of Toronto Press, 1954.

Innis, H.A. *The Fur Trade in Canada: An Introduction to Canadian Economic History*. Toronto: University of Toronto Press, 1970.

International Commission for the Study of Communication Problems. *Report: Many Voices, One World*. Paris: UNESCO, 1980.

Johnson, A.W. *Touchstone for the CBC*. Ottawa: Canadian Broadcasting Corporation, June, 1977.

Johnson, Leland L. *Communications Satellites and Telephone Rates: Problems of Government Regulations*. Santa Monica, Rand Corporation, 1961. (Reprinted in U.S. Senate. Committee on the Judiciary, Subcommittee on Antitrust and Monopoly, Hearings, S. Res. 258, Part 2, pp. 603–652.)

Johnson, Leo A. "The Development of Class in Canada in the Twentieth Century," in Teeple, Gary, Ed. *Capitalism and the National Question in Canada*. Toronto: University of Toronto Press, 1972.

Jones, Charles R. *Facsimile*. New York: Murray Hill Books, 1949.

Kampf, Louis. "A Course in Spectator Sports," *College English*, Vol. 38, No. 8, April 1977, pp. 835–842.

Kaplin, Max. *Leisure in America: A Social Inquiry*. New York: Wiley, 1960.

Kaplin, Max. *Leisure: Theory and Policy*. New York: Wiley, 1975.

Katz, E., Blumler, J.G., and Gurevitch, M. "Uses and Gratification Research," *Public Opinion Quarterly*, Vol. 37, Winter 1973–74, pp. 509–523.

Katz, E., and Foulkes, D. "On the Use of the Mass Media as 'Escape': Clarification of a Concept," *Public Opinion Quarterly*, Vol. 26, No. 3, Fall, 1962, pp. 377–388.

Kekkonen, Urho. "The Free Flow of Information: Towards A Reconsideration of National and International Communication Policies," Symposium on the International Flow of Television Programmes, University of Tampere, Tampere, Finland, May 21, 1973.

Kellner, Douglas. "Ideology, Marxism, and Advanced (pitalism," *Socialist Review*, Vol. 8, No. 6, November–December 1978, pp 37–65.

Kellner, Douglas. "TV, Ideology and Emancipatory Pop lar Culture," *Socialist Review*, Vol. 9, No. 3, May–June 1979, pp. 13–53.

Kendall, Donald M. (Chairman, Pepsico, Inc.), "United States-Soviet Trade Relations," before National Press Club, Washington, D.C. 21 February, 1978.

Kesterton, W.H. *A History of Journalism in Canada.* Toronto: McClelland and Stewart, 1967.

Kittross, M., Ed. *Documents in American Communications Policy. New York:* Arno Press, 1977.

Klapper, Joseph T. *The Effects of Mass Communications.* New York: Free Press, 1960.

Klapper, Joseph T. *The Effects of the Mass Media.* New York: Columbia University Bureau of Applied Social Research, 1949.

Knight, M.M., Barnes, H.E., and Flugel, F. *The Economic History of Europe.* New York: Houghton Mifflin, 1928.

Kolko,Gabriel. *The Triumph of Conservatism.* New York: Free Press, 1963.

Kotler, Philip. *Marketing Management,* 2d ed. Englewood Cliffs, New Jersey: Prentice-Hall, 1972.

Kristeller, Paul Oskar. "The Modern System of the Arts," in Weitz, Morris, Ed., *Problems in Aesthetics.* London: Macmillan, 1970.

Ladd, E.C. "The Polls: The Question of Confidence," *Public Opinion Quarterly,* Vol. 40, Winter 1976–77, pp. 544–552.

Larrabee, E., and Meyersohn, R., Eds. *Mass Leisure.* Glencoe, Ill.: Free Press, 1958.

Lasswell, H.D. "The Structure and Function of Communication in Society," in Bryson, L., Ed., *The Communication of Ideas.* New York: Harper & Row, 1948, pp. 37–51.

Laxer, J., and Laxer, R. *The Liberal Idea of Canada.* Toronto: James Lorimer, 1977.

Lazarsfeld, P.F., and Merton, R.K. "Mass Communications, Popular Taste, and Organized Social Action," in Bryson, L., Ed., *The Communication of Ideas.* New York: Harper & Row, 1948. (Also published in Schramm, W., Ed., *Mass Communications.* Urbana: University of Illinois Press, 1949.)

Leiss, W.A. *The Domination of Nature.* New York: Braziller, 1972.

Leiss, William. *The Limits to Satisfaction: An Essay on the Problems of Needs and Commodities.* Toronto: University of Toronto Press, 1976.

Leiss, William, and Kline, Stephen. "Advertising, Needs, and 'Commodity Fetishism,'" *Canadian Journal of Political and Social Theory,* Vol. 2, Winter 1978, pp. 3–32.

Leith, James A. *The Idea of Art as Propaganda in France, 1750–1799.* Toronto: University of Toronto Press, 1965.

Lessing, Lawrence. *Man of High Fidelity.* New York: Lippincott, 1956.

Levitt, Kari. *Silent Surrender*. Toronto: Macmillan, 1970.

Levitt, T. N. "The Industrialization of Service," *Harvard Business Review*, September–October 1976, pp. 63–74.

Lewis, Ben W. "Emphasis and Misemphasis in Regulatory Policy," in Shepherd, W.C. and Gies, T.G., Eds., *Utility Regulation: New Directions in Theory and Policy*. New York: Random House, 1966.

Liebling, A.J. *The Press*. New York: Ballantine, 1961.

Linder, Staffen B. *The Harried Leisure Class*. New York: Columbia University Press, 1970.

Livant, Bill. "The Audience Commodity: On the 'Blindspot' Debate," *Canadian Journal of Political and Social Theory*, Vol. 3, No. 1, Winter 1979a, pp. 91–106.

Livant, Bill. "The Communication Commodity," University of Regina, 25 December, 1975a. (Unpublished paper.)

Livant, Bill. "More on the Production of Damaged Labour Power," 1 April, 1975b. (Unpublished paper.)

Livant, Bill. "Notes on the Development of the Production of Labour Power," 22 March, 1975c. (Unpublished paper.)

Livant, Bill. "On Two Emerging Features in Communication and Their Relation," June, 1979b. (Unpublished paper.)

Loercher, Diana. "Publishing: Hype vs. Integrity, Mergers," *Christian Science Monitor*, 2 June, 1978, p. 16, (1978a).

Loercher, Diana. "Publishing: Hype vs. Integrity, The Media Tie-in," *Christian Science Monitor*, 5 June, 1978, p. 20, (1978b).

Lorimer, James. "The Politics of Publishing." (Unpublished paper.)

Lough, John. *Paris Theatre Audiences in the Seventeenth and Eighteenth Centuries*. London: Oxford University Press, 1957.

Lowenthal, Max. *The Federal Bureau of Investigation*. New York: William Sloane, 1950.

Lukacs, George. *Realism in Our Time*. New York: Harper & Row, 1964.

Lumsden, I., Ed., *Close the 49th Parallel, Etc.: The Americanization of Canada*. Toronto: University of Toronto Press, 1970.

Lyle, Jack. "Television in Daily Life: Patterns of Use," in Rubenstein, E.A., Comstock, G.H., and Murray, J.P., Eds., *Television and Social Behaviour*, Vol. IV, pp. 1–32. Rockville, Md., National Institute of Mental Health, 1972.

Lynd, Robert S., and Lynd, Helen M. *Middletown, A Study in Contemporary American Culture*. New York: Harcourt Brace, 1929.

McDermott, John. "Technology: The Opiate of the Intellectuals," in Teich, A.H., Ed., *Technology and Man's Future*. New York: St. Martin's Press, 1972.

McKechnie, Samuel. *Popular Entertainment through the Ages*. New York: Benjamin Blom, 1969.

MacPherson, C.B. *Property: Mainstream and Critical Positions*. Toronto: University of Toronto Press, 1978.

McQueen, Humphrey. *Australia's Media Monopolies.* Camberwell, Victoria, Australia.

Magdoff, Harry. "Is There a Non-Capitalist Road?" *Monthly Review*, Vol. 3, No. 8, December 1978, pp. 1–16.

Man, Science, Technology. Moscow/Prague: Academia Prague, 1973.

Mander, Jerry. *Four Arguments for the Elimination of Television.* New York: Morrow, 1978.

Mander, Raymond, and Mitchenson, Joe. *British Music Hall.* Edinburgh: R. & R. Clarck, Ltd., 1965.

Mao Zedong. *Four Essays on Philosophy.* Beijing: Foreign Language Press, 1968.

Marcuse, H. *One-Dimensional Man.* Boston: Beacon Press, 1964.

Marschak, T.A. "On the Study of Taste-Changing Policies," *American Economic Review*, Vol. 68, No. 2, May 1978, pp. 386–391.

Marshall, Herbert, Southard, Frank, and Taylor, Kenneth W. *Canadian American Industry.* New York: Carnegie Endowment for International Peace, 1936. (Toronto: McClelland and Stewart, 1976.)

Martines, Lauro. *Power and Imagination: City States in Renaissance Italy.* New York: Knopf, 1979.

Marx, Karl. *Capital.* New York: Modern Library Edition, 1959.

Marx, Karl. *Grundrisse.* London: Pelican Books, 1973.

Marx. Karl, and Engels, Frederick. *The German Ideology*, edited by C.J. Arthur, New York: International Publishers, 1970.

Matson, Floyd W. *The Broken Image.* Garden City, N.Y.: Anchor Books, Doubleday, 1964.

Mattelart, Armand. *Multinational Corporations and the Control of Culture.* Brighton, England: Harvester Press, 1979.

Mattelart, Michelee. "Las Communicaciones Populares en Chile, 1971–73," in Vidal Benyto, Jose, Ed., *Alternativas Populares a las Communicaciones de Masa.* Madrid: Centro de Investigaciones Sociologicas, 1979.

Mayer, David. *Harlequin in His Element.* Cambridge, Mass.: Harvard University Press, 1969.

Melody, William H. "Are Satellites the Pyramids of the 20th Century? *Search*, Vol. 6, No. 2, Spring 1979, pp. 2–9.

Melody, William H. "Market Structures and Public Policy in Communications," Paper presented at American Economics Association, New York, 28 December, 1969.)

Melody, William H., and Smythe, Dallas W. *Telecommunications Equipment Inquiry*, before the Restrictive Trade Practices Commission, Vancouver, 19 September, 1977. (Unpublished paper.)

Milgram, Stanley. *Obedience to Authority: An Experimental View.* New York: Harper & Row, 1974.

Mill, John Stuart. *On Liberty.* London: Oxford University Press, 1963.

Millett, Kate. *Sexual Politics.* New York: Doubleday, 1970.

Millionshchikov, M. "The Crucial Test for Mankind," *The Scientific and Technological Revolution: Social Effects and Prospects*, Moscow: Progress Publishers, 1972.

Mitchell, Juliet. *Women's Estate*. New York: Pantheon, 1971.

Moffett, Samuel E. *The Americanization of Canada*. Toronto: University of Toronto Press, 1906 (1971).

Mowlana, Hamid. "Technology versus Tradition: Communication in the Iranian Revolution," *Journal of Communication*, Vol. 29, No. 3, Summer 1979, pp. 107–112.

Mulock Committee, see, Canada. House of Commons (1905).

Murdock, Graham. "Blindspots about Western Marxism: A Reply to Dallas Smythe," *Canadian Journal of Political and Social Theory*, Vol. 2, No. 2, 1978, pp. 109–119.

"Native Art." *The Native Perspective*, Vol. 3, No. 2, 1978, pp. 31–90.

Naylor, R.T. "The Rise and Fall of the Third Commercial Empire of the St. Lawrence," in Teeple, Gary, Ed., *Capitalism and the National Question in Canada*. Toronto: University of Toronto Press, 1972.

Newman, Peter. *The Canadian Establishment*. Toronto: McClelland and Stewart, 1975.

Noble, David F. *America by Design: Science, Technology and the Rise of Corporate Capitalism*. New York: Knopf, 1977.

O'Leary Report, see, Canada. Royal Commission on Publications (1961).

Ollman, B. *Alienation: Marx's Conception of Man in Capitalist Society*. New York: Cambridge University Press, 1971 (1976).

On Khrushchov's Phoney Communism and Its Historical Lessons for the World. Beijing: Foreign Languages Press, 1964.

"On Policy Towards Intellectuals," *Beijing Review*, No. 5, 2 February, 1979.

Ontario. Royal Commission on Violence in the Communications Industry, *Approaches, Conclusions and Recommendations*, Vol. 1, 1978.

Ouimet, J.A. "Report on Television," *The Engineering Journal*, V. 83, pp. 172-176, 187, March 1950.

Palamountain, Joseph C., Jr. "Vertical Conflict," in Stern, Louis W., *Distribution Channels: Behavioural Dimensions*, New York: Houghton Mifflin, 1969.

Palmer, Bryan. "Class, Conception and Conflict: The Thrust for Efficiency, Managerial Views of Labor and the Working Class Rebellion, 1903–1922," *Review of Radical Political Economy*, Vol. 7, No. 2, Summer 1975, pp. 31–49.

Parkinson, C.N. *The Evolution of Political Thought*. New York: Viking, 1958.

Parsons, Frank. *The Telegraph Monopoly*. Philadelphia: C.F. Taylor, 1899.

Pawley, Martin. *The Private Future: Causes and Consequences of Community Collapse in the West*. New York: Random House, 1974.

Peers, Frank. *The Politics of Canadian Broadcasting*. Toronto: University of Toronto Press, 1969.

Persin, Jean. "On the Eve of the Seventh World Radio Conference—The ITU and the International Regulation of Radio," *Telecommunications Journal*, March 1959.

Pessemier, Edgar A. "Stochastic Properties of Changing Preferences," *American Economic Review*, Vol. 68, No. 2, May 1978, pp. 380–385.

Plant, Christopher. *PEACESAT and Development in the Pacific Islands*. M.A. Thesis, Simon Fraser University, 1980.

Ploman, Edward W. "Vulnerability in the Information Age," *Intermedia*, Vol. 6, November 1978.

Pollak, Robert A. "Endogenous Taste in Demand and Welfare Analysis," *American Economic Review*, Vol. 68, No. 2, May 1978, pp. 374–379.

Pope, Daniel A. *The Development of National Advertising, 1865–1920*. New York: Columbia University Press, 1973. (Ph.D. dissertation.)

Porat, Marc Uri. "Global Implications of the Information Society," *Journal of Communication*, Vol. 28, No. 1, Winter 1978, pp. 70–80.

Porat, Marc Uri. *The Information Economy: Definition and Measurement*. Washington, D.C.: United States Government Printing Office, 1977.

Posner, Richard A. "Natural Monopoly and Its Regulation," *Stanford Law Review*, Vol. 21, February 1969, pp. 548–643.

Presbrey, Frank. *The History and Development of Advertising*. New York: Greenwood, 1929 (1968).

Probst, S.E. "International and United States Preparation for the 1979 World Administrative Radio Conference," *IEEE Transactions on Electromagnetic Compatibility*, August 1977, pp. 166–170.

Prothro, James W. *Dollar Decade*. Baton Rouge: Louisiana State University Press, 1954.

Reiger, S.H., Nichols, R.T., Early, I.B., and Dews, E. *Communications Satellites: Technology, Economics and System Choices*. Santa Monica: RAND, 1963.

Renmin Ribao Special Commentator, "On Policy Towards Intellectuals," *Beijing Review*, Vol. 22, No. 5, 2 February, 1979, pp. 10–15.

Resnick, Phillip. "Canadian Defense Policy," in Lumsden, Ian, Ed., *Close the 49th Parallel, Etc.: The Americanization of Canada*. Toronto: University of Toronto Press, 1970.

Ricardo, David. *Principles of Political Economy*. London: J.M. Dent, 1819 (1926).

Richeri, Giuseppe. "Italy: A Democratizaton of the Media," Paper at Congress of International Association for Mass Communication Research, Warsaw, Poland, September 1978.

Riesman, David. *The Lonely Crowd*. New Haven: Yale University Press, 1950.

Rinehart, James W. *The Tyranny of Work*. Don Mills, Ontario: General Publishing, 1975.

Roberts, Vera. *On Stage: A History of Theatre*. New York: Harper & Row, 1962.

Robinson, Joan. *The Cultural Revolution in China*. London: Penguin, 1969.

Robinson, Joan. *The New Mercantilism*. London: Cambridge University Press, 1966.

Rockefeller Brothers Fund, Inc. *The Performing Arts*. New York: McGraw-Hill, 1965.

Rogers, Everett. *Communication of Innovators: A Cross-Cultural Approach*. New York: Free Press, 1962.

Rohmer Report, see, Canada. Royal Commission on Book Publishing (1972).

Rohmer Report, *Background Papers*, see Gundy (1972).

Rosenberg, B., and White, D.M., Eds. *Mass Culture: The Popular Arts in America*. Glencoe, Ill.: Free Press, 1964.

Rosenberg, B., and White, D.M., Eds. *Mass Culture Revisited*. New York: Van Nostrand, 1971.

Rosenfeld, Sybil. *The Theatre of the London Fairs*. London: Cambridge University Press, 1960.

Rostow, Eugene V. *The Use and Management of the Electromagnetic Spectrum*. Part 1, Washington: United States Department of Commerce, 1969.

Rubenstein, E.A., Comstock, G.A., and Murray, J.P., Eds. *Television and Social Behaviour*, Vol. IV., "Television in Day-to-Day Life: Patterns of Use." Rockville, Md.: National Institute of Mental Health.

Rutkowski, A.M. "Six Ad-hoc Two: The Third World Speaks Its Mind," 1979. (Unpublished paper.)

Sanches Vasguez, Adolfo. *Art and Society: Essays in Marxist Aesthetics*. New York: Monthly Review Press, 1973.

Sauvy, Alfred. *La Nature Social*. Paris: Armand Colin, 1959.

Schiller, Herbert I. *Communications and Cultural Domination*. White Plains, N.Y.: International Arts and Sciences Press, 1976.

Schiller, Herbert I. "Decolonization of Information: Efforts Towards a New International Order," *Latin American Perspectives*, Vol. 5, No. 1, Winter 1978, pp. 35–48.

Schiller, Herbert I. *Mass Communications and American Empire*. New York: A.M. Kelley, 1969.

Schiller, Herbert I. *The Mind Managers*. Boston: Beacon Press, 1973.

Schiller, Herbert I. "The Transnational Corporation and the International Flow of Information Challenges National Sovereignty," *Current Research on Peace and Violence*, Vol. 2, No. 1, 1979, pp. 1–11.

Schiller, Herbert, I., and Phillips, J.D. *Superstate*. Urbana: University of Illinois Press, 1976.

Schmalensee, R. *The Economics of Advertising*. Amsterdam: North Holland Publishing Company, 1972.

Schramm, W., Ed. *Mass Communications*. Urbana: University of Illinois Press, 1949.

Schumacher, E.F. *Small is Beautiful*. London: Sphere Books, 1973.

Scott, Jack. *Plunderbund and Proletariat*. Vancouver: New Start Books, 1975.

Seldes, Gilbert. *The Great Audience*. New York: Viking, 1950.

Siepmann, Charles. "Radio," in Bryson, Lyman, *The Communication of Ideas*. New York: Harper & Row, 1948.

Simon, Julian L. *Issues in the Economics of Advertising*. Urbana: University of Illinois Press, 1970.

Sinclair, Upton. *The Brass Check*. New York: Arno Press, 1920.

Sinclair, Upton. *the Goose Step*. Pasadena, Author, 1923.

Sinclair, Upton. *The Goslings*. Pasadena, Author, 1924.

Singham, A., and Tran van Dinh, Eds. *From Bandung to Colombo: Conferences of the Non-aligned Countries, 1955–1975*. New York: Third Press Review Books, 1976.

Skinner, B.F. *Verbal Behaviour*. New York: Appleton-Century-Crofts, 1957.

Skinner, B.F. *Walden Two*. New York: Macmillan, 1949.

Smith, A.D. *The Development of Rates of Postage*. New York: Macmillan, 1918.

Smythe, Dallas W. "Communications: Blindspot of Economics," in Melody, W., Ed., *Culture, Communication and Dependency: The Tradition of H.A. Innis*. Norwood, N.J.: Ablex Publishing Corporation, 1980.

Smythe, Dallas W. "Communications: Blindspot of Western Marxism," *Canadian Journal of Political and Social Theory*, Vol. 1, No. 3, Fall 1977, pp. 1–28.

Smythe, Dallas W. "Rejoinder to Graham Murdock," *Canadian Journal of Political and Social Theory*, Vol. 2, No. 2, 1978, pp. 120–127.

Smythe, Dallas W. *The Relevance of United States Telecommunications Experience to the Canadian Situation*. Department of Communications Telecommission Study 2(c), Ottawa: DOC, 1970.

Smythe, Dallas W. *The Structure and Policy of Electronic Communications*. Urbana: University of Illinois Press, 1957. (Reprinted in Kitross, J.M., *Documents in American Telecommunications Policy*, Vol. II. New York: Arno Press, 1977.)

Smythe, Dallas W. A Study of Saskatchewan Telecommunications, 1974. (Unpublished paper.)

Spry, Graham. "The Costs of Canadian Broadcasting," *Queen's Quarterly*, Vol. 67, No. 4, Winter 1961, pp. 505–513.

Steffens, Lincoln. *The Shame of the Cities*. New York: Arno Press, 1920.

Stephenson, H.E., and McNaught, Carolton. *The Story of Advertising in Canada*. Toronto: Ryerson, 1940.

Stephenson, Marylee. "Never Done, Never Noticed: Women's Work in Canada," *This Magazine*, Vol. 11, No. 6, December 1977, pp. 31–33.

Stern, Louis, W. *Distribution Channels: Behavioural Dimension*. Boston: Houghton Mifflin, 1969.

Stigler, George J., and Friedland, Claire. "What Can Regulators Regulate?" *Journal of Law and Economics*, Vol. 5, October 1962, pp. 1–16.

Stone, Catherine. "The Origins of Job Structures in the Steel Industry," *Review of Radical Political Economy*, Vol. 6, No. 2, Summer 1974, pp. 113–173.

Stone, I.F. *The Hidden History of the Korean War*. New York: Monthly Review Press, 1952.

Tarbell, Ida. *History of the Standard Oil Company*. New York: McClure, Phillips & Company, 1904.

Teeple, Gary, Ed. *Capitalism and the National Question in Canada*. Toronto: University of Toronto Press, 1972.

Teich, A.H., Ed. *Technology and Man's Future*. New York: St. Martin's Press, 1972.

Terkel, Louis. *Working*. New York: Pantᵢ on, 1974.

Trainor, Lynn. "Science in Canada, Ameᵢ an Style," in Lumsden, I., Ed., *Close the 49th Parallel, Etc.: The Americanization of Canada*. Toronto: University of Toronto Press, 1970.

Tran Van Dinh. "The Third World and the 1979 World Administrative Radio Conference (WARC)," 1979. (Unpublished paper.)

Trebing, Harry M. "Common Carrier Regulation—the Silent Crisis," *Law and Contemporary Problems*, Part I. Vol. 34, No. 2, Spring 1969a, pp. 299–329.

Trebing, Harry M. "Government Regulation and Modern Capitalism," *Journal of Economic Issues*, Vol. 3, March 1969b, pp. 87–109.

Tribolet, Leslie B. *The International Aspects of Electrical Communications in the Pacific Area*. Baltimore: Johns Hopkins Press, 1929.

Tunstall, Jeremy. *The Media are American*. New York: Columbia University Press, 1977.

U.S. Congress. House of Representatives. Subcommittee on International Organizations and Movements, Committee on Foreign Affairs, Report No. 5, *Winning the Cold War: The United States Ideological Offensive*. 90th Congress, 1st Session, House of Representatives, 1967.

U.S. Senate. Committee on Interstate Commerce. *Hearings* on S. 6, 71st Congress, 1st Session, 1919.

U.S. Congress. Senate. *Government Ownership of Electrical Communications Industry*. S. Doc. 399, 63rd Congress, 2nd Session, 1914.

U.S. Senate. Subcommittee of the Committee on Interstate Commerce. *Hearings Pursuant to S. Res. 187*, 79th Congress, 1st Session, Part 1, 1945.

U.S. Federal Communications Commission. *Proposed Report, Telephone Investigation*. Washington, D.C.: Government Printing Office, 1937.

U.S. Federal Communications Commission. *Report of the Investigation of the Telephone Industry in the United States*. Washington, D.C.: Government Printing Office, 1939.

U.S. Federal Communications Commission. *Rules and Regulations for Facsimile Broadcasting and Multiplex Transmission*. Report and Order, Docket 8751, June 9, 1948.

Veblen, Thorstein. *Absentee Ownership and Business Enterprise in Recent Times: The Case in America*. New York: Viking, 1923 (1954).

Veblen, Thorstein. *The Engineers and the Price System*. New York: A.M. Kelley, 1903 (1965).

Veblen, Thorstein. *The Higher Learning in America*. New York: Huebsch, 1918.

Veblen, Thorstein. *The Theory of Business Enterprise*. New York: C. Scribner's Sons, 1904.

Veblen, Thorstein. *The Theory of the Leisure Class*. New York: Macmillan, 1899 (1927).

Viner, Jacob. *Canada's Balance of International Indebtedness, 1900–1913.* Cambridge, Mass.: Harvard University Press, 1924.

Wang, Yao-ting. "China's Foreign Trade," *China Reconstructs,* Vol. 28, No. 1, January 1979, pp. 24–28.

Ward, S., Wackman, D.B., and Wartella, E. *How Children Learn to Buy.* Beverly Hills, Calif.: Sage, 1977.

Warnock, John W. "All the News it Pays to Print," in Lumsden, Ian, Ed., *Close the 49th Parallel, Etc.: The Americanization of Canada.* Toronto: University of Toronto Press, 1970a.

Warnock, John W. *Partner to Behemoth: The Military Policy of a Satellite Canada.* Toronto: New Press, 1970b.

Watson, J.B. *Behaviourism.* Chicago: University of Chicago Press, 1924 (1958).

Watson, K., Sunter, A., and Ermuth, F. *A Financial Analysis of the Private Radio Sector in Canada and the United States.* A Report by Abt Associates Research of Canada Ltd., Ottawa, 31 March, 1978.

Watt, Ian. *The Rise of the Novel.* Harmondsworth: Penguin Books, 1963.

Weir, E. Austin. *The Struggle for National Broadcasting in Canada.* Toronto: McClelland & Stewart, 1965.

Weitz, Morris, Ed. *Problems in Aesthetics.* London: The Macmillan Company, 1970.

Wells, Alan. *Picture Tube Imperialism.* Maryknoll: Orbis Press, 1972.

Westfield, Fred M. "Regulation and Conspiracy," *American Economic Review,* Vol. 55, June 1965, pp. 424–443.

Wheelwright, E.L., and McFarlane, Bruce. *The Chinese Road to Socialism.* New York: Monthly Review Press, 1970.

"Why China Imports Technology and Equipment," *Beijing Review,* Vol. 21, No. 41, 13 October, 1978, pp. 11–13.

Wiener, Norbert. *The Human Use of Human Beings.* New York: Doubleday, 1950.

Wilcox, Clair. *Public Policies Toward Business.* Chicago: Irwin, 1955.

Williams, Raymond. *Marxism and Literature.* Oxford: Oxford University Press, 1978.

Williams, Raymond. *Television: Technology and Cultural Form.* New York: Schocken Books, 1975.

Xiaoping, Deng. "Greeting the Great Task," *Beijing Review,* Vol. 21, No. 42, 20 October, 1978. pp. 5–8.

Young, Allyn A. *The Single Tax Movement in the United States.* Princeton: Princeton University Press, 1916.

Zaretsky, Eli. "Capitalism, The Family and Personal Life," *Socialist Revolution,* Vol. 3, January–April; May–June, 1973, pp. 69–125; 19–70.

INDEX